The Marginal Cost of Public Funds

The Marginal Cost of Public Funds

Theory and Applications

by Bev Dahlby

The MIT Press
Cambridge, Massachusetts
London, England

MIT Press books may be purchased at special quantity discounts for business or sales promotional use. For information, please e-mail special_sales@mitpress.mit.edu or write to Special Sales Department, The MIT Press, 55 Hayward Street, Cambridge, MA 02142.

This book was set in Times New Roman on 3B2 by Asco Typesetters, Hong Kong, and was printed and bound in the United States of America.

Library of Congress Cataloging-in-Publication Data
Dahlby, B.
The marginal cost of public funds : theory and applications / Bev Dahlby.
    p.   cm.
Includes bibliographical references and index.
ISBN 978-0-262-04250-5 (hbk. : alk. paper)
1. Expenditures, Public—Cost effectiveness. I. Title.
HJ7461.D34   2008
336.3′9—dc22   2007032264

10   9   8   7   6   5   4   3   2   1

In memory of my parents,
George and Laurraine Dahlby,
who instilled in their children
a love of books

Contents

Preface

I began work on this book in 1998 when I was awarded a McCalla Research Professorship by the University of Alberta. At the time I did not realize how long it would take to complete this project because I did not realize how little I knew about the marginal cost of public funds (MCF). Chapter 2 was completed in Edmonton in May 1999, and the first draft of Chapter 10 was completed in August 2006 in Rio de Janeiro. In the intervening years I have worked on various projects, including two editions of *Public Finance in Canada* co-authored with Harvey Rosen, Roger Smith, and Paul Boothe, but almost all of my work during these years has been related to the marginal cost of public funds. Most of those projects have found their way, in one form or another, into this book. I like to think that the long gestation period has produced a more interesting and well-rounded offspring.

Because this book was produced over a long period of time, I have many people to thank.

First, I would like to thank my co-authors—Worawan Chandoevwit of the Thailand Development Research Institute (TDRI) in Bangkok, Nipon Poapongsakorn, Kovit Charnvitayapong, Duangmanee Laovakul, and Somchai Suksiriserekul of Thammasat University in Bangkok, Neil Warren of ATAX at the University of New South Wales, and especially Sam Wilson, my colleague at the University of Alberta, friend and long-time tennis partner. Working with them has allowed me to tackle projects that I would not have been able to undertake on my own. Our joint work has greatly enhanced the applications sections of the book.

I am very grateful to the Donner Canadian Foundation for a research grant and their very patient support for this project. I would also like to thank the Australian Taxation Studies Program at the University of New South Wales in Sydney Australia for an Abe Greenbaum Visiting Fellow, which allowed me to pursue research with Neil Warren on the effects of the Australian equalization system on the state governments' marginal cost of public funds. Alberta Finance provided financial support for my research on provincial tax subsidies for R&D. The results of that research have been incorporated in chapter 10. I would like to thank Bob Howard of

Alberta Finance for his comment on early drafts of that report and his support for my work over the years. I am also grateful to the Canadian International Development ment Agency and the Thailand Development Research Institute for providing financial support for my visit to TDRI in February 2006 to complete the research with Worawan Chandoevwit on the MCFs for excise taxes in Thailand in chapter 4. Robin Boadway and Frank Flatters of Queen's University arranged for my visits to TDRI in the mid-1990s to work on the cost–benefit study of the Thai Taxpayer Survey, which appears in chapter 6. Richard Harris at Simon Fraser University asked me to write a paper on the implications of economic integration for business taxation for an Industry Canada sponsored volume that he was editing. That research ultimately led to the analysis of the MCF for capital taxes and corporate income taxes in chapter 7. Bill Watson at McGill University suggested that I tackle the MCF from public sector borrowing for a conference volume on public debt that he was editing with Chris Ragan. That paper ultimately led to the analysis in chapter 8. Finally, I am especially grateful to Anwar Shah of the World Bank Institute who has been a supporter of my research on the MCF and fiscal federalism over the last fifteen years. The fruits of that research appear in chapters 9 and 10.

Major sections of the book were written in 2004 while I was on sabbatical at the Graduate School of Economics, Getulio Vargas Foundation, Rio de Janeiro, Brazil. I would like to thank Carlos da Costa, Luis Braido, Paulo Klinger, Renato Fragelli, Ricardo Cavalcanti, and Samuel Pessôa for providing an extremely friendly and intellectually exciting environment during my sabbatical and subsequent visits. Two PhD students at FGV, Claudio Wanderley and Régio Martins, attended lectures that I gave on draft chapters of book and in response to their comments and probing questions, I wrote the section on the optimal flat tax. I will always be grateful to them for pushing me to delve deeper into the optimal income tax problem.

I am grateful to the following publishers for permitting me to use sections of the following previously published material in this book: Australian School of Taxation (ATAX) for "The Marginal Cost of Public Funds for Excise Taxes in Thailand," *eJournal of Tax Research*, vol. 5, no. 1 (2007): 135–67; Berkeley Electronic Press for "The Marginal Cost of Funds from Public Sector Borrowing," *Topics in Economic Analysis and Policy*, vol. 6, no. 1 (2006), article 1; Blackwell Publishing for "The Fiscal Incentive Effects of the Australian Equalisation System," *Economic Record*, vol. 79, no. 247 (2003): 435–46; Canadian Public Policy for "A Framework for Evaluating Provincial R&D Tax Subsidies," *Canadian Public Policy*, vol. 31, no. 1 (2005): 45–58; Elsevier for "Progressive Taxation and the Social Marginal Cost of Public Funds" *Journal of Public Economics*, vol. 67, no. 1 (1998): 105–22 and "Vertical Fiscal Externalities in a Federation" *Journal of Public Economics*, vol. 87 (2003): 917–30; Institute for Public Policy for "What Does the Debt Cost Us?" in C. Ragan and W. Watson, eds., *Is the Debt War Over? Dispatches from Canada's Fiscal Frontline*,

Institute for Research on Public Policy, Montreal, 2004, pp. 207–34; Springer publishing for "A Cost–Benefit Analysis of the Thailand Taxpayer Survey" *International Tax and Public Finance*, vol. 7, no. 1 (2000): 63–82; University of Calgary Press for "Economic Integration: Implications for Business Taxation" in R. Harris, ed., *North American Linkages: Opportunities and Challenges For Canada*, Industry Canada Research Series, University of Calgary Press, 2003, pp. 487–532.

Michael Lundholm, Gareth Myles, and Matti Tuomala read drafts of the chapters and provided many helpful suggestions. I am especially indebted to Charles Ballard for his detailed comments, which significantly improved the final product. Ian Parry at Resources for the Future also provided me with comments on chapters 3 and 4, and Mario Jametti at York University provided many helpful suggestions on chapters 9 and 10. I would further like to thank John Covell and Dana Andrus of The MIT Press for their assistance in the preparation of this book. While I am very grateful to all of the people mentioned above, they are not responsible for any errors or shortcomings.

Finally, it is with great happiness that I acknowledge that I would not have been able to complete this book without the love and support of my wife, Mery Clementino dos Santos.

1 Introduction

There are many fascinating theoretical and empirical issues to be addressed in public finance. But none is more important than measuring the effects of tax rate changes and the costs of incremental tax revenue.
—Feldstein (1997, pp. 211–12)

The marginal cost of public funds measures the loss incurred by society in raising additional revenues to finance government spending. As the quotation by Martin Feldstein indicates, the marginal cost of public funds (MCF) has emerged as one of the most important concepts in the field of public economics. It is the key component in evaluations of tax reforms, public expenditure programs, and other public policies, ranging from tax enforcement to privatization of public enterprises.

Taxes can affect the allocation of resources in an economy by altering taxpayers' consumption, labor supply, and investment decisions. If the "invisible hand" of the market produces an efficient or Pareto optimal allocation of resources, then taxes will result in a less efficient allocation of resources to the extent that they alter households' and firms' decisions. We can think of this efficiency loss as a decline in the size of the "economic pie"—the value of goods and services produced and consumed in the economy, including the value of leisure time and the quality of the environment. The shrinkage of the economic pie is what economists mean by the efficiency cost of the tax system. The MCF is a summary measure of the additional distortion in the allocation of resources that occurs when a government raises additional revenues. However, minimizing the efficiency losses is not the only criteria for evaluating tax measures. Taxes that impose heavy burdens on low income individuals are also "costly" taxes. The MCF concept can be used to combine equity or distributional concerns with efficiency effects in a summary measure of the total cost to a society of raising tax revenues.

Insight is the economist's Holy Grail. The MCF concept is especially valuable because it gives us insight into policies issues, ranging from the desirability of deficit-financing public infrastructure spending to evaluating the bias in fiscal decision-making caused by tax competition in a federation. It is a very intuitive way of describing fiscal choices, and therefore it can be readily used to convey economists' insights to policy makers and the general public.

While a substantial literature on the MCF has developed over the last twenty years, much of this literature is fragmented because authors have used different measures for the MCF, or its associated concept, the marginal excess burden, MEB. Over the last ten years, my research has focused on the measurement and application of the MCF, especially with regard to the MCFs in federal systems of government. In this book, I bring together the results of my research over the last ten years, providing a unified treatment of the MCF concept and showing how it can be applied in a wide variety of contexts, ranging from computing the MCFs for excise taxes in Thailand to evaluating the fiscal incentive effects of equalization programs in Australia. Hence the title conveys the book's two main contributions—a careful development of the theoretical foundations of the MCF in a variety of contexts and its application to a wide range of public policy issues.

The Marginal Cost of Public Funds: Theory and Application is intended for economists and public policy analysts working for governments, think tanks, and international institutions. While not intended as a textbook, it could be used as a supplementary textbook in advanced undergraduate or first-year graduate courses in economics. I have used drafts of the chapters in my graduate and undergraduate courses on the economics of taxation at the University of Alberta, at the University of Innsbruck, and at the Graduate School of Economics, Getulio Vargas Foundation, in Rio de Janeiro. To enhance its usefulness as a supplementary textbook, I have included exercises and further reading sections at the end of each of the main chapters.

Chapter 2 describes the theoretical foundations of the MCF using the tools of welfare economics. Section 2.1 begins with a review of the concept of the excess burden of taxation—also known as the deadweight loss from taxation—and its measurement using the equivalent variation, compensating variation, and consumer surplus measures of welfare change. This section also introduces a measure of the gain from a tax reform. A point that is emphasized throughout the chapter is that the measurement of the efficiency loss from taxation depends on the prices that are used to evaluate the welfare changes of consumers and producers.

Section 2.2 introduces the concept of the social marginal cost of public funds in a very general context and shows how the conditions defining an optimal tax system and optimal spending on public services are based on this concept. Section 2.3 shows how the MCF concept can be used to calculate the gain, or the loss, from a tax reform, by way of the pre–tax reform and post–tax reform MCFs and a price index that reflects the change in the "value" of a dollar arising from changes in prices caused by the tax reform.

Section 2.4 uses the concepts of consumer and producer surplus to provide an intuitive derivation of a formula for the MCF for an excise tax in a competitive market. This formula allows one to calculate the MCF based on the elasticities of demand and supply and the tax rate.

Section 2.5 explores the relationship between the MCF and the MEB, which is the additional excess burden generated in raising an additional dollar of tax revenue. This section shows that the $MCF = (1 + MEB_{EV})P$, where MEB_{EV} is the equivalent variation-based MEB and P is a price index that converts the equivalent variation of welfare changes, which are measured at before-tax prices, into a dollar measure of the welfare change at the after-tax prices, the MCF.

Section 2.6 applies the conceptual framework developed in the preceding sections to a standard economic problem—measuring the gain from tariff reductions. A simple partial equilibrium model is used to illustrate why tariffs have high MCFs and how the gains from tariff reductions can be computed using the MCFs for tariffs and their replacement taxes. Some illustrative calculations show that there are potentially large efficiency gains if a tariff is replaced by a broad consumption tax in a country that is highly dependent on tariff revenues.

Section 2.7 shows how distributional concerns can be incorporated in the definition and measurement of the MCF. The social marginal cost of public funds, the SMCF is shown to be the product of two factors—Ω, which is the distributionally weighted cost of all of the consumer and producer prices changes resulting from an increase in the tax rate on commodity i, and the MCF, which is the aggregate efficiency loss caused in raising an additional dollar of tax revenue. Section 2.8 provides a brief review of a few key studies that have contributed to the development of the concept and the interpretation of the MCF. Other studies that have made specific contributions to the calculation of the MCFs for commodity, labor and capital taxes are discussed in sections 3.8, 5.6, and 7.5.

Chapter 3 focuses on the MCFs for commodity taxes. The model developed in chapter 2 is extended by measuring the MCF when there are other distortions in the economy. These distortions include taxes on other commodities, positive and negative externalities in the production and consumption of commodities, imperfect competition, smuggling and tax evasion, and addiction. Thus a major theme of chapter 3 is how market distortions can be incorporated in the measurement of the MCF. The final section of the chapter contains a summary of studies of the marginal distortionary costs of commodity taxes. These studies are divided into those that focus on the MCFs for taxes on specific commodities, those that calculate the MCFs for general sales taxes, and those that calculate the MCFs for taxes on imports and exports.

Chapter 4 contains studies of the MCFs for excise taxes in Thailand and the United Kingdom. In Thailand commodity taxes represent 59.1 percent of total tax revenues, with excise taxes contributing 25.6 percent of tax revenues. Given its heavy reliance on excise taxes, the equity and efficiency effects of excise taxes are important aspects of tax policy in Thailand. Estimates of the own- and cross-price elasticities of demand are used in this chapter for ten categories of goods and services in Thailand to capture the interdependence of the various commodity tax bases in Thailand in computing the MCFs. In section 4.1 the nontax distortions created by (1) environmental externalities, (2) public expenditure externalities, (3) addiction, (4) market power, and (5) smuggling are incorporated in the computation of the MCFs. The analysis indicates that the MCF for the fuel excise tax is relatively low while the MCFs for the tobacco and alcohol excise taxes exceed 2.00. Also calculated are distributionally weighted MCFs, which do not change the ranking of the social marginal cost of the excise taxes. Finally, this section shows that a revenue-neutral marginal tax reform—reducing the excise tax rates on alcohol and tobacco by one percentage point and increasing the fuel excise tax—will result in a net efficiency gain equal to 1.72 Baht for every additional Baht of fuel tax revenue.

Section 4.2 calculates the MCFs for the 1999 excise taxes on petroleum, alcoholic beverages, and cigarettes in the United Kingdom, taking as a starting point a study by Parry (2003). Like Parry, the analysis shows that petroleum taxes are the most distortionary and that cigarette taxes are the least distortionary, but the analysis extends Parry's findings in three ways. First, the section's calculations reveal that it is potentially important to distinguish between direct consumption externalities and public expenditure externalities, whereas Parry treated all externalities as direct consumption externalities. Second, from the tax shifting and conjectural variations parameter estimates for the cigarette industry by Delipalla and O'Donnell (2001), the calculations reveal that it is important to incorporate the market power distortion in measuring the MCF for excise taxes on cigarettes. Third, the calulations reveal that it is important to distinguish between the MCFs for the ad valorem and per unit excise levied on cigarettes.

Chapter 5 focuses on the MCF from taxing labor income because taxes on labor income—either levied directly through income, payroll, and social security contributions or indirectly through broadly based sales taxes—represent the most important source of tax revenues in most countries. Indeed much of the literature on the MCF deals with taxes on labor income. The chapter begins by deriving the MCF for a proportional wage tax in a perfectly competitive labor market where magnitude of the MCF depends on the elasticities of supply and demand of labor, and it briefly reviews some of the empirical evidence concerning labor supply elasticities. Section 5.2 uses the framework developed in Dahlby (1998) to consider the marginal cost of funds from imposing a progressive income tax with increasing marginal tax rates. The section develops a generic measure of the SMCF that can be used to evaluate any arbitrary increase in one or more of the marginal tax rates that are imposed under a progressive personal income tax. The section also reviews the calculation of the

SMCFs for three alternative progressivity-preserving tax rate increases from a study of the Japanese income tax system by Bessho and Hayahi (2005).

Section 5.3 uses a model developed by Kleven and and Kreiner (2006) to show how the labor force participation effects from tax rate changes can be incorporated in the MCF. Computations of the MCFs for five European countries by Kleven and Kreiner show that incorporating the participation or "extensive margin" responses can significantly increase estimates of the MCFs for some countries.

Most of this chapter uses the conventional labor supply model to analyze the MCF from taxes on earnings. However, in recent years, the most important research concerning the disincentive effects of taxation has tried to measure the wide range of adjustments that individuals can make to their reported incomes in response to a tax rate increase. Section 5.4 shows how the estimates of the elasticity of taxable income can be used to calculate the MCF. Section 5.5 shows that the MCF concept is at the heart of three standard models of political economy—the median voter model, the probabilistic voting model, and the Leviathan model. These models show that the MCF is important for predicting how a government will tax, not just for guiding prescriptions for how it should tax.

There have been many studies of the MCF from taxing labor income that have used frameworks similar to the one adopted in this book, but there are also many other empirical studies have used a wide variety of concepts—marginal welfare cost, marginal excess burden, marginal efficiency cost, and marginal deadweight loss—and other frameworks to calculate the marginal distortionary cost of taxes on labor income. Section 5.6 provides a brief survey of the wide range of empirical studies of the marginal distortionary cost of taxing labor income.

Chapter 6 contains three applications of the MCF concept to the taxation of labor income. Section 6.1 incorporates one of the most important labor market distortions in the measurement of the MCF: involuntary unemployment. The section uses the Shapiro and Stiglitz (1982) efficiency wage model to explain the existence of involuntary unemployment. The analysis, based on numerical values of the Canadian labor market, shows that incorporating involuntary unemployment significantly increases the MCF for an employer payroll tax.

Section 6.2 uses the MCF concept to evaluate a tax enforcement program in Thailand, based on a case study in Thailand by Poapangsakorn et al. (2000). The section develops a measure of the marginal social cost of raising revenue from increased tax enforcement activity, the $SMCF_p$, and shows that more resources should be devoted to tax enforcement if (and only if) the $SMCF_p$, is lower than the social marginal cost of raising revenue by increasing tax rates, the $SMCF_t$. The Poapangsakorn et al. (2000) study found that the $SMCF_p$ was high for the Thai tax enforcement program, indicating that it was a high-cost source of additional tax revenue for the government of Thailand.

Section 6.3 uses the MCF concept to derive the optimal "flat tax." The flat tax is a progressive tax that can be made more progressive, for a given tax yield, by increasing the basic exemption and the marginal tax rate on earnings above the exemption. The section uses the model to compute the optimal flat tax for a government that needs to raise the same revenues as a 20 percent proportional tax on earnings. The computations indicate that the optimal exemption level can be relatively high (43 percent of earners would not pay the tax) and the optimal marginal tax rate can be over 40 percent even with relatively modest distributional objectives.

Chapter 7 investigates the optimal taxation treatment of the return to capital in a small open economy using the marginal cost of public funds concept. The chapter starts with a simple two-period life cycle model, which is used to examine one of the most hotly contested tax policy issues: whether governments should levy income taxes or consumption taxes. The optimal tax rule from the Corlett and Hague model—tax at a higher rate the good that is most complementary with leisure—implies that there should be a tax on the return on savings if future consumption is more complementary with leisure than current consumption. This insight, stemming from the work of Feldstein (1978) and Atkinson and Sandmo (1980), provides an alternative intuitive explanation of the optimal tax treatment of savings. Section 7.1 presents some calculations of the optimal tax or subsidy on the return on savings and the gain or loss in moving from a proportional income tax to an equal yield (in present value terms) consumption tax system. These calculations indicate that shifting to a consumption tax may entail either a large gain or a large loss depending on the value of the compensated cross-price elasticity of demand between future consumption and leisure, the elasticity of the supply of savings, and the labor supply elasticity.

Section 7.2 turns the attention from a residence-based tax on the return to savings to a source-based tax on the return to capital. The section begins by deriving expressions for the MCFs for capital and labor taxes in a small open economy where there are pure profits because of a fixed supply of a third input (interpreted as land or natural resources). The section derives a closed form expression for the optimal tax rate on capital, and shows that the optimal tax depends on the own- and cross-price elasticities of demand for labor and capital, the labor supply elasticity, the tax rates on labor income and pure profits, and on distributional preferences. It shows that if the government only cares about the tax burden on labor and the production function is Cobb-Douglas, then the optimal tax rate on capital is the after-tax share of profits in total income.

Section 7.3 analyzes the MCF for a corporate income tax (CIT) levied by a small capital-importing economy when the home country adopts (1) a foreign tax credit system, (2) an exemption system, or (3) a deduction system. The expressions for the MCFs are used to calculate the optimal CIT rate and wage tax rate under the three international tax regimes. The overall conclusion is that although capital mobility puts downward pressure on CIT rates, especially if capital-exporting countries adopt exemption or deduction systems, relatively high rates can be chosen by a small capital-importing country if pure profits are a relatively large share of domestic income and low distributional weights are applied to profits. Chapter 7 concludes with a brief survey of the results of previous studies of the marginal distortionary cost of taxing the return on capital.

Chapter 8 focuses on the MCF from public sector borrowing. Section 8.1 begins with a brief overview of the postwar literature on the burden of the public debt. This historical background helps put into context the models of the public debt that are considered in this chapter. The postwar debates over the burden of the public debt identified two main mechanisms by which the public debt can impose a burden on the economy—through a wealth effect and through a distortionary tax effect. Section 8.2 uses the Diamond (1965) overlapping generations model to analyze the wealth effect of the public debt and to derive a measure of the marginal cost of funds from public sector borrowing.

Section 8.3 uses a simple model, originally developed by Elmendorf and Mankiw (1999), to analyze the MCF from public sector debt when interest payments on the debt are financed by a distortionary tax on total output. This framework is used in section 8.4 to derive a rule for the optimal financing of lumpy expenditure projects—use debt financing to equalize over time the marginal cost of public funds through taxes. A numerical example shows that there can be significant welfare gains from debt-financing lumpy expenditures. Finally, section 8.5 uses a simple endogenous growth model, which incorporates the Ricardian equivalence effect and the distortionary tax effect, to derive a measure of the marginal cost of funds from public sector borrowing and to explore the connection between the level of public debt and the rate of economic growth. This model is used to compute the marginal cost of public funds from public sector borrowing in the Canada and the United States and to consider the effect of higher public debt on the optimal level of public expenditures.

Chapter 9 focuses on the potential biases in the perceived MCFs of subnational governments in a federation. These biases can arise because of vertical and horizontal fiscal externalities among the governments in federation. Section 9.1 begins with a brief discussion of the nature of the tax externalities that arise in a federation and the associated problem of fiscal imbalance—misallocations of the tax burden and the provision of public services among subnational governments and between the levels of government. The conventional definition of fiscal imbalance is not very useful for policy purposes. Defining fiscal imbalances in terms of differences in the marginal cost of public funds provides valuable insights concerning this issue.

Section 9.2 develops a simple model of horizontal tax externalities in which subnational governments levy taxes on a mobile tax base. Each government's perceived

MCF is biased upward because it does not take into account the positive fiscal externality that its taxes create for other subnational governments. Section 9.3 considers how intergovernmental grants can be structured to correct the fiscal distortions caused by horizontal tax and expenditure externalities and to address horizontal fiscal imbalances. In the latter case equalization grants can help achieve an optimal allocation of the tax burden across the federation by equalizing the MCFs across subnational governments. The section shows that the optimal equalization grants will depend on the relative sizes of the tax bases of the subnational governments as well as on the relative tax sensitivity of their tax bases.

Section 9.4 examines the vertical fiscal externalities that can occur in a federal state because of the interdependence of the central and subnational governments' tax bases. The framework developed in Dahlby and Wilson (2003), where both central and subnational governments levy taxes on labor income and profits, is used to show that the subnational governments' MCFs may be biased either up or down because of the vertical tax externality.

Section 9.5 uses a model developed by Keen and Kotsogiannis (2002) to describe the conditions under which either the vertical or the horizontal tax externalities dominate and whether subnational governments' spending is too low or too high. This framework is also used to illustrate situations where there is a vertical fiscal imbalance in the sense that the MCFs of the federal and state governments are not equal, and either too little or too much state spending results relative to federal spending.

Chapter 10 analyzes three policy issues that arise in a federations. Section 10.1 uses the marginal cost of funds concept to analyze the provision of investment incentives by subnational governments. In particular, this framework is used to evaluate the provision of R&D tax subsidies by provincial governments in Canada. Almost all previous studies of R&D tax policies have focused either on the tax sensitivity of R&D or on external rate of return from R&D. The main contribution of this section is to show how the tax sensitivity of R&D, its external rate of return, and the marginal cost of public funds can be combined in evaluating tax subsidies for R&D.

In most federations the federal and subnational governments have different "fiscal capacities" because either the sizes of their tax bases differ or the tax sensitivity of their tax bases differ. These differences in fiscal capacities can give rise to horizontal and vertical fiscal imbalances within a federation. Intergovernmental grants are part of the fiscal architecture of most federations in order to address these imbalances, but the intergovernmental grants can have unintended effects on the tax and expenditure decisions of national and subnational governments. Section 10.2, which is based on Dahlby and Warren (2003), shows how fiscal equalization grants may have affected the perceived MCFs of the state governments in Australia.

Section 10.3 applies a modified version of the Kanbur and Keen (1993) cross-border shopping model to the effects of an equalization grant system on the horizontal and vertical fiscal imbalances in a federation. The section explores how the financing of equalization grants—either funding by the federal government out of general tax revenues or direct contributions by the state governments—affects the ability of equalization grants to address vertical and horizontal fiscal imbalances. A simulation model is used to show that the efficient allocation of the tax burden in a federation may require higher tax rates in regions with the less sensitive tax bases. These simulations show how regionally differented tax rates would implement the equivalent of the Ramsey rule for optimal taxation by shrinking the regional tax bases in the same proportion. The simulations also show that an equalization grant system can improve welfare, as measured by a utilitarian social welfare function, if states vary in the size of their tax bases or the tax sensitivity of their tax bases.

2 Conceptual Foundations of the MCF

This chapter uses the tools of welfare economics to describe the theoretical foundations of the MCF and shows how this concept can be used to evaluate tax and expenditure policies in the public sector. Section 2.1 begins with a review of the concept of the excess burden of taxation and its measurement using the equivalent variation (EV), compensating variation (CV), and consumer surplus (CS) measures of welfare change. This chapter also introduces a measure of the gain from a tax reform, based on the pre–tax reform prices. This measure is shown to be proportional to the equivalent variation based measure of excess burden when an excise tax is replaced by a lump-sum tax. The proportionality factor that links the two measures is a price index because, as is emphasized throughout this chapter, the measurement of the efficiency loss from taxation depends on the prices that are used to evaluate the welfare changes of consumers and producers.

Section 2.2 introduces in a very general context the concept of the social marginal cost of public funds and shows how the conditions defining an optimal tax system and optimal spending on public services are based on this concept. In most countries, tax reform is almost always on the policy agenda, suggesting that tax systems are rarely "optimal." Section 2.3 shows how the MCF concept can be used to calculate the gain, or the loss, from a tax reform, using the pre-reform and post-reform MCFs and a price index P that reflects the change in the "value" of a dollar arising from changes in prices caused by the tax reform.

Section 2.4 uses the concepts of consumer and producer surplus to provide an intuitive derivation of a formula for the MCF for an excise tax in a competitive market. This formula allows us to calculate the MCF based on the elasticities of demand and supply and the tax rate. It indicates that the MCF is equal to 1.00 if either the uncompensated elasticity of demand or the elasticity of supply is zero because in these cases production and consumption of the taxed good does not change when the tax is imposed.

These results seem to contradict the idea that a tax system causes an excess burden even if the demand for the taxed commodity is completely inelastic. Section 2.5

explores how this paradox can be resolved by way of the relationship between the
MCF and the marginal excess burden of taxation (MEB), which is the additional
excess burden generated in raising an additional dollar of tax revenue. The section
shows that the $MCF = (1 + MEB_{EV})P$, where MEB_{EV} is the equivalent variation
based MEB and P is a price index that converts the EV welfare changes, which are
measured at the pre-tax prices, into a dollar measure of the welfare change at the
post-tax prices, the MCF. For the case where the demand for the taxed commodity is completely inelastic, it turns out that while the $(1 + MEB_{EV})$ is greater than
one because the tax increases the excess burden, the price index P is equal to
$(1 + MEB_{EV})^{-1}$. Therefore the $MCF = 1.00$. The section also shows that the MCF
is equal to one plus the compensating variation-based marginal excess burden, multiplied by a factor that converts income-compensated revenue changes into uncompensated revenue changes. In summary, this section shows that the MCF is grounded in
the established measures of excess burden, but it is a more flexible tool for evaluating
tax reforms and expenditure programs than the excess burden concept.

Section 2.6 applies the conceptual framework developed in the preceding sections
to a standard economic problem—measuring the gain from a tariff reduction. Most
of the literature on free (or freer) trade is by international trade economists who,
since the time of Ricardo, have emphasized the efficiency gains from reallocating
resources from the import-competing sectors to the rest of the economy through tariff reductions. However, a tariff reduction can also be viewed as a tax reform, in
which a highly distortionary tax—the tariff—is replaced by some less distortionary
form of taxation. The section uses a simple partial equilibrium model to illustrate
why tariffs have high MCFs and how the gains from a tariff reduction can be computed using the MCFs for a tariff and its replacement tax. Some illustrative calculations show that there are potentially large efficiency gains if a tariff is replaced by a
broad consumption tax in a country that is highly dependent on tariff revenues.

While most of this chapter focuses on the efficiency effects of distortionary taxes,
the distributional effects of taxes, and the expenditures that they finance, cannot be
ignored. Taxes that impose heavy burdens on poor people also have a high social
marginal cost even if they do not distort the allocation of resources. Section 2.7 shows
how distributional concerns can be incorporated in the definition and measurement
of the MCF. Implicit in any social welfare function that is used to evaluate tax and
expenditure policies is a set of distributional weights that reflect a society's willingness to trade off gains and losses among different households. Usually these distributional weights are pro-poor, meaning an additional dollar received by a poor
household has a higher social value than a dollar received by a richer household.
The section shows how distributional weights can be used in a consistent fashion
to incorporate equity concerns into the measurement of the marginal cost of funds.
The social marginal cost of public funds, SMCF, is defined as the distributionally

weighted cost of raising an additional dollar of tax revenue from a particular tax source. The SMCF for a tax on commodity i is defined as the product of two factors—Ω_i, which is the distributionally weighted cost of all consumer and producer prices changes resulting from an increase in the tax rate on commodity i and the MCF_i, which is the aggregate efficiency loss caused in raising an additional dollar of tax revenue. Thus the social marginal cost of public funds provides a convenient and consistent framework for incorporating both the equity and the efficiency aspects of tax reform.

The final section of the chapter provides a review of the key papers that have contributed to the development and interpretation of the MCF concept.

2.1   The Excess Burden of Taxation

2.1.1   Measuring Excess Burden

The excess burden of a tax system is the difference between a money measure of the welfare loss caused by the tax system and the tax revenue that is collected.[1] The concept of excess burden is illustrated in figure 2.1 under the assumptions that an excise tax is imposed on a single commodity x_1, that all markets are perfectly competitive, and that the supply of the taxed commodity is perfectly elastic at a given producer price. The prices of all other commodities are normalized to equal one and treated

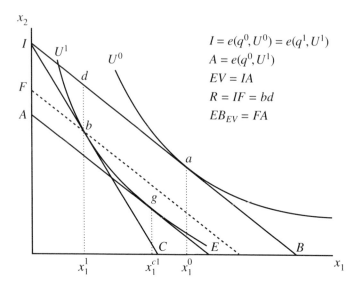

Figure 2.1
Equivalent variation-based measure of excess burden, EB_{EV}

as a single composite commodity, x_2. The consumer has a fixed amount of money income of I. In the absence of taxation, the consumer would face a set of prices represented by the vector q^0 and would consume the bundle of commodities at point a where his indifference curve U^0 is tangent to his before-tax budget line, IB. If an excise tax of t_1 is imposed on x_1, its price will increase by the full amount of the tax. Let this new price vector be represented by q^1. The consumer now faces the new budget line, IC, and maximizes utility by purchasing the combination of commodities at point b on the indifference curve U^1.

Economists use the *expenditure function*, $e(q, U)$, to measure a consumer's welfare loss from a price increase. The expenditure function measures the amount of money that a consumer needs at a given set of prices, q, to attain a given level of well being or utility, U. The difference in the value of the expenditure function, $e(q, U^1) - e(q, U^0)$ is a money measure of the consumer's change in welfare between situation 1 and situation 0. This measure of welfare change depends on the preferences of the individual and the particular set of prices that is used to value the welfare change. The derivative of the expenditure function with respect to the price of commodity i is the *compensated demand function* for commodity i, which indicates the quantity of x_i that would be demanded at various prices if the consumer's income were adjusted so that his utility remained constant; that is, $\partial e / \partial q_i = x_i^c(q, U)$. The compensated demand function is a useful analytical device because it shows the substitution effect of the price change, whereas the ordinary demand curve shows both the substitution and the income effects of a price change. The derivative of the expenditure function with respect to the level of utility is the inverse of the marginal utility of income, $\partial e / \partial U = 1/\lambda(q, U)$. It indicates the rate at which utility increases when the individual receives an additional dollar of lump-sum income. The marginal utility of income is positive because it is assumed that the consumer is never satiated, and it will generally be a function of the prices of the goods and services consumed by the individual, and the individual's utility level.

The *equivalent variation* is one of the most widely used measures of welfare change. It provides a monetary measure of the utility change, $U^1 - U^0$, based on the initial or before-tax prices, or $EV = e(q^0, U^1) - e(q^0, U^0)$. The equivalent variation measures the maximum amount that an individual would be willing to pay to avoid a price increase. Note that since, in these examples, we are dealing with an increase in a consumer price, $U^1 < U^0$, and therefore the $EV < 0$. However, excess burden is usually defined to be a positive number, and therefore the equivalent variation based measure of the excess burden is defined as follows:

$$EB_{EV} = [e(q^0, U^0) - e(q^0, U^1)] - R, \tag{2.1}$$

where R is the amount of tax revenue raised, $R = t_1 x_1^1$.

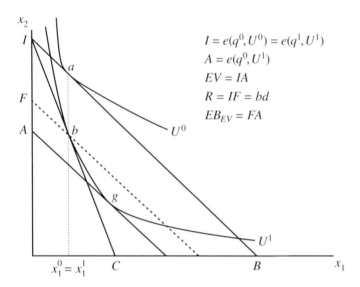

$$I = e(q^0, U^0) = e(q^1, U^1)$$
$$A = e(q^0, U^1)$$
$$EV = IA$$
$$R = IF = bd$$
$$EB_{EV} = FA$$

Figure 2.2
EB_{EV} when demand is completely inelastic

In figure 2.1 the EV is given by the distance IA, since $I = e(q^0, U^0) = e(q^1, U^1)$ and $A = e(q^0, U^1)$. The amount of tax revenue collected is the vertical distance between point b and point d or FI, and therefore the excess burden of the tax is equal to FA.

Figure 2.2 shows the interesting special case where the demand for the taxed commodity is completely price inelastic, and therefore the output of the tax commodity does not change when the tax is imposed, that is $x_1^0 = x_1^1$. As in figure 2.1, the EV of the tax is IA, the tax revenue collected is FI, and the excess burden is FA. This illustrates the important point that the excess burden depends on the substitution effect of the price change, which is the movement from point b to point g on indifference curve U^1 in response to the relative price change.[2] There is no excess burden from taxation if the individual has Leontief or "elbow" shaped indifference curves, in which case the individual always consumes goods in a fixed proportion and there is no substitution effect, or if the tax is a *lump-sum* or fixed amount that is independent of the actions or choices of the taxpayer.[3] Since by definition a taxpayer cannot influence the size of his lump-sum tax, it does not distort his behavior. A lump-sum tax only has an income effect—there is no substitution effect. Given the limited information that governments have about taxpayers' preferences and opportunities to earn income, lump-sum taxes cannot be based on each taxpayer's potential economic well-being. Consequently feasible lump-sum taxes must be more or less uniform

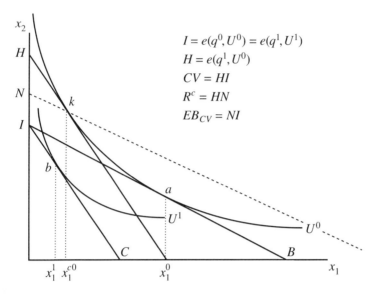

$$I = e(q^0, U^0) = e(q^1, U^1)$$
$$H = e(q^1, U^0)$$
$$CV = HI$$
$$R^c = HN$$
$$EB_{CV} = NI$$

Figure 2.3
Compensating variation-based measure of excess burden, EB_{CV}

across taxpayers. Governments tend to shy away from lump-sum taxes because they are regressive.

Another common approach to the measurement of excess burden uses the *compensating variation* to measure welfare changes. The compensating variation is a money measure of the utility change, $U^1 - U^0$, based on the current or post-tax prices, such that $CV = e(q^1, U^1) - e(q^1, U^0)$. The compensating variation measures the amount that we would have to pay the individual to compensate him for the increase in prices caused by the taxes. The compensating variation approach to the measure of excess burden is illustrated in figure 2.3. As before, in the absence of taxation, the individual would consume the combination of commodities at point a on the indifference curve U^0. In order to compensate the consumer for the increase in the price of x_1 caused by the tax, the consumer's income would have to be increased to $H = e(q^1, U^0)$. With this level of income the consumer would purchase the bundle of commodities at point k on U^0. The tax revenue that would be collected if the individual were compensated for the price increase will be defined as $R^c = t_1 \cdot x(q^1, U^0)$ or equal to HN. The compensating variation measure of the excess burden of the tax is defined as the difference between the CV and the compensated tax revenue or

$$EB_{CV} = [e(q^1, U^0) - e(q^1, U^1)] - R^c. \tag{2.2}$$

In figure 2.3 the EB_{CV} is the distance NI.

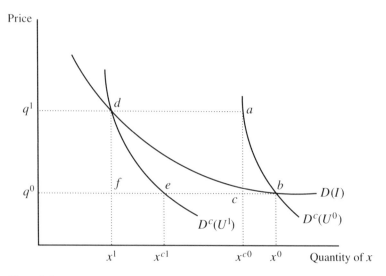

Figure 2.4
Measuring excess burden using demand curves

The EB_{EV} and the EB_{CV} are also illustrated in figure 2.4 using demand curves. The consumer's ordinary or Marshallian demand curve is $D(I)$. When the price of the commodity increases from q^0 to q^1, the quantity of the good consumed declines from x^0 to x^1. Figure 2.4 also shows the consumer's *compensated demand* curves, denoted as D^c. The EV for a price change is equal to the area to the left of the compensated demand curve $D^c(U^1)$, or the area $q^1 deq^0$. (See appendix 2.1 for the derivation of this result.) Total tax revenue is equal to the area $q^1 dfq^0$, and the EB_{EV} is the triangular area def. Similarly the CV for the price increase is equal to the area to the left of the compensated demand curve $D^c(U^0)$, or the area $q^1 abq^0$. The compensated tax revenue is equal to the area $q^1 acq^0$, and therefore the EB_{CV} is the triangular area abc.[4] These measures of excess burden can be approximated using the formula for the area of triangle as

$$EB \approx \frac{1}{2}(\Delta x^c)t = \frac{1}{2}\left(-\frac{dx^c}{dq}\frac{dq}{dt}\right)t = \frac{1}{2}\left(-\left(\frac{q^1}{x}\frac{dx^c}{dq}\right)\cdot\frac{t}{q^1}\right)tx = \frac{1}{2}(-\varepsilon^c\tau)R, \qquad (2.3)$$

where Δx^c is the reduction in the compensated demand for x, and t is the per unit tax rate, $q^1 - q^0$. This formula indicates that the excess burden per dollar of tax revenue, EB/R, is proportional to the compensated elasticity of demand for the taxed commodity, $\varepsilon^c < 0$, and the ad valorem tax rate, $\tau = t/q^1$. Consequently the higher the tax rate, the greater is the excess burden per dollar of tax revenue, provided that the compensated elasticity of demand remains constant as the tax rate rises.

Figure 2.4 also illustrates the *consumer surplus* (CS) measure of excess burden. As a result of the price increase the welfare loss sustained by the individual can be approximated by the reduction in consumer surplus, which is the area $q^1 dbq^0$. The consumer surplus measure of excess burden is defined by

$$EB_{CS} = \int_{q^0}^{q^1} x(q, I)dq - t_1 x_1 \tag{2.4}$$

and is equal to the area *dbf*. The consumer surplus measure of excess burden is often used as a heuristic device for describing excess burden, but it is not a rigorously defined measure of welfare change because (1) it is not clear what "question" consumer surplus is the answer to, (2) it may give misleading answers (as in the case where demand is completely inelastic and the CS-based measure of excess burden is zero, even though there is an excess burden) and (3) when there are multiple price changes the CS measure may depend on the order in which the price changes are assumed to occur (see Dahlby 1977). However, in evaluating tax policy, the consumer surplus measure often provides an intuitively appealing way of explaining welfare changes. As we will see in section 2.4, consumer surplus provides a useful way of interpreting the marginal cost of public funds.

2.1.2 Measuring the Gain from Tax Reform

We now turn to the measurement of the welfare gains (or losses) from a revenue-neutral tax reform. Extending the example developed in the previous section, suppose the government substituted a lump-sum tax for the excise tax on x_1. See figure 2.5. With a lump-sum tax of $R = FI$, but with the excise tax removed, the individual's budget line would be FH, and the individual would consume the combination of goods at point g on the indifference curve U^2. This tax revenue neutral reform would result in an improvement in the individual's well-being because the indifference curve U^2 lies above the indifference curve U^1. Let $\Delta M = e(q, U^2) - e(q, U^1)$ represent a money measure of the welfare improvement from this revenue-neutral tax reform, where U^1 represents the current level of well-being, and U^2 represents the post-reform level of well-being. While, in theory, any arbitrary set of prices can be used to measure this welfare gain, we will argue that the use of current market prices, which incorporate the effects of the current set of taxes, makes the evaluation of the welfare changes transparent and intuitive. The public has great difficulty interpreting, and accepting as valid, measures of benefits and costs based on some "arbitrary" set of prices that is far removed from their day-to-day experience. Since the ultimate goal of a tax policy evaluation, or a cost–benefit analysis of a public expenditure program, is to be a "useful" guide for policy making, we think that analysts should use current prices to measure benefits and costs, including the marginal cost of public

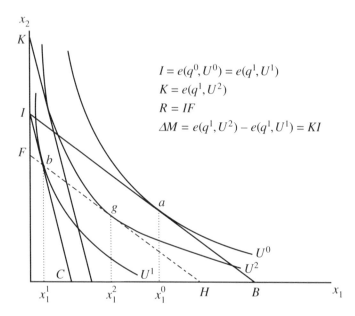

$$I = e(q^0, U^0) = e(q^1, U^1)$$
$$K = e(q^1, U^2)$$
$$R = IF$$
$$\Delta M = e(q^1, U^2) - e(q^1, U^1) = KI$$

Figure 2.5
Gain from tax reform

funds. Therefore we will argue that the most useful definition of ΔM is the one that uses current market prices, denoted by the vector q^1. We will define ΔM as

$$\Delta M = e(q^1, U^2) - e(q^1, U^1), \tag{2.5}$$

where q^1 represents the current or pre-reform prices. In terms of figure 2.5, ΔM is equal to the distance KI. Note that while the tax reform illustrated in figure 2.5 involves the substitution of a lump-sum tax for a distortionary excise tax, this measure of the gain from tax reform in (2.5) is completely general and could be used to measure any revenue-neutral tax reform that substitutes one distortionary tax for another.

The gain from tax reform is illustrated using demand curves in figure 2.6. With the excise tax imposed, the individual consumes x^1 at the point g on his ordinary demand curve $D(I)$. The tax revenue generated by the excise tax, which we will denote by R, is equal to the area $q^1 g f q^0$. If the excise tax is removed and a lump-sum tax of R is imposed instead, the price of the taxed good declines to q^0 and the ordinary demand curve shifts to the left, given our assumption that it is a normal good. With this revenue-neutral tax reform, the individual consumes at point k on his new ordinary demand curve $D(I - R)$. From the definition of ΔM in (2.5) we obtain

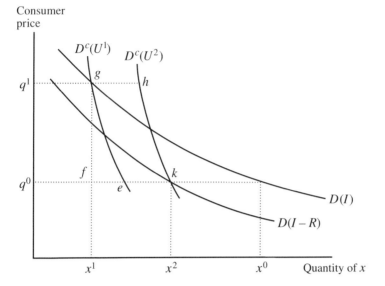

Figure 2.6
Gain from replacing an excise tax with a lump-sum tax

$$\Delta M = e(q^1, U^2) - e(q^1, U^1) = e(q^1, U^2) - [e(q^0, U^2) + R] = \text{area } q^1 h k q^0 - R$$

$$= EB_{EV} + \text{area } ghke \tag{2.6}$$

based on the relationships $I = e(q^1, U^1)$, $I - R = e(q^0, U^2)$, $e(q^1, U^2) - e(q^0, U^2) =$ area $q^1 h k q^0$ and $EB_{EV} =$ area gfe. This analysis shows that ΔM will be larger than the EB_{EV} by an amount which is equal to the area between the two compensated demand curves, $D^c(U^1)$ and $D^c(U^2)$ or the area $ghke$. This area can be approximated as $t(gh) = t(dx/dI) \cdot \Delta M = \tau b \mu \Delta M$, where $b = qx/I$ is the budget share of the commodity and $\mu = (dx/dI)(I/x)$ is the income elasticity of demand for the taxed commodity. Consequently the gain per dollar of tax revenue from substituting an equal yield lump-sum tax for an excise tax is equal to

$$\frac{\Delta M}{R} = \frac{1}{2}\left(\frac{-\tau \varepsilon^c}{1 - \tau b \mu}\right), \tag{2.7}$$

which exceeds the equivalent variation-based measure of excess burden by the factor of $(1 - \tau b \mu)^{-1} > 1$.

The relationship between ΔM and EB_{EV} can be explained as follows. EB_{EV} is a measure of the efficiency loss caused by the excise tax measured at the pre-tax prices q^0. ΔM is a money measure of the efficiency gain from switching to an equal-yield lump-sum tax measured at the current post–tax reform prices, q^1. To convert the EB_{EV} measure into the equivalent ΔM, we have to multiply EB_{EV} by $\lambda(q^0, U^1)$, which converts EB_{EV} into the equivalent utility loss. Dividing this utility loss by $\lambda(q^1, U^1)$ converts it into a money measure of the efficiency gain at the post-tax prices, q^1. Thus ΔM is related to EB_{EV} as follows:

$$\Delta M = EB_{EV} \cdot \frac{\lambda(q^0, U^1)}{\lambda(q^1, U^1)} = EB_{EV} \cdot P(q^0, q^1, U^1), \tag{2.8}$$

where $P(q^0, q^1, U^1)$ is a price index, which converts welfare changes measured at q^0 into welfare changes measured at q^1. This price index is the ratio of the marginal utilities of income for pre- and post-tax prices measured at the same level of utility, U^1.

Below we examine some of the properties of the price index $P(q^0, q^1, U^1)$. First, we examine the effect of a change in the price of a commodity on the marginal utility of income, holding utility constant. Let $V = V(q, I)$ denote the consumer's indirect utility function, with $\lambda(q, I) = \partial V/\partial I$. By Roy's theorem, $\partial V/\partial q = -\lambda x(q, I)$, the ordinary demand function for x.

If a price increases by dq, and the individual's utility remains constant, then there must be an increase in income such that $dI = x \, dq$ as is shown below:

$$\frac{dV}{dq} \cdot dq + \frac{dV}{dI} \cdot dI = 0 \quad \text{or} \quad -\lambda x dq + \lambda dI = 0 \quad \text{or} \quad \frac{dI}{dq}\bigg|_U = x. \tag{2.9}$$

Therefore

$$\frac{\partial \lambda(q, U)}{\partial q} = \frac{d\lambda}{dq} + \frac{d\lambda}{dI} \cdot \frac{dI}{dq}\bigg|_U = \frac{d\lambda}{dq} + x \cdot \frac{d\lambda}{dI}. \tag{2.10}$$

The total derivative of λ with respect to q is equal to

$$\frac{d\lambda}{dq} = \frac{d}{dq}\left(\frac{dV}{dI}\right) = \frac{d}{dI}\left(\frac{dV}{dq}\right) = \frac{d}{dI}(-\lambda x) = -\left(\lambda \frac{dx}{dI} + x \frac{d\lambda}{dI}\right). \tag{2.11}$$

Substituting the equation above into (2.10) yields

$$\frac{\partial \lambda(q, U)}{\partial q} = -\left(\lambda \frac{dx}{dI} + x \frac{d\lambda}{dI}\right) + x \cdot \frac{d\lambda}{dI} = -\lambda \frac{dx}{dI}. \tag{2.12}$$

Since $\lambda > 0$, this implies that $\partial \lambda/\partial q$ and dx/dI have opposite signs. In other words, for utility held constant, an increase in the price of a normal good leads to a decline in the marginal utility of income. Consequently, when an excise tax is imposed on a normal good, $P(q^0, q^1, U^1) > 1$ and $\Delta M > EB_{EV}$. Furthermore use of the first-order Taylor series approximation obtains

$$\lambda(q^1, U^1) \approx \lambda(q^0, U^1) + \frac{\partial \lambda(q^0, U^1)}{\partial q}(q^1 - q^0)$$

$$= \lambda(q^0, U^1) - \lambda(q^0, U^1)\frac{\partial x}{\partial I}(q^1 - q^0)$$

or

$$\frac{\lambda(q^1, U^1)}{\lambda(q^0, U^1)} \approx 1 - \frac{q^0 x^0}{I}\left(\frac{\partial x}{\partial I}\right)\left(\frac{I}{x^0}\right)\left(\frac{q^1 - q^0}{q^0}\right). \tag{2.13}$$

Thus $P(q^0, q^1, U^1) \approx (1 - \tau b \mu)^{-1}$, and this is why ΔM is approximately $(1 - \tau b \mu)^{-1}$ times as large as EB in (2.7). It can also be shown that if there are taxes on n commodities the price index can be approximated as $P(q^0, q^1, U^1) \approx (1 - \sum_{i=1}^{n} b_i \tau_i \mu_i)^{-1}$ As we will see in section 2.5, the price index $P(q^0, q^1, U^1)$ also plays a similar role in linking the marginal excess burden of taxation with the marginal cost of public funds.

2.2 Optimal Taxation and Public Expenditures

We will derive here a general expression for the social marginal cost of public funds (SMCF) and the conditions for optimal taxation and public spending, within the following simple, yet general, framework. Suppose that the government levies taxes on n tax bases. We let τ_i represent the tax rate imposed on tax base i. The government uses its tax revenue to finance m publicly provided goods, so we let G_j represent good j provided by the government. Total tax revenue $R(\tau, G)$ will, in general, be a function of all the tax rates and public services provided by the government. Remember, public good provision can affect the level of tax revenues. That is, for tax rates held constant, public services will affect the demand for, or the supply of, the tax bases. Also the tax bases will, in general, be interrelated so that an increase τ_i will affect the tax revenues generated from tax base j. In this case the government's budget constraint is $R(\tau, G) = C(G)$, where $C(G)$ is the cost of producing public services.

It is assumed here that tax and expenditure policies are evaluated using a social welfare function based on the well-being of the members of the society, $S = S(U^1, U^2, \ldots, U^H)$. This social welfare function implicitly uses a set of distributional weights to evaluate gains or losses by different individuals in the society. Since the tax rates and public services affect individuals' well-being, $U^i = U^i(\tau, G)$, we will simply express the social welfare function in terms of the tax rates and the public services $S(\tau, G)$. (A more conventional treatment of distributional issues using a social welfare function is contained in section 2.7.) Although an increase in a tax rate may make some individuals better off (e.g., if the tax reduces the production of a private good that generates harmful externalities), in general, we expect that $\partial S / \partial \tau_i < 0$

because taxes raise consumer prices or reduce the net incomes of producers. Further-more, although some people may be made worse off by the provision of the public good,[5] we will assume that on balance $\partial S / \partial G_j > 0$, either because more people gain than lose from the provision of the good or because it provides benefits to individuals who have particularly high distributional weights in the social welfare function. The problem for the government is to choose the values of τ and G that maximize the social welfare function subject to its budget constraint. To solve this maximization problem, we set up the Lagrange equation

$$\Lambda = S(\tau, G) + \mu(R(\tau, G) - C(G)), \tag{2.14}$$

where μ is the Lagrange multiplier on the government's budget constraint. The first-order conditions are

$$\frac{\partial S}{\partial \tau_i} + \mu \frac{\partial R}{\partial \tau_i} = 0 \qquad \text{for } i = 1, 2, 3, \ldots, n, \tag{2.15}$$

$$\frac{\partial S}{\partial G_j} - \mu \left(\frac{\partial R}{\partial G_j} - \frac{\partial C}{\partial G_j} \right) = 0 \qquad \text{for } j = 1, 2, 3, \ldots, m. \tag{2.16}$$

The conditions in (2.15), which can be rewritten in the form

$$SMCF_{\tau_i} \equiv \frac{-\partial S / \partial \tau_i}{\partial R / \partial \tau_i} = \mu \qquad \text{for } i = 1, 2, 3, \ldots, n, \tag{2.17}$$

indicate that the social marginal cost of raising an additional dollar of revenue from tax base i, $SMCF_{\tau_i}$, should be the same for all tax bases. Just as a multi-plant firm can minimize the total cost of producing a given level of output by allocating produc-tion among its factories so that the marginal cost of production is the same in each plant, a government can minimize the total social cost of generating a given level of tax revenue by setting its tax rates so as to equalize the SMCF for each tax base. The definition of the SMCF in (2.17) is very general, and much of this book is devoted to measuring the SMCF for different taxes and in different contexts.

The first-order conditions determining the optimal provision of each publicly pro-vided good can be written as

$$SMB_{G_j} = SMCF(MC_{G_j} - R_{G_j}), \tag{2.18}$$

where $SMB_{G_j} \equiv \partial S / \partial G_j$ is the social marginal benefit of an additional unit of public good j, $MC_{G_j} \equiv \partial C / \partial G_j$ is the marginal cost of producing good j, $R_{G_j} \equiv \partial R / \partial G_j$ is the change in total tax revenues caused by the provision of an additional unit of the public service, and SMCF is the social marginal cost of funds from all tax bases. This condition is known as the Atkinson-Stern (1974) rule for the optimal provision of a public good financed by distortionary taxation. It implies that the marginal production cost minus the gain in tax revenues from provision of the public good should be multiplied by the SMCF to derive the total social marginal cost of producing and financing an additional unit of the public good. Alternatively, the Atkinson-Stern condition can be written as $SMB_{G_j} + SMCF \cdot R_{G_j} = SMCF \cdot MC_{G_j}$, where the left-hand side represents the sum of the direct social marginal benefit plus the social marginal value of additional tax revenue caused by the provision of the good. Thus the social marginal cost of public funds is a key concept in the normative theory of public finance, defining an optimal tax system and providing a link between optimal taxation and expenditure decisions.

Four points should be noted about the Atkinson-Stern condition. First, the Samuelson condition for the optimal provision of a public good—the sum of the marginal benefits to individuals should equal the marginal cost of producing the public good—is a special case to the Atkinson-Stern condition because the Samuelson condition assumes that lump-sum taxes are used to finance the public good. Therefore $SMCF = 1$, $R_G = 0$, and the SMB would be the sum of the marginal benefits. Second, the R_G will generally vary with different types of public expenditures if they are financed by distortionary taxes, and R_G may be positive or negative. For example, if G_j represents a lump-sum income transfer to low-income individuals, the R_{Gj} may be negative if it reduces their labor supplies. (Alternatively, it might be argued that such transfer can have a positive revenue effect if they allow credit market constrained individuals to acquire more human capital and become more productive.) If G_j is infrastructure, such as a road or bridge, it may improve the productivity of private inputs, labor and capital. In many instances the improvement in private sector productivity will lead to higher tax revenues, but it is also possible that tax revenues will decline. For example, an improvement in recreational facilities might increase time devoted to leisure and reduce income and payroll tax revenues. Third, both the SMBs and the SMCF should be measured using the same prices to evaluate the individuals' gains and losses from public good provision and taxation and that same social welfare function or distributional weights should be used in evaluating these gains and losses. Fourth, optimal taxation is a goal that is seldom realized in practice. To evaluate public expenditures when taxes are not set optimally, the analyst can still use the Atkinson-Stern condition but use the SMCF for the tax base that will be used to finance the additional spending.

2.3   The MCF and the Gain from Tax Reform

Because tax systems are rarely "optimal," economists need to evaluate various tax reform proposals that may or may not move the tax system closer to the "optimal system." In this section we will learn how the marginal cost of public funds (MCF) can be used to determine the net gain to a society from a revenue-neutral tax reform. To keep the analysis as simple as possible, we will ignore distributional issues by assuming that the economy only consists of a single individual whose well-being is represented by the indirect utility function $V(q, I)$, where q is the vector of consumer prices that depend on the tax rates imposed on the n commodities and I is lump-sum income. (Incorporating distributional concerns in the measurement of the SMCF is considered in section 2.7). Total tax revenues, $R = \sum_{i=1}^{n} t_i x_i$ will depend on the tax rates imposed on n commodities that are consumed by the individual.

Suppose that the government engages in a revenue-neutral tax reform by reducing t_i and increasing t_j. It is assumed that $dR/dt_i > 0$ and $dR/dt_j > 0$. This tax reform will be welfare improving if

$$dV = \frac{dV}{dt_i} dt_i + \frac{dV}{dt_j} dt_j > 0. \tag{2.19}$$

The government's budget constraint implies that the $dt_i < 0$ and $dt_j > 0$ must satisfy the following condition:

$$\frac{dR}{dt_i} dt_i + \frac{dR}{dt_j} dt_j = 0. \tag{2.20}$$

Solving (2.20) for dt_i in terms of dt_j and substituting in (2.19), we can write the condition for a welfare-improving tax reform as

$$dV = \left[\frac{-dV/dt_i}{dR/dt_i} + \frac{dV/dt_j}{dR/dt_j} \right] \frac{dR}{dt_j} dt_j \geq 0. \tag{2.21}$$

A money measure of the welfare gain from the tax reform can be obtained by dividing dV by the marginal utility of income:

$$\frac{dV}{\lambda(q, I)} = (MCF_{t_i} - MCF_{t_j}) \frac{dR}{dt_j} dt_j \geq 0, \tag{2.22}$$

where the marginal cost of raising an extra dollar of tax revenue by increasing tax rate t_i is defined by the expression

$$MCF_{t_i} = -\frac{-[1/\lambda(q, I)]dV/dt_i}{dR/dt_i}. \tag{2.23}$$

The MCF_{t_i} measures the monetary cost (at the price vector q and the lump-sum income level I) to the individual of raising an additional dollar of tax revenue from tax base i. In defining the MCF_{t_i}, we can assume that dR/dt_i is positive, meaning the government is operating on the upward-sloping section of its Laffer curve with respect to t_i.[6]

Equation (2.22) shows that switching revenues from tax base i to tax base j will improve the taxpayer's well-being if $MCF_{t_i} > MCF_{t_{ji}}$. With the optimal tax system, where the marginal cost of raising revenue is the same for all tax sources, there is no potential gain from a revenue-neutral tax reform.

It is again important to emphasize that the measured welfare gain in (2.22) depends on the particular set of prices that are used to measure the welfare changes. In particular, the MCFs are money measures of the welfare cost of raising an additional dollar of tax revenues, and these will depend on the particular set of prices that are used to measure the welfare changes. While, in theory, any arbitrary set of prices can be used to measure the MCFs, we will argue that using current market prices, which reflect the current set of taxes, makes the analysis intuitively meaningful for policy makers and the public. The most useful definition of the MCF is one that uses current market prices to measure welfare changes. We will define the MCF using $\lambda(q^1, I)$, or equivalently $\lambda(q^1, U^1)$, to convert utility changes into money measures of welfare change. The implications of using current market prices in measuring the MCF will be discussed at greater length in section 2.4.

Equation (2.22) provides a measure of the gain for small changes in the tax rates on two commodities. However, tax reforms often involve large tax rate changes. To evaluate these more realistic tax reforms, we need to be able to measure the gains from discrete tax rate changes. To illustrate the gains from discrete tax rate changes, consider the following example, illustrated in figures 2.7, where in the initial situation the tax rate on x_i is t_i^1 and the tax rate on x_j is zero. Then there is a revenue-neutral substitution, with the elimination of the tax on x_i and a tax of t_j^2 imposed on x_j. Although this tax reform could occur instantaneously, for the purposes of calculating the gain from the tax reform, we can think of the tax rates being varied in a revenue-

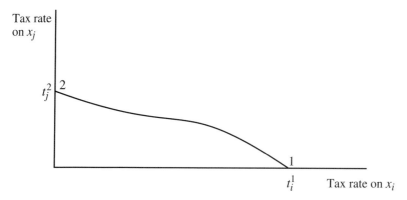

Figure 2.7
Revenue-neutral tax reform

neutral way along the path from point 1 to point 2 depicted in figure 2.7. The welfare gain along this path, measured at current prices, can be derived as follows by way of equation (2.22):

$$\frac{\Delta V}{\lambda^1} = \int \left(\frac{\lambda}{\lambda^1}\right) \frac{dV}{\lambda} = \int (MCF_{t_i} - MCF_{t_j}) P \frac{dR}{dt_j} dt_j, \tag{2.24}$$

where λ^1 is the marginal utility of income in the initial situation, and $P = (\lambda/\lambda^1)$ is a price index that converts the gains from the tax reform at a particular point on the path to a welfare gain measured at current prices. The MCFs and the P are measured at the tax rates (and prices) along the revenue-neutral path for the tax rates, such as the one shown in figure 2.7. Equation (2.24) indicates that the gain from the tax reform is equal to the difference in the MCFs of the two taxes multiplied by the price index and summed over the changes in tax revenue collected from x_j.

The gain from substituting the tax on x_j for the tax on x_i is illustrated in figure 2.8. Initially no revenue is collected from the tax on x_j, and the gap between the MCFs for the two taxes is given by the distance ac. Substituting the first dollar of tax revenue from x_i to x_j results in a net social gain equal to if $MCF_{t_i}^1 - MCF_{t_j}^1$. Each additional dollar of tax revenue that is substituted from the x_i tax base to the x_j tax base generates a net gain equal to the difference between the MCFs for the two taxes. Multiplying by the price index P converts them to gains measured at current prices. As t_i and t_j change, the MCFs for the two taxes will also change. Eliminating the last

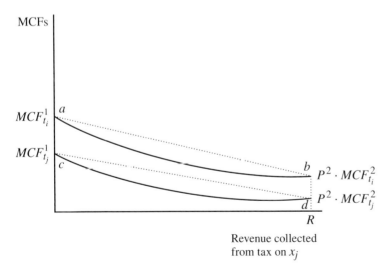

Figure 2.8
Measuring the gain from a tax reform using the MCFs

dollar of tax revenue collected on x_i yields a net social gain equal to the distance bd multiplied by the price index $P^2 = \lambda(q^2, U^2)/\lambda(q^1, U^1)$. Therefore the net gain from the revenue neutral tax reform is equal to the area between the two solid lines in figure 2.8.[7]

Equation (2.24), or equivalently the area between the solid lines in figure 2.8, is an exact measure of the gain from a revenue-neutral tax reform. However, in many instances it will be convenient to approximate this gain by the area between the dashed lines ab and cd. This approximation, expressed as the gain per dollar of tax revenue, is equal to

$$\Gamma \approx \frac{1}{2}[(MCF^1_{t_i} - MCF^1_{t_j}) + P^2(MCF^2_{t_i} - MCF^2_{t_j})]. \tag{2.25}$$

In other words, we can approximate Γ, the gain per dollar of revenue from a tax reform, by using estimates of the MCFs in the pre-reform and post-reform situations and the price index P^2. Note that P^2 is the ratio of the post-reform and pre-reform marginal utilities of income and that, in general, $U^1 \neq U^2$. Indeed one would expect that with a significant tax reform U^2 would be substantially greater than U^1. Therefore P^2 is not the same as the price index in (2.8) to equate ΔM with EB_{EV}. We will see in section 2.5 how (2.25) can be used to evaluate the gains from tariff reform, but before doing so, we will require some background on the interpretation of the MCF.

2.4   Interpreting the MCF Using Demand and Supply Curves

An intuitive interpretation of the marginal cost of public funds can be obtained using the familiar demand and supply framework. Suppose that there is only one taxed commodity, all markets are perfectly competitive, and all producers and consumers are identical so that the distributional effects of imposing the tax can be ignored. In figure 2.9, D and S are the ordinary (uncompensated) market demand and supply curves for x. In the absence of taxation, the price of the good would be q^0, and x^0 units would be produced and consumed. When a tax of t^1 dollars per unit of x is imposed on the producers of this commodity, the consumer price increases to q^1, and the price that producers receive declines to $p^1 = q^1 - t^1$. The quantity of x produced and consumed declines to x^1. The total tax revenue collected by the government is $R^1 = t^1 \cdot x^1$ or the area $q^1 agp^1$.

The increase in the price paid by consumers reduces consumer surplus by an amount equal to the area $q^1 abq^0$, and the decline in the producer price causes a loss of producer surplus equal to the area $q^0 bgp^1$. The loss of consumer and producer surplus exceeds the revenue raised by the tax by the area of the triangle abg, which is the equivalent of the EB_{CS}.

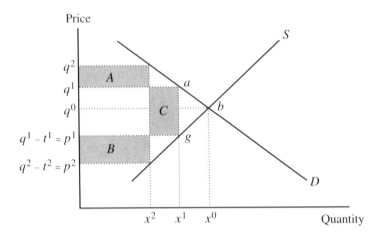

Figure 2.9
The MCF with demand and supply curves

Now consider the cost of raising additional tax revenue by increasing the tax rate to t^2. The consumer price increases to q^2, the producer price declines to p^2, and output declines to x^2. The change in total tax revenue, $\Delta R = t^2 x^2 - t^1 x^1$, would be equal to shaded areas $A + B - C$. The reduction in the value of the economy's net output (the value of the lost output to consumers less the opportunity cost of the resources to producers) is given by the area between the demand and supply curves over the output range $x^1 - x^2$. The area C is an approximation to the decline in the value of net output.

The MCF of the tax is equal to the additional dollar that the private sector surrenders to the government plus the reduction in the net output of the private sector per dollar of revenue, or

$$MCF = 1 + \frac{C}{A + B - C} = \frac{A + B}{A + B - C}.$$ (2.26)

Since, for a small tax rate increase, $A + B$ is the loss of consumer and producer surpluses, the MCF can also be interpreted as the loss of consumer and producer surplus per dollar of additional tax revenue. Equation (2.26) indicates that the MCF is greater than one if the output of x declines, or in other words if $C > 0$.

To derive a formula for the MCF, we write the individual's indirect utility functions as $V(q, p, I)$, where $\partial V / \partial p = \lambda x > 0$; that is, an increase in the producer price of a commodity increases the individual's utility in proportion to the amount of the good supplied. The effect of an increase in the tax rate on the individual's utility is equal to

$$\frac{dV}{dt} = \frac{\partial V}{\partial q}\frac{dq}{dt} + \frac{\partial V}{\partial p}\frac{dp}{dt} = -\lambda x^1 \frac{dq}{dt} + \lambda x^1 \frac{dp}{dt} = -\lambda x^1, \tag{2.27}$$

where we use the fact that $dq/dt = dp/dt + 1$.

The rate of change in tax revenues is equal to:

$$\frac{dR}{dt} = x^1 + t\frac{dx}{dq}\frac{dq}{dt} = x^1\left(1 + \frac{t}{q}\left(\frac{q}{x^1}\frac{dx}{dq}\right)\frac{dq}{dt}\right) = x^1\left(1 + \tau\varepsilon\frac{dq}{dt}\right)$$

$$= x^1\left(1 + \tau\varepsilon\left(\frac{\eta}{\eta - (1-\tau)\varepsilon}\right)\right), \tag{2.28}$$

where η and ε are the ordinary or uncompensated elasticities of supply and demand and τ is the ad valorem tax rate, t/q. In the case illustrated in figure 2.9, $\eta > 0$ and $\varepsilon < 0$.

The substitution for dq/dt in the right-hand side of (2.28) is based on a formula for the degree of forward shifting of a per unit tax levied on producers in a perfectly competitive market. See appendix 2.1 for the derivation of this formula.

Substituting (2.27) and (2.28) in the definition of the MCF in (2.23) yields the following formula for the MCF:

$$MCF_t = \frac{(-1/\lambda)dV/dt}{dR/dt} = \frac{x^1}{dR/dt} = \frac{\eta - (1-\tau)\varepsilon}{\eta - (1-\tau)\varepsilon + \tau\varepsilon\eta}, \tag{2.29}$$

where the λ in (2.29) is measured at the current market prices, q^1 and p^1, and therefore it is equal to the λ in (2.27). The formula indicates that the MCF will be larger the more elastic the demand and supply of the taxed commodity and the higher the existing tax rate.

Equation (2.29) encompasses some important special cases. If demand is perfectly elastic and the demand curve is horizontal line, the MCF is equal to $(1 - (\tau/(1-\tau))\eta)^{-1}$. If the supply is perfectly elastic and the supply curve is horizontal line, the MCF is equal to $(1 + \tau\varepsilon)^{-1}$. On the other hand, if either the demand or the supply of the taxed commodity is completely inelastic, $\varepsilon = 0$ or $\eta = 0$, then the MCF will be equal to one because the total output of the taxed commodity is unchanged when the tax rate is increased. This result is puzzling because it seems to be inconsistent with the analysis in figure 2.2, which showed that a tax imposes an excess burden even if the ordinary demand curve for the taxed commodity is completely inelastic. This seems to suggest that the MCF should be greater than one even if $\varepsilon = 0$. To resolve this puzzle, we will explore in the next section the connection between the MCF and the marginal excess burden of a tax.

2.5   Relationship between the MCF and the MEB

Marginal excess burden (MEB) is defined as the rate at which the excess burden increases when an additional dollar of tax revenue is raised, $MEB = dEB/dR$. We will begin by deriving the MEB using the equivalent variation-based measure of excess burden. Taking the derivative of (2.1) with respect to the tax rate, and noting that $e(q^0, U^0)$ is a constant, yields

$$\frac{dEB_{EV}}{dt} = -\frac{\partial e(q_0, U^1)}{\partial U} \cdot \frac{dU}{dq^1} \cdot \frac{dq^1}{dt} - \frac{dR}{dt}$$

$$= -\frac{1}{\lambda(q^0, U^1)} \cdot [-\lambda(q^1, U^1)x(q^1, U^1)] - \frac{dR}{dt}, \qquad (2.30)$$

where Roy's theorem is used to substitute $-\lambda x$ for dU/dq, and it is assumed that $dq^1/dt = 1$. It is important to note that the two λ in (2.30) are measured at different sets of prices and therefore they do not, in general, cancel out. Dividing (2.30) by dR/dt yields

$$MEB_{EV} = \frac{dEB_{EV}/dt}{dR/dt} = \frac{x}{dR/dt} \cdot \frac{\lambda(q^1, U^1)}{\lambda(q^0, U^1)} - 1 = MCF \cdot \frac{\lambda(q^1, U^1)}{\lambda(q^0, U^1)} - 1, \qquad (2.31)$$

since from (2.29) the $MCF = x/(dR/dt)$. Clearly, MCF is equal to[8]

$$MCF = (1 + MEB_{EV}) \cdot \frac{\lambda(q^0, U^1)}{\lambda(q^1, U^1)}. \qquad (2.32)$$

As in section 2.1.2, the price index $P(q^0, q^1, U^1) = \lambda(q^0, U^1)/\lambda(q^1, U^1)$ converts a loss measured at the pre-tax prices to a loss measured at the post-tax prices. In other words, $(1 + MEB_{EV})$ is the monetary measure of the harm inflicted on the private sector from raising an additional dollar of tax revenue, measured at the pre-tax prices q^0. Multiplying $(1 + MEB_{EV})$ by $\lambda(q^0, U^1)$ converts it into a utility measure of the loss based on the pre-tax prices, q^0. Dividing this utility loss by $\lambda(q^1, U^1)$ converts it into a utility measure of the loss based on the pre-tax prices, q^0. The MCF measures the cost of raising an additional dollar of tax revenue measured at current tax distorted prices, while $(1 + MEB_{EV})$ measures the cost of raising an additional dollar of tax revenue at pre-tax prices. Using the approximation to $P(q^0, q^1, U^1) \approx (1 - \tau b\mu)^{-1}$, we obtain

$$MCF \approx (1 + MEB_{EV})(1 - \tau b\mu)^{-1}. \qquad (2.33)$$

This implies that the MCF is only equal to $(1 + MEB_{EV})$ if the income elasticity of demand for the taxed commodity is zero. If a tax is imposed on a normal good, then

$\lambda(q^0, U^1) > \lambda(q^1, U^1)$ and $MCF > 1 + MEB_{EV}$. Conversely, if a tax is imposed on an inferior good, then $\lambda(q^0, U^1) < \lambda(q^1, U^1)$ and $MCF < 1 + MEB_{EV}$. This is the situation depicted in figure 2.2 because a good with completely inelastic demand is an inferior good.

The approximation $P(q^0, q^1, U^1) \approx (1 - \tau b \mu)^{-1}$ helps to explain why the $MCF = 1$ if $\varepsilon = 0$ even though the MEB_{EV} is positive. Using (2.3), we find that the MEB_{EV} is approximately equal to

$$MEB_{EV} \approx \frac{-\frac{1}{2}\varepsilon^c R - \frac{1}{2}\tau \varepsilon^c (\partial R/\partial \tau)}{\partial R/\partial \tau} = -\frac{1}{2}\tau \varepsilon^c \left(1 + \frac{1}{(\tau/R)(\partial R/\partial \tau)}\right)$$

$$= -\frac{1}{2}\tau \varepsilon^c \left(\frac{2 + \tau \varepsilon}{1 + \tau \varepsilon}\right), \tag{2.34}$$

since $(\tau/R)(\partial R/\partial \tau) = (1 + \tau \varepsilon)$. When $\varepsilon = 0$, $(1 + MEB_{EV}) = 1 - \tau \varepsilon^c$. From the Slutsky condition, $\varepsilon^c = b\mu$ when $\varepsilon = 0$. Therefore $(1 + MEB_{EV}) = 1 - \tau b \mu$, the reciprocal of $\lambda(q^0, U^1)/\lambda(q^1, U^1)$. Consequently, from (2.32), we have that the MCF is equal to one when $\varepsilon = 0$.

Now we will derive the relationship between the compensating variation-based measure of the marginal excess burden, MEB_{CV}, and the MCF. Both the MCF and the CV measure the losses at the current tax-distorted prices. However, the EB_{CV} is based on compensated tax revenue, and therefore it is natural to define the MEB_{EV} as the additional excess burden generated in raising an additional dollar of compensated tax revenue, or

$$MEB_{CV} = \frac{dEB_{CV}/dt}{dR^c/dt}$$

$$= \frac{\partial e(q^1, U^0)/\partial t - \partial e(q^1, U^1)/\partial t - (\partial e(q^1, U^1)/\partial U)(\partial U^1/\partial t) - \partial R^c/\partial t}{\partial R^c/\partial t}$$

$$= \frac{x(q^1, U^0) - x(q^1, U^1) - (-\lambda(q^1, U^1)x(q^1, U^1))/\lambda(q^1, U^1)}{dR^c/dt} - 1$$

$$= \frac{x(q^1, U^0)}{dR^c/dt} - 1 = \frac{1}{1 + \tau \varepsilon^c} - 1 = \frac{-\tau \varepsilon^c}{1 + \tau \varepsilon^c}, \tag{2.35}$$

where ε^c is evaluated at (q^1, U^0). It is assumed that the government is operating on the upward-sloping section of its (compensated) Laffer curve and therefore $1 + \tau \varepsilon^c > 0$. Since $(1 + MEB_{CV}) = (1 + \tau \varepsilon^c)^{-1}$ and $MCF = (1 + \tau \varepsilon)^{-1}$, the relationship between the MCF and the MEB_{CV} is as given below:

$$MCF = (1 + MEB_{CV})\left(\frac{1 + \tau\varepsilon^c}{1 + \tau\varepsilon}\right). \tag{2.36}$$

Thus the MCF is equal to $(1 + MEB_{CV})$ multiplied by the factor $(1 + \tau\varepsilon^c)/(1 + \tau\varepsilon)$, which is equal to dR^c/dR. This factor converts the loss per dollar of compensated revenue into a loss per dollar of actual revenue, which is what is needed to measure the marginal cost of the government's net expenditure on a public service. From the Slutsky condition, $\varepsilon = \varepsilon^c - b\mu$, we can conclude that the MCF will equal $(1 + MEB_{CV})$ only if the income elasticity of demand for the taxed commodity is zero. If the taxed commodity is a normal good, $(1 + \tau\varepsilon^c)/(1 + \tau\varepsilon)$ will be greater than one, and the MCF greater than $(1 + MEB_{CV})$. If the good is inferior, the MCF will be less than $(1 + MEB_{CV})$. In the special case where $\varepsilon = 0$, $(1 + MEB_{CV})$ is equal to the reciprocal of $dR^c/dR = (1 + \tau\varepsilon^c)$, and therefore the MCF is equal to one.

The consumer surplus-based measure of excess burden is equal to

$$MEB_{CS} = \frac{dEB_{CS}/dt}{dR/dt} = \frac{x(q^1, I)}{dR/dt} - 1. \tag{2.37}$$

Consequently $MCF = 1 + MEB_{CS}$, which confirms the intuition conveyed in figure 2.9 that the MCF can be viewed as the loss of consumer (and producer) surplus in raising an additional dollar of tax revenue through a tax rate increase.

To summarize, we have defined the MCF as the cost to the private sector of raising an additional dollar of tax revenue, measured at the current tax-distorted prices. The MCF is equal to (1) one plus the MEB_{CS}, (2) one plus the MEB_{EV} multiplied by a price index, and (3) one plus the MEB_{CV} multiplied by a factor relating marginal compensated revenues to actual revenues. In the latter two cases the difference between the MCF and $(1 + MEB)$ is increasing in the tax rate, the income elasticity of demand, and the budget share of the taxed commodity. These relationships imply that $MCF = 1$ does not mean that a tax is nondistortionary; that is, $MCF = 1$ does not mean that the marginal excess burden, as measured by the EV or the CV, is zero. Furthermore they also imply that a tax with $MCF > 1$ is not necessarily a distortionary tax. Consequently one must be very cautious in interpreting the MCF, and no special significance should be attributed to the MCF when it is greater than or less than one.

2.6 Application: The MCF for a Tariff and the Gain from Free Trade

In the nineteenth century, tariffs were the most important source of revenue in most countries. Over the last fifty years, most developed countries have reduced their tariffs because of the GATT and the emergence of free trade zones such as NAFTA and the European Union, and tariffs are no longer an important source of tax revenue in developed countries. However, tariffs continue to be an important source of tax revenue for some developing countries, in part because the cost of administering tariffs may be low compared to the administrative and compliance costs of value-added, payroll, or income taxes. For example, in sub-Saharan Africa in 1994 to 1996, taxes on international trade represented 36.2 percent of total tax revenue, while domestic taxes on goods and services were 31.3 percent and taxes on income, profits and capital gains were 27.6 percent of tax revenue.[9] The small island countries of the Caribbean are also heavily dependent on tariffs for tax revenues. The movement to free trade zones, such as the Free Trade Area of the Americas, presents special challenges for these countries because they need to adopt alternative sources of tax revenue when they lower their tariff barriers.

In this section we analyze the MCF for a tariff and derive a measure of the net gain from a revenue-neutral switch from a tariff to a broad consumption tax.[10] This framework can be used to compare the efficiency gain from the improvement in resource allocation obtained by eliminating tariffs to the additional administrative and compliance costs that may have to be incurred in levying some other form of taxation. (See Slemrod 1990 on optimal tax systems and tax collection costs.)

The analysis proceeds within a very simple framework. It is assumed that we are dealing with a small economy that faces a perfectly elastic supply of the goods at exogenously determined world prices. For simplicity we treat all goods as a single commodity x that can be imported at the world price, normalized to equal one. The domestic price is therefore equal to $1 + \tau_m$, where τ_m is the ad valorem tax rate on imports M, which is the difference between domestic demand and domestic supply. Domestic production of x is an increasing function of the domestic price of the commodity, and domestic demand is a decreasing function of the domestic price. Figure 2.10 shows the initial situation when the tariff is τ_m^1, the domestic supply curve is S, and the domestic demand curve is D. Initially imports are equal to M^1, and total tariff revenues are equal to the area $abcd$. It is assumed that there are no other taxes.

An increase in the tariff to τ_m^2 raises the domestic price of the good, leading to an increase in domestic production from S^1 to S^2, a reduction in domestic consumption from D^1 to D^2, and a decline in total imports to M^2. It is assumed that the economy is operating on the upward-sloping section of the Laffer curve for tariff revenues, and that tariff revenues increase, from $abcd$ to $efgh$, as a result of the tax rate increase.

The increase in the tariff makes domestic producers better off and domestic consumers worse off. In this analysis we will ignore distributional considerations and measure the net social loss by the difference between the change in consumer surplus and the change in producer surplus, which for a small tariff increase is approximately equal to $M^1 d\tau_m$ = area $ifgj$. In other words, for this increase in the tariff, the MCF

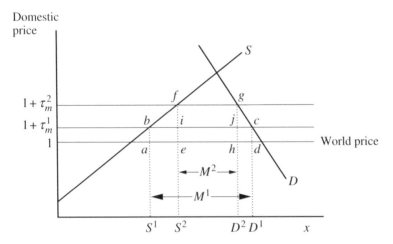

Figure 2.10
The MCF for a tariff

(assuming that there are no other distortions in the economy) is approximately equal
to

$$MCF_{t_m} = \frac{\text{area } ifgj}{\text{area } ifgj - \text{area } abie - \text{area } hjcd} = \frac{1}{1 + \tau_m[(D/M)\varepsilon - (S/M)\eta]}, \quad (2.38)$$

where $\varepsilon \leq 0$ is the price elasticity of domestic demand and $\eta \geq 0$ is the price elasticity
of domestic supply.

We want to compare the tariff's MCF with that of a broad consumption tax, τ_c,
which is levied on both domestic and foreign-produced goods. Based on our analysis
in section 2.3, the MCF for a consumption tax with a perfectly elastic world supply
curve is equal to[11]

$$MCF_{\tau_c} = \frac{1}{1 + \tau_c \varepsilon}. \quad (2.39)$$

Comparing (2.38) with (2.39), we see that at the same tax rates, the tariff's MCF will
be higher than the MCF from a consumption tax for two reasons. First, imports are
a more tax-sensitive tax base than total consumption because domestic production
increases when the tariff increases, causing imports and the tax base to shrink. (This
increase in production, in the absence of other distortions, is a misallocation of scarce
resources that have alternative uses.) The MCF for a tariff will be higher the greater
the elasticity of the domestic supply of the imported good. Second, even if the domestic supply is completely inelastic, the tariff's MCF is greater than the consumption
tax's MCF because the consumption tax is broader than the tariff tax base. As

imports become a larger share of total consumption, the tariff's MCF approaches the MCF for a consumption tax. In the limit, if a small country imports all of its consumer goods, the tariff is equivalent to a consumption tax.

This comparison of the MCFs of a tariff and a consumption tax has been based on the assumption that the tax rates are the same. However, since imports are less than domestic consumption, a consumption tax can raise the same revenue at a lower tax rate. That is, $\tau_c < (M^1/D^1)\tau_m$. The lower tax rate is another reason why a broad consumption tax will have a lower MCF and be a more efficient method of raising tax revenues than a tariff. (This relation, of course, assumes that supply and demand do not become much more elastic when prices decline.)

As previously noted, small developing countries may rely on tariffs as a revenue source because the cost of administering a tariff may be lower than the cost of collecting a broad consumption tax. Therefore policy makers need to know whether the efficiency gain from improved resource allocation, caused by the elimination of the tariff, is greater than the increase in administration and compliance costs. In this section we develop a simple measure of the efficiency gain from a revenue-neutral switch from a tariff to a broad consumption tax.

As noted in section 2.3, the gain per dollar of tax revenue from tax reform can be approximated by

$$\Gamma \approx \frac{1}{2}[(MCF^1_{\tau_m} - MCF^1_{\tau_c}) + P^2(MCF^2_{\tau_m} - MCF^2_{\tau_c})]. \tag{2.40}$$

The MCFs can be calculated from the formulas

$$MCF_{\tau_m} = \frac{1}{1 + (\tau_m + \tau_c)(D/M)\varepsilon - \tau_m(S/M)\eta}, \tag{2.41}$$

$$MCF_{\tau_c} = \frac{1}{1 + (\tau_c + \tau_m)\varepsilon}. \tag{2.42}$$

Note that these formulas differ from those in (2.38) and (2.39) because they take into account the interaction between the tariff and consumption tax bases. (This topic will be discussed in more detail in chapter 3.)

The price adjustment factor, P^2, can be approximated using a first-order Taylor series as

$$\lambda^2 \approx \lambda^1 + \sum_{j=1}^{n} \frac{\partial \lambda}{\partial q_j}(q_j^2 - q_j^1) + \sum_{k=1}^{m} \frac{\partial \lambda}{\partial p_k}(p_k^2 - p_k^1). \tag{2.43}$$

From (2.11), we can express $d\lambda/dq_j = -\lambda x_j(\rho + \mu_j)$, where ρ is the elasticity of the marginal utility of income and μ_j is the income elasticity of demand for commodity j. A similar expression can be obtained for $\partial \lambda / \partial p_j$. Therefore P^2 can be approximated as

$$P^2 = \frac{\lambda^2}{\lambda^1} \approx 1 - \sum_{j=1}^{n} b_j [\rho + \mu_j] \left(\frac{q_j^2 - q_j^1}{q_j^1} \right) + \sum_{k=1}^{m} f_k [\rho + \mu_k] \left(\frac{p_k^2 - p_k^1}{p_k^1} \right), \qquad (2.44)$$

where b_j is the budget share of commodity j, μ_j is the income elasticity of demand for commodity j, f_k is the share of income from input k, and μ_k is the income elasticity of supply for input k.

In the context of this simple model of tariff reform, it can be shown (see appendix 2.1) that P^2 can be approximated as

$$P^2 \approx 1 + \left[1 - \frac{M^1}{D^1} q^1 \frac{dD}{dI} \right] \left(\frac{\tau_m^1}{1 + \tau_m^1} \right), \qquad (2.45)$$

where $q^1 dD / dI$ is the marginal propensity to consume out of lump-sum income. Given equations (2.41), (2.42), and (2.45), we can approximate the efficiency gain per dollar of revenue in switching from a tariff to a general consumption tax using (2.40).

Table 2.1 gives some illustrative calculations based on the assumption that we are dealing with a country that is highly reliant on imports and tariffs for revenues. It is assumed that the initial tariff rate is 30 percent and that the marginal propensity to spend out of lump-sum income is 0.8.[12] In case 1, where imports are initially 40 percent of total consumption and the elasticities of supply and demand are 0.5, the MCF for the tariff is 2.50, which is substantially higher than the MCF for a general consumption tax, 1.80. The elimination of the tariff would actually reduce the MCF for the general consumption tax so that it would equal 1.06 if the tariff were replaced by the general consumption tax. The calculations indicate that the gains

Table 2.1
Gain from eliminating tariffs

	Case 1 $M/D = 0.40$, $\varepsilon = -0.50$, $\eta = 0.50$	Case 2 $M/D = 0.60$, $\varepsilon = -0.50$, $\eta = 0.50$	Case 3 $M/D = 0.40$, $\varepsilon = -0.25$, $\eta = 0.25$
$MCF_{\tau_m}^1$	2.50	1.54	1.43
$MCF_{\tau_c}^1$	1.18	1.18	1.08
$MCF_{\tau_m}^2$	1.18	1.18	1.08
$MCF_{\tau_c}^2$	1.06	1.10	1.03
P^2	1.16	1.12	1.16
Γ	0.727	0.224	0.203

Notes: The calculations are based on $\tau_m^1 = 0.30$, $\tau_c^1 = 0.00$, $\tau_m^2 = 0.00$, and $\tau_c^2 = (M/D)\tau_m^1$. The marginal propensity to consume is 0.80.

from replacing the tariff are substantial—72.7 cents for each dollar of tariff revenue replaced. Therefore, unless the additional administrative and compliance costs with the general consumption tax are more than 72.7 cents per dollar of tax revenue, replacing the tariff with a general consumption tax would generate a net social gain.

Cases 2 and 3 illustrate how the calculated gain from removing a tariff is affected by different values for the key parameters. In Case 2, if imports are 60 percent of total consumption instead of 40 percent, then the gain from eliminating the tariff is reduced to 22.4 cents per dollar of tariff revenue. This shows that the gain from replacing a tariff with a general consumption tax is smaller the more dependent the economy is on imports, but this gain can still be very substantial. Case 3 shows that if demand and supply are relatively inelastic, then (as expected) the gain from eliminating a tariff is reduced to 20.3 cents per dollar of tariff revenue, but this gain is still substantial.

These calculations are only illustrative, and they have been included here primarily to show how the concept of the marginal cost of public funds can be used to measure the efficiency gain from a tax reform. Nonetheless, they are at least suggestive that there may be substantial gains from eliminating tariffs, even for small countries that are highly dependent on imports.[13]

2.7   Incorporating Distributional Preferences in the MCF

To this point we have focused on the efficiency aspects of the marginal cost of public funds. However, all societies are concerned about the distributional impact of their tax system, and a tax that is borne mainly by the poor has a high social cost. Indeed governments use distortionary taxes because of their concern for distributional equity. In the absence of distributional concerns, governments could simply rely on lump-sum taxes. Consequently we need to incorporate distributional concerns in the measurement of the social marginal cost of public funds to fully evaluate tax and expenditure reforms.[14]

Suppose there are H households in the economy. Household h purchases x_i^h units of commodity i at the price q_i and supplies y_j^h units of input j at the price p_j. The household's budget constraint is $\sum_{i=1}^{n} q_i x_i^h = \sum_{j=1}^{m} p_j y_j^h + I^h$, where I^h is the household's lump-sum income. The level of utility or well-being that household h can obtain, given consumer and producer prices, its lump-sum income, its ownership of inputs, and its preferences, is indicated by its indirect utility function, $V^h = V^h(q, p, I^h, G)$, where q is the vector of consumer prices, p is the vector of producer prices, and G is a vector of publicly provided goods and services. By Roy's theorem, $\partial V^h / \partial q_i = -\lambda^h x_i^h < 0$, where $\lambda^h(q, p, I^h, G)$ is the household's marginal utility of income and $x_i^h(q, p, I^h, G)$ is the household's ordinary demand function for commodity *i*. Similarly $(1/\lambda^h)\partial V^h/\partial p_j = y_j^h(q, p, I^h, G)$ is the household's supply function for input *j*. The total demand for commodity *i* is $x_i = \sum_{h=1}^{H} x_i^h$ and the total supply of input *j* is $y_j = \sum_{h=1}^{H} y_j^h$.

It is assumed that tax and expenditure decisions are based on the social welfare function, $S = S(V^1, V^2, \ldots, V^H)$, which reflects the trade-off that a society is willing to make when a policy makes some households better off and other households worse off. The distributional weight, $\beta^h = (\partial S/\partial V^h)\lambda^h$, represents the value that the society places on an extra dollar of lump-sum income received by household *h*. It will be assumed that the social welfare function reflects a "pro-poor" preference such that β^h is higher when V^h is lower.

The social valuation of the households' welfare loss from an increase in the price of commodity *i* is

$$\frac{\partial S}{\partial q_i} = \sum_{h=1}^{H} \frac{\partial S}{\partial V^h} \cdot \frac{\partial V^h}{\partial q_i} = -\sum_{h=1}^{H} \beta^h \cdot x_i^h = -\left(\sum_{h=1}^{H} \beta^h \cdot s_i^h \right) x_i = -\omega_i x_i, \tag{2.46}$$

where $s_i^h = x_i^h/x_i$ is household *h*'s share of the total consumption of commodity *i*. The ω_i parameter is known as the distributional characteristic of commodity *i*, and it measures the social harm caused by increasing total household expenditure on x_i by a dollar. Note that ω_i will tend to be larger when β^h and s_i^h are positively correlated. This means that ω_i will be high for commodities that are consumed mainly by the poor. Similarly $\omega_j = \sum_{h=1}^{H} \beta^h s_j^h = \sum_{h=1}^{H} \beta^h (y_j^h/y_j)$ denotes the social value of an extra dollar of income paid to the owners of input *j*.

We will define the social marginal cost of public funds, SMCF, as the distributionally weighted cost of raising an additional dollar of tax revenue from a particular tax source. To evaluate the distributional effect of a tax increase, it is important to incorporate all of the consumer and producer price changes that result from it. In most economies, markets for commodities and inputs are interrelated, and a tax imposed on one commodity or tax base will, in general, result in price changes for some inputs and some other commodities. For example, a tax on x_i causes q_i to increase. The reduction in the demand for x_i also reduces the demand for inputs that are used intensively in the production of x_i, causing the relative prices of these inputs to decline. These relative input price changes, in turn, lead to changes in the prices of other commodities.

Let Ω_i denote the distributionally weighted cost of all of the consumer and producer prices resulting from an increase in the tax rate on commodity *i*:

$$\Omega_i = \frac{1}{x_i} \left[\sum_{k=1}^{n} \omega_k x_k \frac{dq_k}{dt_i} - \sum_{j=1}^{m} \omega_j y_j \frac{dp_j}{dt_i} \right]. \tag{2.47}$$

The $SMCF_{t_i}$ is equal to

$$SMCF_{t_i} = \frac{-dS/dt_i}{dR/dt_i} = \frac{\Omega_i x_i}{dR/dt_i} = \Omega_i \cdot MCF_{t_i}. \tag{2.48}$$

If producer prices were fixed, then $dq_i/dt_i = 1$, $dq_k/dt_i = 0$, and $dp_j/dt_i = 0$ for $i \neq k$, and $SMCF_{t_i} = \omega_i \cdot MCF_{t_i}$. (In the absence of distributional concerns, $\beta^h = 1$ for all h, $\omega_i = 1$ and $\Omega_i = 1$ for all i.) Thus the social marginal cost of public funds can be viewed as the product of an equity factor, Ω_i, and an efficiency factor, MCF_{t_i}.[15] Each of the three main components of Ω_i—the β^h and the s_i^h, which together determine the ω_i, and the tax-shifting parameters, the dq_k/dt_i and the dp_j/dt_i—will be discussed below.

The β^h reflect a society's, or perhaps more accurately its policy makers', willingness to trade-off gains and losses sustained by different segments of society. The distributional weights are based on value judgments, and economists have no special insights into what constitutes the appropriate set of distributional weights. Economists, however, have tried to help policy makers apply a consistent set of distributional weights. One approach is to use an explicit functional form for the relative distributional weights such as

$$\frac{\beta^h}{\beta^r} = \left(\frac{Y^h}{Y^r}\right)^{-\xi}, \tag{2.49}$$

where Y^r is the income of a reference household (e.g., a household with the average income) and $\xi \geq 0$ is a parameter that measures the society's aversion to inequality. A standard normalization is to set $\beta^r = 1$. If $\xi = 0$, $\beta^h = 1$ for all h, and no consideration is given to distributional concerns. On the other hand, if $Y^h = 0.5Y^r$, then $\beta^h = 1.414$ if $\xi = 0.5$ and $\beta^h = 2$ if $\xi = 1$. Thus, as figure 2.11 indicates, a larger value for ξ implies a more pro-poor set of distributional weights.[16] An example of the computation of the distributional characteristics of commodities in Thailand is contained in section 4.1.3.

The main problem with incorporating distributional concerns in the measurement of the marginal social cost of taxation is that there may be may be little agreement concerning the magnitudes of the distributional weights to be used. Sensitivity analysis might reveal the range of values of ξ that would generate a net social gain from a tax reform, but this might not be convincing for those who have strong views about distributional concerns. For example, Harberger (1978, p. S113) argued:

When distributional weights are used together with weighting functions of the type most commonly employed in writings on the subject, the result is to open the door to projects and programs whose degree of inefficiency by more traditional (unweighted) cost-benefit measures would . . . be unacceptable to the vast majority of economists and the informed public.

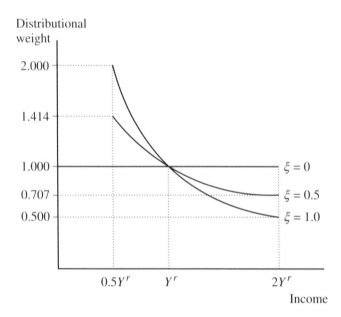

Distributional
weight

Figure 2.11
Distributional weights and the inequality aversion parameter

In view of the lack of consensus regarding the appropriate range of values for distributional weights, Mayshar and Yitzhaki (1995) developed an alternative procedure
that focuses on the tax reforms that would generate net social gains for any social
welfare function yielding the same ordinal ranking of the β^h. There is more like-
lihood of consensus on the ranking of the "deservedness" of different households,
than on the numerical values of the β^h, and therefore the identification of the
"Dalton-improving" tax reforms using the Mayshar-Yitzhaki approach may provide
a more credible analysis of the distributional impact of tax policy changes.

The tax-shifting parameters dq_k/dt_i and dp_j/dt_i are also required to determine the
distributional impact of a tax change. As noted above, a tax increase may change the
prices of a range of commodities and inputs because of the interdependence of commodity and input markets. Economists often use computable general equilibrium
(CGE) models to analyze the complex interactions that occur with tax policy changes
(e.g., see Ballard, Shoven, and Whalley 1985; Devarajan, Thierfelder, and Suthiwart-
Narueput 2002). In the absence of a CGE model, economists frequently have to
make "educated guesses" about the incidence of taxes, based on their understanding
of how markets interact. For example, if a country accounts for only a small proportion of total world production and consumption of a commodity, then the supply
curve of the commodity will be perfectly elastic at the world price. Any excise tax

increase will be fully reflected in the consumer price of the commodity. The prices of other commodities and input prices will not be affected. When tax-shifting assumptions have to be made in order to compute the SMCF, it is a good practice for the analyst to make these assumptions explicit and, where possible, to examine how alternative incidence might affect the computed SMCF.

2.8   Alternative Interpretations of the MCF

The literature on the marginal cost of public funds is large and diverse. A search of Google Scholar performed in January 2008 turned up 1,260 hits for "marginal cost of public funds." However, the relevant literature is even broader than this because many authors have used other terminology—marginal excess burden, marginal welfare cost, marginal efficiency cost of funds, and marginal revenue cost of increasing welfare (the inverse in the MCF)—to describe similar or closely related concepts. Summarizing this large and diverse literature is not an easy task. This section will only cover the key studies that have contributed to the development of the concept and the interpretation of the MCF. The papers that have made specific contributions to the calculation of the MCFs for commodity, labor, and capital taxes will be discussed in sections 3.8, 5.6, and 7.5.

I should begin by acknowledging that although I use the definite article to refer to the MCF developed in section 2.2, there are many different ways of defining the marginal cost of public funds, and no single definition has been widely adopted. Other authors have used different conceptual frameworks in defining the MCF. The fact that a wide range of measures have been proposed and used to compute the marginal cost of public funds does not mean there is a "problem" that has to be "resolved." A good analogy is with the literature on the measurement of income inequality, where many indexes, such as the Gini, the Theil, and the Atkinson, have been proposed and are used in empirical studies. No single index of inequality has emerged as dominant because they all have particular strengths and weaknesses, and some are more suited for particular purposes than others. A similar situation has emerged in the MCF literature. It is now generally recognized that there are many valid ways of defining the MCF, and we have to evaluate the usefulness of any particular measure in terms of its properties and the context in which it is being used.

Pigou (1947) is widely acknowledged as the first to point out that when distortionary taxes are used to finance public expenditures, the cost–benefit rule has to be modified. He noted (p. 34):

Where there is indirect damage, it ought to be added to the direct loss of satisfaction involved in the withdrawal of the marginal unit of resources by taxation, before this is balanced against the satisfaction yielded by the marginal expenditure. It follows that, in general, expenditure ought not to be carried so far as to make the real yield of the last unit of resources expended by the government equal to the real yield of the last unit left in the hands of the representative citizen.

In the early 1970s Stiglitz and Dasgupta (1971), Diamond and Mirrlees (1971), and Atkinson and Stern (1974) showed how the conventional Samuelson rule for the optimal provision of public services—equate the sum of the marginal benefits with the marginal cost of production—should be modified when public services are financed by distortionary taxes. Their modified rules incorporated a measure of the marginal cost of public funds and a term that reflected the additional revenues generated by an increase in the provision of the public service. In particular, Diamond and Mirrlees (1971, p. 271) noted:

[T]he cost associated with the raising of government revenue implies that the impact of public consumption on revenue is a relevant part of the first-order conditions . . . [and], for the same reason, the cost of public consumption is measured in terms of *the cost to the government of raising revenue* to finance the expenditure. (italics added)

The other early influence on the development of the MCF concept was Harberger's wide-ranging contributions to the measurement of excess burden. Harberger (1964, 1971) emphasized the important role of substitution effects in the measurement of excess burden caused by taxation. However, Harberger's focus was on the total or average excess burden created by tax systems, not on the marginal excess burden caused by raising a small amount of additional revenue.

One of the first papers that tried to measure the marginal excess burden of taxation was Campbell (1975), who proposed a measure that he called the marginal proportional deadweight loss. Based on parameter estimates from a linear expenditure system for Canada and effective commodity tax rates in 1961, Campbell (p. 444) concluded that "the deadweight loss imposed on the representative individual by the raising of an extra dollar of tax revenue by means of the specific set of unit commodity tax increases, as opposed to a lump-sum tax, is 25 cents."

The first paper that focused on the measurement of the marginal cost of public funds was by Browning (1976).[17] His proposed measure of the MCF was $1 + m\eta^c$, where m is the marginal tax rate on earnings and η^c is the compensated labor supply elasticity. Unfortunately, this measure is flawed because it includes the "substitution effect" in the measurement of the welfare loss from a tax rate increase, and the change in revenue does not reflect any disincentive effects. Still it was a very important contribution in focusing attention on the marginal distortion created in raising additional revenue and, in particular, on how the progressivity of the tax system might affect the marginal cost of raising revenues.[18] Harberger's work on the excess burden of taxation clearly had a strong influence on Browning's approach to the concept of the MCF. The Diamond-Mirrlees, Stiglitz-Dasgupta, and Atkinson-Stern formulations of the MCF in optimal tax or optimal expenditure frameworks were not referenced in his paper. The lack of integration of the two approaches—applied welfare measures versus optimal tax and expenditure analysis—in formulating the MCF introduced some misunderstandings about the definition and role of the MCF in public policy analysis. In particular, Browning and others who followed in his tradition did not develop their measures as part of an optimality condition or a condition for welfare improvement. They simply proposed a particular measure and left undefined how it would be used for tax policy evaluation or public expenditure.

Fullerton (1991) attempted to reconcile the different methodologies or conceptual frameworks that were used in a spate of MCF studies that emerged in the mid-1980s. He showed that there was a great deal of confusion and inconsistency in the definitions of the MEBs used in studies by Stuart (1984), Ballard, Shoven and Whalley (1985), and Browning (1987). Fullerton (p. 305) concluded that "no measure of 'marginal excess burden is necessary. Instead, the marginal cost of funds is enough information. It can be used to compare one tax to another . . . and it can be used to evaluate the public project . . . ." This view about the irrelevance of the MEB for public policy analysis was also endorsed by Triest (1990).

Much of the controversy concerning the MCF revolves around two issues: (1) the relationship between the MCF and the MEB and (2) whether or not the taxpayers' responses to the effects of additional public expenditures (financed by the increase in revenues from the marginal tax rate increase) should be included in the MCF. We will consider each of these issues below.

There is a wide range of opinion on the relationship between the MCF and the MEB. At the one extreme, Auerbach and Hines (2002, p. 1386) have argued:

[T]he deadweight loss of a tax system and the MCPF [marginal cost of public funds] are two entirely separate concepts. Deadweight loss is a measure of the potential gain from replacing distortionary taxes with an efficient lump-sum alternative, and marginal deadweight loss is simply the change in this magnitude as tax revenue changes. By contrast, the MCPF reflects the welfare cost, in units of a numéraire commodity, of raising tax revenue for exhaustive government expenditure.

On the other hand, there is the alternative view, equally forcefully expressed by Jones (2005, p. 156), that the MCF is *by definition* $1 + MEB$.

In my view, these controversies should have been resolved long ago by the analysis in Triest (1990), probably the most important theoretical contribution in the MCF literature, which linked the MCF and the MEB, via equation (2.32), that is, $MCF = (1 + MEB_{EV})[\lambda(q^0, U^1)/\lambda(q^1, U^1)]$. Clearly, Auerbach and Hines' position is untenable. The MCF, defined as a dollar measure of the welfare loss from raising an additional dollar of tax revenue at the current tax-distorted prices q^1, is directly related to the equivalent variation based measure of marginal excess burden.

The definition of the MCF proposed by Jones (2005), which we can write as $MCF^0 = 1 + MEB_{EV}$, is valid if the marginal cost of funds is defined as a money measure of the welfare loss in raising an additional dollar of tax revenue at the pre–tax reform or undistorted prices, q^0. However, using pre-tax prices that are far removed from the current prices that individuals face makes it difficult to interpret such measures.[19] Furthermore, using MCF^0 in a cost–benefit analysis means that the marginal benefits of any project that is financed by distortionary taxation would also have to be valued at these pre-tax or undistorted prices. In his earlier work, Browning (1976, 1987) used the $MCF^0 = 1 + MEB$ (or equivalent) definition of the marginal cost of public funds. However, in a recent paper, Browning, Gronberg, and Liu (2000, pp. 596–97) acknowledged that the definition of the MCF based on the current tax-distorted prices has a significant advantage over MCF^0:

[because] the required marginal benefit measure ... is evaluated at realized prices (i.e., at the distorted preproject equilibrium). All of the appropriate survey (contingent valuation) or econometric methods (such as hedonic or travel cost methods) yield marginal benefits in terms of the current cum-tax prices ... and thus must be compared to costs using MCF [the marginal cost of funds measured at current cum-tax prices].

Ballard and Fullerton (1991) also tried to resolve the seeming inconsistency between two approaches to the measurement of the MCF. One set of measures, based on what they called the Pigou-Harberger-Browning (PHB) tradition used compensated price or labor supply elasticities, and the MCF for a distortionary tax increase was always greater than one because the MEB was positive. The alternative MCF measures, derived from what they called the Stiglitz-Dasgupta-Atkinson-Stern (SDAS) approach, were based on uncompensated price elasticities of demand and labor supply. With these measures the MCF for a distortionary tax could be less than one if, for example, the taxed good was sufficiently inferior. Using the Musgravian distinction between a differential and a balanced budget incidence analysis introduced earlier by Ballard (1990), Ballard and Fullerton (1991) characterized the PHB measures as based on a "differential analysis" in which the increase in a distortionary tax is offset by a reduction in a lump-sum tax. In contrast, they characterized the SDAS measures as based on a "balanced budget analysis" where the additional revenue raised by a distortionary tax is spent on an exhaustive good that is does not directly affect consumption of the taxed goods; that is to say, public services and private consumption goods (including leisure) are weakly separable in the individuals' utility functions.[20] The PHB measures were based on the compensated elasticities because the implied reduction in the lump-sum tax eliminates the income effect of the tax change, whereas the SDAS measures were based on uncompensated elasticities because there were, by assumption, no offsetting income effects.

This neat distinction between the PHB measures, which depend only on compensated elasticities, and the SDAS measures, which only depend on uncompensated elasticities, breaks down, as Ballard and Fullerton pointed out, when dealing with an increase in a marginal tax rate in a progressive income tax system. In that case the MCF in the SDAS framework does not just depend on the uncompensated labor supply elasticity in SDAS framework—both the compensated labor supply elasticity and the income effects are relevant—because, in general, the taxpayers' marginal and average tax rates will increase by different amount. (This point is described in greater detail in section 5.2.)

There seems to be widespread agreement that if the MCF is to be used in the evaluation of public sector projects, then the SDAS approach, which has been adopted in this book, should be used to calculating the MCF. That is, it should be assumed that the additional revenues are spent on a weakly separable project. See Mayshar (1990) and Wilson (1991), and also Sandmo (1998, p. 371) who argued:

Spending on health and education is presumably quite different, both with regard to distributional characteristics and revenue effects, from the use of resources on national defense or communications infrastructure. If these elements were to be incorporated into the MCF, individual agencies doing cost–benefit analyses of their projects would therefore have to be assigned different values for the MCF depending on how completion of their projects would affect the distribution of welfare and tax revenue. This goes against the basic idea of the MCF as a relatively simple measure of the welfare costs of distortionary taxation....

This does not mean that the spending effects are ignored in a cost–benefit analysis using the SDAS-based MCFs. The spending effects will be included in the R_G terms in (2.18) and will be included as an additional benefit (or cost) of the project, evaluated at the MCF.

Further controversy concerning the role of the MCF in public sector decision-making arose with Kaplow's (1996, 2004) claim that the conventional Samuelson rule can be used to determine whether more public services should be provided if the increased expenditure is accompanied by a tax increase that exactly reflects the marginal benefit of the public service to each individual.[21] In this way the labor supply effects produced by distortionary taxes are offset, and the additional provision of the public service is distributionally neutral. Kaplow's proposition generated many commentaries (e.g., see Browning and Liu 1998; Ng 2000; Slemrod and Yitzkaki 2001) because it appeared to deny the need to use the MCF or distributional weights in making public sector decisions. However, it is now generally recognized that Kaplow's proposition does not invalidate the Atkinson-Stern rule. Its main contribution is to identify the conditions for potential Pareto improvements because it is highly unlikely that the required tax adjustments reflecting individuals' marginal benefits are ever applied in practice (see Gahvari 2006).

In a more constructive vein, Liqun Liu has made significant contributions by incorporating the MCF in the standard cost–benefit framework. In Liu (2004), the shadow prices that would be used in a cost–benefit analysis to measure the social opportunity cost of inputs used in a public sector project are shown to consist of a net revenue component and private income component. The latter reflects the expansion in private incomes due to the general equilibrium changes in input prices that occur when the public sector hires an additional unit of the input. The net revenue component indicates by how much the net revenue requirement of the government increases or decrease when it employs an additional unit of the input. Liu showed that net revenue component is multiplied by the government's MCF to reflect its social opportunity cost. Therefore the MCF is an integral part of the shadow price of public inputs. In Liu (2003), the MCF is incorporated in a multi-period cost–benefit framework. Liu showed that to calculate the net social gain, the present value of the net revenue requirements from an increase in a public service should be multiplied by the MCF, defined as the present value of the harm done to individuals from a small tax increase divided by the increase in the present value of the government's revenue stream from a small tax increase. Further integration of the MCF concept in the cost–benefit framework is an important topic for future research.

Further Reading for Chapter 2

The literature on tariff reform has been dominated by trade economists, who have emphasized the efficiency gains from the reallocation of resources from import-competing sectors to the rest of the economy, and they have often assumed that tariffs would be replaced by nondistortionary lump-sum taxes. However, tariff reform can also be viewed as a tax reform measure, and this view is especially important in developing countries that are highly dependent on tariff revenues. Unfortunately, until recently there has been comparatively little research on "tariff reform as tax reform." Some important insights are contained in Keen and Ligthart (2002) who show that in a small open economy in which all goods are traded, a tariff reduction combined with a consumption tax rate increase that leaves the consumer prices of all goods unchanged will increase welfare and government revenues, if it increases the domestic value of production. In other words, if the tariff reform does not further distort production in the economy, it will improve welfare and increase tax revenue—a win–win situation. Anderson (2002) uses a "compensated" MCF to analyze the efficiency and distributional effects of tariff reforms. His definition of the compensated MCF is, in the simplest case that he considers, equivalent to $1 + MEB_{CV}$ (see equation 2.36). Erbil (2004) has computed the compensated MCFs in thirty-three countries using computable general equilibrium models. He found that the MCFs for tariffs were lower than the MCFs for output taxes in only six of these countries, indicating that replacing tariffs with other broader commodity taxes is an efficiency-enhancing tax reform in most countries.

Appendix to Chapter 2

Relationship between the Equivalent Variation and the Compensated Demand Curve

To show that the equivalent variation (EV) of a price change is equal to the area to the left of the corresponding compensated demand curve, we start with the definition of the EV:

$$EV = e(q^0, U^1) - e(q^0, U^0) = e(q^0, U^1) - e(q^1, U^1).$$

From the first theorem of calculus,

$$EV = \int_{q^1}^{q^0} \frac{\partial e(q, U^1)}{\partial q} dq = - \int_{q^0}^{q^1} x^c(q, U^1) dq.$$

Note that the right-hand side of the equation is the (negative) of the area to the left of the compensated demand curve, $x^c(q, U^1)$.

Formula for Tax Shifting under Perfect Competition

Under perfect competition, the market equilibrium is determined by the following equation:

$$D(q) = S(p),$$

where $p = (1 - \tau_{av})q - t$ is the producer price of the good. τ_{av} is the ad valorem tax rate on the commodity and t is the per unit tax rate. Taking the total differential of this equation, we obtain

$$\frac{q}{x} \frac{dD}{dq} dq = \frac{p}{q} \left(\frac{dS}{dp} \frac{p}{x} \right) [(1 - \tau_{av})dq - qd\tau_{av} - dt],$$

$$\varepsilon dq = \frac{1}{1 - \tau_{av} - \tau_{pu}} \eta [(1 - \tau_{av})dq - qd\tau_{av} - dt],$$

where $\tau_{pu} = t/q$ is the ad valorem equivalent rate of the per unit excise tax. Defining the total excise tax rate as $\tau = \tau_{av} + \tau_{pu}$, we obtain the following:

$$(1 - \tau_{av}) \frac{dq}{dt} = (1 - \tau_{av}) \frac{dq}{qd\tau_{av}} = \frac{(1 - \tau_{av})\eta}{(1 - \tau_{av})\eta - (1 - \tau)\varepsilon}.$$

Note that this implies that if producer prices are fixed and supply is perfectly elastic:

$$\frac{dq}{dt} = \frac{dq}{qd\tau_{av}} = \frac{1}{(1 - \tau_{av})} > 1.$$

Derivation of the Equation (2.45)

Using the approximation to P^2 in (2.43), where $p^1 = q^1 = 1 + \tau_m$, $p^2 = 1$, and $q^2 = 1 + \tau_c$, we obtain the following:

$$P^2 \approx 1 - (p + \theta_D)\left(\frac{\tau_c - \tau_m}{1 + \tau_m}\right) + (fp + \theta_S)\left(\frac{-\tau_m}{1 + \tau_m}\right),$$

where p is the elasticity of the marginal utility of income, θ_D is the marginal propensity to spend with respect to lump-sum income, θ_S is the marginal propensity to supply goods with respect to lump-sum income, and f is producers' income as a fraction of total income, where $f = (pS/(I + pS) = 1 - (M/D)$. Also note that $\theta_D = 1 + \theta_S$. If the revenue-neutral τ_c is approximated as $(M/D)\tau_m$, then

$$P^2 \approx 1 + \left(1 - \frac{M}{D}\theta_D\right) \cdot \left(\frac{\tau_m}{1 + \tau_m}\right).$$

This is equivalent to equation (2.45).

Exercises for Chapter 2

2.1 Suppose that the consumer has the following additively separable utility function between the private goods, z and x, and the publicly provided good G:

$$U = \min[z, \alpha x] + \beta G - \gamma G^2,$$

where α, β, and γ are positive constants. Suppose that a per unit tax of t_x is levied on x, that the consumer prices are $q_x = 1 + t_x$ and $q_z = 1$, and that the consumer has a fixed income equal to I.

(a) Show that the excess burden from taxing x is zero by deriving the equivalent variation-based measured of excess burden.

(b) Derive an expression for the MCF_{t_x} and explain why the $MCF_{t_x} > 1$ for $t_x > 0$ even though there is no excess burden from taxing x.

(c) Suppose that G can be provided at a constant marginal cost of production of c. Show, using the Atkinson-Stern condition, that the optimal provision of the public good when it is financed by an excise tax on x is the same as the level that would be provided under a lump-sum tax.

2.2 Suppose the consumer has the following utility function based on the private goods, z and x, and the publicly provided good G:

$$U = G^\beta x^\alpha z^{1-\alpha},$$

where $0 < \alpha < 1$ and $0 < \beta < 1$. The consumer has a fixed income equal to I and the government could levy a lump-sum tax of T or excise taxes on x and z equal to t_x and t_z to finance expenditures on G, which can provided at a constant marginal cost of production of c. The consumer prices are $q_x = 1 + t_x$ and $q_z = 1 + t_z$. In making her consumption decisions, the consumer takes the tax rates and the level of provision of the public good as given.

(a) Derive a formula for the optimal provision of G (in terms of the parameters, α, β, c, and the consumer's income, I) if the government finances the provision of G using only the lump-sum tax T; that is $t_x = 0$ and $t_z = 0$.

(b) Suppose instead that the government only levies an excise tax on x; that is $t_x > 0$, $t_z = 0$, and $T = 0$. Show that the marginal cost of funds for the government is

$$MCF_{t_x} = 1 + t_x.$$

(c) Use the Atkinson-Stern condition to derive a formula for the optimal provision of G in terms of the parameters, α, β, c, and the consumer's income, I, if the government finances the provision of G by only levying an excise tax on x.

(d) Show that the optimal provision of the public good is higher when it is financed by the lump-sum tax than when it is financed by the excise tax on x.

(e) Let $\alpha = 1/3$, $\beta = 1/2$, $c = 1$, and $I = 100$. Calculate a money measure (based on the tax-distorted prices) of the welfare loss from financing the public good using the excise tax instead of a lump-sum tax.

3 The MCF for Commodity Taxes

The purpose of this chapter is to develop a framework for calculating the MCFs for commodity taxes. Building on the basic theory of the MCF developed in chapter 2, we extend the model by measuring the MCF when there are other distortions in the economy, namely taxes on other commodities that drive wedges between the consumer and producer prices, externalities that lead to a divergence between the marginal social benefit from consuming a commodity and the marginal social cost of producing it, imperfect competition whereby producers are able to set consumer prices above the marginal costs of production, addiction, and smuggling. Consequently, although this chapter is about the MCFs for commodity taxes, a major theme is how market distortions can be incorporated in the measurement of the MCF.

The chapter begins by showing, in section 3.1, the link between the MCF and the shape of the Laffer curve—a curve that shows how tax revenues change as the tax rate changes. Intuitively the MCF is higher when the slope of the tangent to the Laffer curve is low because a tax increase that causes a greater distortion in the taxpayers' behavior will produce a smaller increase in tax revenues. (At the peak of the Laffer curve, where tax revenues are a maximum, the MCF is infinite, and it is not defined if the tax rate is so high that the government is on the negatively sloped part of the Laffer curve.) In other words, the MCF for any tax base is inversely related to the elasticity of total tax revenue with respect to the tax rate on that tax base. This way of thinking about the MCF is useful because it provides a way of estimating the MCF from data on tax rates and tax revenues. The application of these ideas is discussed in greater detail in chapter 5.

The interactions and interrelationships between the taxes imposed on different commodities is the main subject of section 3.2. If a tax rate increase on one commodity causes consumers to switch their expenditures to other highly taxed commodities, then the distortionary effect of the tax increase will be mitigated. This is because, while the higher tax will reduce the resources allocated to the taxed commodity, it may improve the allocation of resources to the other taxed commodities. In the absence of nontax distortions, the tax rate on a commodity is the difference between the marginal social benefit and the marginal social cost of commodity. The additional revenue that a tax generates from other tax bases is a measure of the improvement in the allocation of resources in other sectors of the economy. Of course, an increase in the tax rate on one commodity may cause revenues from other tax bases to decline, perhaps because the taxpayer can no longer afford to purchase as much of the other taxed commodities. In this case the MCF will be high because the decline in tax revenues from other bases is a measure of the deterioration in the allocation of resources in the economy. Consequently it is vitally important to incorporate the interdependence of the tax bases in measuring the MCF for any particular tax.

The interdependence of the demands for taxed commodities is at the heart of the optimal commodity tax problem. In this section we also derive the standard results of the optimal tax literature—the Ramsey rule, the inverse elasticity rule, and the Corlett and Hague rule—using the MCF concept as opposed to the conventional optimization framework. This alternative approach provides a simple and intuitive way of deriving and presenting the basic optimal commodity taxation results.

In section 3.4 we see how the MCF formula can be modified to incorporate the distortions caused by externalities. The section begins by discussing a direct consumption externality, whereby the consumption of a good, say gasoline, directly affects the well-being of other individuals in the economy because of harmful emissions. The direct consumption externality can be measured by the gap between the marginal social benefit from the good and its marginal social cost of production, expressed as a percentage of the consumer price, and this measure of the environmental distortion should be included in the numerator of the MCF formula. Its presence will tend to reduce the MCF for taxes on commodities that generate harmful environmental distortions. This way of incorporating environmental distortions in the MCF can be used to derive the simple Pigouvian tax rule—set tax rates equal to the environmental distortion as defined above—and a modified Pigouvian tax rule when there are other distortionary taxes in the system and the government has to trade off environmental protection with revenue generation.

We also see how a public expenditure externality, which occurs when the consumption of a good affects the cost of providing government services, can be incorporated in the MCF. A classic example of a public expenditure externality is cigarette consumption, which increases expenditures in a publicly funded health care system. An excise tax on a good with a public expenditure externality increases the government's net revenues directly (by adding to tax revenues) and indirectly (by reducing its expenditures), and the latter effect reduces its MCF.

Section 3.5 shows how the market distortion caused by imperfect competition can be incorporated in the measurement of the MCF. The section begins with a simple and intuitive derivation of the MCF for a tax on a monopolists' product when the market demand curve is linear and the marginal cost of production is constant. We see how the MCF can be measured for any type of demand curve, and for rising or declining marginal costs of production. The analysis reveals that the MCF from taxing a monopolist's product will often be quite high because the tax reduces the production of a commodity that is already underprovided. Consequently the first dollar of tax revenue obtained by taxing a monopolist's product will cost more than a dollar because a very small tax distortion further exacerbates an existing, and sometimes sizable, market power distortion.

A well-known result in the public finance literature is that ad valorem taxes on a monopolist's product elicit smaller price increases than per unit taxes, and we see how this difference is reflected in the MCFs for ad valorem and per unit taxes on a monopolist's product. However, we also demonstrate that the standard result—ad valorem taxes are less distortionary and therefore superior to per unit taxes—does not necessarily hold when the monopolist's product generates harmful environmental or public expenditure externalities. Later this result is illustrated in the computations of the MCFs for UK excise taxes taxes that we carry out in section 4.2.2.

This section extends the analysis of imperfect competition to a general model of oligopoly using conjectural variations to describe firms' strategic behavior. It shows how the basic ideas developed for a monopoly can be applied to a wide range of market structures using this framework. This result proves very useful because pure private monopoly is relatively rare, and the conjectural variations approach allows us to utilize parameter estimates from the industrial organization literature on the price behavior of oligopolistic industries.

In many countries excise taxes on alcohol and tobacco are viewed favorably as "sin taxes" because higher prices may reduce the degree of excessive consumption. In this view some consumers have self-control (or addiction) problems and consume excessive amounts of these commodities. The simple model used in section 3.6 was developed by O'Donoghue and Rabin (2006) to illustrate the way in which the self-control distortion can be incorporated in the evaluation of a tax increase on these commodities. Incorporating self-control distortions into the calculation of the MCF is controversial, but the perception that some individuals have self-control problems appears to be reflected in public opinion and policy makers' views concerning the use of excise taxes. For this reason it seems important to incorporate defective decision-making explicitly in the model so that it can be compared with the other distortions that affect the MCF.

Smuggling commodities that are subject to excise taxes is a major problem in many countries. Section 3.7 shows how smuggling raises the MCF of an excise tax by reducing the size of the government's tax base and increasing the tax sensitivity of the tax base.

Section 3.8 contains a summary of studies of the marginal distortionary costs of commodity taxes. These studies are divided into those that focused on the MCFs for taxes on specific commodities, those that calculated the MCFs for general commodity and sales taxes, and those that calculated the MCFs for taxes on imports and exports.

3.1   The MCF and the Laffer Curve

Recall from section 2.3 that when there is only one taxed commodity, the MCF has the following form:

$$MCF = \frac{x}{dR/dt} = \frac{R/t}{dR/dt} = \frac{1}{\rho}, \tag{3.1}$$

where x is the quantity of the taxed good, $R = tx$ is the total tax revenue, dR/dt is the derivative of total tax revenues with respect to the tax rate, and ρ is the elasticity of tax revenue with respect to the tax rate. As equation (3.1) indicates, the MCF can be interpreted as the inverse of the elasticity of tax revenues with respect to the tax rate. In other words, if tax revenues are relatively unresponsive to changes in the tax rate because of tax avoidance or evasion, then the marginal cost of public funds will be high. For example, if a 10 percent increase in the tax rate leads to a 5 percent increase in total tax revenues, the elasticity of tax revenue to the tax rate is 0.5, and the marginal cost of public funds is 2.0. If, however, there are no behavioral responses to the changes in the tax rate, then ρ will be equal to one because revenue will be proportional to the tax rate, and the MCF will be equal to one. The key point is that the MCF depends on how tax bases, and therefore tax revenues, respond to changes in tax rates.

The relationship between tax revenue and the tax rate can be depicted by the *Laffer curve*. Figure 3.1 shows the Laffer curve when the output of the taxed commodity declines as the tax rate increases. The dR/dt is the slope of a tangent line to the Laffer curve, and R/t is the slope of a line from the origin to a point on the Laffer curve. Therefore the MCF at t^1 is the ratio of the slopes of $0a$ to bb'. If, as shown in figure 3.1, the Laffer curve is strictly concave, then the slope of bb' will be less than the slope of the ray $0a$, and the MCF will be greater than one. Tax revenues are a maximum when the tax rate is t^* and at that point, the MCF is infinite. If the government is operating on the negatively sloped section of the Laffer curve, the MCF is not defined. Neither a Leviathan nor a benevolent government should operate on the downward-sloping section of the Laffer curve because a tax rate decrease would make taxpayers better off and the government would collect more tax revenues.[1]

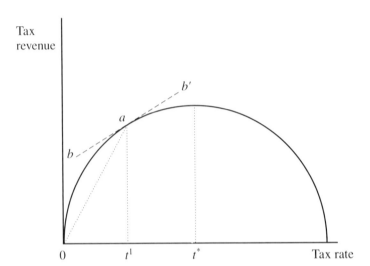

Figure 3.1
Relationship between the MCF and the Laffer curve

3.2   The MCF with Multiple Tax Bases

In the previous section we had assumed that only one commodity is taxed. However, most governments obtain revenue from more than one tax source, and therefore it is important to measure the MCF when taxes are imposed on multiple tax bases. In most tax systems the tax bases are at least to some degree interdependent. In measuring the MCF for a particular tax, it is important to capture these interactions and to measure the effects of a tax increase on total tax revenues collected, and not just the additional tax revenues from that particular tax base.

Suppose that a government imposes taxes on n different tax bases. The size of the ith tax base will, in general, depend on τ_i as well as the tax rates that are imposed on other tax bases because of substitution or complementarity relationships among the tax bases. The revenue obtained from tax base i is equal to $R_i = \tau_i B_i(\tau)$ where τ is a vector of tax rates $(\tau_1, \tau_2, \ldots, \tau_n)$ and B_i is size of the tax base i. (In the case of commodity taxes, τ_i is t_i/q_i and $B_i = q_i x_i$.) Total tax revenue, R, is the sum of the tax revenues obtained from the tax sources, or $R(\tau) = \sum_{i=1}^{n} R_i = \sum_{i=1}^{n} \tau_i B_i$.

Since the harm inflicted on the taxpayer from a small increase in τ_i is $B_i d\tau_i$, while the change in total revenue is $(\partial R/\partial \tau_i)\, d\tau_i$, a general expression for the MCF_{τ_i} is

$$MCF_{\tau_i} = \frac{B_i}{\partial R/\partial \tau_i} = \frac{\tau_i B_i/R}{(\tau_i/R)(\partial R/\partial \tau_i)} = \frac{\alpha_i}{\rho_i}, \tag{3.2}$$

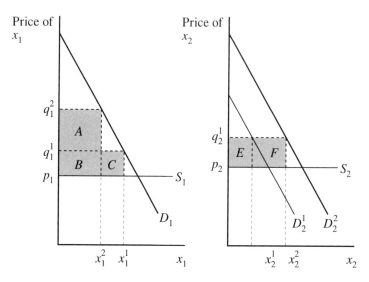

Figure 3.2
The MCF when a substitute good is also taxed

where $\alpha_i = (\tau_i B_i)/R$ is the proportion of total tax revenue obtained from tax base i and $\rho_i = (\tau_i/R)(\partial R/\partial\tau_i)$ is the elasticity of total tax revenue with respect to tax rate i. Note that ρ_i is equal to $\sum_{j=1}^{n}\alpha_j\rho_{ji}$, where ρ_{ji} is the elasticity of revenue from tax base j with respect to τ_i. If a change in τ_i does not affect the tax revenue obtained from other tax sources, such that $\rho_{ji} = 0$ for all $j \neq i$, then the MCF_{τ_i} is $1/\rho_{ii}$ which, except for the subscripting, is the same formula as in (3.1). If an increase in τ_i causes tax revenues from other sources to increase, then the ρ_{ji} $(j \neq i)$ will be positive, and for a given ρ_{ii} and α_j, the MCF_{τ_i} will be smaller. If an increase in τ_i causes revenues from other tax bases to decline, then ceteris paribus, the MCF_{τ_i} will be larger.

The implications of tax base interactions for the MCF_{τ_i} are illustrated in figure 3.2 where it is assumed that there are only two taxed commodities, x_1 and x_2, which are substitutes, and therefore $\varepsilon_{21} = (\partial x_2/\partial q_1)(q_1/x_2) > 0$. Initially, $q_1^1 = p_1 + t_1^1$ and $q_2^1 = p_2 + t_2^1$, and the tax revenue from commodity 1 is area $B + C$ and the tax revenue from commodity 2 is area E. If the tax rate on x_1 is increased by Δt_1, the price of x_1 increases by the amount of the tax. The consumption of x_1 declines to x_1^2, and the consumption of x_2 increases to x_2^2. The money measure of the harm inflicted on the consumer is approximately $x_1\Delta t_1$, and the MCF_{τ_i} is equal to $(x_1\Delta t_1)/(\Delta R_1 + \Delta R_2)$, where ΔR_1 is equal to the shaded areas A minus the shaded area C and ΔR_2 is area F. Note that ΔR_2 is also a money measure of the improvement in the allocation of resources because each addition unit of x_2 is valued by the consumer at q_2^1, but it only cost society p_2 to produce each unit. When ΔR_2 is positive, the MCF_{τ_1} is lower because of the improvement in resource allocation due to the increase in x_2. On the other hand, if x_1 and x_2 were complements and $\varepsilon_{21} < 0$, then ΔR_2 would be negative, and the calculated MCF_{τ_1} would be higher.

The interdependence of tax bases is a general phenomenon. For example, an increase in the personal income tax (PIT) reduces disposable income, which will reduce sales and excise tax revenues because consumer expenditures will decline. Thus the MCF_{PIT} is larger than would be indicated by focusing only on its effect on PIT revenues. On the other hand, an increase in the PIT rate may lead some taxpayers to increase the amount of income that is earned through, or retained by, corporations. The increase in CIT revenues from a PIT rate increase would reduce the magnitude of the MCF_{PIT}.

In the case of commodity taxes the MCF_{τ_i} is equal to the following:

$$MCF_{\tau_i} = \frac{x_i}{x_i + \sum_{j=1}^{n} t_j (dx_j/dq_i)} = \frac{b_i}{b_i + \sum_{j=1}^{n} \tau_j b_j \varepsilon_{ji}}, \tag{3.3a}$$

where ε_{ji} is the elasticity of demand for commodity j with respect to the price of commodity i and b_j is the budget share of commodity j. An important special case is where all commodities that the individual consumes are taxed at the same rate τ and the consumer has a fixed amount of income to spend on these commodities. From (3.3a) the marginal cost of funds from a common tax rate on all commodities would be equal to

$$MCF_{\tau_i} = \frac{b_i}{b_i + \tau \sum_{j=1}^{n} b_j \varepsilon_{ji}} = \frac{1}{1 - \tau}, \tag{3.3b}$$

since $\sum_{j=1}^{n} b_j \varepsilon_{ji} = -b_i$ if the individual's total expenditure on all commodities is fixed. If total income is fixed, a common tax rate on all commodities would be equivalent to a nondistortionary lump-sum tax levied on the consumer with no excess burden. The marginal excess burden would also be zero and from (2.32) the marginal cost of public funds would be equal to $\lambda(q^0, U^1)/\lambda(q^1, U^1) = (1 - \tau)^{-1}$. In other words, the MCF would be greater than one with a nondistortionary general sales tax on all commodities because the MCF measures the welfare loss in raising additional tax revenue at the post–tax reform prices.

However, tax systems do not tax all commodities at a common rate. In particular, leisure is not taxed under a general sales tax, and this distorts an individual's labor–leisure decision. The theory of optimal commodity taxation, which is summarized in the following section, emphasizes the interaction between the demands for the taxed commodity and the nontaxed goods such as leisure.

3.3   Optimal Commodity Taxation

In this section we will use the MCF framework to derive the main results in the optimal commodity tax literature—the Ramsey rule, the inverse elasticity rule, and the
Corlett and Hague rule. (For more conventional treatments of the optimal commodity tax problem, see Sandmo 1976; Diamond 1976; Auerbach and Hines 2002; Salanié 2003, ch. 3.) With the optimal tax system, the distributionally weighted MCFs
will be the same for each taxed commodity. That is, to raise a given amount of tax
revenue at the lowest social cost, the tax rates should be adjusted so that $SMCF_{\tau_i} =
SMCF_{\tau_j}$ for all tax bases i and j. From section 2.7 we know that the SMCF for a tax
on commodity i is the product of a distributional component Ω_i and an efficiency
component MCF_{τ_i}. We will focus on the case where producer prices are fixed, in
which case the distributional component is simply the distributional characteristic of
the commodity, ω_i. With the optimal set of tax rates, the MCF from taxing each
commodity will be inversely related to its distributional characteristic. However, we
will begin by ignoring distributional concerns and focus only on the "efficiency"
effects of commodity taxes by equating their MCFs. Putting distributional concerns
to one side allows us to develop the intuition regarding those factors which affect the
efficiency component of the optimal tax system. Later we will show how distributional concerns modify the efficiency-based rules for optimal taxation.

   In the absence of distributional concerns, the optimal set of tax rates on n commodities that raises a given amount of tax revenue R will be the solution to $(n-1)$
equations of the form $MCF_{\tau_i} = MCF_{\tau_j}$ (where the MCF for each tax is given by
equation 3.3) plus an additional equation, the budget constraint $R = \sum \tau_j q_j x_j$. It is
very difficult to characterize the general solution to this system of equations because
the MCF for each tax may depend on all of the tax rates. In addition the budget
shares and the elasticities of demand will (in general) depend on the tax rates. However, a basic insight into the nature of the optimal commodity taxes rates can be
obtained by using the Slutsky condition, $\varepsilon_{ji} = \varepsilon_{ji}^c - b_i \mu_j$ to replace the ε_{ji} in (3.3).
Using the symmetry condition of consumer demand, $b_j \varepsilon_{ji}^c = b_i \varepsilon_{ij}^c$, we can write the
MCF for each tax in the form

$$MCF_{\tau_i} = \frac{1}{\sum_{j=1}^{n} \tau_j \varepsilon_{ij}^c + [1 - \sum_{j=1}^{n} \tau_j b_j \mu_j]}. \qquad (3.4)$$

The first term in the denominator can be interpreted as the compensated proportional reduction in the demand for commodity i, $\Delta x_i^c / x_i$, that results from the given
set of tax rates. The term in square brackets can be interpreted as the inverse of the
price index $P(q^1, q^0, U^1)$ that converts welfare changes measured at the undistorted
prices to money measures of the welfare changes at the current tax-distorted prices.

(See section 2.1.2 on the price index.) Consequently the MCF for any commodity tax can be written in the form

$$MCF_{\tau_i} = \frac{P}{1 + P(\Delta x_i^c / x_i)}. \tag{3.5}$$

Of course, the price index P depends on the tax rates, but it is the same for each MCF_{τ_i}. Consequently, if $MCF_{\tau_i} = MCF_{\tau_j}$, it must be the case that $\Delta x_i^c / x_i = \Delta x_j^c / x_j$. In other words, in the absence of distributional concerns, the optimal set of commodity taxes results in the same compensated proportional reduction in the demands for all taxed commodities. This property of the optimal commodity tax system is known as the *Ramsey rule*.[2]

How should the Ramsey rule be modified to take into account distributional concerns? With the optimal tax system $SMCF = \omega_i MCF_{\tau_i} = \omega_j MCF_{\tau_j}$, and therefore the relative reductions in the compensated demands for any two taxed commodities will be equal to the following:

$$\frac{\Delta x_i^c / x_i}{\Delta x_j^c / x_j} = 1 + \frac{\omega_j - \omega_i}{\omega_j} \cdot \frac{1}{MEB_{EV_j}}, \tag{3.6}$$

where MEB_{EVj} is the marginal excess burden from taxing commodity j:

$$MEB_{EV_j} = \frac{-P(\Delta x_j^c / x_j)}{1 + P(\Delta x_j^c / x_j)}. \tag{3.7}$$

Equation (3.6) indicates that if the distributional characteristics of the two goods are the same, then the proportional compensated reductions in the demands for the two goods should be the same. If ω_i is less than ω_j (because the poor consume a smaller proportion of good i than good j), then there should be a larger compensated reduction in demand for commodity i compared to commodity j. Note that when the marginal excess burden of taxation is higher, the deviation from the Ramsey rule will be smaller. In other words, when the efficiency losses from taxation are very high, the optimal tax system will implement a resource re-allocation that is very close to the Ramsey rule.

The Ramsey rule implies that there should be a uniform proportional reduction in the compensated demands for the taxed goods, rather than uniform tax rates.[3] To gain some appreciation of the factors that determine the optimal tax rate pattern, economists have examined two special cases. In the first case, it is assumed that all of the (uncompensated) cross-price elasticities of demand are zero so that the MCF for each commodity only depends on its own price elasticity of demand and its tax rate. With $\varepsilon_{ij} = 0$ for $i \neq j$ in (3.3), the optimal tax rates will satisfy, in the absence of distributional concerns, the condition $(1 + \tau_i \varepsilon_{ii})^{-1} = (1 + \tau_j \varepsilon_{jj})^{-1}$. This implies that the optimal tax rates should be inversely related to the commodities' demand elasticities, which is known as *the inverse elasticity rule*. This rule implies that price sensitive commodities should be taxed at proportionately lower rates in order to achieve the uniform proportional reductions in the compensated demands for the commodities as is required by the Ramsey rule. For example, if the $\varepsilon_{ii} = -0.5$, $\varepsilon_{jj} = -2.0$, and $\varepsilon_{ij} = \varepsilon_{ji} = 0$, then the tax rate on commodity i should be four times as large as the tax rate on commodity j. The inverse elasticity rule is often criticized as a guide for tax policy because the assumption that all cross-price elasticities of demand are zero is clearly unrealistic and because it may result in a regressive tax system. (Necessities, which are disproportionately consumed by the poor, are usually thought to be price inelastic, whereas luxuries, which are disproportionately consumed by the rich, have more price sensitive demands. Note that the Ramsey rule may also imply regressive taxes. In the case of the inverse elasticity rule, the potential for regressivity is more obvious.)

Distributional concerns would modify the optimal pattern of taxation, under the strong assumption of zero cross-price elasticities of demand, in the following manner:

$$\frac{\tau_i}{\tau_j} = \frac{\varepsilon_{jj}}{\varepsilon_{ii}} \left(1 + \frac{\omega_j - \omega_i}{\omega_j} \cdot \frac{1}{MEB_{CS_j}} \right), \tag{3.8}$$

where MEB_{CS_j} is the consumer surplus based measure of the marginal excess burden from taxing commodity j defined in (2.37). If the distributional characteristic for commodity i is higher than the distributional characteristic for commodity j, commodity i should be taxed at a proportionately lower rate than is implied by their relative price elasticities of demand. For example, if $\omega_i = 1.20$, $\omega_j = 1.00$, $\varepsilon_{ii} = -0.5$, $\varepsilon_{jj} = -2.0$, $MEB_{CS_j} = 0.25$, and $\tau_j = 0.10$, then τ_i should be 0.08, not 0.40, as is implied by the inverse elasticity rule. Note that the deviation from the inverse elasticity rule will become smaller the larger the MEB_{CS_j} (i.e., when efficiency effects of taxation are more important).

The Corlett and Hague rule for optimal taxation is derived under the special assumption that there are two taxed commodities, x_1 and x_2, and a third untaxed good, x_0, that is conventionally viewed as leisure. This assumption is sometimes motivated by the observation that the government may not be able to observe the number of hours of leisure that an individual takes and therefore may not be able to tax leisure. The price of leisure, q_0, is the wage rate that the individual can earn because it represents the opportunity cost, in terms of forgone consumption, of an hour of leisure. (Chapter 5 contains a more detailed analysis of taxation on labor–leisure choices.) The individual's budget constraint is $q_0 x_0 + q_1 x_1 + q_2 x_2 = I$, where I is the individual's "full income." (If x_0 is leisure, then $I = q_0 T + M$, where T is the individual's endowment of T, $L = T - x_0$ is the number of hours spent working at the wage rate q_0, and M is nonlabor income.) The government can affect the consumer prices of x_1 and x_2 by setting the tax rates, but it cannot directly affect q_0. Note, however, that taxing x_1 and x_2 at the same rate τ is equivalent to imposing a proportional wage tax at the rate τ_L if $M = 0$ and $\tau_L = \tau/(1 + \tau)$.

Using the definition of the MCF in (3.4), we can write the MCF from taxing commodity 1 as

$$MCF_{\tau_1} = \frac{1}{P^{-1} + \tau_1 \varepsilon_{11}^c + \tau_2 \varepsilon_{12}^c}. \tag{3.9}$$

Because an equiproportional increase in all prices will leave the compensated demand for a commodity unchanged, we have the following relationship for the compensated elasticities of demand for commodity 1:

$$\varepsilon_{11}^c + \varepsilon_{12}^c + \varepsilon_{10}^c = 0. \tag{3.10}$$

We use this relationship to eliminate ε_{12}^c in (3.9), the MCF from taxing so that commodity 1 becomes

$$MCF_{\tau_1} = \frac{1}{P^{-1} + (\tau_1 - \tau_2)\varepsilon_{11}^c - \tau_2 \varepsilon_{10}^c}; \tag{3.11}$$

the MCF for the tax on commodity 2 would have a similar form:

$$MCF_{\tau_2} = \frac{1}{P^{-1} + (\tau_2 - \tau_1)\varepsilon_{22}^c - \tau_1 \varepsilon_{20}^c}. \tag{3.12}$$

In the absence of distributional concerns, the condition $MCF_{\tau_1} = MCF_{\tau_2}$ determines the optimal tax rates, τ_1 and τ_2. To determine the optimal pattern of tax rates, we evaluate the MCFs for the two taxes when both commodities are taxed at the uniform tax rate $\tau = \tau_1 = \tau_2$:

$$MCF_1 = \frac{1}{P^{-1} - \tau \varepsilon_{10}^c} \quad \text{and} \quad MCF_2 = \frac{1}{P^{-1} - \tau \varepsilon_{20}^c}. \tag{3.13}$$

From the expression above, it can be seen that $MCF_1 \gtreqless MCF_2$ as $\varepsilon_{10}^c \gtreqless \varepsilon_{20}^c$. Therefore at a uniform tax rate the good that is more complementary with leisure has the lower MCF (i.e., we should tax at a higher rate the good that is a poorer substitute for the untaxed good). For concreteness, suppose that commodity 1 is a (net) substitute for leisure (e.g., clothing) and commodity 2 is a (net) complement for leisure (e.g., golf clubs). This means that $\varepsilon_{20}^c < 0 < \varepsilon_{10}^c$ and that $MCF_1 > MCF_2$. We will assume that the MCF for each good is increasing in its own tax rate, so this implies that $\tau_2 > \tau_1$ with the optimal tax system. In other words, the optimal commodity tax system imposes a higher tax rate on the good that is more complementary with leisure.

The intuition behind the *Corlett and Hague rule* can be explained as follows[4]: if commodity 2 is more complementary with leisure than commodity 1, an increase in the tax rate on commodity 2 will lead to a reduction in the demand for leisure and an increase in the amount of labor supplied by the individual. The increased earnings will be spent on both taxed goods, generating additional tax revenues and allowing the government to decrease one or both tax rates, and thereby reduce the deadweight loss from taxation. In other words, taxing at a higher rate the good that is more complementary with leisure helps reduce the distortion in the labor–leisure choice caused by the government's inability to tax leisure.

The Ramsey rule, the inverse elasticity rule and the Corlett and Hague rule provide us with some intuition about the properties of the optimal taxes on commodities. However, as stressed at the beginning of this section, the computation of the optimal tax rates is very difficult because it involves the solution to a complex system of highly nonlinear equations.[5] This solution may depend on how the own- and cross-price elasticities of demand change as tax rates change, and we have only a limited knowledge about these properties of consumer demand systems. The computation of a complete set of optimal tax rates is somewhat ambitious, given our current knowledge of the behavior of the own- and cross-price elasticities of demand. However, Decoster and Schokkaert (1990, p. 295) have concluded that the "sensitivity to the specification of the demand system is less severe for a tax reform exercise than it is for the calculation of optimal tax rates." Reasonably reliable indications of the directions for social welfare improving tax reforms can often be obtained by computing of the distributionally weighted MCFs at current tax rates. The computation of the SMCFs for commodity taxes can often provide useful information for policy makers in the reform of commodity tax systems.

To this point it has been assumed that only taxes drive a wedge between the consumer price, which indicates the marginal social benefit of a commodity, and the producer price, which measures its marginal social cost. Implicitly it has been assumed that the market would produce an efficient allocation of resources if the government levied only lump-sum taxes. However, markets may fail to allocate resources efficiently if there are externalities, such as pollution, in consumption or production activities, or if some firms can exercise monopoly power in setting the prices of their products. The next two sections show how these nontax distortions in private sector can be incorporated in the measurement of the marginal cost of public funds.

3.4 The MCF with Externalities

The price system can also fail to allocate resources efficiently if there are external benefits or costs in production or consumption activity. Pigou (1920) was the first to point out that an efficient allocation of resources could be achieved if taxes were imposed on activities that generate harmful externalities so that their market prices reflect the true social cost of the activity. In recent years many governments have become interested in *green taxes* that yield a *double dividend*—a cleaner environment plus the "social value" of the additional tax revenue generated by these taxes. In this section the MCFs for taxes on commodities that generate positive or negative externalities are derived. We then derive the optimal green taxes when other distortionary taxes are also imposed to finance government spending. (The literature on optimal green taxes is discussed in section 3.8.)

3.4.1 Environmental Externalities

Suppose that consumers purchase a commodity x_i that produces a marginal external benefit of d_E. (In the case of a harmful externality, such as pollution, $d_E < 0$.) The left-hand side of figure 3.3 shows the initial equilibrium where the consumer price is q_i^1 and x_i^1 units of the commodity are consumed. The area under the d_E curve represents the total external benefit that accrues to individuals who do not purchase x_i. If the tax rate on x is increased to t^2, then the demand for x_i will decline, and the total

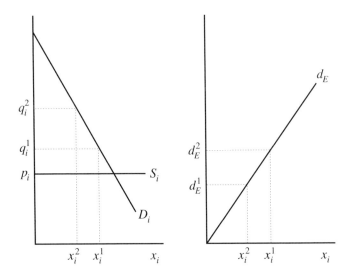

Figure 3.3
The MCF when the taxed good generates a positive externality

external benefit will also decline. For a small increase in the tax rate, the harm inflicted on the producers and consumers of the commodity is $x_i dt$, and the reduction in the value of the external benefit is $-d_E \Delta x_i$, where $\Delta x_i = x_i^2 - x_i^1 < 0$.

The MCF from taxing commodity i (assuming a perfectly competitive market and no other distortions) is

$$MCF_{\tau_i} = \frac{x_i dt_i - d_{E_i} \Delta x_i}{(\partial R / \partial t_i) \cdot dt_i} = \frac{1 - \delta_{E_i} \varepsilon_{ii} (dq_i / dt_i)}{1 + \tau_i \varepsilon_{ii} (dq_i / dt_i)} = \frac{\alpha_i (1 - \delta_{E_i} \varepsilon_{ii})}{\rho_i}, \tag{3.14}$$

where $\delta_{E_i} = d_{E_i} / q_i$ is the proportional marginal external benefit generated by x_i, and $\varepsilon_{ii} < 0$ is the own-price elasticity of demand for x_i. (In deriving the equation above, we make use of the fact that $\Delta x_i = (x_i \varepsilon_{ii} / q_i) dt_i$. The last expression is based on the assumption that producer prices are fixed and therefore $dq_i / dp_i = 1$.) The MCF for an externality-generating activity only differs from the expression for the MCF in the absence of nontax distortions if the $-\delta_{E_i} \varepsilon_{ii}$ term in the numerator is nonzero. If the activity generates a positive externality, then $-\delta_{E_i} \varepsilon_{ii}$ is positive and the MCF is higher because taxing the commodity reduces the positive external benefit from the commodity. If the activity produces a harmful externality, then $-\delta_{E_i} \varepsilon_{ii}$ is negative, and the MCF is lower, reflecting a social gain from reducing a harmful externality when the commodity is taxed. Finally, note that from (3.14) the optimal tax rate on commodity 1 is the Pigovian tax $\tau_i = -\delta_{E_i}$ if the government can levy lump-sum taxes and its MCF is one.

The existence of distortionary taxes elsewhere in the economy has raised the possibility of a double dividend from levying green taxes. The notion of a double dividend from taxing a polluting activity is simply that the MCFs for green taxes are lower than the MCFs for other sources of tax revenue. Suppose that a government's alternative tax revenue source is a tax on commodity j with MCF_{τ_j}. If we replace a dollar of tax revenue from x_j with a dollar from taxing a pollutant x_i, there is a net social gain equal to $MCF_{\tau_j} - MCF_{\tau_i}$. The "first dividend," $MCF_{\tau_j} - \alpha_i / \rho_i$, is the net gain from raising the additional revenue from taxing x_i rather than x_j in the absence of external effects. For this externality to be positive, it must be the case that the elasticity of total tax revenue from taxing x_i will be relatively high. The additional tax dividend in turn means that the demand for x_i is relatively inelastic and that taxing i increases (or at least does not significantly reduce) the demand for x_j. The second dividend per dollar of tax revenue is $\alpha_i \delta_{E_i} \varepsilon_{ii} / \rho_i$, the value of the reduction in external damages when an additional dollar of tax revenue is raised from x_i. Note that the second dividend will be smaller when the demand for x_i is relatively inelastic, and therefore the magnitude of the ε_{ii} has offsetting effects on the two dividends.

With the optimal green tax rate on x_i, the MCF from taxing x_i is equal to the MCF from all other revenue sources. For simplicity, assume that producer prices are fixed, that the only other taxed commodity is j, and that $MCF_{\tau_j} = (1 + \tau_j \varepsilon_{jj})^{-1}$. In other words, the tax on x_j does not affect the demand for x_i. The optimal green tax is then equal to[6]

$$\tau_i = \frac{-\delta_{E_i}}{MCF_{\tau_j}} + \left[\frac{b_i \varepsilon_{jj} - b_j \varepsilon_{ji}}{b_i \varepsilon_{ii}}\right] \tau_j, \tag{3.15}$$

where b_j is the budget share of commodity j. The first term on the right-hand side of (3.15) is the component that is required to correct the externality, and the second term is the tax rate that should be imposed on x_i in the absence of the externality. Note that the externality term will be smaller when the MCF from the alternative tax source is larger. As Bovenberg (1999, p. 430) has explained, this inverse relationship arises for the following reason:

If public revenues become scarcer, as indicated by a higher marginal cost of public funds, the optimal tax system focuses more on generating revenues and less on internalizing pollution externalities. The conflict between raising revenues and protecting the environment exists because an environmental levy reduces pollution by encouraging taxpayers to avoid taxes. Tax avoidance not only reduces pollution but also makes it necessary to levy higher distortionary taxes to finance public spending. Accordingly, the larger the government's revenue needs are ... the less the government can afford tax differentiation aimed at environmental protection.

Ballard and Medema (1993, tab. 2, p. 212) calculated the MCFs for various taxes using a computable general equilibrium model for the US economy based on 1983 data that incorporated estimates of harmful environmental externalities. They found that the MCF for Pigouvian tax on harmful goods had the lowest MCF equal to 0.731. The MCF for an output tax on polluters was higher at 0.925 because it did not induce additional abatement activity. Other broad taxes had MCFs greater than one. The MCF for a labor income tax was 1.067. The MCF for an output tax on all industries was 1.113, and the MCF for a sales tax was 1.082.[7]

3.4.2 Public Expenditure Externalities

To this point it has been assumed that the taxed commodity directly affects the well-being of other individuals in the economy, even though they do not purchase the commodity. There is another type of externality that can affect the well-being of other individuals in the economy, and this is an indirect effect that occurs through the government's budget constraint. For example, an increase in cigarette consumption may increase public expenditures on health care. Even in the absence of a "second-hand" smoke externality, nonsmokers as well as smokers will be adversely affected by the higher taxes that they have to pay as a result of higher public health care expenditures. The health care costs associated with smoking are often used to justify high taxes on tobacco products. Below we show how these public expenditure effects can be incorporated in the MCF for a taxed product.

Suppose that the government provides a service G, and let the cost of providing this service be $C(G, x)$ where $\partial C/\partial G > 0$ is the marginal cost of providing the service and $\partial C/\partial x$ is the increase in the cost of providing a given level of service (e.g., health care) as a result of an increase in the consumption of a private good x. For simplicity we will ignore the taxes that are levied on other goods (that might be substitutes or complements of x), and therefore the public sector's budget constraint requires that $tx = C(G, x)$. Increasing the tax rate on x can increase the public sector's net revenues either directly by increasing total revenues or indirectly by reducing net expenditures. Consequently the MCF for taxing x will be equal to

$$MCF_t = \frac{x}{x + t(dx/dt) - [(\partial C/\partial x)(dx/dt)]} = \frac{1}{1 + (\tau - \delta_G)\varepsilon}, \qquad (3.16)$$

where it is assumed that the supply of the taxed commodity is perfectly elastic so that $dq/dt = 1$ and $\delta_G = (\partial C/q\partial x)$ is the change in the cost of public expenditures when individuals spend another dollar on x. Assuming that $\delta_G > 0$, we see that the public expenditure effect reduces the MCF when a higher tax rate reduces the demand for the commodities that are responsible for higher costs of providing a given level of public services. If government could impose lump-sum taxes, and if the MCF were one, then the optimal tax rate on x would be $\tau = \delta_G$. In other words, the commodity would be taxed at a rate that reflects its public expenditure externality, just as in the case of the Pigouvian tax for a direct consumption externality.

3.5   The MCF with Imperfect Competition in Commodity Markets

Now we will consider how market power distortions affect the marginal cost of public funds for commodity taxes. We begin with monopoly because it provides a relatively simple framework within which we can show how market power affects the measurement of the MCF. We also show how the form of taxation—per unit taxes or ad valorem taxes—affects the MCF under monopoly. This provides a useful framework for showing that in the absence of other distortions, the MCF for an ad valorem excise tax is lower than the MCF for a per unit excise tax. However, in section 3.5.2 we will see that the superiority of ad valorem under monopoly does not necessarily hold when there are externalities in consumption or public expenditure. Finally, in section 3.5.3 we will see how the same basic method for calculating the MCF can be applied to a conjectural variations model of oligopoly. This framework allows us to calculate the MCF from taxing commodities for market structures ranging from monopoly to perfect competition.

Price of x

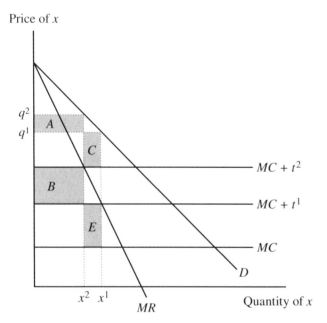

Figure 3.4
The MCF for a tax on a monopolist's product

3.5.1   The MCF under Monopoly

We begin with an intuitive derivation of the marginal cost of public funds when a tax is imposed on a commodity produced by a monopoly. In figure 3.4 it is assumed that a monopolist faces a linear demand curve for its product. An important characteristic of a linear demand curve is that the marginal revenue curve, MR, is twice as steep as the demand curve. For simplicity it is also assumed that the marginal cost of production is constant in the long run and that there are no other distortions in the economic system. Initially the per unit tax on the monopolist's product is t^1, profit-maximizing output is x^1, the price is q^1, and the monopolist's after-tax profit is $\pi^1 = q^1 x^1 - (MC + t^1)x^1$. The firm maximizes profits when the following markup condition is satisfied:

$$q^1 = \left[\frac{\varepsilon}{1 + \varepsilon}\right](MC + t^1). \tag{3.17}$$

The firm's markup over its marginal cost plus tax is $\varepsilon(1 + \varepsilon)^{-1}$, which is greater than one because the firm is maximizing profits when its marginal revenue is positive, and therefore the demand for its product is price elastic, $\varepsilon < -1$.

When the tax rate is increased to t^2, the consumer price increases to q^2, and output declines to x^2. Given a linear demand curve and the assumption of constant marginal cost, the price increase is equal to half of the tax increase, $\Delta q = 1/2\Delta t$, because the marginal revenue curve is twice as steep as the demand curve. As a result of the price increase, consumers suffer a decline in consumer surplus that can be approximated for a small tax rate increase by the shaded area A. As a result of the tax increase, there is a decline in the monopolist's profit equal to areas $B + C - A$. Intuitively area B is the decline in the monopolist's profits due to the tax rate increase, with output held constant, area C is the decline in monopoly profit due to the decline in output, and area A is the offsetting increase in profit due to the price increase. The change in total tax revenue is area B minus E.

An intuitive derivation of the MCF from taxing a monopolist's product is outlined below.[8] The MCF measures the reduction in consumer surplus and monopoly profit per dollar of additional tax revenue or

$$MCF = \frac{-\Delta CS - \Delta\Pi}{\Delta R} = \frac{B + C}{B - E}. \tag{3.18}$$

The MCF has two components. The first is $B/(B - E)$, which is the inverse of the elasticity of tax revenue with respect to the tax rate, ρ. However, this elasticity of tax revenue is determined by the shape of the marginal revenue curve, not the demand curve as in section 3.1. Alternatively, $B/(B - E)$ can be viewed as the loss of consumer surplus, per dollar of additional tax revenue, that would occur in absence of the firm's monopoly power. The second component, $C/(B - E)$, measures the social loss per dollar of additional revenue due to the distortion in the allocation of resources caused by the firm's monopoly power, $d_M = q - (MC + t)$. Let δ_M be the market power distortion as a percentage of the consumer price, $\delta_M = d_M/q$. The area C is equal to $(q - (MC + t)\Delta x$ or $(-\delta_M\varepsilon dq/dt)x\Delta t$. Since B is equal to $x\Delta t$ and $B - E$ is equal to $x(1 + \tau\varepsilon dq/dt)\Delta t$, the MCF for a tax on a monopolist's product is

$$MCF = \frac{1 - \delta_M\varepsilon(dq/dt)}{1 + \tau\varepsilon(dq/dt)} = \frac{1 + (dq/dt)}{1 + \tau\varepsilon(dq/dt)}, \tag{3.19}$$

where the condition for the proportional markup over the marginal cost, $\delta_M = -1/\varepsilon$, is used to derive right-hand side of equation (3.19). Consequently the first dollar of tax revenue obtained by taxing a monopolist's product will cost more than one dollar. Note that the "first dollar" of tax revenue obtained by taxing a monopolist's product has an MCF of $(1 + dq/dt)$, which is greater than one because a very small tax distortion further exacerbates the existing market power distortion. Finally, note the similarity between the expression above for the MCF for a monopolist's product and the MCF for an externality-generating product in (3.14). In both cases the numerator in the MCF formula includes a term that reflects the additional efficiency gain from an additional unit of the commodity caused by a nontax distortion.

If the government levied lump-sum taxes and its MCF were one, then the optimal tax rate on the monopolist's product would be $\tau = -\delta_M = \varepsilon^{-1} < 0$. In other words, the government should subsidize the monopolist's product in order to induce it to produce more output if lump-sum taxes could be used to finance government expenditures.

The formula in (3.19) indicates that the MCF for a tax on a monopolist's product is higher when the degree of forward tax shifting, dq/dt, is higher. As noted above, with a linear demand curve and constant marginal cost, $dq/dt = 1/2$, and therefore the $MCF = 3/(2 + \tau\varepsilon)$. By comparison, as noted in section 2.3, the MCF under perfect competition with perfectly elastic supply is $1/(1 + \tau\varepsilon)$.

The case where the monopolist has a linear demand curve and its marginal cost is constant has been used to develop the intuition concerning the MCF for a tax on a monopolist's product, but it leads to a very restrictive conclusion regarding the degree of tax shifting under monopoly. A general expression of the degree of tax shift under monopoly is[9]

$$\frac{dq}{dt} = \frac{\varepsilon}{1 + \varepsilon - E - v\varepsilon(1 + (1 - \tau)\varepsilon)}, \tag{3.20}$$

where E is the elasticity of the elasticity of demand with respect to price, $(d\varepsilon/dq)(q/\varepsilon)$ and v is the elasticity of marginal cost with respect to output, $(dMC/dx)(x/MC)$. It can be shown that $1 + (1 - \tau)\varepsilon < 0$, and therefore the last term in the formula, $-v\varepsilon(1 + (1 - \tau)\varepsilon)$, will be negative (positive) if the firm's marginal cost curve has a positive (negative) slope.

The degree of forward shifting will be smaller when the marginal cost curve has a positive slope and $v > 0$ because marginal cost will decline as the price increases, and this will help to moderate the price increase. Conversely, dq/dt will be larger if the firm experiences increasing returns to scale and marginal cost declines as output increases. For the remainder of the discussion on tax shifting, we will focus on the case where the marginal cost is constant and $v = 0$.

The formula for tax shifting indicates that the degree of forward shifting depends not only on the elasticity of demand ε but also on E, which indicates how the elasticity of demand varies as the price of the product varies. If demand becomes more elastic as the price increases, the monopolist will apply a smaller markup over $MC + t$, thereby moderating the price increase in response to a tax increase. For example, with a linear demand curve, the price elasticity of demand becomes larger (in absolute value) as the price of the commodity increases, and $E = 1 - \varepsilon > 1$. Substituting this value for E in (3.20) yields $dq/dt = 0.5$. Therefore the increased sensitivity of demand to price increases explains why the monopolist only passes on half of a tax increase when the demand curve is linear. If, on the other hand, the elasticity of demand is a constant, then $E = 0$, and $dq/dt = \varepsilon/(1+\varepsilon) > 1$, meaning the monopolist will raise the price of his product by more than the full amount of the tax. A third interesting case occurs when the demand function has the form $\ln x = a - bq$, where a and b are positive constants. With this demand function, $E = 1$ and $dq/dt = 1$. In general, $dq/dt \gtreqqless 1$ as $E \gtreqqless 1$ when the firm has constant marginal costs of production.

The following numerical calculations with $\varepsilon = -1.5$ and $\tau = 0.20$ indicate how the degree of tax shifting under monopoly affects the MCF. With a linear demand curve, $dq/dt = 0.5$ and the MCF is 1.77. With $E = 1$, $dq/dt = 1$, and MCF is 2.86. With a constant elasticity of demand of -1.5, $dq/dt = 3$, and the MCF is 40. Thus a wide range of values for the MCF can be obtained for the same values for ε and τ, depending on how ε varies along the demand curve. Consequently measuring the degree of tax shifting is critical for measuring the MCF from taxing a monopolist's product.

3.5.2 Ad valorem versus Per Unit Taxes on a Monopolist's Product

In the preceding section it was assumed that a per unit tax was imposed on the monopolist's product. However, per unit and ad valorem excise taxes will illicit different price responses from a monopolist, and therefore the MCFs for these two types of excise tax will also be different. This contrasts with the situation under perfect competition where per unit and ad valorem taxes have equivalent effects on price and output if they raise the same amount of revenue. In order to highlight the different effects that per unit and ad valorem taxes have under monopoly, we will denote the ad valorem tax rate on the monopolist's product as τ_{av}, the per unit tax rate as t, the per unit tax expressed as a proportion of the consumer price as $\tau_{pu} = t/q$, and the total ad valorem equivalent tax rate on the commodity as $\tau = \tau_{pu} + \tau_{av}$. Then it can be shown that[10]

$$\frac{dq}{dt} = \left[\frac{\varepsilon}{1+\varepsilon}\right]\left(\frac{dq}{qd\tau_{av}}\right). \tag{3.21}$$

In other words, the increase in the price of the monopolist's product with a per unit tax exceeds the increase with an equivalent ad valorem tax by a factor that is equal to the firm's markup over marginal cost. Tax revenues will be equal to $R = (t + \tau_{av}q)x$, and the MCFs for the per unit and ad valorem taxes will be equal to the following:

$$MCF_t = \frac{1 + (dq/dt)}{1 + [\tau_{pu}\varepsilon + \tau_{av}(1+\varepsilon)](dq/dt)}, \tag{3.22}$$

$$MCF_{\tau_{av}} = \frac{1 + (dq/qd\tau)}{1 + [\tau_{pu}\varepsilon + \tau_{av}(1+\varepsilon)](dq/qd\tau_{av})}. \tag{3.23}$$

Note that the first term in square brackets represents the loss of revenue due to the shrinkage of the per unit tax revenues, x, while the second term in square brackets represents the loss of revenues due to the shrinkage of the ad valorem tax base, qx, caused by the tax-induced price increases. The increase in the price of the product partially offsets the decline in output when the tax rate is increased, and the decline in the ad valorem tax base is smaller than the decline in the per unit tax base. Consequently, for a given total tax rate, $\tau_{pu} + \tau_{av}$, the MCFs will be lower when the per unit tax rate is lower. In addition note that the two formulas for the MCFs only differ in the tax-shifting responses and since $dq/dt > dq/(qd\tau_{av})$, the $MCF_t > MCF_{\tau_{av}}$. Therefore, if a government has to raise revenues by taxing a monopolist's product, ad valorem taxes are less distortionary than per unit taxes.

The superiority of levying ad valorem taxes on a monopolist's product is no longer so clear-cut when there are consumption and public expenditure externalities in the economy. The MCFs for per unit and ad valorem excise taxes on a monopolist's product are equal to

$$MCF_t = \frac{1 - (\delta_M + \delta_E)\varepsilon(dq/dt)}{1 + \tau_{av}(dq/dt) + (\tau - \delta_G)\varepsilon(dq/dt)}, \tag{3.24}$$

$$MCF_\tau = \frac{1 - (\delta_M + \delta_E)\varepsilon(dq/qd\tau)}{1 + \tau_{av}(dq/qd\tau_{av}) + (\tau - \delta_G)\varepsilon(dq/qd\tau_{av})}, \tag{3.25}$$

where $\delta_M = -1/\varepsilon$ is the monopoly tax distortion, δ_E is the environmental distortion, with $\delta_E > 0$ (<0) if the good produces a positive (negative) externality, and δ_G is the public expenditure distortion, with $\delta_G > 0$ (<0) if an increase in the consumption of the good increases (decreases) the cost of providing a given level of a public service. The numerator of each expression includes the social loss from the reduction in the output of the taxed product due to monopoly power and the environmental externality. The second term in the denominator is the increase in revenues that results from an increase in the price of the product, given that the government levies an ad valorem tax, and the third term is the impact on the government's net revenues as a result of the reduction in the production of the commodity. Note that the two expressions for the MCFs only differ in the $dqdt$ and $dq/qd\tau_{av}$. Since dq/dt exceeds $dq/qd\tau_{av}$ by the factor $\varepsilon/(1+\varepsilon) > 1$, sufficient conditions for the MCF_t to be less than MCF_τ are

$$\delta_E + \delta_M < 0 \quad \text{and} \quad \delta_G > \tau_{pu} + \frac{(1+\varepsilon)\tau_{av}}{\varepsilon}. \tag{3.26}$$

In other words, if the marginal environmental damage from the product exceeds the price distortion caused by monopoly, implying that the monopoly price of the product is too low, and if the marginal expenditure distortion exceeds the total tax rate on the commodity, then a per unit tax has a lower MCF than an ad valorem tax. Intuitively the per unit tax has a lower MCF under these conditions because social welfare is improved by raising the price of the product, and a per unit tax is more effective in raising the price of the product than an ad valorem tax. Note that under these conditions the MCF_t is less than one.

The combinations of ad valorem and per unit tax rates that satisfy the optimality condition $MCF_t = MCF_{\tau_{av}}$ are given below:

$$\tau_{pu} = \delta_G - \delta_E - \delta_M - \left(\frac{1+\varepsilon}{\varepsilon}\right)\tau_{av}. \tag{3.27}$$

With this combination of per unit and ad valorem tax rates, $MCF_t = MCF_{\tau_{av}} = 1$. Figure 3.5 shows the combinations of per unit and ad valorem tax rates that satisfy the conditions in (3.26) and (3.27). Combinations of τ_{pu} and τ_{av} that lie below the dotted line satisfy the sufficient conditions for $MCF_t < MCF_\tau$, and the combinations that lie along the solid line satisfy the condition $MCF_t = MCF_\tau = 1$. It is easy to generate numerical examples where $MCF_t < MCF_\tau < 1$ holds in this region, and in section 4.2.2, we will see that this condition holds for cigarette taxes in the United

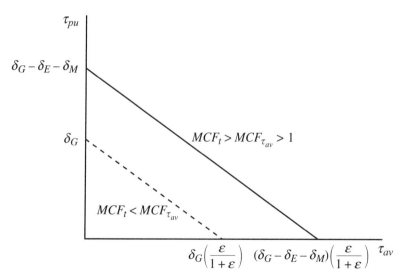

Figure 3.5
The MCFs with per unit and ad valorem taxes

Kingdom. Therefore it seems likely that if the government cannot levy lump-sum taxes and its need for tax revenue is high, such that $MCF > 1$, then it should only impose an ad valorem tax on the monopolist's product and that the tax rate should be greater than $(\delta_G - \delta_E - \delta_M)(\varepsilon/(1 + \varepsilon))$. However, if a government's optimal tax policy implies that the $MCF < 1$ (perhaps for distributional reasons), then the government should only impose a per unit tax on the monopolist's product at a rate that is less than $(\delta_G - \delta_E - \delta_M)$. Finally, the model indicates that if the government can levy lump-sum taxes and its MCF is one, it can levy any combination of per unit and ad valorem taxes that satisfy condition (3.27).

3.5.3 The MCF under Oligopoly

In the preceding section we derived the MCFs for excise taxes imposed on a good produced by a monopolist. However, pure private monopolies (as opposed to publicly owned monopolies) are relatively rare. Most imperfectly competitive markets are best characterized as oligopolies where a small number of firms dominate the market. Fortunately the basic results on the MCFs for excise taxes on monopoly products can be extended to imperfectly competitive markets if a simple conjectural variations model of oligopoly is adopted.[11] In this type of oligopoly model, n firms produce an identical product. Total industry output is $X = \sum x_j$. A firm's strategic behavior is captured by its conjectural variation parameter, $\gamma_j = (dX/dx_j)(x_j/X)$, which reflects the firm's beliefs concerning how other firms in the industry will respond to a change in its output. We assume that all firms have identical costs and the same conjectural variations. For a perfectly competitive industry, $\gamma = 0$, because each firm expects the price of the product (and hence total output) to remain constant when it increases its output. With a symmetric Cournot duopoly, $\gamma = 0.5$ because $dX/dx_j = 1$ and $X = 2x_j$. If the n firms in the industry collude to maximize their joint profits, then $\gamma = 1$. This is equivalent to the monopoly case. Thus the conjectural variations parameter can be interpreted as a measure of the market power that is exercised by firms in the industry, and the model can be used to reflect a wide range of market structures.

Let the profit earned by firm j be equal to

$$\Pi_j = (1 - \tau_{av})qx_j - C(x_j) - tx_j, \tag{3.28}$$

where q, the market price, is a function of aggregate output. The first-order condition for profit maximization is

$$\frac{d\Pi_j}{dx_j} = (1 - \tau_{av})\left[q + x_i\frac{dq}{dX}\frac{dX}{dx_i}\right] - MC - t = 0. \tag{3.29}$$

This can be rewritten as

$$q\left[1 + \frac{\gamma}{\varepsilon}\right] = \frac{MC + t}{1 - \tau_{av}}, \tag{3.30}$$

where $\varepsilon = (dX/dq)(q/X)$ is the elasticity of market demand for the product. Therefore the markup over the tax-adjusted marginal cost of production will be

$$q = \left[\frac{\varepsilon}{\gamma + \varepsilon}\right]\left(\frac{MC + t}{1 - \tau_{av}}\right). \tag{3.31}$$

The distortion caused by the exercise of market power will be equal to

$$\delta_M = \frac{q - [(MC + t)/(1 - \tau_{av})]}{q} = \frac{-\gamma}{\varepsilon}. \tag{3.32}$$

The degree of tax shifting will be equal to

$$\frac{(1 - \tau_{av})dq}{dt} = \frac{\varepsilon}{\varepsilon + \gamma(1 - E) - v\varepsilon\{\gamma + [(1 - \tau_{pu} - \tau_{av})/(1 - \tau_{av})]\varepsilon\}}, \tag{3.33}$$

where τ_{pu} is t/q and τ_{av} is the ad valorem tax rate. Analogous to the pure monopoly case,[12] $dq/dt = \varepsilon(\gamma + \varepsilon)^{-1}dq/(qd\tau_{av})$. The MCF for a per unit has the same general form as in section 3.5.1:

$$MCF_t = \frac{1 - \delta_M\varepsilon(dq/dt)}{1 + [\tau_{pu}\varepsilon + \tau_{av}(1 + \varepsilon)](dq/dt)} = \frac{1 + \gamma(dq/dt)}{1 + [\tau_{pu}\varepsilon + \tau_{av}(1 + \varepsilon)](dq/dt)}. \tag{3.34}$$

The MCF for an ad valorem tax has the same form as (3.34) but with $dq/(qd\tau_{av})$ substituted for dq/dt. Thus the expressions in (3.33) and (3.34) allow us to calculate the MCFs for excise taxes imposed in market structures ranging from perfect competition ($\gamma = 0, v = (1 - \tau)\eta^{-1}$) to pure monopoly ($\gamma = 1$).

The cigarette industry is highly concentrated in most countries, and there is considerable evidence of noncompetitive behavior in cigarette pricing. In a recent paper Delipalla and O'Donnell (2001) used a conjectural variations framework, similar to the one outlined above, to estimate the responsiveness of cigarette prices to tax-changes in European countries. Their estimates of the tax-shifting parameters were consistent with the theoretical prediction that ad valorem taxes produce smaller price increases than per unit taxes in an imperfectly competitive market. The ratio of the tax-shifting parameters for per unit and ad valorem taxes implies that the distortion in the market price caused imperfect competition is 0.219 if the price elasticity of demand for cigarettes is -0.40. Thus the imperfect competition is a potentially important distortion in cigarette market. In chapter 4 we will use their parameter estimates to calculate the MCF for excise taxes on cigarettes in the United Kingdom.

3.6   Addiction/Self-control Problems

Many individuals regret excessive consumption of some commodities, such as alcohol, tobacco, and fatty foods. "For example, during 2000, 70 percent of current smokers expressed a desire to quit completely and 41 percent stopped smoking for at least one day in an attempt to quit, but only 4.7 percent successfully abstained for more than three months."[13] Individuals who are prone to excessive drinking or smoking are said to have self-control or addiction problems. In many countries excise taxes on alcohol and tobacco are viewed favourably as "sin taxes" because higher prices may reduce the degree of excessive consumption. (See Badenes-Plá and Jones 2003 for a survey of the economics literature on addiction and taxes, Gruber and Köszegi 2004 and Gruber and Mullainathan 2005 for recent empirical studies of the implications of addiction for efficiency and distributional effects of cigarette taxes, and *The Economist* 2006 for a discussion of public policies based on the "new paternalism.")

We use a simple model developed by O'Donoghue and Rabin (2006) to illustrate the way in which the self-control distortion can be incorporated in the evaluation of a tax increase on these commodities. Suppose that an individual consumes only two goods, x_1 and x_2. The consumption of x_2 provides constant marginal utility, normalized to equal one. The consumption of x_1 provides the individual with a benefit $V(x_1)$ and also a psychic cost $C(x_1)$, which could be interpreted as a cost that arises from a future health problem. The individual make consumption decisions according to the following utility function

$$U^* = V(x_1) - \Phi C(x_1) + x_2, \tag{3.35}$$

where Φ is a positive parameter. If $\Phi < 1$, the individual is said to have a self-control problem because he does not take into account the full personal cost consuming x_1. The individual's budget constraint is $q_1 x_1 + x_2 = I$, where the price of x_2 is set equal to one. The individual consumes x_1^* based on the first order condition, $V_{x_1} = \Phi C_{x_1} + q_1$.

However, the individual's long-run happiness is based on the utility function:

$$U^{**} = V(x_1) - C(x_1) + x_2, \tag{3.36}$$

which fully reflects the cost that the individual incurs when he consumes x_1. The individual with self-control problems overconsumes x_1 because the ideal consumption is based on $V_{x_1} = C_{x_1} + q_1$

To evaluate the effects of a tax rate change, we will assume that the individual and society are concerned with the impact of the tax increase on the individual's long-run utility. (See Bernheim and Rangel 2005 on using the individual's long-term welfare in assessing policies.) The welfare effect of a tax increase is equal to

$$\frac{dU^{**}}{dt_1} = (V_{x_1} - C_{x_1})\frac{dx_1}{dq_1} + \frac{dx_2}{dq_1} = -x_1^* + (V_{x_1} - C_{x_1} - q)\frac{dx_1}{dq_1}, \qquad (3.37)$$

since, from the individual's budget constraint, $dx_2/dq_1 = -x_1^* - q_1 dx_1/dq_1$. Using the individual's first-order condition, we have the following expression that measures the harm caused by a tax increase:

$$-\frac{dU^{**}}{dt_1} = x_1^*\left[1 + \left(\frac{(1-\Phi)C_x}{q_1}\right)\varepsilon_{11}\right] = x_1^*(1 - \delta_{A1}\varepsilon_{11}), \qquad (3.38)$$

where $\varepsilon_{11} = (dx_1/dq_1)(q_1/x_1) < 0$ is the price elasticity of demand for x_1. The distortion caused by the individual's self-control problem is defined as

$$\delta_{A_1} = \frac{V_{x_1} - C_{x_1} - q_1}{q_1} = \frac{(\Phi - 1)C_{x_1}}{q_1}. \qquad (3.39)$$

The δ_{A_1} parameter reflects the distortion that arises because there is a wedge between marginal value of an additional unit of x to the individual and its true marginal cost. It can be interpreted as the *neglected* proportion of the additional cost incurred in spending an additional dollar on x_1. If the individual has a self-control problem and $\Phi < 1$, δ_{A_1} is negative, and this factor tends to reduce the social harm from a tax increase. Indeed it is possible for a price increase to make the individual better off, at least as judged by his long-run utility function if $\delta_{A_1}\varepsilon_{11} > 1$, and in this case the MCF would be a negative number. The formula for the marginal cost of public funds for the commodity tax is

$$MCF_{t_1} = \frac{1 - \delta_{A_1}\varepsilon_{11}}{1 + \tau_1\varepsilon_{11}} \qquad (3.40)$$

provided that there are no other distortions in the economy. If the government could raise revenue by imposing a lump-sum tax such that its MCF is 1.00, then the optimal tax rate on the commodity would be $\tau_i = -\delta_{A_i} = (1 - \Phi)(C_x/q_i)$. The optimal sin tax rate would reflect the *neglected* proportion of the additional cost incurred in spending an additional dollar on x_1.

Obviously incorporating these self-control distortions into the calculation of the MCF is controversial. To some extent lack of self-control problems, especially with regard to tobacco products, does reflect public opinion and policy makers' views concerning the use of excise taxes. For this reason it is important to incorporate defective decision-making explicitly in the model so that it can be compared with the other distortions that affect the MCF. This way better judgment can be made concerning the relative importance of self-control problems in the overall assessment of the appropriate level of excise taxation.

3.7 Smuggling

The smuggling of commodities that are subject to high excise taxes is a major problem in many countries.[14] This section outlines a simple model that incorporates smuggling into the MCF for an excise tax.[15] We will suppose that the elasticity of the supply of the smuggled commodity is $\eta^s > 0$. The price of the smuggled commodity will reflect its production cost plus the smuggling costs that are incurred by the smugglers, $q^s = p + c^s$. Let us assume then that these smuggling costs are less than the per unit excise tax imposed on the legitimate goods. Consumers are willing to buy smuggled goods as long as the price of a smuggled good plus the search costs, f, are less than the price of a legitimate good cigarette, $q^s = q - f$. Let us further assume that the excise tax increases are fully reflected in the price of legitimate the legitimate good; this implies that $dq/dt = dq^s/dt = 1$ if search costs are relatively constant. The demand for the legitimate goods that are fully taxed is the difference between the total demand and the demand for smuggled goods, or $x^l = x^T(q) - x^s(q^s)$, where x^T is the total number of cigarettes consumed. The government's tax revenue (ignoring all other taxes) is $R = tx^l$. The marginal cost of public funds from taxing cigarettes can then be expressed as

$$MCF = \frac{x^l(dq/dt) + x^s(dq^s/dt)}{x^l + t[(dx^l/dq)(dq/dt)]} = \frac{1}{(1-v)(1+\tau\varepsilon^l)}, \qquad (3.41)$$

where $v = x^s/x^T$ is the share of the smuggled goods in total consumption and ε^l is the elasticity of demand for legitimate goods. Smuggling increases the MCF because the tax base is smaller and the tax base is more tax sensitive because smuggling gives individuals the opportunity to switch to a nontaxed alternative. The elasticity of demand for legitimate goods is related to the elasticity of demand for total consumption and the smuggling supply elasticity as follows:

$$(1-v)\varepsilon^l = \varepsilon^T - v\left(\frac{q}{q^s}\right)\eta^s, \qquad (3.42)$$

where $(q/q^s) = (p + c^s + f)/(p + c^s) < (1 - \tau)^{-1}$. When the tax rate is raised, the volume of taxed goods decreases because total consumption falls and the volume of smuggled goods increases. For example, if 20 percent of the cigarettes are smuggled and if the elasticity of total demand for cigarettes is −0.40, the elasticity of demand for legitimate cigarettes could be as high as −0.813—provided that the elasticity of the supply of smuggled cigarettes is 0.50—and as much as −1.44—provided that the elasticity of the supply of smuggled cigarettes is 1.50. Therefore ignoring the impact of smuggling by using the elasticity of total demand for cigarettes in the calculation of the MCF, rather then the elasticity of demand for legitimate cigarettes, can significantly underestimate the MCF for cigarette taxes.

In the next chapter we will use the concepts and frameworks developed in this chapter to evaluate the MCFs for excise taxes on alcohol, tobacco, and fuel in Thailand and the United Kingdom.

3.8   Studies of the Marginal Distortionary Cost of Taxing Commodities

Table 3.1 summarizes studies of the marginal distortionary costs from taxing commodities. These studies have used a variety of frameworks and concepts—marginal cost of public funds (MCF), marginal excess burden (MEB), marginal efficiency cost (MEC)—to measure the marginal distortionary costs and therefore it is difficult to summarize and compare their results. Here we only note that the studies by Ahmad and Stern (1984, 1990) were pathbreaking studies in extending concept and measurement of the MCF to commodity taxes and incorporated distributional concerns in the manner described in section 2.7. These studies are grouped into those that deal with the marginal distortionary costs of taxes on specific commodities, those that deal with general commodity and sales taxes, and those that deal with taxes on exports and imports.

Further Reading for Chapter 3

Besley and Jewitt (1995) show that a necessary condition for a uniform rate of taxation of commodities to be optimal is that the wage-compensated supply of labor is independent of goods prices; namely the tax rate depends only on the level of utility.

Myles (1987) examines the optimal commodity taxes for an economy with both competitive and imperfectly competitive industries. The optimal tax rates for the competitive industries satisfy a condition that combines the Ramsey rule with another factor that reflects the price, tax revenue, and profit changes induced in the noncompetitive industries by the tax rate increase on a competitive industry's products. For the goods produced by noncompetitive industries, the standard Ramsey rule is modified by the degree to which the tax is shifted forward and the degree of imperfect competition.

Skeath and Trandel (1994) derive conditions under which ad valorem taxes on an oligopoly's product are superior to per unit taxes. Using a linear demand curve model, they show that ad valorem taxes are not Pareto superior if tax rates are low or the number of firms in the industry is sufficiently high.

Table 3.1
Studies of the marginal distortionary cost of commodity taxes

Author	Data	Results	Comments
Specific commodity and excise taxes			
Ahmad and Stern (1984)	India, 1979–1980	MCFs for 9 commodity groups ranged from 1.0037 for milk and milk products to 1.245 for clothing.	With an inequality aversion parameter value of 1.00, fuel and light had the highest SMCF and milk and milk products had the lowest SMCF.
Ahmad and Stern (1990)	Pakistan, 1975–1976	MCFs ranged from 0.999 for meat and eggs to 1.122 for edible oils.	Specific commodity tax increases given for 13 commodity groups. With an inequality aversion parameter value of 1.00, wheat had the highest SMCF while meat and eggs has the lowest.
Cragg (1991)	Canada, 1978	MCFs ranged from 0.769 for recreation to 1.429 for food.	Specific commodity tax increases given for 10 commodities. With an inequality aversion parameter of 1.00, tobacco had the lowest SMCF and alcoholic beverages had the highest, followed by food.
Decoster and Schokkaert (1990)	Belgium, 1978–1979	MCFs for 12 commodity groups ranged from 0.8096 for services to 2.7963 for tobacco with the Rotterdam model and from 0.9438 for beverages to 1.3677 for transportation with the AIDs model. The rank correlation coefficient between the two sets of MCFs was 0.16.	The authors concluded that "the rankings of the marginal welfare costs are affected by imposing the restriction of symmetry of the Slutsky matrix." (p. 295). However, the differences between the SMCFs were reduced as the coefficient of inequality aversion became larger.
Devarajan et al. (2002)	Bangladesh	MCFs ranged from 0.95 for fisheries to 1.07 for tobacco. A uniform tax increase had an MCF of 1.05	CGE models were used to calculate MCFs. The authors concluded that the MCFs in these developing countries were substantially higher than in developed economies and that the MCFs were not uniform across sectors or taxes, indicating the potential for efficiency-enhancing reforms.
	Cameroon	MCFs ranged from 0.48 for cash crops to 0.96 for food and forestry. A uniform tax increase had an MCF of 0.90.	
	Indonesia	MCFs ranged from 0.97 for liquid natural gas to 1.11 for electricity and gas. A uniform tax increase had an MCF of 0.90.	
Diewert and Lawrence (1996)	New Zealand, 1971–1991	MEBs for a tax on motor vehicles ranged from −0.056 in 1986 to 0.0071 in 1975, with an average value of −0.0246.	Calculations were based on an econometric model of demand and supply elasticities of seven goods, including labor demand and supply.

Table 3.1
(continued)

Author	Data	Results	Comments
Madden (1995)	Ireland	MCFs for 10 commodity groups ranged from 1.079 for clothing and footwear to 1.664 for alcohol.	Calculations were based on a demand system with labor supply responses to commodity tax increases. With an inequality aversion parameter value of 2.00, services had the lowest SMCF and tobacco highest SMCF (more discussion in section 4.1.1).
Parry (2003)	United Kingdom, 1999	MEBs for excise taxes on cigarettes, 0.11, alcohol, 0.24, and petrol, 1.00.	Calculations included distortions caused by externalities (more detail provided in section 4.2).
West and Williams (2006)	United States, 1997	MCF for taxing gasoline was between 1.01 and 1.03.	This estimate of the MCF did not include marginal environmental damage (MED) from gasoline. They use an estimate of the MED of $0.77 per liter to calculate an optimal tax rate for gasoline.

General commodity and sales taxes

Author	Data	Results	Comments
Ballard, Shoven and Whalley (1985)	United States, 1973	MEBs for consumer sales taxes ranged from 0.251 to 0.388, depending on labor supply and savings elasticities. The MEBs for output taxes ranged from 0.147 to 0.279.	MEBs were calculated using a large scale CGE model of the US economy. The MEBs for sales on commodities other than alcohol, tobacco, and gasoline had the lowest MEBs (0.026 to 0.119) of any of the taxes studied.
Baylor and Beausejour (2004)	Canada, 1996–1998	Welfare gain per dollar of reduction in the present value of sales tax revenue was 0.13.	Sales tax was calculated using a dynamic CGE model. The sales tax was the least distortionary of any of the taxes that they studied.
Campbell (1975)	Canada, 1961	MEB was 0.25 for a general commodity tax increase.	Pioneering study of marginal distortions caused by tax increases.
Diewert and Lawrence (1996)	New Zealand, 1971–1991	MEBs for a general consumption tax ranged from 0.049 in 1972 to 0.137 in 1991, with an average value of 0.083. MEBs for a general production tax or subsidy ranged from 0.037 in 1972 to 0.147 in 1990 with an average value of 0.070.	Calculations were based on an econometric model of demand and supply elasticities of seven goods including labor demand and supply.
Erbil (2004)	31 countries, 1995 and 1997	MCFs for taxes on domestic output ranged from 1.000 for Uganda to 1.442 for Japan.	CGE models were used for calculations. See also results for tariffs.

Table 3.1
(continued)

Author	Data	Results	Comments
Jorgenson and Yun (1991)	United States, 1986	MEC of a sales tax on consumer and investment goods was 0.262.	Calculations were based on a dynamic general equilibrium model. MECs for property taxes were 0.176 in 1986 and 0.139 in 1996. Sales taxes had the next lowest MEC in both years.
Jorgenson and Yun (2001)	United States, 1996	MEC of a sales tax on consumer and investment goods was 0.175.	
Warlters and Auriol (2005)	38 African countries, 1998 to 2002	MCFs for taxes on domestic consumer goods ranged from 0.97 in Namibia to 1.27 in São Tomé. The average value was 1.09.	CGE models were used for calculations. Authors concluded that an economy's MCF rose substantially with the size of the informal sector.
Taxes on imports and exports			
Devarajan et al. (2002)	Bangladesh	MCFs for import taxes ranged from 1.17 for livestock to 2.18 for sugar. A uniform import tax increase had an MCF of 1.20.	CGE models were used to calculate MCFs. The import taxes generally had higher MCFs than commodity taxes.
	Cameroon	MCFs for import taxes ranged from 1.05 for intermediate goods to 1.37 for food and consumption. A uniform import tax increase had an MCF of 1.05.	
	Indonesia	MCFs for import taxes ranged from 0.99 for business services to 1.18 for other industries. A uniform import tax increase had an MCF of 0.99.	
Diewert and Lawrence (1996)	New Zealand, 1971–1991	MEBs for import taxes ranged from 0.019 in 1972 to 0.042 in 1990, with an average value of 0.026.	Calculations were based on an econometric model of demand and supply elasticities of seven goods including labor demand and supply.
Diewert and Lawrence (1996)	New Zealand, 1971–1991	MEBs for export taxes (or subsidies) ranged from 0.037 in 1984 to 0.077 in 1988, with an average value of 0.052.	
Erbil (2004)	31 countries, 1995 and 1997	MCFs for tariffs ranged from 1.013 for Denmark to 1.556 in China. In 27 countries, the MCFs for tariffs exceeded the MCFs for domestic output.	CGE models were used for calculations. For Japan, Mexico, Sri Lanka, Sweden, United Kingdom, and Denmark, tariffs had a lower MCF than taxes on domestic output.
Warlters and Auriol (2005)	38 African countries, 1998–2002	MCFs for taxes on imports ranged from 0.97 in Uganda to 1.23 in Sudan. The average value was 1.08.	CGE models were used for calculations.
Warlters and Auriol (2005)	38 African countries, 1998–2002	MCFs for taxes on exports ranged from 0.63 in Eritrea to 3.14 in Ethiopia. For Burkina Faso and Rwanda, export taxes reduced revenues. The average MCF, excluding these countries, was 1.21.	CGE models were used for calculations.

Abbreviations: MCF is marginal cost of public funds, SMCF is a distributionally weighted MCF, MEC is marginal efficiency cost, MEB is marginal excess burden, and CGE is computable general equilibrium model.

Delipalla and Keen (1992, prop. 6) show that an ad valorem tax welfare dominates a per unit tax that raises the same revenue. (Welfare dominance means that it raises as least as much revenues, generates more profits for the firm, and leaves consumers better off.) Note, however, the relevant comparison for purposes of tax policy is not a comparison of ad valorem and specific taxes that generate the same revenue but rather which tax has the lower MCF.

Appendix to Chapter 3

Derivation of the MCF for a Per Unit Tax on a Monopolist's Product

The after-tax profit of the monopolist is

$$\Pi = (1 - \tau_\pi) \cdot [qx - C(x) - \tau_{av}qx - tx], \tag{A3.1}$$

where τ_π is the profit tax rate, τ_{av} is the ad valorem tax rate, and t is the per unit tax rate. Differentiating after-tax profit with respect to the per unit tax rate, we obtain

$$\frac{d\Pi}{dt} = (1 - \tau_\pi)\left[x\frac{dq}{dt} + q\frac{dx}{dq}\frac{dq}{dt} - MC\frac{dx}{dq}\frac{dq}{dt} - x - t\frac{dx}{dq}\frac{dq}{dt}\right]$$

$$= (1 - \tau_\pi)\left[x\frac{dq}{dt} - x + (q - MC - t)\frac{dx}{dq}\frac{dq}{dt}\right], \tag{A3.2}$$

where MC is the marginal cost of production. The first term in square brackets corresponds to area A in figure 3.4, the second term corresponds to area B, and the third term corresponds to area C.

We ignore distributional concerns and represent social welfare by an indirect utility function $V(q, \Pi)$ for a representative individual. The social welfare cost of an increase in the tax rate on the monopolist's product is

$$-\frac{1}{\lambda}\frac{dV}{dt} = -\frac{1}{\lambda}\left(\frac{dV}{dq}\frac{dq}{dt} + \frac{dV}{d\Pi}\frac{d\Pi}{dt}\right)$$

$$= x\frac{dq}{dt} - (1 - \tau_\pi)x\left[\frac{dq}{dt} - 1 + \delta_M\varepsilon\frac{dq}{dt}\right]$$

$$= x\left[(1 - \tau_\pi) + \tau_\pi\frac{dq}{dt} - (1 - \tau_\pi)\delta_M\varepsilon\frac{dq}{dt}\right], \tag{A3.3}$$

where $\delta_M = (q - MC - t)/q$, ε is the elasticity of demand, $\lambda = dV/d\Pi$ is the marginal utility of income, and $dV/dq = -\lambda x$ by Roy's theorem. The first term in square brackets represents the net increase in taxes paid by the private sector, given that excise taxes are deductible in computing the firm's profit tax liability. The second term represents the additional profit tax that is paid as a result of the increase in the price of the monopolist's good. The third term is the reduction in after-tax profits sustained by the monopolist as a result of the decline in output caused by the tax.

Total tax revenue is equal to $R = tx + \tau_\pi \Pi/(1 - \tau_\pi)$. Differentiating with respect to t, we obtain

$$\frac{dR}{dt} = x\left(1 + \tau_{pu}\varepsilon\frac{dq}{dt}\right) + \frac{\tau_\pi}{1 - \tau_\pi}\left[(1 - \tau_\pi)\left[x\frac{dq}{dt} - x + (q - MC - t)\frac{dx}{dq}\frac{dq}{dt}\right]\right]$$

$$= x\left[(1 - \tau_\pi) + \tau_\pi\frac{dq}{dt} + (\tau_{pu} + \tau_\pi\delta_M)\varepsilon\frac{dq}{dt}\right]. \tag{A3.4}$$

The first term in square brackets represents the net increase in tax revenues, for a given level of output by the monopolist, the second term is the increase in profit tax revenues from the induced increase in the price of the monopolist's product, and the third term is reduction in total tax revenues from the reduction in the output produced by the monopolist. Note that the government sustains a reduction in profit taxes, $\tau_\pi\delta_M$, as a result of the reduction in the monopolist's profit.

Combining (A3.3) with (A3.4), we obtain the following expression for the marginal cost of public funds:

$$MCF_t = \frac{(1 - \tau_\pi) + \tau_\pi(dq/dt) - (1 - \tau_\pi)\delta_M\varepsilon(dq/dt)}{(1 - \tau_\pi) + \tau_\pi(dq/dt) + (\tau_{pu} + \tau_\pi\delta_M)\varepsilon(dq/dt)}. \tag{A3.5}$$

Note that (A3.5) corresponds to (3.19) for the case where τ_π is zero. An interesting special case is where $\tau_\pi = 1$, which could correspond to a situation where the monopoly is owned by the government and all of the profits and taxes on the product are received by the public treasury. (This may correspond to the publicly owned tobacco monopolies in some European countries.) In this situation the MCF is equal to

$$MCF_t(\tau_\pi = 1) = \frac{1}{1 + (\tau_{pu} + \delta_M)\varepsilon}, \tag{A3.6}$$

which is independent of the degree of tax shifting. In this case the total tax rate on the product is effectively $\tau_{pu} + \delta_M$.

Exercises for Chapter 3

3.1 The almost ideal demand system (AIDS), developed by Deaton and Muellbauer (1980), is frequently used to estimate the parameters of consumer demand functions. In this system the indirect utility function has the following form:

$$V(q, M) = \frac{\ln(M) - \ln(Q)}{\beta_0 \cdot \prod_i (q_i)^{\beta_i}},$$

where the prices of the n goods purchased by the consumer, M is the consumer's total income (and expenditure), the β are parameters that satisfy the restriction given below, and the Q is a price index that is defined as

$$\ln(Q) = \alpha_0 + \sum_j \alpha_j \cdot \ln(q_j) + \frac{1}{2} \cdot \sum_i \sum_j \gamma_{ij} \cdot (\ln(q_i) \cdot \ln(q_j)).$$

Here the α and γ are parameters that have the following restrictions:

$$\sum_{i=1}^{n} \alpha_i = 0, \quad \sum_{i=1}^{n} \gamma_{ij} = 0, \quad \sum_{j=1}^{n} \gamma_{ij} = 0, \quad \sum_{i=1}^{n} \beta_i = 0.$$

The expenditure function that corresponds to the indirect utility function is

$$\ln e(q, U) = \ln(Q) + U \cdot \beta_0 \cdot \prod_i (q_i)^{\beta_i}.$$

Utility maximization subject to the budget constraint, $\sum_i q_i x_i = M$, generates the following budget share equations:

$$b_i = \alpha_i + \sum_j \gamma_{ij} \cdot \ln(q_j) + \beta_j \cdot \ln\left(\frac{M}{Q}\right).$$

Suppose that there are only three goods consumed by this individual and that the parameter values are as follows:

$$\alpha_0 = 0, \quad \alpha_1 = 0.20, \quad \alpha_2 = 0.40, \quad \alpha_3 = 0.40,$$

$$\beta_0 = 1.00, \quad \beta_1 = 0.30, \quad \beta_2 = 0.20, \quad \beta_3 = -0.50,$$

$$\gamma = \begin{pmatrix} 0.5 & -0.25 & -0.25 \\ -0.25 & -0.25 & 0.50 \\ -0.25 & 0.50 & -0.25 \end{pmatrix}.$$

Suppose that individual's total income is $M = 1$ and that in the absence of taxation, $q_i = 1$ for $i = 1, 2$, and 3.

(a) In the initial situation, the government imposes a 30 percent ad valorem tax rate on good 1 and a 20 percent ad valorem tax rate on good 2. Good three is not taxed. As a result the consumer price for good 1 is $(1 - \tau_1)^{-1} = 1.429$ and the consumer price of good 2 is $(1 - \tau_2)^{-1} = 1.25$. The consumer price of good three is assumed to remain at 1.00. Calculate the equivalent variation based measure of the excess burden per dollar of tax revenue with this tax regime, and calculate the gain from replacing this tax regime with an equal yield lump-sum tax. Why does the gain per dollar of tax revenue from this tax reform exceed the excess burden per dollar of tax revenue?

(b) Suppose that the government cannot impose lump-sum taxes and that it cannot tax good 3 for political or administrative reasons. Would the efficiency of the tax system be improved with a uniform rate of taxation on goods 1 and 2 that raised the same revenue as the tax system described in (a)? [*Hint:* Find the uniform tax rate on goods 1 and 2 that raises approximately the same revenue—with a deviation of less than 1 percent from the original revenue—and calculate the excess burden associated with this uniform tax rate.]

3.2 Let t be the per unit excise tax imposed on a good that is produced by a duopoly. Suppose that the two firms produce an identical product, have the same costs of production, and exhibit Cournot-Nash strategic behavior. The market demand curve for their product is linear and has the following form:

$$q = a - bX,$$

where $X = x_1 + x_2$ is aggregate output, q is the consumer price, and a and b are positive constants. The total profit earned by each firm is

$$\Pi_i = (q - t - c)x_i, \qquad i = 1, 2,$$

where t is the per unit tax imposed on the product and c is the constant marginal cost of production. There are no other taxes or distortions in the economy, and society places the same distributional weights on firms' shareholders and the consumers of the product.

(a) Calculate the marginal cost of public funds, and explain why it is greater than one, when $t = 0$, $a = 20$, $b = 1$, and $c = 5$.

(b) Now suppose that one of the firms is owned by foreigners and the other firm is owned by domestic residents. As in the question above, t is the tax rate imposed on the output of both producers and t_f is a per unit tax imposed on imports of the good by the foreign producer. The profits of the domestically-owned and the foreign-owned firms are given below:

$$\Pi_n = (q - t - c_n)x_n,$$

$$\Pi_f = (q - t - t_f - c_f)x_f,$$

where $X = x_n + x_f$. Show that the MCFs for the two types of taxes have the following form if the government ignores the impact of its taxes on the shareholders of the foreign-owned firm:

$$
MCF_t = \frac{\left(\frac{x_f}{X}\right)\frac{dq}{dt} + \left(\frac{x_n}{X}\right)\left(1 + \gamma \cdot \frac{dq}{dt}\right)}{1 + \tau \cdot \varepsilon \cdot \frac{dq}{dt} + \tau_f \cdot \left(\frac{q}{X} \cdot \frac{dx_f}{dt}\right)},
$$

$$
MCF_{tf} = \frac{x_f \cdot \frac{dq}{dt_f} - \delta_M \cdot q \cdot \frac{dx_n}{dt_f}}{x_f + (t_f + t) \cdot \frac{dx_f}{dt_f} + t \cdot \frac{dx_n}{dt_f}},
$$

where $\tau = t/q$, $\tau_f = t_f/q$, γ is the firms' conjectural variations parameter, and $\delta_M = (q - c_n - t)/q$ is the domestic distortion caused by the firms' market power.

(c) If the domestic and foreign firms have Cournot-Nash conjectural variations and the market demand curve and marginal costs are the same as in exercise 3.2a, calculate the MCFs for t and t_f when $t = 0$, $t_f = 0$, $a = 20$, $b = 1$, and $c = 5$. Explain why the MCF_t is now lower than in exercise 3.2a. Explain why the marginal cost of funds from the tariff on imported production, MCF_{tf}, is lower than the MCF_t, whereas the analysis of the tariff in section 2.5 indicated a consumption-based tax was more efficient than the tariff.

4 The MCFs for Excise Taxes in Thailand and the United Kingdom

Excise taxes, commodity taxes, and import duties are important sources of tax revenue in most countries, but they are especially important in developing countries. In 1995 to 1997 these taxes represented 60.6 percent of tax revenues in developing countries in compared to 32.5 percent in OECD countries.[1] Among Southeast Asian countries, reliance on taxes on goods and services ranges from 13.0 percent of total tax revenue in Brunei to 82.3 percent in Cambodia. See table 4.1. In this chapter we use the framework that was developed in chapter 3 to calculate the MCFs for alcohol, tobacco, and fuel taxes in Thailand and the United Kingdom.

In Thailand commodity taxes represent 59.1 percent of total tax revenues, with excise taxes contributing 25.6 percent of tax revenues. Given its heavy reliance on excise taxes, the equity and efficiency effects of excise taxes are important aspects of tax policy in Thailand. The study in section 4.1 is based on Chandoevwit and Dahlby (2007). We use estimates of the own- and cross-price elasticities of demand for ten categories of goods and services in Thailand to capture the interdependence of the various commodity tax bases in Thailand in computing the MCFs, and we incorporate in the computation of the MCFs the nontax distortions created by (1) environmental externalities, (2) public expenditure externalities, (3) addiction, (4) market power, and (5) smuggling. Based on the benchmark parameter values, the MCFs are 0.532 for fuel excise taxes, 2.187 for tobacco excise taxes, 2.312 for alcohol excise taxes, and 1.080 for a VAT increase. Pro-poor distributional weights and data on the spending patterns of 90 household groups in Thailand are also used to calculate distributionally weighted MCFs, but this procedure does not change the ranking of the social marginal cost of the excise taxes. Finally, we show that a revenue-neutral marginal tax reform—reducing the excise tax rates on alcohol and tobacco by one percentage point and increasing the fuel excise tax—results in a net efficiency gain equal to 1.72 Baht for every additional Baht of fuel tax revenue.

In section 4.2 we calculate the MCFs for UK excise taxes on petrol, alcoholic beverages, and cigarettes in 1999, using, as a starting point, a study by Parry (2003) who computed the MEBs for these excise taxes as well as for taxes on labor. Parry's basic

Table 4.1
Taxes on goods and services in ASEAN countries (percentage of total tax revenues)

Country	Excise taxes	Consumption taxes	Import duties	Total commodity taxes
Brunei	—	—	13.0	13.0
Cambodia	16.3	33.6	32.4	82.3
Indonesia	6.4	19.3	2.4	28.1
Laos	18.7	26.0	16.0	60.7
Malaysia	10.5	12.3	5.7	28.5
Myanmar	1.7	45.2	9.6	56.5
Philippines	12.9	14.4	16.1	43.4
Singapore	25.9	8.5	0.0	34.4
Thailand	25.6	21.2	12.3	59.1
Vietnam	8.8	29.8	24.0	62.6

Source: Cnossen (2005a, tab. 3, p. 508).

parameter values, including his estimates of the environmental externalities associated with the consumption of petrol, alcohol and tobacco, are used to calculate the MCFs using the framework developed in this chapter. Like Parry, we find that petrol taxes are the most distortionary and that cigarette taxes are the least distortionary, but our analysis extends Parry's analysis by showing three things. First, our calculations reveal that it is potentially important to distinguish between environmental externalities and public expenditure externalities, whereas Parry treated all externalities as environmental externalities. Second, using the tax-shifting and conjectural variations parameter estimates for the cigarette industry by Delipalla and O'Donnell (2001), we find that it is important to incorporate the market power distortion in measuring the MCF for excise taxes on cigarettes. Third, we also find that it is important to distinguish between the MCFs for ad valorem and per unit excises levied on cigarettes.

4.1 The MCFs for Excise Taxes in Thailand

The basic theory behind the calculations of the MCFs for excise taxes is contained in chapter 3. The general formula that we use is

$$SMCF_{t_i} = \omega_i \cdot \frac{b_i - \sum_{j=1}^{n} b_j(\delta_{E_j} + \alpha_j \delta_{A_j} + (1 - \tau_{\pi_j})\delta_{M_j})\varepsilon_{ji}^T}{b_i(1 - v_i) + \sum_{j=1}^{n} b_j(1 - v_j)(\tau_j + \tau_{\pi_j}\delta_{M_j})\varepsilon_{ji}^I - \sum_{j=1}^{n} b_j\delta_{G_j}\varepsilon_{ji}^T}, \qquad (4.1)$$

where ω_i is the distributional characteristic of commodity i; b_i is the budget share of commodity i; the δ are the distortion caused by environmental externalities (E),

Table 4.2
Tax rates and budget shares for commodities in Thailand

Commodity	Tax rate, τ_i	Budget share, b_i
Food	0.016	0.234
Alcohol	0.393	0.042
Tobacco	0.587	0.017
Clothing	0.018	0.131
Health	0.035	0.064
Electricity and fuels	0.536	0.024
Telecommunications	0.035	0.017
Housing and water	0.036	0.126
Entertainment	0.037	0.042
Other goods and services	0.032	0.302

Source: Chandoevwit and Dahlby (2007).

addiction (A), market power (M), and public expenditure externalities (G); α_i is the proportion of the population that is addicted to commodity i; τ_{π_i} is the tax rate on profits for firms producing commodity i; ε_{ji}^T is the elasticity of total demand for the commodity j (i.e., both legitimate and smuggled) with respect to the price of commodity i; ε_{ji}^l is the elasticity of demand for the legitimate sales of commodity j with respect to the price of commodity i; and v_i is the proportion of the smuggled commodity that is not taxed.

4.1.1   Parameter Values

The average tax rates and budget shares for the ten commodity groups included in the analysis are shown in table 4.2. The average tax rates for all commodities, except alcohol, tobacco, and electricity and fuels, were calculated using value-added tax divided by value added for 2002. Data for the value-added taxes were obtained from the Ministry of Finance and for value added from the National Economic and Social Development Board (NESDB). These data were disaggregated by commodity using an I–O table for 1998. The statutory value added tax was 7.0 percent, but the average tax rates are around 3.5 percent for most commodities except for food and clothing because some items and small firms are exempt from VAT.

   The average tax rates for alcoholic beverage and tobacco were calculated using tax revenue collected by Excise Department divided by consumption. Alcoholic beverage and tobacco consumption data are from the National Income Account provided by NESDB. The average tax rates for these two commodities are 39 and 59 percent. Note that the tax rate for tobacco does not include the profit earned by the Thai Tobacco Monopoly (TTM), the state-owned company that has a monopoly in the production of domestic cigarettes. (The profit rate for the TTM is discussed in the section dealing with market power distortions.) The average tax rate for fuel, 54 percent, was calculated by dividing tax revenue collected by Excise Department divided by total output of refined petroleum as reported by NESDB.

The budget shares were calculated from the aggregate consumption data from the NESDB's *Gross Domestic Product Report*. The budget share of alcohol was 4.2 percent, tobacco was 1.7 percent, and electricity and fuels was 2.4 percent of aggregate consumption spending in 2002.

The estimated demand elasticities are given in the matrix below. (The own-price elasticities along the diagonal are highlighted.)

−0.1033	−0.0959	0.0818	0.1940	−0.0262	−0.0730	0.0545	−0.6860	−0.0486	0.0649
0.7103	−0.8429	−0.0125	−0.2744	0.4372	0.5244	−0.9369	0.1127	0.8354	−0.8950
−0.0348	−0.5159	−0.7992	−0.0835	0.1114	−0.0185	−0.1424	0.2369	0.1969	−0.3799
−0.5169	−0.3983	0.0281	−0.8380	0.1388	−1.1741	0.5797	0.2243	−0.6041	0.4520
0.0206	1.0223	−0.6111	1.8406	−1.5239	1.2575	−1.1766	1.8135	1.4716	−1.6749
−0.2923	−0.3043	0.2181	0.6647	−0.0927	−0.1833	0.2832	−0.5222	−0.1347	−0.0513
−0.2673	0.2926	0.1845	−1.4932	0.9452	1.2515	−0.2462	−0.2629	0.6606	−2.5485
0.1650	0.1295	−0.0802	0.7296	−0.5065	−0.0600	−0.2327	−0.0228	0.3480	−0.3652
0.0851	−0.1283	0.1458	0.0926	−0.4631	−0.3089	0.1216	−0.1335	−0.5734	0.1231
−0.9002	0.0565	0.0221	−1.1178	0.3235	0.2813	0.1250	−0.2827	−0.3962	−0.4540

The price elasticities of demand for the ten commodities were estimated, using the almost ideal demand system (AIDS) developed by Deaton and Muellbauer (1980), based on data on consumption expenditures from 1983 to 2002 in the Thailand National Income Account. The observations for 1998 and 1999 were omitted because of the nonnormal consumption shares in that year due to the economic crisis that began in the fall of 1997.

The estimated own-price elasticity for alcoholic beverages is quite high, −0.8429, compared to the −0.54 estimate obtained by Sarntisart (2003). However, it is less elastic than the values in the TDRI (2005) study where the price elasticities for color liquor, white liquor, imported liquor, beer and wine were −1.56, −2.73, −0.61, −2.68, and −0.60. One reason for the differences in these estimates may be that Sarntisart used household consumption data that included both tax and untaxed consumption while TDRI (2005) study used the data from taxed consumption provided by the Excise Department. Other empirical studies of the demand for alcohol have found that the demand for beer is relatively price insensitive (around −0.3) and the demand for spirits is price elastic (around −1.5), with the demand for wine having an intermediate price elasticity (around −1.00). Our estimate of the elasticity of the total demand for taxed alcohol falls within the usual range of estimates from other countries.[2]

Our elasticity estimates indicate that alcohol is a gross complement for tobacco (−0.5159) and for electricity and fuel (−0.3043), while tobacco is a very weak complement for alcohol (−0.0125) but a substitute for electricity and fuel (0.2181).[3] Therefore an alcohol tax rate increase will reduce the demand for both tobacco and fuel, and therefore some of the increase in the alcohol tax revenues from an alcohol tax rate increase will be offset by declines tobacco and fuel excise tax revenues. (The net effect on other commodity tax revenues is indeterminate but likely to be relatively small.) This negative effect on tobacco and fuel excise tax revenues will tend to raise the MCF for alcohol excise taxes. However, the reductions in the consumption of tobacco and fuel would also reduce the MCF for alcohol excise taxes if the net distortion for these commodities, captured by the $\delta_{E_j} + \delta_{A_j} + (1 - \tau_{\pi_j})\delta_{M_j}$ terms in the MCF formula, are negative, meaning marginal social cost exceeds marginal social benefit.

The price elasticity for tobacco products is −0.7992, which is close to the −0.83 value obtained in a study by Pattamasiriwat (1989) but substantially higher than the −0.39 price elasticity found by Sarntisart (2003) based on household tobacco consumption data.[4] The differences may be due to smuggled or nontaxed cigarettes, which the study by Sarntisart indicated are fairly prevalent in Thailand. (He found that about 46 percent of imported cigarette package littering in five provinces across Thailand were untaxed cigarette.) In other words, the price elasticity using data from the National Income Account is higher than for total household cigarette consumption, where taxed and untaxed cigarettes are included. Galbraith and Kaiserman (1997) found the same relationship in Canada where the price elasticity for taxed cigarettes was higher (−1.01) than that for total (taxed and untaxed) cigarette consumption (−0.4). Another study from Canada by Gruber, Sen, and Stabile (2002) also found that the demand for taxed cigarettes was higher than the total demand (−0.70 versus −0.45). Our cross-price elasticities of demand imply that an increase in tobacco taxes will increase excise tax revenues from fuel but increase distortion in the allocation of resources if there is a negative distortion in the market for fuel.

The demand for fuel and electricity consumption is quite price inelastic (−0.1833). Econometric studies of price elasticity of gasoline in the United States reviewed by Parry and Small fall in the −0.3 to −0.90 range,[5] and therefore our estimate of the own-price elasticity is considerably lower than that found in other countries. However, Wade (2003) showed that the short-run price elasticities of distillate fuel for residential and commercial uses were −0.15 and −0.13. In his review he showed that short-run price elasticity of fuel oil for residential use in the United States was −0.10 to −0.59 and for commercial use was −0.07 to −0.19. Our econometric estimates indicate that electricity and fuel is a substitute for alcohol (0.5244) and a weak complement for cigarettes (−0.0185). Consequently a fuel tax increase would tend to increase alcohol excise tax revenues and improve the allocation of resources if the net nontax distortion in the alcohol market is positive.

Our demand estimation is based on the assumption that total consumer expenditure is exogenously determined. In particular, it assumes that variations in the prices of commodities do not affect labor supply decisions. Most of the previous studies of commodity tax reform such as Ahmad and Stern (1984) and Decoster and Schokkaert (1990) have either adopted this assumption or assumed separability between leisure and all other goods in consumers' utility functions. These assumptions imply that in the absence of nontax distortions the optimal commodity tax rate is a uniform tax rate because all good are equally "substitutable" with leisure, the nontaxed good.

Given the importance that the theoretical literature on optimal taxation has attached to the cross-price elasticities between leisure and commodities, it is important to briefly review the few papers have examined the empirical significance of the separability assumption for computing MCFs for commodity taxes. Madden (1995, p. 497), noting that several econometric studies of consumer demands and labor supplies reject the separability assumption, estimated models with and without the separability assumption, based on data for Ireland between 1958 and 1988, and concluded that the MCF "rankings do not appear to be very sensitive to assumptions regarding separability between goods and leisure." In particular, he found that the MCFs for alcohol, tobacco, and fuels were 1.664, 1.397, and 1.193, respectively, without imposing separability and 2.304, 1.504, and 1.418 when separability was imposed.[6] Although Madden's estimates of the MCFs were higher when separability between leisure and commodities was imposed in estimating the demand elasticities, the rankings of the MCFs for the three commodities subject to high levels of excise taxation did not change. In his computations of the efficiency effects of UK excise taxes, Parry (2003) assumed that petrol and alcoholic beverages were substitutes for leisure and that cigarettes were a complement. However, the implied cross-price elasticities between leisure and the price of these commodities were very low and did not have a material effect on Parry's measures of the marginal excess burdens imposed by the excise taxes.[7]

Other studies have obtained conflicting results concerning the importance of the separability assumption. Ebrahimi and Heady (1988, tab. 4) using commodity and labor supply estimates by Blundell and Walker (1983) found that imposing separability reduced the optimal UK tax rate on energy from 35 to 29 percent. More recently West and Williams (2006) found that including the cross-price effect between labor supply and the price of gasoline substantially increased the optimal gasoline tax rate in the United States. They estimated a model based on individual household's expenditures gasoline and all other goods and their labor income, and found that higher gasoline prices increased labor income (reduced the demand for leisure). This reduced the MCF from taxing gasoline and increased the optimal gasoline tax rate.

However, only one of the three cross-price elasticity between labor income and the price of gasoline that they estimated was significantly different from zero (males in households with two adults) and that point elasticity was very low 0.013.

In view of the previous conflicting results, it is difficult to assess the importance of the separablility assumption for our calculations and the cross-price effects between excise taxes and labor supplies clearly need further investigation. Given our current and very limited knowledge about the importance of these effects, we have proceeded by adopting the conventional assumption that these effects do not have a material effect on the rankings of the MCFs for excise taxes.

Despite a significant body of research there is a great deal of uncertainty regarding the appropriate values to use for the δ_E parameters for developed countries, such as the United States or the United Kingdom. There is even greater uncertainty for a developing country, such as Thailand, where much less empirical research has been done on the environmental impacts of alcohol, tobacco, and fuels and where economic, social, and environmental conditions may be substantial different than in the developed countries. Nonetheless, we have had to make some choices regarding these parameters, which are shown in table 4.3. A detailed description of the benchmark parameter values is given in the following sections of this chapter.[8]

The externalities caused by alcohol consumption and tax policies to deal with these issues has received wide spread attention from economists.[9] As noted by Grossman (2004, p. 25), the measurement of the externalities caused by alcohol consumption is even more problematic than for cigarette consumption for the following reasons:

[M]ost individuals who consume alcohol do not harm themselves or others; indeed, moderate alcohol consumption has been shown to lower the risk of coronary heart disease in men. Instead, the adverse effects of alcohol spring from the overuse or misuse of this substance. Examples include cirrhosis of the liver, drunk driving crashes, workplace accidents, various forms of violent behavior, risky sexual behavior, and failure to complete college.

Our estimates for the "environmental" externalities from alcohol are based on Smith (2005)'s recent survey of alcohol excise taxes because he decomposed these externalities in a way that is consistent with our framework. Smith estimated the total UK externality cost of alcohol to be 17 percent of the before-tax price. Based on his breakdown of the social costs of alcohol, one can decompose his total externality into an 8.2 percent private sector "environmental" externality (losses sustained by employers, etc.), a 1.31 percent public expenditure externality (health costs, crime, and social responses), and 7.3 percent "internality" from unemployment and premature death. (The latter is included in the δ_A parameter for alcohol.) The δ_E parameter for the benchmark case was calculated as $-0.082(1 - 0.393)0.27 = -0.014$. The 0.393 is the tax rate on alcohol in Thailand. We multiply by $(1 - 0.393)$ to express the externality as a percentage of the tax inclusive price. We then multiply by the

Table 4.3
Parameter values for non–tax distortions

	Low case	Benchmark case	High case
Environmental externality, δ_E			
Alcohol	−0.007	−0.014	−0.05
Cigarettes	0	−0.025	−0.05
Fuel	−0.05	−0.10	−0.38
Public expenditure externality, δ_G			
Alcohol	0.001	0.002	0.008
Cigarettes	0.004	0.05	0.30
Fuel	0.09	0.18	0.27
Addiction, δ_A and α			
Alcohol	−0.03, 0.017	−0.06, 0.052	−0.12, 0.071
Cigarettes	−0.80, 0.18	−1.65, 0.18	−3.3, 0.18
Fuel	0, 0	0, 0	0, 0
Market power, δ_M			
Alcohol	0.065	0.13	0.26
Cigarettes	0.10	0.20	0.30
Fuel	0	0	0
Telecom	0.10	0.25	0.55
Net non–tax distortion: $\delta_E - \delta_G + \alpha\delta_A + (1 - \tau_\pi)\delta_M$			
Alcohol	0.037	0.072	0.115
Cigarettes	−0.148	−0.372	−0.944
Fuel	−0.140	−0.280	−0.65
Telecom	0.070	0.175	0.385
Smuggling, ε^T and v			
Alcohol	−0.54, 0.080	−0.54, 0.160	−0.54, 0.240
Cigarettes	−0.40, 0.023	−0.40, 0.155	−0.40, 0.300
Fuel	na	na	na

0.27, which is the ratio of the purchasing power parity of the Thai GDP per capita to the UK GDP per capita.[10] The high case is the benchmark case without the adjustment for the relative GDPs in Thailand and the United Kingdom. The low case is 50 percent of the benchmark case.

The environmental externality from tobacco is mainly secondhand smoke, and we do not know of any estimates for this type of externality. As noted in the literature, much of the secondhand smoke problem occurs within the family, and therefore it is debatable whether this is an "externality." The incidence of secondhand smoke in Thailand has also been reduced with nonsmoking in public transit, schools, and public offices, but smoking is still permitted in bars and non–air-conditioned restaurants in Thailand. Overall, it appears that the secondhand smoke externality is small (not many people offer to pay smokers to butt out their cigarettes), but obviously this is controversial and based on a value judgment that admittedly is difficult to defend.

Newbery's (2005) estimate of the environmental cost is 14 pence per liter for gasoline in United Kingdom, excluding road costs which can be treated as a public expenditure externality, and including 3.2 pence per liter for accidents. The benchmark value for the fuel environmental externality is $-(0.14\pounds/\text{liter})(67.8\text{B}/\pounds)(0.27)/$ $(25\text{B}/\text{liter}) = -0.10$, given that the Thai GDP per capita is 27 percent of the UK GDP per capita. For the high case, we do not adjust for differences in Thai to UK real GDP per capita $-(0.14\pounds/\text{liter})(67.8\text{B}/\pounds)/(25\text{B}/\text{liter}) = -0.38$. The low case is 50 percent of the benchmark case.

As is widely recognized, alcohol, tobacco, and fuel consumption can directly or indirectly drive up public expenditures, forcing taxpayers to pay higher taxes to finance their externalities or crowding out other valuable public services. This distortion operates through the government's budget constraint, and therefore it has a distinct effect on the marginal cost of public funds, even though most studies do not distinguish between environmental externalities and public expenditure externalities.

The public expenditure externality for alcohol is based on an estimate of 1.3 percent of the before-tax UK price by Smith (2005). The distortion parameter was calculated as $0.013(1 - 0.393)0.27 = 0.002$ where, as before, we multiply by $(1 - 0.393)$ to express the externality as a percentage of the tax inclusive price. We then multiply by the 0.27, which is the ratio of the purchasing power parity Thai GDP per capita to the UK GDP per capita. The high case is the benchmark case without the adjustment for the relative GDPs in Thailand and the United Kingdom. The low case is 50 percent of the benchmark case.

The benchmark value for the impact of smoking on health care costs uses the estimates from Manning et al. (1989) of US$0.25 per package (figures updated to 2003; see Cnossen 2005b, p. 37). This value was multiplied by 0.20 to reflect the relative GDP in Thailand and divided by 1.08, the price of a package of cigarettes in Thailand. The resulting estimate of the δ_G parameter is $(0.25)(0.20)/(1.08) = 0.046$, rounded to 0.05. The high case was obtained using the position expressed by the Director-General for WHO, Dr. Lee Jong-wook, that 15 percent of all health care costs in high-income countries are due to smoking. Public health care costs are two-thirds of total health care costs in Thailand. Total health care costs in 2002 were 333,798 million Baht (US$8.01 billion), and total value of cigarette consumption was 55,832 million Baht (US$1.34 billion). Therefore the high-case parameter value was calculated as $(0.32)(0.15)(333,798)/(55,832) = 0.29$, rounded to 0.30. The low case parameter value was based on the Sarntisart (2003, p. 43) estimate that the direct health care costs of tobacco were 249 million Baht ($US5.98 million) in 2003. This would imply that the δ_G parameter would be $(249)/(55,832) = 0.004$.

Newbery's (2005) estimate of road costs are 25.2 pence/liter in the United Kingdom. The benchmark value for fuel public expenditure externality is $(0.252\pounds/\text{liter})(67.8\text{ Baht}/\pounds)(0.27)/(25\text{ Baht}/\text{liter}) = 0.18$. The high case is 50 percent higher and the low case is 50 percent lower than the benchmark case.

As noted in chapter 3, excise taxes are often viewed as "sin taxes," levied in order to discourage the consumption of products that are "bad for people." In section 3.6

we used the O'Donoghue and Rabin (2006) model to formalize the view that some individuals engage in excessive consumption of alcohol and tobacco because of defective decision-making. Obviously the choice of the parameters is difficult in the absence of empirical research that might shed light on the degree of excessive consumption. Some progress in this direction has made with the study by Gruber and Mullainathan (2005) which suggested that cigarette taxes in the United States and Canada might make some individuals better off by inducing them to quit smoking, or at least reduce their consumption of cigarettes. More research on this topic is obviously needed before anyone can feel fully comfortable in incorporating addiction in the MCF calculations. However, strong views about addiction dominate public views about the importance of excise taxes on alcohol and tobacco. Our formalization of these views here should help assess their importance relative to the other factors, such as externalities, market power, and smuggling, which also influence public policy regarding excise taxes.

The calculation of the addiction parameter was based on Smith's estimate that the income loss from unemployment and premature death in the United Kingdom was 7.3 percent of the before-tax price of alcohol. The value of value C_x/q_x was calculated as $(0.073(1 - 0.373)0.27)/(0.05) = 0.24$. (The division by 0.05 represents the calculation of the present value of the annual stream of lost income at a 5 percent discount rate.) Gruber and Köszegi (2004, tab. 2, p. 1977) used values of $\Phi = 0.60$ to $\Phi = 0.9$ to reflect hyperbolic discounting of future costs and benefits by individuals with addiction problems. We use the midrange value of 0.75. This implies that our benchmark parameter value for δ_A for alcohol is $(0.75 - 1)0.24 = -0.06$. The low case is 50 percent of the benchmark case and the high case is twice the benchmark case. The proportion of the population addicted to alcohol, α, is the 3.34 percent of the population who reportedly drink every day plus 50 percent of the 3.79 percent who drink three to four times a week.[11] Thus the benchmark figure for α is $3.34 + (0.5)3.79 = 5.2$ percent. The high case figure is $3.34 + 3.79 = 7.1$ percent. The low case figure is half the percentage that drinks every day.

The benchmark value for the addiction distortion for cigarettes was obtained using Gruber and Köszegi's (2004, p. 1979) estimate that the cost in terms of life years lost per pack of cigarettes in the United States is $35.64. The purchasing power equivalent per capita GDP in Thailand is 20 percent of that of the US GDP and the price of cigarettes in Thailand is US$1.08. (see Guindon, Tobin, and Yach 2002). We also used a value of 0.75 for Φ as in the alcohol addiction calculations. Taken together, our benchmark value for δ_A for cigarettes is $(0.75 - 1)(35.64/1.08)(0.20) = -1.65$, implying that the "neglected cost" for a package of cigarettes in Thailand is 165 percent of the actual price. The low case is 50 percent of the benchmark case and the high case is twice the benchmark case. The estimate for the proportion of addicted smokers is the 18 percent of Thais who are reported to be regular smokers.[12]

Imperfect competition is a market distortion, but it has played little role in the discussion of excise tax policy, even though in beer and tobacco markets are highly concentrated in many countries.[13] For example, Cnossen and Smart (2005) do not discuss the implications of firms' market power for setting cigarette taxes. In our calculation we incorporate a measure of the distortion caused by market power in the beer and white whiskey market, the tobacco market, and the mobile phone market in Thailand. The latter is included, even though an excise tax was not levied on telecommunication services in 2002 because excise tax increases on alcohol, tobacco, and fuels might increase (decrease) the demand for telecommunication services leading to an improvement (deterioration) in resource allocation.

The domestic beer market in Thailand is dominated by two large firms—Boon Rawd Brewery Co. and Thai Beverage PLC. Prior to 1995 the domestic beer market was monopolized by the Boon Rawd Brewery Co., a privately owned company founded by members of a prominent elite in 1933. The company produces a famous brand beer "Singha," which used to have 80 to 90 percent of sales in the beer market. In 1994 Thai Beverage PLC entered the market and produced a beer they called "Chang." After a period of fierce competition in the market, the Thai Beverage PLC had 65 percent of the beer market in 2002 and Boon Rawd Brewery Co. had 26 percent. Thai Beverage PLC also has a monopoly power over the white liquor market.

The market power parameter for alcohol was based on the assumption that the sale of beer and white liquor, which represent approximately 70 percent of total alcohol sales, is a Cournot duopoly. Therefore $\delta_M = 0.5(1/-2.7)0.70 = 0.13$, where the 0.5 is 1 divided by the number of firms and -2.7 is an estimate of the elasticity of demand for beer and white liquor from the study by TDRI (2005).[14] This calculation implies that the firms earn a pure profit margin of 13 percent. The high case is twice the benchmark case and the low case is 50 percent of the benchmark case. It is assumed that marginal changes in pure profits are taxed at the statutory Thai corporate income tax rate of 30 percent. Our analysis is based on the assumption that excise taxes are fully shifted to consumers. However, a study by Young and Bielińska-Kwapisz (2002) indicates that taxes on beer and spirits are overshifted in the United States. In their study, taxes on beer and spirits increased consumer prices by approximately 1.7 times the tax rate. We also briefly consider the impact of the overshifting of alcohol excise taxes on the MCF for alcohol.

The Thai Tobacco Monopoly (TTM) controls the production of domestic brands. The market power distortion in the benchmark case, $\delta_M = 0.20$, is based on an estimate of the market power of European tobacco companies from a study by Delipalla and O'Donnell (2001).[15] We have assumed that all of the profits of the TTM go to the Thai government, or $\tau_\pi = 1$. Therefore the total effective tax rate on cigarettes in the benchmark case is $0.587 + 0.20 = 0.79$, which is very close to the effective tax rate that Sarntisart (2003, p. 43) used in his study of tobacco control in Thailand.

The high case is twice the benchmark case and the low case is half the benchmark case.

The mobile phone market in Thailand is dominated by two large firms—Advance Info Service PLC and Total Access Communication PLC. In the absence of other information about the degree of market power exercised by these firms, we have assumed that the δ_M is 0.25 in the benchmark case, 0.55 in the high case, and 0.10 in the low case.[16]

Table 4.3 also shows the net nontax distortions created by the environmental and public expenditure externalities, addiction, and market power. For the benchmark parameter values, the positive values for alcohol and telecommunications imply that the market price exceeds the net social cost and an increase in output would produce a net social gain. Therefore a tax increase that reduces the consumption of these commodities will produce high efficiency loss because of the underprovision of these commodities. The negative values for tobacco and fuel imply that the marginal social costs of these commodities exceed their consumer price and a reduction in the consumption of these goods produces a net social gain. Thus the net nontax distortions tend to lower the MCFs for these commodities. Of course, the tax distortions, exacerbated by smuggling, also affect the MCFs, and we consider this source of distortion below.

To capture the effect of alcohol smuggling, we use a total demand elasticity of $\varepsilon_{22}^T = -0.54$ based on the estimate of the demand for alcohol in Sarntisart (2003). A study of alcohol smuggling in Thailand by TDRI (2006) indicates that illegally produced and smuggled alcohol is about 16 percent of alcohol consumption.[17] For the low case, we use 8 percent, and for the high case, we use 24 percent.

To capture the effect of tobacco smuggling, we use a total demand elasticity of $\varepsilon_{33}^T = -0.40$ based on this widely used value of the elasticity of demand for cigarettes. The benchmark value for the proportion of smuggled cigarettes is from a survey by Sarntisart (2003, p. 26), who found that "15.5% of their cigarettes packages had warning labels in English or other nonThai languages or no warning labels, and were probably illegally imported." The low-case estimate was based on the results of a different survey, also described in Sarntisart (2003), where it was found that 46 percent of discarded imported cigarette packages had warning label in wrong language or no warning labels. Given that imports represent 4.89 percent of total consumption of cigarettes, the proportion of smuggled cigarettes in the low case was calculated as $0.46(4.89) = 2.22$ percent. (The share of imported cigarettes was based on figures in Sarntisart 2003, tab. 3.4, p. 9.) The high-case figure is twice the benchmark figure.

4.1.2   Calculations of the MCFs

The calculations of the MCFs for the benchmark parameter values are shown in table 4.4. Alcohol taxes have the highest MCF at 2.312, followed by tobacco at

Table 4.4
MCFs for excise taxes and the VAT: Benchmark parameter values

	Excise tax on alcohol	Excise tax on tobacco	Excise tax on fuel	VAT
MCFs	2.312	2.187	0.532	1.080
Contribution of non–tax distortions to the MCFs[a]				
Environmental externalities, δ_E	−0.075	0.052	−0.004	−0.004
Public expenditure externalities, δ_G	−0.275	0.182	−0.012	−0.007
Market power, δ_M	0.335	0.457	−0.212	−0.005
Addiction, δ_A	−0.156	−0.298	−0.0007	−0.012
Smuggling	0.323	0.618	0.022	0.019
MCFs in the absence of non–tax distortions	1.985	1.566	0.737	
MCFs in the absence of non–tax distortions and interactions with other tax bases	1.496	1.882	1.109	

a. A positive (negative) value means that the factor increases (reduces) the MCF.

2.187, and fuels at 0.532. The large gaps between the MCFs for alcohol and tobacco and the MCF for fuels indicate that there could be a substantial welfare gain from a revenue-neutral tax reform, which would reduce tax rates on alcohol and tobacco and increase the tax rate on fuel. However, this conclusion has to be tempered by the fact that the low MCF for fuel is likely due to our low estimate of the elasticity of demand for fuel—the elasticity of demand is one-quarter that of alcohol and tobacco.

Although the excise taxes are the focus of our analysis, we have also calculated the MCF for a VAT increase, based on the assumption that the VAT increase would be fully reflected in the prices of alcohol, cigarettes, and fuel and increase the prices of the other expenditure categories to the same degree that their current effective tax rates reflect the VAT. Thus, for example, we assume that the prices of food, clothing, and housing would increase by 0.230, 0.251, and 0.506 percentage points with a 1 percentage point VAT increase. The MCF for the VAT increase with the benchmark parameter values was 1.080, much lower than the MCFs for alcohol and cigarette excise taxes but higher than for the fuel excise tax. It should be borne in mind that the VAT increase is similar (although not exactly equivalent) to a proportional wage tax increase because it reduces workers' real wage rates. Our relatively low estimate for MCF_{VAT} reflects our assumption of fixed labor supplies. However, a computations of the MCF for an income tax increase in Thailand in the mid-1990s by Poapangsakorn et al. (2000, tab. 6, p. 76) were in the 1.04 to 1.11 range, and therefore comparable to our estimate of the MCF for a VAT increase.

Our main contribution to the calculation of MCFs for commodity taxes is that we have incorporated most of the key factors that affect decisions or attitudes concerning excise taxes—environmental externalities, public expenditure externalities, imperfect competition, addiction, smuggling, and the interactions of tax bases—in a single model. Table 4.4 shows how each of these distortions affects the MCFs for alcohol, tobacco, and fuel. The contribution of each distortion to the MCFs is set in turn equal to zero and then the MCFs are recalculated. For example, these calculations indicate that if all environmental externalities are ignored, the MCF for alcohol will be 2.387 instead of 2.312. Therefore incorporating the environmental externalities at the benchmark parameter values reduces the MCF for alcohol by 0.075. Similarly environmental externalities increase the MCF for tobacco taxes by 0.052. This may seem surprising, but it can be explained by the fact that the δ_E for tobacco is quite low and an increase in tobacco taxes will increase the demand for fuels (with a cross-price elasticity of 0.218) where the δ_E parameter is four times larger (in absolute value). Similarly, incorporating the public expenditure externalities reduces the MCF for alcohol taxes by 0.275 but increases the MCF for cigarette taxes by 0.182.

The market power distortion raises the MCFs for alcohol and tobacco by 0.335 and 0.457, respectively, but lowers the MCF for fuel by 0.212, even though the fuel industry is assumed to be competitive. The reason for the reduction in the MCF for fuel is that a fuel tax increase raises the demand for alcohol (with a cross-price elasticity of 0.524), and this helps to offset the alcohol market power distortion.

As might be expected, incorporating addiction significantly reduces the MCFs for excise taxes on alcohol and cigarettes. The 0.298 reduction in the MCF for cigarettes is relatively large because addicted smokers are assumed to ignore costs of smoking that are 165 percent of the product price in our benchmark case. However, smuggling has an even greater impact on the MCFs for alcohol and tobacco, raising them by 0.323 and 0.618 respectively; that is, the impact of smuggling more than offsets the impact of addiction on the MCFs. The second last row in table 4.4 shows the MCFs in the absence of the nontax distortions (including smuggling). These calculations indicate that the combined effect of the nontax distortions and smuggling increase the MCFs for alcohol and tobacco excises, but reduces the MCF for fuel taxes.

The last row of table 4.4 shows how the MCF is affected by a failure to account for the effect of an excise tax rate change on tax revenues from other tax bases. (Most discussions of tobacco taxation, e.g., Sunley et al. 2000, tab. 17.5, p. 423, only focus on the effect of a tobacco tax increase on tobacco tax revenues and ignore the effects on other sources of tax revenue.) The calculations in the table show that incorporating the effects on other tax revenue sources is very important in evaluating an alcohol excise increase. The MCF for alcohol would be significantly underestimated if we ignore the effects of an alcohol tax rate increase on the revenues from other commodity taxes. Recall that our demand estimation indicates that alcohol is a complement for both tobacco and fuel, with cross-price elasticities of −0.516 and −0.304, respectively. Increasing the alcohol excise tax reduces revenues for these other two heavily taxed commodities, and this account in part for alcohol's relatively high MCF. Conversely, incorporating the interactions with the other tax bases lowers the MCFs for tobacco and fuel taxes.

The computations in table 4.4 are based on the assumption that excise taxes are fully reflected in consumer prices. However, in imperfectly competitive markets, taxes may be undershifted or overshifted even if the marginal cost of production is constant in the long run. As previously noted, Young and Bielińska-Kwapisz (2002) found that beer and spirit prices in the United States increased by about $1.70 for a $1.00 excise tax increase. If the same degree of overshifting of the alcohol excise taxes occurs in Thailand, then the MCF for the alcohol excise tax would be 8.927, making it an extremely expensive source of tax revenue. The sensitivity of the calculation of the MCFs to the degree of tax shifting indicates that future research should try to determine the degree to which excise taxes are over- or undershifted in imperfectly competitive markets.

To summarize, this analysis indicates that smuggling, market power, and addiction have potentially large impacts on the MCFs, especially for tobacco taxes, and that interactions with other tax bases is especially important for calculating the MCFs for excise taxes.

These conclusions are based on a particular set of parameter values. To determine the sensitivity of these results to the choice of the parameter values, the MCFs were recalculated using the high-case and low-case values for the parameters. Table 4.5 indicates that the MCFs are lower in the high case. This means that the higher parameter values for the environmental and public expenditure externalities and addiction more than offset the use of the higher parameter values for market power and smuggling. The contributions of the various distortions to the MCFs are also generally larger (in absolute value) than in the benchmark case. The only major anomaly is that the public expenditure externality now reduces the MCF for tobacco.

Table 4.5
MCFs for excise taxes and the VAT: High distortion case

	Excise tax on alcohol	Excise tax on cigarettes	Excise tax on fuel	VAT
MCFs	1.95	2.10	0.32	1.05
Contributions of non–tax distortions to the MCFs[a]				
Environmental externalities, δ_E	−0.243	0.257	−0.016	−0.012
Public expenditure externalities, δ_G	−0.725	−0.220	−0.010	−0.021
Market power, δ_M	0.388	0.442	−0.424	−0.004
Addiction, δ_A	−0.304	−0.629	0.00006	−0.024
Smuggling	0.269	1.178	0.019	0.031

a. A positive (negative) value means that the factor increases (reduces) the MCF.

Table 4.6
MCFs for excise taxes and the VAT: Low distortion case

	Excise tax on alcohol	Excise tax on cigarettes	Excise tax on fuel	VAT
MCFs	2.220	1.794	0.645	1.083
Contributions of distortions to MCF[a]				
Environmental externalities, δ_E	−0.028	0.029	−0.002	−0.001
Public expenditure externalities, δ_G	−0.090	0.086	−0.007	−0.003
Market power, δ_M	0.182	0.200	−0.095	0.004
Addiction, δ_A	−0.069	−0.109	−0.001	−0.006
Smuggling	0.198	0.142	0.014	0.009

a. A positive (negative) value means that the factor increases (reduces) the MCF.

Table 4.6 shows similar calculations for the low case parameters values. The MCFs for alcohol and tobacco are lower than in the benchmark case, but the MCF for fuels increases from 0.532 to 0.645. Thus the rankings of the MCFs for the three excise taxes are the same in the benchmark and low cases, but rankings of alcohol and tobacco are reversed in the high case.

The large gap between the MCFs for the excise taxes on alcohol and cigarettes and the MCF for the fuel excise tax indicates that there is a potentially large efficiency gain from a revenue-neutral tax reform that can increase the fuel excise tax and re- duce the excise taxes on alcohol and cigarettes. An indication of the potential size of these gains can be obtained by considering small cuts in the alcohol and cigarette excise taxes, offset by a revenue-neutral increase in the fuel excise tax. The gains and losses from these tax revenue changes can be evaluated at the average of the pre–tax reform and post–tax reform MCFs and compared to the total increase in fuel tax revenue. For example, using the benchmark parameter values, the fuel excise tax would have to be raised by a 0.688 percentage point to maintain revenues if the excise taxes on alcohol and tobacco were each cut by one percentage point. This revenue-neutral tax reform would increase the MCF for the fuel excise tax from 0.532 to 0.536 and lower the MCFs for alcohol and tobacco excises from 2.312 to 2.269 and from 2.187 to 2.137, respectively. Evaluated at the average of the pre- reform and post-reform MCFs, there would be a net efficiency gain of 1.72 Baht for each additional Baht of fuel tax revenue collected. One limitation of this approach is that does not allow us to determine how large the revenue-neutral fuel tax increase should be to maximize the net efficiency gain from this type of excise tax reform.

4.1.3   Calculations of the SMCFs

To calculate the distributionally weighted MCFs for the three excise taxes, the β are computed here using (2.49) and using a fairly conventional range of values for ξ, 0.25 to 1.00. The average per capita monthly income in Thailand of 3,844 Baht

Distributional weights

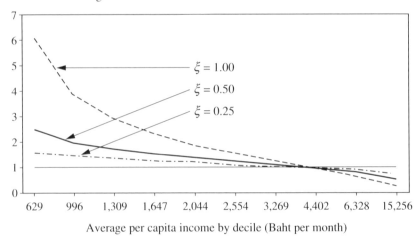

Figure 4.1
Distributional weights by decile

(US$92.26) in 2002 was used as the reference income level.[18] Figure 4.1 shows the distributional weights at the average income levels in the ten deciles. The distributional weights range between 1.572 and 6.114 at the average income in the first decile, 629 Baht (US$15.10) per month, and between 0.708 and 0.252 at the average income level in the tenth decile, 15,256 Baht (US$366.14) per month, when the values of ξ range between 0.25 and 1.00. To compute the distributional characteristics of the commodities, the expenditure patterns of 90 household groups are used (based on data from five urban areas and four rural regions in each decile) from the Socio-Economic Survey (SES 2002). Table 4.7 shows the computed distributional characteristics for all of the commodities for values of ξ between 0.25 and 1.00, normalized so that the distributional characteristic for food is equal to one. Note that when $\xi = 0.25$, alcohol, tobacco, and fuel have almost identical distributional characteristic values, around 0.88. Therefore, with a moderate set of distributional weights, the relative SMCFs are the same as their efficiency components, the MCFs. Divergences in the distributional characteristics appear when larger values of ξ are used. Among the three commodities subject to the excise taxes, tobacco has the lowest ω. Electricity and fuels has the highest when $\xi = 0.50$ and alcohol has the highest when $\xi = 1.00$. Therefore the relative ranking of the distributional characteristics varies with the magnitudes of the distributional weights.

The bottom panel of table 4.7 shows the SMCFs for the three excise taxes using the distributional characteristics for the three goods. Note that the ranking of the SMCFs is the same as the MCFs—the fuel excise tax always has the lowest social

Table 4.7
Distributional characteristics of commodities in Thailand

	$\xi = 0.00$	$\xi = 0.25$	$\xi = 0.50$	$\xi = 1.00$
Normalized distributional characteristics				
Food	1.000	1.00	1.000	1.000
Alcohol	1.000	0.882	0.835	0.762
Tobacco	1.000	0.885	0.821	0.707
Clothing	1.000	0.942	0.893	0.828
Health	1.000	0.940	0.849	0.721
Electricity and fuels	1.000	0.957	0.874	0.754
Telecommunications	1.000	0.888	0.799	0.660
Housing and water	1.000	0.987	0.922	0.824
Entertainment	1.000	0.904	0.801	0.659
Other	1.000	0.910	0.827	0.700
SMCFs[a]				
Alcohol excise	2.311	2.038	1.930	1.761
Tobacco excise	2.183	1.932	1.792	1.543
Fuel excise	0.533	0.510	0.465	0.402

a. Based on the benchmark parameter values.

cost, followed by tobacco, and the alcohol excise has the highest SMCF. Consequently placing higher weights on the losses sustained by lower income groups does not alter the view, based solely on efficiency considerations, that a revenue-neutral increase in fuel excise taxes and a cut in alcohol and tobacco excise taxes would represent an improvement in social welfare.

4.1.4 Summary and Extensions

The analysis of this section has expand the Ahmad-Stern framework for evaluating marginal commodity tax reforms by incorporating the most important non-tax distortions that influence the setting of excise taxes on alcohol, tobacco and fuels in Thailand. Some of these distortions, such as environmental externalities and addiction, reduce the social marginal cost of imposing excise taxes; other distortions, such as the exercise of market power by producers of alcohol and tobacco and smuggling, tend to raise the MCFs for these excise taxes. While there is a great deal of uncertainty about the appropriate values for these parameters, our analysis provides a framework within which the net effects of these offsetting distortions can be evaluated. The results here indicate that smuggling, market power, and addiction have potentially large impacts on the MCFs, especially for tobacco taxes, and that interactions with other tax bases is especially important for calculating the MCFs for excise taxes. The overall conclusion we can make is that the MCFs for alcohol and tobacco excise taxes in Thailand are much higher than for fuel excise taxes and that there would be substantial welfare gain from a revenue-neutral reduction in the excise tax rates on alcohol and tobacco and an increase in fuel excise tax rates.

There are a number of areas where more research and data collection would help in the evaluation of the excise taxes in Thailand. First, the interaction between commodity prices and labor income should be investigated in light of the recent results obtained by West and Williams (2006) for the United States. Second, the possibility of overshifting of excise taxes, which has been recorded in the market for alcohol in the United States by Young and Bielińska-Kwapisz (2002), should be investigated in Thailand. Third, tourism is an important industry in Thailand, and foreign tourists may bear a significant portion of the excise taxes on alcohol and tobacco. Significant levels of "tax exporting" to tourists might reduce the MCFs for these excise taxes. Finally, businesses and industry pay some of the fuel excise taxes, and to the extent that the fuel excises exceed their marginal externality costs, they may create relatively large welfare losses by distorting firm's production decisions. These effects should also be included in the computation of the MCF for the fuel taxes.

4.2   The MCFs for Excise Taxes in the United Kingdom

Parry (2003) calculated the marginal excess burdens for excise taxes on petrol, alcoholic beverages, and cigarettes in the United Kingdom in 1999. In this section we use Parry's benchmark parameter values to calculate the MCFs for these taxes using the methodology developed in chapter 3. We also incorporate other elements of the tax system—commodity taxes on all other goods, the existence of per unit and ad valorem taxes on cigarettes, public expenditure externalities, and distortions caused by imperfect competition in the cigarette market—that were not incorporated in Parry's model. The calculations of this section are primarily intended to illustrate how the various factors that affect the MCFs, as covered in chapter 3, can be incorporated in the calculation for these excise taxes, and that they reveal the importance of including the market power of firms in the cigarette industry in calculating the MCF from cigarette taxes.

The MCFs for the excise taxes are calculated in the context of a model where a representative individual allocates his expenditures among four commodities and his time between work and leisure. His budget constraint is

$$\sum_{j=1}^{4} q_j x_j = (1 - \tau_L) w L, \tag{4.2}$$

where the after-tax wage rate is $(1 - \tau_L)w$, and L is amount of labor supplied. Since $L = T - x_0$, where x_0 is the individual's leisure time and T is total amount of time available for work or leisure, the budget constraint can also be written in the following form:

$$\sum_{j=0}^{4} q_j x_j = q_0 T, \tag{4.3}$$

where $q_0 = (1 - \tau_L)w$ is the "price" of leisure, and $q_0 T$ is the individual's total potential net earnings. Total tax revenues are equal to

$$R = \sum_{j=1}^{4} \tau_j q_j x_j + \tau_L w L = \sum_{j=0}^{4} \tau_j q_j x_j + \tau_L w T, \tag{4.4}$$

where the effective tax rate on leisure, $\tau_0 = -\tau_L/(1 - \tau_L)$, is negative, reflecting the fact that wage taxes reduce the opportunity cost of leisure. In applying this model to UK excise taxes, we will define commodity 1 as petrol, commodity 2 as alcoholic beverages, commodity 3 as tobacco products, and commodity 4 as all other goods.

Combining the various factors that have been discussed in chapter 3—the price sensitivity of the tax bases, the interactions between tax bases based on their substitutability or complementarity, and the market distortions caused by externalities and imperfect competition—the MCF for a tax on commodity i can be calculated using the following formula:

$$MCF_{t_i} = \frac{b_i(1 - \tau_{\pi_i}) + b_i \tau_{\pi_i}(dq_i/dt_i) - \sum_{j=0}^{4} b_j(\delta_{E_j} + (1 - \tau_{\pi_j})\delta_{M_j})\varepsilon_{ji}(dq_i/dt_i)}{b_i(1 - \tau_{\pi_j}) + b_i \tau_{\pi_i}(dq_i/dt_i) + \sum_{j=0}^{4} b_j(\tau_j + \tau_{\pi_j}\delta_{M_j} - \delta_{G_j})\varepsilon_{ji}(dq_i/dt_i)}, \tag{4.5}$$

where b_i is the budget share of commodity i, $q_i x_i/q_0 T$ and τ_{π_i} is the tax rate on pure profits in industry i. This equation is similar to equation (4.1), except that we now allow for the possibility that dq_i/dt_i is not equal to one, although we assume $dq_j/dt_i = 0$ for $j \neq i$. It is also assumed that monopoly profits are small in relation to total income, and therefore we can ignore the effect of changes in monopoly profits on the demands for commodities. In the context of this application, this seems to be reasonable, given that the cigarette industry is only a small part of the UK economy.

4.2.1 Parameter Values

Some of the key parameter values used in the calculations of the MCFs are shown in table 4.8. Parry used a value of 0.42 for τ_L in his calculation, based on a study of effective tax rates on labor by Mendoza, Razin, and Tesar (1994). His measure of the effective tax rate on labor income included the value-added taxes on commodities in addition to income and payroll taxes. In our model those taxes are reflected in the

Table 4.8
Key parameter values for the United Kingdom

Commodity	Tax rates, τ_i	Budget shares, b_i	Distortions		
			Environmental, δ_E	Public expenditure, δ_G	Market power, δ_M
Leisure	−0.466	0.500	0	0	0
Petrol	0.863	0.0284	−0.160	0.018	0
Alcohol	0.450	0.0177	−0.083	0.028	0
Tobacco	0.823	0.00910	−0.071	0.212	0.219
All other goods	0.109	0.445	0	0	0

commodity tax rates, including the tax rate on commodity 4, and therefore they should not be included in our measure of τ_L. In our calculations the average commodity tax rate is about 17.6 percent and therefore the wage tax rate that is equivalent to Parry's tax wedge is a tax rate of 31.8 percent. The effective tax rate on leisure is $\tau_0 = -0.318/(1 - 0.318) = -0.466$.

The excise tax rates—86.3 percent on petrol, 45.0 percent on alcoholic beverages, and 82.3 percent on cigarettes—are based on the tax rate data for 1999 in the Institute for Fiscal Studies publication by Chennells, Dilnot, and Roback (1999).[19] Note that these tax rates are expressed as a percentage of the consumer price and include the VAT rate of 17.5 percent, whereas Parry expressed tax rates as a percentage of the producer price and excluded the VAT from the tax rates on these commodities. The VAT on petrol, alcoholic beverages, and cigarettes is included in the effective tax rates because it contributes to the tax wedge between the consumer price and the producer price. The excise tax on petrol generated £23.1 billion in 1999–2000. The excise taxes on alcoholic beverages generated £6.1 billion, and the cigarette taxes yielded £7.0 billion. Using the commodity tax rates, with an adjustment for the VAT component in the tax rates, the resulting calculations are $q_1x_1 = £32.25$ billion, $q_2x_2 = £20.26$ billion, and $q_3x_3 = £10.38$ billion. Given that total UK consumer expenditure was £570.44 billion in 1999, this implies that $q_4x_4 = £507.44$ billion. In 1999–2000, VAT revenues were £54 billion and other excise taxes, such as vehicle excise duties and betting and gambling duties, were £10.5 billion. After adjusting for the VAT collected from sales of petrol, alcohol beverages, and tobacco products, we have that the average tax rate on all other goods was 10.9 percent.[20] Petrol and alcohol taxes are levied as per unit taxes in the United Kingdom while the tobacco taxes are a mix of per unit and ad valorem taxes, with per unit taxes representing 54.41 percent of the total tax rate. As noted below, the fact that tobacco taxes are a combination of ad valorem and per unit taxes will affect the extent to which consumer prices increase when tobacco taxes are increased. It is assumed that profits are taxed at a standard corporate income tax rate of 30 percent.

The budget share calculations were based on the assumption that half of the representative individual's available time is devoted to leisure (nonmarket activities), and therefore $b_0 = 0.5$. Since $(1 - b_0)q_0 T$ is equal to £570.44 billion, total potential net earnings, $q_0 T$, were estimated to be £1.114 trillion. This figure was used to calculate the budget shares of the other commodities given the values for the $q_j x_j$ calculated in the previous section. Consequently other commodities represent 44.5 percent of total net potential earnings, and total expenditures on petrol, alcoholic beverages, and cigarettes collectively represent only 5.5 percent of total potential earnings.

Parry (2003) provided an extensive review of the empirical literature measuring the values of the externalities generated by the consumption of gasoline, alcohol and cigarettes. Obviously there is still a great deal of uncertainty concerning the magnitudes of these parameters, but Parry's choices for his base case estimates seem reasonable, and we have adopted them for the benchmark computations. Based on his review of the literature, Parry concluded tobacco products impose the largest harmful externalities, representing 28.3 percent of the consumer price of the product, and alcohol consumption imposes the smallest harmful externality, at just 11 percent of the product price. Parry treated all of the externalities as if they were environmental externalities, even though some of the most important externalities are better classified as public expenditure externalities. Here the estimates of the "total" externality are the same as in Parry's benchmark, but they are allocated between environmental externalities and public expenditure externalities. We have somewhat arbitrarily assumed that 10 percent of the petrol externalities, 25 percent of the alcohol-related externalities, and 75 percent of the tobacco-related externalities are public expenditure externalities.[21]

Parry did not consider the implications of imperfect competition in his measures of the efficiency cost of taxes. As noted in section 3.5.3, the cigarette industry is highly concentrated in most countries, and there is considerable evidence of noncompetitive behavior in cigarette pricing. Delipalla and O'Donnell (2001) obtained the following estimates of the responsiveness of cigarette prices to per unit and ad valorem tax rate increases:

$$(1 - \tau_{av}) \frac{dq}{dt} = 0.92 \quad \text{and} \quad (1 - \tau_{av}) \frac{dq}{qd\tau} = 0.72. \tag{4.6}$$

Their estimates were consistent with the theoretical prediction that ad valorem taxes lead to smaller price increases than per unit taxes in an imperfectly competitive model, and imply that the distortion in the market price caused imperfect competition is 0.219 if the price elasticity of demand for cigarettes is -0.40. Their estimates also imply that the cigarette excise taxes are not fully shifted to consumers because the firms' after-tax price decreases when the excise taxes are increased. Here these estimates of tax shifting and market power are used to calculate the MCFs for excise taxes on cigarettes in the United Kingdom. For the other commodities we assume, as did Parry, that producer prices are fixed and the other excise taxes are fully shifted to consumers and that an excise tax increase for one commodity does not affect the prices of the other commodities. The implication is that a tax on labor is borne by workers. Consequently a per unit labor tax reduces the price of leisure by the amount of the tax, which in our notation is $dq_0/dt_L = -1$.

The price and income elasticities of demand used in computing the MCFs are given below:

$$\varepsilon = \begin{pmatrix} -0.200 & 0.008 & 0.001 & -0.001 & 0.191 \\ -0.060 & -0.700 & -0.012 & -0.006 & 0.779 \\ 0.190 & 0 & -0.600 & 0 & 0.410 \\ 0.110 & 0 & 0 & -0.400 & 0.290 \\ 1.343 & -0.028 & -0.017 & -0.011 & -1.287 \end{pmatrix}, \quad \mu = \begin{pmatrix} 0.300 \\ 0.700 \\ 0 \\ 0 \\ 1.867 \end{pmatrix}. \tag{4.7}$$

Although the income elasticities of demand, the μ_i, do not appear in (4.2), estimates of the income elasticities are used to derive the complete set of price elasticities, and together with the price elasticities, they determine the magnitudes of the substitution effects that underlie the efficiency losses from taxation. The normal practice for economists is to state the income effects of a change in the wage rate in terms of changes in the supply of labor, and not leisure. Let $\theta = (1 - \tau_L)wdL/dM$ be the income effect on labor supply. Parry adopted a widely used value of -0.15 in his calculations. It can be shown that income elasticity of demand for leisure is equal to $\mu_0 = -\theta/b_0$. Given our assumption that b_0 is 0.50, this implies that the equivalent income elasticity of demand for leisure is 0.30. We have also adopted Parry's assumptions regarding the income elasticities of demand for petrol, alcoholic beverages, and cigarettes, 0.7, 0.0, and 0.0, respectively. Since $\sum_{j=0}^{4} b_j\mu_j = 1$, our budget share estimates imply that the income elasticity of demand for all other good is 1.867.

The price elasticities of demand for the leisure, petrol, alcohol, and cigarettes used above are equivalent to those used by Parry. He assumed in his benchmark estimates that the labor supply elasticity, η, is 0.20. The equivalent value for the own-price elasticity of demand for leisure is $\varepsilon_{00} = -\eta(1 - b_0)/b_0 = -0.20$. In addition his values of $\varepsilon_{11} = -0.70$ were used for the price elasticity of demand for gasoline, $\varepsilon_{22} = -0.60$ for the price elasticity of demand for alcoholic beverages, and $\varepsilon_{33} = -0.40$ for the price elasticity of demand for cigarettes.

Parry used a parameter, ϕ_j, to reflect the cross-price elasticity between leisure and the other taxed goods in his model. In our notation, $\phi_j = (-\varepsilon_{0j}/\varepsilon_{00})(1 - b_0)/b_j$. In other words, if commodity j is a substitute for leisure and $\varepsilon_{0j} > 0$, then ϕ_j is positive given that $\varepsilon_{00} < 0$, and if $\phi_j < 0$, then commodity j is a complement with leisure. In his base case scenario, Parry assumed values of $\phi_1 = 0.70$, $\phi_2 = 0.20$, and $\phi_3 = -0.20$. Given our estimates of the budget shares and price elasticity of demand for leisure, Parry's parameter values imply $\varepsilon_{01} = 0.008$, $\varepsilon_{02} = 0.001$, and $\varepsilon_{03} = -0.001$. In other words, Parry assumed that petrol and alcoholic beverages are substitutes for leisure and that cigarettes are a complement. However, the values of these cross-price elasticities are close to zero, implying that the excise tax changes will have little direct effect on labor supply. In the absence of better information regarding these cross-price elasticities, we have adopted these values for the base case calculations.

Parry's assumption that $\varepsilon_{j0} = 0$ is inconsistent with his assumptions regarding the income elasticities of demand because the symmetry condition in consumer demand implies that $b_j \varepsilon_{ji}^c = b_i \varepsilon_{ij}^c$ or, using the Slutsky equation,

$$b_j(\varepsilon_{ji} + b_i \mu_j) = b_i(\varepsilon_{ij} + b_j \mu_i)$$

or

$$\varepsilon_{ji} = \frac{b_i}{b_j} \varepsilon_{ij} + b_i(\mu_i - \mu_j). \tag{4.8}$$

In the ε matrix, condition (4.8) was used to calculate the ε_{j0}, given the ε_{0j} and the income elasticities. This condition was also used to compute ε_{12}, ε_{13}, and ε_{23}, given Parry's assumption that $\varepsilon_{21} = \varepsilon_{31} = \varepsilon_{32} = 0$. Finally, given the revised values for these cross-price elasticities, the homogeneity, $\sum_{i=0}^{4} \varepsilon_{ji} = 0$, $j = 0, 1, \ldots, 4$, and the Cournot aggregation $\sum_{j=0}^{4} b_j \varepsilon_{ji} + b_i = 0$, $i = 1, 2, \ldots, 4$, conditions were used to compute the cross-price elasticities. In other words, the price elasticities in each column of the matrix above should sum to zero because an equiproportional increase in all prices, including q_0, does not change the budget constraint of the individual. The

Table 4.9
Calculations of the MCFs for excise taxes in the United Kingdom

Tax base	Parry's MEBs	MCFs		
		$b_0 = 0.50$	$b_0 = 0.40$	$b_0 = 0.60$
Labor	0.30	1.290	1.294	1.286
Petrol	1.00	3.008	3.008	3.008
Alcohol	0.24	1.424	1.429	1.419
Cigarettes	0.11			
per unit tax		0.978	0.981	0.976
ad valorem		0.981	0.984	0.979
All other commodities	a	1.242	1.246	1.238

Source: Based on the benchmark calculation in Parry (2003).
a. Parry did not model or compute the MEB for taxes on all other goods.

Cournot aggregation condition requires that the weighted sum of the price elasticities in rows 1 to 4 of the matrix equal the (negative) budget share of the commodity in that row. These nine equations were used to calculate the nine price elasticities in the last column and the last row of the ε matrix.

4.2.2   Computations of the MCFs

Given these parameter values, the MCFs were calculated using (4.2), and they are shown in table 4.9.[22] For purposes of comparison, Parry's MEBs for his benchmark case are also shown. A direct comparison of the magnitudes of his MEBs and our calculated MCFs is not possible because the MCFs will not in general be equal to $1 + \text{MEBs}$. However, a comparison of the ordinal ranking is valid and important because an efficiency-enhancing tax reform would (in general) increase the tax with the lowest MEB or MCF and reduce the tax rate with the highest MEB or MCF. As can be seen, petrol taxes have the highest efficiency cost, and cigarette taxes have the lowest efficiency cost, in both sets of calculations.[23] Parry's MEBs indicate that alcohol taxes have a lower marginal efficiency cost than a tax on labor, whereas the MCF calculations indicate that the labor taxes have lower efficiency costs than alcohol taxes. MCF calculations also indicate that a tax on labor has a slightly higher marginal efficiency cost than a tax on all other goods.[24] In summary, calculations of the MCFs using Parry's benchmark parameter values produce a very similar ranking of the marginal efficiency costs of the various taxes, but our MCF calculations emphasize the substantial gains from raising cigarette taxes and lowering petrol taxes because the differences in the MCFs is 2.03 whereas the differences in Parry's MEBs for the two taxes is only 0.89.

Incorporating the market power distortion in cigarettes reduced the overall distortion in the cigarette market from -0.283 to -0.064, but the MCFs were still less than one and cigarette taxes had the lowest MCFs for all of the excise taxes. Despite the relatively low total distortion the MCFs for the excise taxes on cigarettes were still less than one, in part because Deliapalla and O'Donnell's estimates imply that producer prices do not increase by the amount of the tax and therefore consumers do not bear the full amount of the tax burden. Finally, note that the MCFs for per unit and ad valorem excise taxes on cigarettes were virtually identical, with the MCF for the per unit excise tax slightly lower than the MCF for the ad valorem taxes. These calculations indicate that the standard result—ad valorem taxes are superior to per unit excise taxes in an imperfectly competitive market—is not valid when there are other distortions in the market, a point that was emphasized in section 3.5.2. Table 4.9 also shows that the calculated MCFs for two alternative assumptions about the budget share of leisure, $b_0 = 0.40$ and $b_0 = 0.60$. These calculations show that the magnitudes of the MCFs are not very sensitive to the assumed values of b_0.

5 The MCF from Taxing Labor Income

Taxes on labor income—levied directly through income, payroll, and social security contributions, or indirectly through broadly based sales taxes—represent the most important source of tax revenues in most countries, hence the importance of the MCF for taxes on labor income. In this chapter we begin by deriving the MCF for a proportional wage tax in a perfectly competitive labor market. The concept and expressions for the MCF parallel those in section 2.3. The analysis developed in section 2.4 is also used to explain why the MCF is equal to one if labor supply is completely inelastic, even though the tax distorts the individual's labor–leisure choice and creates an excess burden. The magnitude of the MCF depends on the elasticities of supply and demand, and this section briefly reviews some of the empirical evidence concerning labor supply elasticities. It shows the appropriate definition of the labor demand elasticity to be used in computing the MCF for a general payroll tax, and argues that the long-run elasticity of the demand for labor is likely to be much higher than the labor supply elasticity. This implies that most of the burden of a payroll tax will be borne by workers. In addition this argument implies that computations of the MCF that assume a perfectly elastic demand for labor, a common assumption in the literature, will not produce large errors.

Section 5.2 uses the framework developed in Dahlby (1998) to consider the marginal cost of funds from imposing a progressive income tax with increasing marginal tax rates. Such progressive taxes are motivated by the desire to achieve fairness or equity in taxation, and therefore, it is vital to incorporate distributional preferences in the analysis in order to measure the social marginal cost of funds (SMCF). The generic measure of the SMCF developed in this section can be used to evaluate any arbitrary increase in one or more of the marginal tax rates that are imposed under a progressive personal income tax. The section shows that the labor supply effects depend on the magnitude of the compensated labor supply elasticity multiplied by the marginal tax rate increase in the taxpayer's current tax bracket and the income elasticity of labor supply multiplied by the change in the taxpayer's average tax rate. These two effects have offsetting impacts on labor supply, but the income effect is

muted under a progressive tax structure because the average tax rate increase, especially for high-income workers, is typically less than their marginal tax rate increase.
This implies that disincentive effects, especially for high-income workers, become important even if their uncompensated labor supply elasticities are close to zero. The
MCFs for three alternative progressivity-preserving tax rate increases are illustrated
based on a study of the Japanese income tax system by Bessho and Hayahi (2005).

Most of the analysis in this chapter uses the conventional labor supply model to
analyze the MCF from taxes on earnings. Sections 5.3 and 5.4 show how a broader
range of labor market adjustments affects the MCF. A model developed by Kleven
and and Kreiner (2006) is used to show how the labor force participation effects from
tax rate changes can be incorporated in the MCF. In this model the MCF depends
on the elasticity of participation, which empirical studies indicate may be larger than
the conventional labor supply elasticities that reflect adjustment in hours of work by
those who are already employed, and the "participation" tax rate, which may be substantially different from the marginal and average tax rates on earnings. Computations of the MCFs for five European countries by Kleven and Kreiner show that
incorporating the participation or "extensive margin" responses can significantly increase estimates of the MCFs for some countries.

Section 5.4 reviews important research, based on the pioneering work by Martin
Feldstein (1995, 1999), which has tried to measure the wide range of adjustments
that individuals can make to their reported incomes in response to a tax rate increase. The "new tax responsiveness" (NTR) literature focuses on the changes in the
ways employees are compensated, the timing of reported income, the utilization of
deductions, and the amount of evasion or underreporting. All these adjustments can
make tax bases shrink in responsive to tax rate increases, and therefore they affect
the MCF. The estimates of the elasticity of taxable income, η_Y, are used in this section to calculate the MCF. The general expressions for the MCF, developed in
section 5.2, are also applied with estimates of η_Y substituted for the conventional labor supply elasticity.

Up to this point we used the MCF concept to address normative issues, such as how
the tax system should be reformed and what the optimal level of spending is on a
public service financed by public goods. However, the MCF also plays an important
role in political economy models that explain the fiscal policies that governments
actually adopt. Section 5.5 shows that the MCF concept is at the heart of three standard
political economy models—the median voter model, the probabilistic voting model,
and the Leviathan model. Thus knowledge of the MCF is important for predicting
how a government will tax, not just for guiding prescriptions for how it should tax.

There have been many studies of the MCF from taxing labor income that have
used frameworks similar to the one adopted in this book, but there are also many
other empirical studies have used a wide variety of concepts—marginal welfare cost,

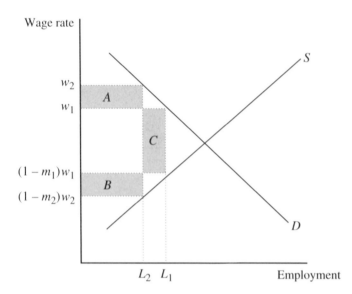

Figure 5.1
The MCF for a proportional tax on labor income

marginal excess burden, marginal efficiency cost, and marginal deadweight loss—and frameworks to calculate the marginal distortionary cost of taxes on labor income. Section 5.6 provides a brief survey of the wide range of empirical studies of the marginal distortionary cost of taxing labor income.

5.1 The MCF for a Proportional Tax on Labor Income

The MCF for a proportional tax on wage income earned in a competitive labor market can be derived using the same approach as in section 2.4. Figure 5.1 shows the equilibrium in a competitive labor market, where D is the aggregate demand curve for labor and S is the supply curve of labor. To simplify matters, we will assume here that a single homogeneous product is produced using labor and capital.[1] Output is the numéraire, and the real wage rate paid to workers is w. The wage rate and the real rate of return on capital, r, are assumed to adjust to ensure the full employment of the labor force and the capital stock. Initially a proportional tax rate of m_1 is imposed on earnings, the gross-of-tax wage rate is w_1, and the employment level is L_1. If the tax rate increases to m_2, part of the burden is shifted from workers through a higher wage rate where the degree of tax shifting is

$$\frac{dw}{wdm} = \frac{\eta_L}{(1-m)(\eta_L - \varepsilon_{Lw})},$$ (5.1)

where η_L is the elasticity of the supply of labor, L, with respect to the net wage rate, $(1 - m)w$ and ε_{Lw} is the elasticity of demand for labor. As a result of the increase in the tax rate, employment declines to L_2 because of the increase in the wage rate to w_2. We will discuss the shifting of the burden in greater detail in section 5.1.2.

The MCF for a proportional wage tax can be derived, in the same way that the MCF for an excise tax was derived in section 2.4, by calculating the welfare loss in the private sector per dollar of additional tax revenue. The burden that is borne by the recipients of capital income is equal to area A in figure 5.1 where

$$A = Ldw = \left(\frac{\eta_L}{(1 - m)(\eta_L - \varepsilon_{Lw})}\right)wLdm. \tag{5.2}$$

The burden of the tax increase that falls on workers is equal to the area B or

$$B = (1 - m)Ldw = \left(\frac{-\varepsilon_{Lw}}{\eta_L - \varepsilon_{Lw}}\right)wLdm. \tag{5.3}$$

The increase in tax revenues is $A + B - C$, where area C can be approximated as

$$C = -mwdL = -mwL\varepsilon_{Lw}\frac{dw}{w} = \left(\frac{-m\varepsilon_{Lw}\eta_L}{(1 - m)(\eta_L - \varepsilon_{Lw})}\right)wLdm. \tag{5.4}$$

The MCF can therefore be expressed as

$$MCF_\tau = \frac{A + B}{A + B - C} = \frac{\eta_L - (1 - m)\varepsilon_{Lw}}{\eta_L - (1 - m)\varepsilon_{Lw} + m\varepsilon_{Lw}\eta_L}. \tag{5.5}$$

This general formula for the MCF for a proportional wage tax has the same form as (2.29). It indicates that the MCF will be higher when the tax rate is higher or when either the demand for labor or the supply of labor is more elastic because this will increase the size of area C. This area can be interpreted as the "net output" that is lost when the tax rate is increased, where net output is defined as the difference between the value of the output produced by a worker, which is reflected in his market wage rate, and the value of the worker's leisure time, which is reflected by the after-tax wage rate. In the following two sections we will consider in more detail the factors that affect the elasticities of the supply and demand for labor.

5.1.1 Elasticity of Labor Supply

The η_L parameter in (5.5) is the uncompensated aggregate labor supply elasticity. Each worker's labor supply elasticity can be decomposed as $\eta_L = \eta_L^c + \theta$, where $\eta_L^c \geq 0$ is the compensated labor supply elasticity, which reflects the substitution effect of a net wage rate change on the supply of labor, and $\theta = (1 - m)w\partial L/\partial I$, which can be interpreted as the income elasticity of labor supply or the effect of a one dollar

increase in nonlabor income on after-tax earnings. It is reasonable to assume that leisure is a normal good, and therefore an individual's supply of labor will decline when
his nonlabor income increases, and therefore $\theta < 0$. Depending on the relative magnitudes of these income and substitution effects, an individual's supply of labor may
either increase or decrease when his wage rate increases.

Note that the MCF will be greater than, equal to, or less than one as if the labor
supply curve has a positive, zero, or negative slope given that $m > 0$ and $\varepsilon < 0$. From
the discussion in section 2.4, it should be clear that an $MCF \leq 1$ does not imply that
a proportional wage tax is nondistortionary. As long as there is a positive substitution effect between consumption and leisure, the MEB_{EV} is positive for a proportional wage tax. As noted in section 2.4, the marginal cost of public funds is related
to the equivalent variation based marginal excess burden by the relationship $MCF = (1 + MEB_{EV})(\lambda(w, U^1))/\lambda((1 - m)w, U^1)$, where $\lambda(\cdot)$ is the marginal utility of income. A decline in the net wage rate can be interpreted as a decline in the opportu-
nity cost, or the "price," of leisure. As (2.12) indicates, a reduction in the price of a
normal good, holding utility constant, causes λ to increase. Therefore the price index
$\lambda(w, U^1)/\lambda((1 - m)w, U^1)$ will be less than one if leisure is a normal good, and the
MCF will be less than $1 + MEB_{EV}$. Thus the puzzle concerning the interpretation of
an MCF that is less than one for a distortionary payroll tax can be explained by the
fact the MCF measures the additional burden in raising an additional dollar of revenue when the price of leisure is $(1 - m)w$, whereas the $(1 + MEB_{EV})$ measures the
additional harm when the price of leisure is w and the marginal utility from an additional dollar of income is lower.[2] It is worth repeating the lesson from section 2.4—
an MCF that is less than one does not mean that a tax is nondistortionary.[3]

Another point worth noting is that the MCF for a lump-sum tax increase will be
less than one if the government also imposes a proportional wage tax. A one dollar
increase in a lump-sum tax will induce an individual to supply more labor, which will
increase wage tax revenues by $-\theta m/(1 - m)$. Therefore the MCF for a lump-sum tax
is

$$MCF_{LST} = \frac{1}{1 - [m/(1 - m)]\theta}. \tag{5.6}$$

The MCF_{LST} will be less than one if leisure is a normal good and $\theta < 0$. In other
words, the lump-sum tax imposes a one dollar burden on the taxpayer but generates
more than one dollar of tax revenue. The reason is that individuals work more and
wage tax revenues increase when a lump-sum tax is imposed.

The factors that affect labor supply have been examined in numerous econometric
studies, and yet there is still a great deal of uncertainty regarding the effects of
tax rate changes because labor supply is difficult to define and measure. The supply
of labor has many dimensions, including the number of hours worked per week/

month/year, the length of time the individual is attached to the labor market (labor force participation and retirement decisions), occupation choice and human capital acquisition, and last but not least, the amount of effort actually expended on the job. Furthermore government regulations, labor union agreements, and the fixed costs associated with employment mean that some individuals will not be working their desired number of hours given the wage rate that they can earn. Despite these difficulties in defining and measuring labor supply, economists have attempted to measure labor supply elasticities. (See Blundell 1996 for a listing of parameter estimates for the labor supply responses of married women and men in the United States and the United Kingdom.) These studies show that the uncompensated labor supply elasticities for married women tend to relatively large (0.45 and 0.65 in two US studies) and that the UK studies indicate that the presence of young children, not surprisingly, reduces the labor supply elasticities. It should always be borne in mind that labor supply elasticities are generally not constants, and there can be considerable variation in the labor supply elasticities for individuals earning different wage rates. Furthermore some econometric studies indicate that married males' labor supply elasticities may be negative, even though the substitution effects are positive and non-negligible, because the income effects from wage rate changes are large.[4]

As mentioned at the beginning of this section, it is the aggregate uncompensated labor supply elasticity that is relevant for the measurement of the MCF, and this aggregate elasticity can be viewed as a weighted average of the individuals' labor supply elasticities where the weights are each individual's share of total labor income. Since males have higher average earnings than females and married males have higher labor force participation rates than married females in most countries, the appropriate aggregate labor supply elasticity should be a weighted average of male and female labor supply elasticities. For example, if the male labor supply elasticity is 0.00 and the female labor supply elasticity is 0.30, if females earn 70 percent of what males earn, and if the female participation rate is 70 percent while the male participation rate is 80 percent, then the aggregate labor supply elasticity is 0.114. However, most studies that have calculated the MCF for taxes on labor incomes have used somewhat higher values—typically in the 0.10 to 0.20 range—in part because aggregate labor supply responses may be greater than the labor supply elasticities obtained from estimating individuals' labor supply responses. For example, if everyone's net wage rate falls as a result of a general tax rate increase, the standard hours of work per week may decline, whereas an individual who has a lower net wage rate may not be able to work fewer hours because the standard hours of work are based on the average number of hours of work desired by the employer and the other employees.

Tax evasion affects the MCF, in much the same way as a labor supply reduction, if individuals respond to an income tax rate increase by reducing their reported income.

For example, Usher (1986) showed that in taking the tax evasion responses into account, the MCF for a proportional income tax is equal to

$$MCF_\tau = \frac{1}{1 - [m/(1-m)](1-v)\eta_L - [v/(1-v)]\varphi}, \tag{5.7}$$

where v the proportion of total income that is evaded and φ is the elasticity of tax evaded with respect to the tax rate. Thus, even if the aggregate amount of labor supplied to the economy is constant, the MCF may be greater than one if more tax is evaded when the tax rate is increased. In section 6.2 we will consider the MCF from measures to reduce the degree of tax evasion.

As was emphasized in chapter 3, the MCF is inversely related to the elasticity of total tax revenue with respect to the tax rate. This means that we need to take into account all of the adjustments that taxpayers make that can cause tax bases to shrink when we measure the MCF. In section 5.4 we will review the econometric studies that have estimated the elasticity of taxable income to tax rate changes and show how this parameter can be used to calculate the MCF.

5.1.2 Elasticity of Demand for Labor

There are a number of alternative ways of defining the elasticity of demand for labor. For example, it is possible to define ε_{Lw} as the responsiveness of the demand for labor to a wage rate increase, with output fixed or the prices of the other inputs held constant. Since we are interested in the efficiency and distributional effects of taxes, neither of these ways of defining ε_{Lw} is appealing because they ignore the output changes and tax-shifting effects that we consider important in measuring the MCF. In the context of the model outlined in section 5.1, a more appropriate measure of the elasticity of demand for labor is one that indicates how the demand for labor varies as the wage rate increases when the price of output, the numéraire, is held constant but r, the return on capital, varies so that the capital stock remains fully employed. It can be shown that this labor demand elasticity is equal to[5]

$$\varepsilon_{Lw} = -\left(\frac{\sigma + \alpha\eta_K}{1-\alpha}\right), \tag{5.8}$$

where $\sigma \geq 0$ is the elasticity of substitution between labor and capital in production, α is labor's share of the cost of production, and η_K is the elasticity of the supply of capital.

This demand elasticity can be decomposed into two components. The first component is the demand response, with capital stock held constant. This component is $-\sigma/(1-\alpha)$, and the labor demand will be more elastic when it is easier to substitute labor and capital in production and when labor's share of the cost of production are higher. To understand this response, suppose that the real wage rate increases by dw. Since output has been adopted as the numéraire and firms earn zero economic profits in the long run, the return to capital has to decline such that $\alpha(dw/w) + (1 - \alpha)(dr/r) = 0$. The decline in r combined with the increase in w means that firms will try to substitute capital for labor, and the demand for labor will decline. Labor's share of the aggregate cost of production is usually considered to be quite high, between two-thirds and three-quarters of total output. If the aggregate production function is Cobb-Douglas so that $\sigma = 1$ and $\alpha = 2/3$, then $\varepsilon_{Lw} = -3$ even if the supply of capital is fixed. In fact the demand for labor will be in the elastic range as long as $\sigma > 1 - \alpha$.

In considering the second component of the labor demand response, suppose that it is not possible to substitute labor for capital in the production function, $\sigma = 0$, and $\eta_K > 0$. As noted above, an increase in the real wage rate, dw, implies that r must decline. The decline in the return to capital causes the amount of capital employed in the economy to decrease, and this effect is larger when η_K is larger. The decline in the capital stock reduces the marginal product of labor, which causes the demand for labor to decline. If the supply of capital to the economy is perfectly elastic (perhaps because we are dealing with a small open economy that can borrow or lend at a given real after-tax rate of return determined on world markets), then demand for labor will be perfectly elastic.

The implication of this analysis is the aggregate demand for labor will tend to be elastic. This has two consequences. The first is that most of the burden of a payroll tax will tend to be borne by workers because the labor demand elasticity will be much higher than the labor supply elasticity. For example, labor's share of the burden of a proportional wage tax is $1 - (1 - m)dw/(wdm)$. If we assume a Cobb-Douglas production function and a fixed supply of capital, then $\varepsilon_{Lw} = -3$. If we use a relatively high value for the labor supply elasticity, such as $\eta_L = 0.2$, then labor will bear 93.8 percent of the tax burden. The share of the burden borne by labor will be even higher if the supply of capital is even somewhat elastic.

The second implication concerns the calculation of the MCF. Much of the MCF (and optimal income tax) literature has assumed that the demand for labor is perfectly elastic[6], and under this assumption, the formula for the MCF for a proportional wage tax is

$$MCF_\tau = \frac{1}{1 - [m/(1 - m)]\eta_L} . \tag{5.9}$$

If the demand for labor is not perfectly elastic, the correct formula is given by (5.5). However, the magnitude of the error in using (5.9) instead of (5.5) will generally be relatively small. For example, if $\varepsilon_{Lw} = -3$, $\eta_L = 0.2$, and $m = 0.4$, then the "true" value of the MCF is 1.176, whereas the calculation using (5.9) yields 1.154. Hence the assumption of a perfectly elastic demand for labor may simplify the calculation of the MCF, especially in more complex models than the one presented in section 5.1, without producing a significant error.

5.2   The SMCF for a Progressive Wage Tax

Equation (5.5) is the MCF from a proportional tax on wage income, but most countries' personal income tax schedules impose higher marginal tax rates in the upper income tax brackets.[7] Since a progressive income tax is only imposed for reasons of distributional equity, it is important to analyze the MCF in a multi-individual framework that incorporates the society's distributional concerns. The analysis in this section is based on Dahlby (1998).[8]

We will begin by considering the progressive tax system depicted in figure 5.2. An individual receives a constant wage rate w, has zero nonlabor income, and faces the piecewise linear consumption opportunity locus $0acd$, which indicates his consumption level given the amount of income earned. The marginal tax rate is m_1 when income is between 0 and X_1, m_2 when income is between X_1 and X_2, and m_3 when income exceeds X_2, with $m_1 < m_2 < m_3$. Each section of the opportunity locus has a slope equal to $1 - m_j$. An individual's indifference curves in consumption-income space are positively sloped because additional income only results from a reduction

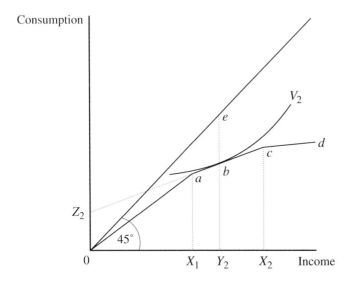

Figure 5.2
Consumption–income decision with increasing marginal tax rates

in leisure time. Therefore an increase in earnings must be accompanied by an increase in consumption to hold well-being constant. Suppose that the individual's indifference curve, V_2, is tangent to the individual's opportunity locus at point b. The individual earns Y_2, his total tax payment, R_2, is equal to the distance eb, and he faces the marginal tax rate of m_2 on his earnings.

It is convenient to use the indirect utility function $V((1 - m_i)w_i, Z_i)$ to represent the well-being of the individual, where w_i is the individual's wage rate and Z_i is individual's "virtual income." Z_i is the income level that makes the utility of the individual facing a constant marginal tax rate of m_i equivalent to the utility level that they obtain under the nonlinear tax system. It can be seen in figure 5.2 that $Z_2 = (m_2 - m_1)X_1$. Note that $R_2 = m_2(Y_2 - X_1) + m_1 X_1 = m_2 Y - Z_2$. Therefore $Z_2 = (m_2 - \tau_2)Y_2$, where τ_2 is the individual's average tax rate R_2/Y_2. Thus the individual's virtual income can be viewed as the implicit income that the individual receives because his average tax rate is less than his marginal tax.

Suppose the tax system has n tax brackets, with the marginal income tax rate of m_j when income is between X_{j-1} and X_j, where $X_0 = 0$ and $X_n = \infty$ and $m_1 < m_2 < m_3 < \cdots < m_n$. The tax revenue collected from individual i will be

$$R_i = m_i(Y_i - X_{i-1}) + \sum_{j=1}^{i-1} m_j(X_j - X_{j-1}), \tag{5.10}$$

where the first term is the tax paid on income earned in the ith bracket and the other terms represents the tax paid on income earned in the lower tax brackets. The virtual income that individual i receives is equal to

$$Z_i = \sum_{j=1}^{i-1}(m_i - m_j)(X_j - X_{j-1}) = m_i X_{i-1} - \sum_{j=1}^{i-1} m_j(X_j - X_{j-1}) = (m_i - \tau_i)Y_i. \tag{5.11}$$

The individual's average tax rate, τ_i, can also be defined by

$$\tau_i = \sum_{j=1}^{n} \chi_{ij} m_j, \tag{5.12}$$

where χ_{ij} is the proportion of individual i's income that is in tax bracket j. If $Y_i > X_j$, then $\chi_{ij} = (X_j - X_{j-1})/Y_i$. If $X_{j-1} < Y_i < X_j$, then $\chi_{ij} = (Y_i - X_{j-1})/Y_i$. If $Y_i < X_{j-1}$, then $\chi_{ij} = 0$. For an arbitrary set of marginal tax rate changes, the change in the individual i's average tax rate, holding Y_i constant, is

$$d\tau_i = \sum_{j=1}^{n} \chi_{ij} dm_j. \tag{5.13}$$

Let the labor supply function of individual i be

$$L_i = L((1 - m_i)w_i, Z_i) \tag{5.14}$$

with $Y_i = w_i L_i$. The effect of a change in the marginal tax rate in the jth tax bracket on the revenue collected from individual i is

$$dR_i = w_i L_i dm_i + m_i w_i \left[\frac{\partial L_i}{\partial (1 - m_i)w_i} \frac{\partial (1 - m_i)w_i}{\partial m_i} dm_i + \frac{\partial L_i}{\partial Z_i} dZ_i \right] - dZ_i \quad \text{for } i = j$$

$$= m_i w_i \left[\frac{\partial L_i}{\partial Z_i} dZ_i \right] - dZ_i \quad \text{for } i > j, \tag{5.15}$$

where the $dZ_i = (dm_i - d\tau_i) Y_i$ and the $d\tau_i$ is computed according to (5.13). First, consider the effect of an increase in the marginal tax rate in the individual's tax bracket. The first term in square brackets in (5.28) shows the uncompensated labor supply response to a reduction in the individual's net wage rate. To decompose the labor supply responses into their income and substitution effects, we will use the same notation as in section 5.1 where the uncompensated labor supply elasticity equals $\eta_i = \eta_i^c + \theta_i$ and $\eta_i^c > 0$ is the compensated labor supply elasticity and $\theta_i < 0$ is the marginal propensity to earn income out of nonlabor income. In particular, $\theta_i = (1 - m_i)w_i(dL_i/dZ_i)$. Second, note that an increase in a marginal tax rate in a tax bracket that is below the individual's tax bracket is equivalent to a lump-sum tax increase that only has an income effect. This is reflected in the $dZ_i = -Y_i d\tau_i < 0$, and it will increase the individual's labor supply, assuming that leisure is a normal good.

Decomposing the labor supply responses into substitution and income effects, the change in the revenues collected from individual i will be equal to

$$dR_i = Y_i \left[d\tau_i - \frac{m_i}{1 - m_i} (\eta_i^c dm_i + \theta_i d\tau_i) \right]. \tag{5.16}$$

The first term in square brackets is the change in taxes paid by the individual if there is no labor supply response. The first term in the round brackets shows the effect on tax revenues due to the adjustment in labor supply caused by the substitution effect $(-\eta_i^c dm_i)$, while the second term represents the income effect $(-\theta_i d\tau_i)$. Note that if the marginal tax rate on the individual's earnings does not change, then $dm_i = 0$, and there is no substitution effect. If the marginal tax rate in a higher income bracket changes, then both dm_i and $d\tau_i$ will be zero.

We will make the simplifying assumption that all households in a given tax bracket are identical and that the tangency occurs in the interior of the tax bracket, i.e. individuals are not at the upper limit of a tax bracket. By Roy's theorem,

$\partial V / \partial ((1 - m_i) w_i) = \lambda_i L_i$, the effect on an individual's well-being from small changes in his marginal and average tax rates is equal to $dV_i = -\lambda_i Y_i dm_i + \lambda_i dZ_i = -\lambda_i Y_i d\tau_i$. Using a general social welfare function, $S(V_1, V_2, V_3, \ldots, V_n)$, as in section 2.7, we write the change in social welfare from a tax rate change as

$$dS = \sum_{j=1}^{n} S_j dV_j = -\sum_{j=1}^{n} f_j \beta_j Y_j d\tau_j, \tag{5.17}$$

where f_j is the number of individuals in tax bracket j and β_j is the distributional weight attached to an additional dollar of lump-sum income received by an individual in tax bracket j. It will be assumed that the distributional weights are "pro-poor," meaning they decrease as individuals' standard of living increases.

Combining the social welfare change in (5.17) with revenue changes in (5.16), the SMCF from an arbitrary set of small changes in the marginal tax rates is therefore equal to the following:

$$SMCF_{PIT} = \frac{\sum_{j=1}^{n} \beta_j s_j d\tau_j}{\sum_{j=1}^{n} s_j [d\tau_j - [m_j/(1 - m_j)](\eta_j^c dm_j + \theta_j d\tau_j)]}, \tag{5.18}$$

where s_j is the proportion of total income that is earned in the jth bracket and $d\tau_j$ is given by (5.13). The numerator is the distributionally weighted cost of raising tax revenue in each tax bracket given some set of marginal tax rate changes, and the denominator the change in total tax revenues.

While the formula in (5.18) can be used to evaluate the SMCF for any combination of marginal tax rate changes, it is useful to consider some specific applications. First we will consider a simple two tax bracket system. The MCFs for m_1 and m_2, with the definitions of the tax brackets held fixed, are

$$SMCF_{m_1} = \frac{\beta_1 s_1 + \beta_2 s_2 \chi_{21}}{s_1 + s_2 \chi_{21} - [m_1/(1 - m_1)](s_1 \eta^c + (s_1 + s_2 \chi_{21})\theta)}, \tag{5.19}$$

$$SMCF_{m_2} = \frac{\beta_2 \chi_{22}}{\chi_{22} - [m_2/(1 - m_2)](\eta^c + \chi_{22}\theta)}, \tag{5.20}$$

where, for simplicity, it is assumed that all individuals have identical labor supply elasticities. Note that in the formula for the $SMCF_{m_2}$ the income effect is weighted by the fraction of the individual's income that is in the top tax bracket, whereas the substitution effect is unweighted. When only a small fraction of taxpayer's income is in the top tax bracket, the substitution effect of an increase in m_2 dominates, and the reduction in labor supply can be quite significant even when the uncompensated labor supply elasticity is zero or negative. This effect tends to reduce the revenue maximizing marginal tax rate in the top tax bracket, which is equal to the following:

$$m_n^* = \frac{\chi_{nn}}{\eta^c + \chi_{nn}(1 + \theta)}. \tag{5.21}$$

Finally, note that in the formula for the $SMCF_{m_1}$, the income effect of the tax rate change has more weight than the substitution effect, reflecting the fact that the individuals in the second tax bracket only have an income effect when m_1 increases. The greater weight attached to the income effect will tend to reduce the $SMCF_{m_1}$.

The SMCFs for progressivity-preserving tax rate increases can be derived from the general formula in (5.18).[9] Three alternative local measures of progressivity were proposed by Musgrave and Thin (1948), viz average rate progression, $ARP = (m_i - \tau_i)/Y_i$, liability progression, $LP = m_i/\tau_i$, and residual income progression, $RIP = (1 - m_i)/(1 - \tau_i)$. An ARP preserving tax rate increase occurs when all marginal tax rates are increased by the same amounts in all brackets and therefore $dm_i = d\tau_i$. An LP-preserving tax rate increase occurs when all marginal tax rates are increased in the same proportion and therefore $dm_i/m_i = d\tau_i/\tau_i$. This implies that individuals in higher income brackets face larger absolute marginal tax rate increases. An RIP-preserving tax rate increase occurs $dm_i/(1 - m_i)$ is the same for all i. This implies that individual in higher brackets face smaller absolute increases in their marginal tax rates. After making the appropriate substitutions, we write the formulas for the SMCFs for the three types of tax changes as

$$SMCF_{ARP} = \frac{\sum_{j=1}^{n} \beta_j s_j}{\sum_{j=1}^{n} s_j \left[1 - \frac{m_j}{1 - m_j} \eta_j \right]}, \tag{5.22}$$

$$SMCF_{LP} = \frac{\sum_{j=1}^{n} \beta_j r_j}{\sum_{j=1}^{n} r_j \left[1 - \frac{m_j}{1 - m_j} \left(\frac{m_j}{\tau_j} \eta_j^c + \theta_j \right) \right]}, \tag{5.23}$$

$$SMCF_{RIP} = \frac{\sum_{j=1}^{n} \beta_j a_j}{\sum_{j=1}^{n} a_j \left[1 - \frac{m_j}{1 - m_j} \left(\frac{1 - m_j}{1 - \tau_j} \eta_j^c + \theta_j \right) \right]}, \tag{5.24}$$

where s_j, r_j, and a_j are respectively the proportions of total income, tax revenue, and after-tax income in tax bracket j. Note that the three types progressivity-preserving tax rate changes put different emphasis on the income and substitution effects of the tax rate changes. The ARP only depends on the uncompensated labor supply elasticity

Table 5.1
Calculations of the SMCFs in Japan in 1997 and 2002

	$\xi = 0.000$		$\xi = 1.000$		$\xi = 2.000$	
	1997	2002	1997	2002	1997	2002
ARP	1.017	1.042	0.846	0.811	0.676	0.545
LP	1.077	1.141	0.841	0.832	0.633	0.521
RIP	1.003	1.023	0.848	0.807	0.685	0.549

Source: Bessho and Hayahi (2005, tabs. 2a, 2b, 3a, 3b).
Note: SMCFs have been normalized by the average distributional weights in each year.

because average and marginal tax rates increase by the same amounts. The LP places more weight on the substitution effects than the income effects, since $(m_i/\tau_i) > 1$, and the RIP places a less weight on the substitution effect than the income effect, since $(1 - m_i)/(1 - \tau_i) < 1$.

Bessho and Hayahi (2005) have applied the formulas above for the SMCFs for ARP, LP, and RIP to the Japanese income tax system. They estimated of the labor supply responses of prime age males in Japan in 1997 and 2002 based on a linear labor supply function, which implies that the labor supply elasticities vary with the worker's wage rate. For 1997 they found that the compensated labor supply elasticity varied between 0.09 and 0.91 with an average value of 0.34 and a standard error of 0.11. The income effect ranged from -0.08 to -0.79 with an average value of -0.30 and a standard error of 0.10. The average labor supply responses were somewhat larger in 2002 with an average compensated labor supply elasticity of 0.67 and an average income effect of -0.56.

Table 5.1 shows their computations of the SMCFs for the three types of progressivity-preserving tax rate changes with distributional weights based on income inequality aversion parameter values of $\xi = 0, 1$, and 2. With $\xi = 0$ and distributional weights equal to one for all individuals, the LP had the highest, and the RIP the lowest, SMCF in 1999 and 2002. With $\xi = 2$, the ranking was reversed, with the RIP the highest and the LP the lowest in both years. With $\xi = 1$, the RIP was highest in 1997 and the lowest in 2002. Thus the ranking of the SMCFs depends not only on the degree of inequality aversion but also on the tax rates, the income distribution, and the labor supply responses that may have changed between the two years.

5.3   Incorporating Labor Force Participation Effects in the MCF

In analyzing the effects of a tax rate increase, the literature on the MCF from taxing labor has mainly focused on the adjustment in the "intensive" margin, such as the change in the number of hours worked per month, rather than on the adjustment in the "extensive" margin—the decision to participate in the labor market. The absence of any extensive margin response in the formulas for the MCF is a concern because adjustments in participation rates are one of the most important sources of labor market adjustments (see Heckman 1991; Blundell and MaCurdy 1999). A recent paper by Kleven and and Kreiner (2006) has filled this gap in the literature, and in this section their framework is used to show how the effects of taxes on labor force participation can be incorporated in the MCF. In particular, the Kleven and Kreiner model shows that the "participation" tax rate may be substantially different from the marginal and average tax rates on earnings and that the participation effect may be especially important for some subgroups of the population, such as low-income earners or men over age 55.

A country's tax-transfer function can be represented by $R(Y_i, v)$, where $Y_i = w_i L_i$ is the labor market earnings of an individual with a wage rate of w_i who works L_i hours and v is a shift parameter in the tax-transfer function, which can be interpreted as an increase in marginal tax rates. The individual's marginal and average tax rates are $m_i = \partial R / \partial Y_i$ and $\tau_i = R(Y_i, v) / Y_i$. If an individual does not work, he receives a transfer equal to $-R(0, v)$, and his consumption level is $c_0 = -R(0, v)$. The benefit rate from the transfer will be defined as $b_i = R(0, v) / Y_i$, where Y_i is the labor market earnings of an individual who receives a wage of w_i. An individual who works has a consumption level equal to $c_i = w_i L_i - R(Y_i, v)$ and a utility level equal to $U(c_i, T - L_i) - Q$, where T is the total amount of time available for work and leisure and Q is a fixed cost associated with working (e.g., transportation and clothing expenditures plus the physical and mental costs of working). It is assumed that these fixed costs of working are distributed across individuals who receive a wage rate equal to w_i according to the cumulative distribution function $P_i(Q)$. An individual with fixed costs of working equal to $\bar{Q}_i$, who could receive a wage rate of w_i, will be indifferent between working and not working where

$$\bar{Q}_i = U(c_i, T - L_i) - U(c_0, T). \tag{5.25}$$

$P_i(\bar{Q}_i)$ can be interpreted as the labor force participation rate among individuals who could receive a wage rate equal to w_i and earn Y_i if employed. To simplify the notation, it will be denoted as P_i. Individuals with Q greater than $\bar{Q}_i$ are voluntarily unemployed. We will denote the elasticity of the participation rate for group i with respect to their net wage rate $w_{ni} = (1 - m_i) w_i$ as $\vartheta_i = (dP_i / dw_{ni})(w_{ni} / P_i)$. The participation elasticity is positive, and empirical studies indicate that it is larger than the conventional (uncompensated) labor supply elasticity, η_i, which measures the responsiveness of the labor supplied by those who are already in the workforce.

The per capita net revenue raised from the individuals who could earn w_i is given by $R_i = P_i R(Y_i) + (1 - P_i) R(0)$. A small change in the shift parameter would have the following effect on the per capita revenues from group i:

$$\frac{dR_i}{d\upsilon} = P_i\frac{\partial R(Y_i)}{\partial \upsilon} + (1 - P_i)\frac{\partial R(0)}{\partial \upsilon} + P_i m_i\frac{dY_i}{d\upsilon} + (\tau_i + b_i)Y_i\frac{dP_i}{d\upsilon}. \tag{5.26}$$

The first two terms in this expression are the direct effects of changes in the tax-transfer parameters on the net revenues collected from workers and nonworkers in the absence of labor supply adjustments. The third term is the effect on tax revenues of the "intensive margin" adjustment by labor force participants, and the fourth term in the "extensive margin adjustment" by nonparticipants. For concreteness, suppose that the change in the tax transfer system is an increase in the marginal tax rate imposed on group i. As in section 5.2, the intensive marginal adjustment will be given by (5.16) where $d\tau_i$ is the average tax rate change associated with the marginal tax rate increase dm_i. The effect on per capita tax revenues will be equal to

$$dR_i = P_i Y_i\left[d\tau_i - \frac{m_i}{1 - m_i}(\eta_i^c dm_i + \theta_i d\tau_i) - \frac{\tau_i + b_i}{1 - m_i}\vartheta_i\right], \tag{5.27}$$

since $\partial R(0)/\partial m_i = 0$. The key difference between the expression above and (5.16) is the participation elasticity multiplied by $(\tau_i + b_i)/(1 - m_i)$. Note that $(\tau_i + b_i)$ is the participation tax rate and that it may be substantially different than m_i.

In the Kleven and Kreiner model, individuals choose not to work because the cost of working is relatively high for them. Unemployment in their model is voluntary and not a labor market distortion, and the welfare loss that any individual suffers from a small tax rate change is equal to their tax increase. Consequently the expression for the social cost of a tax rate change can be derived in the same manner as (5.17), and the expression for the SMCF for an arbitrary set of marginal tax rate increases can be written as

$$SMCF_{PIT} = \frac{\sum_{j=1}^{n}\beta_j s_j d\tau_j}{\sum_{j=1}^{n}s_j[d\tau_j - [m_j/(1 - m_j)](\eta_j^c dm_j + \theta_j d\tau_j) - [(\tau_i + b_i)/(1 - m_i)]\vartheta_i]}, \tag{5.28}$$

where s_j is the proportion of income earned by group j and β_j is now interpreted as the average distributional weight applied to an income earner in tax bracket j.

Kleven and Kreiner (2006) argued that the additional term in the denominator of (5.28) may have a significant effect on the measured revenue response to a marginal tax rate change because (1) the participation elasticity, ϑ_i, is positive and possibly quite large especially for low-income groups, (2) the participation tax rate $(\tau_i + b_i)$ is high in some countries because of generous social welfare programs, and (3) $(1 - m_i)$ is low because of high marginal tax rates on earnings.

Kleven and Kreiner (2006, tabs. 1 and 2) illustrate the impact of incorporating the participation effect using data on the marginal and average tax rates from the tax-

Table 5.2
Incorporating labor force participation effects in the MCF

	Average marginal tax rate on earnings, m_{ave}	Average participation tax rate, $\tau_{ave} + b_{ave}$	MCF for a proportional tax rate increase	
			$\eta_i = 0.10$ and $\vartheta_i = 0$	$\eta_i = 0.10$ and $\vartheta_{ave} = 0.20^a$
Denmark	0.68	0.75	1.29	2.20
France	0.62	0.71	1.21	1.72
Germany	0.66	0.68	1.23	1.85
Italy	0.60	0.54	1.19	1.52
United Kingdom	0.47	0.49	1.10	1.26

Source: Kleven and Kreiner (2006, tabs. 1 and 3).
a. The participation rate elasticity was assumed to be 0.4 in the first two deciles, 0.3 in the third and fourth deciles, 0.2 in the fifth and sixth deciles, 0.1 in the seventh and eighth deciles, and 0.0 in the top two deciles.

transfer systems for five European countries, and some of their results are summarized in table 5.2. The first column indicates that the average marginal tax rate on earnings, as computed in Immervoll et al. (2007), ranged from 0.68 in Denmark to 0.47 in the United Kingdom. The average participation tax rates are higher than the marginal tax rates on earnings in all countries except Italy, and range from 0.75 in Denmark to 0.49 in the United Kingdom. The last two columns show Kleven and Kreiner's calculations of the MCF for a proportional tax rate increase (an equal marginal tax rate increase in all tax brackets such that $dm_i = d\tau_i$ for all income earners). In the third column the participation elasticity was set equal to zero for all income groups, while the uncompensated labor supply elasticity is assumed to be 0.10 for all groups. Computations were based on tax rates and income shares for 10 deciles in each country. The computed MCFs ranged from 1.29 in Denmark to 1.10 in the United Kingdom. The fourth column shows the impact of incorporating the participation effect, when the average participation elasticity declines from 0.4 in the bottom quintile to zero in the top quintile. The computed MCFs are substantially higher for all countries and especially for Denmark where the MCF increases from 1.29 to 2.20. Thus the Kleven and Kreiner results indicate the potential importance of incorporating labor force participation effects in the computation of the MCF from changes in marginal tax rates on labor income.

Because unemployment is voluntary in the Kleven and Kreiner model, changes in the employment rate due to marginal adjustments in tax rates do not create a direct welfare loss. However, if unemployment is involuntary, changes in the level of employment can have significant direct effects on individuals' well-being and these should be incorporate in the numerator of the MCF formula. In section 6.2 we use an efficiency wage model of involuntary unemployment to incorporate changes in the rate of unemployment in the MCF.

5.4   Using the Elasticity of Taxable Income to Calculate the MCF

To this point we have used the conventional labor supply model, where taxes distort an individual's leisure-consumption choice, as the framework for analyzing the MCF from taxes on earnings. However, labor supply has many dimensions, and the econometric studies have found that individuals' hours of work do not reflect the most significant responses to a tax rate change. As Feldstein (1997, p. 209) argues:

[T]he relevant labor supply elasticity is much larger than the traditional estimates imply. The relevant distortion to labor supply is not only the effect of tax rates on participation rates and hours but also their effect on education, occupational choice, effort, location, and all of the other aspects of behavior that affect the short-run and long-run productivity and income of the individual.

Thus we need to take into account changes in the ways employees are compensated (e.g., in the substitution of nontaxable fringe benefits, employer-provided health care, for wage income), the timing of reported income (e.g., when deductions are made or when bonuses and options are realized), the utilization of deductions (e.g., charitable contributions or tax-deductible savings), and the amount of evasion or underreporting. All these adjustments make the tax base more responsive to tax rate changes than the traditional labor supply model would suggest, and therefore they increase the MCF.

Over the past decade a number of US studies have used cross-sectional and panel data to estimate the response of taxpayers' reported incomes to marginal tax rate changes, using the "natural experiments" that have occurred as a result major changes to the US personal income tax system. Early studies found that the taxable income was very sensitive to marginal tax rates. For example, the Feldstein (1995) study of the effects of the 1986 tax reforms, which substantially reduced marginal tax rates especially for high-income earners, indicated that the elasticity of taxable income with respect to the net of tax share, defined as one minus the taxpayer's marginal tax rate, was somewhere between 1.00 and 3.00. However, there are a host of empirical problems connected with properly isolating the permanent changes in taxpayer behavior, which are the relevant issues, from the short-term timing and relabeling effects that are much less important for determining the MCF from a permanent tax reform. Furthermore, as with many other policy issues such as the effects of free trade, it is difficult to disentangle the effects of tax reforms from other factors, such as technological changes, that affect the long-run trends in the distribution of wages and forms of compensation. More recent studies of the responses to tax reforms have attempted to distinguish between long-term adjustments in behavior and short-term timing responses and other factors that affect the trends in reported incomes, and they have obtained much lower estimates of elasticity of taxable income. We will not review these empirical studies here because they have been recently described in detail by Goolsbee (1999, 2000), Gruber and Saez (2002), and Saez (2004). We will be content to show how the empirical results from the "new tax responsiveness" (NTR) literature can be used to compute the marginal cost of public funds.

We will use the same basic framework as in section 5.2 to develop a model by which to calculate the MCF based on the parameter values of the Gruber and Saez (2002) study. We will assume that the representative individual's reported income is Y and his total tax payment is $R = mY - Z$, where Z is his virtual income because only income in excess of X is taxed. As in section 5.2 the virtual income arises because the average tax rate, τ, is less than the individual's marginal tax rate; that is, $Z = (m - \tau)Y = mX$. A small increase in the individual's marginal tax rate imposes a loss equal to $(Y - X)dm$. The increase in tax revenue is equal to $Y + dY/dm - dZ/dm$. We will write the behavioral response in terms of the elasticity of reported income with respect to the net of tax share, $\eta_Y = (1 - m)(dY/d(1 - m))(1/Y)$, so that the MCF can be calculated as

$$MCF = \frac{1}{1 - [m/(1 - m)]\eta_Y(m/\tau)},$$ (5.29)

where we make use of the identity, $\tau Y \equiv m(Y - X)$. The m/τ ratio is included in the denominator of this expression, which reflects the progressivity of the tax system. The elasticity η_Y encompasses a broader range of taxpayer responses than the labor supply responses that formed the basis of that model. In particular, adjustments in Y can occur through changes in deductions and the substitution of nontaxed forms of consumption, such as fringe benefits, for taxable income.

Gruber and Saez's (2002) study was based on a panel of individual tax returns in the United States from 1979 to 1990. Over this period the top federal marginal income tax rate declined from 70 percent in 1980 to 28 percent in 1988. The authors included in their analysis the variations in the state personal taxes. Their econometric model indicated that the overall elasticity of taxable income was around 0.40. In addition they found that "income effects" were not significant, and therefore their estimate of η_Y can be interpreted as a "compensated" response as well as a total response. Finally, they found that high-income individuals were much more responsive to tax rate changes, in part because these taxpayers have more scope for varying the form and timing of their remuneration. Their estimate of η_Y for high-income earners was 0.57. By contrast, the η_Y for middle- and low-income earners was not significant. For their study, $m = 0.27$ and $\tau = 0.18$, and $\eta_Y = 0.4$, and therefore the implied MCF is 1.285. This should be interpreted as the MCF for a uniform increase in marginal tax rates. Note that it is considerably lower than the MCF of 3.00 that Feldstein (1999) calculated using an estimated value of η_Y of 1.04.

The main point being stressed here is that the same basic model that was developed within the conventional labor supply model can be used to calculate the MCF using econometric results from the NTR literature. Obviously more refinements and extensions are possible. As previous chapters have shown, it is important to include nontax distortions and the effects on revenues from other tax sources in calculating the MCF for a particular tax. The latter effect may be important for computing the MCF from personal income tax changes, especially related to the US 1986 tax reform, where there is evidence that high-income investors shifted their income form taxable corporations to "S corps" where the income was taxed as personal income. Incorporating the interactions between the personal, corporate, and sales tax bases would be an important step toward a full implementation of the NTR methodology in computing the MCF.

5.5   The MCF in Models of Political Choice

Most of this book is concerned with exploring the role of the MCF in the normative theory of public finance. However, the MCF also plays an important role in economic models which attempt to explain the level of taxation and the tax mix. Here we will briefly examine the role that the MCF plays in three standard models of political economy of taxation.[10]

5.5.1   Median Voter Model

The first model that we consider is the median voter model.[11] Suppose that H individuals have indirect utility functions $V^h((1 - \tau)w_h, G)$, where τ is a proportional wage tax that is used to finance expenditures on a public good, G. Each individual's earnings are equal to $Y_h = w_h L((1 - \tau)w_h, G)$, where $L(.)$ is the individual's labor supply function. Note that an increase in the provision of the public good may increase, decrease, or leave unchanged the individual's labor supply, and that G is not necessarily a pure public good, such as national defense. It could, for example, be a lump-sum income transfer or a publicly provided private good such as a recreation facility. The government's total tax revenue is $R(\tau, G) = \tau \sum Y_h = \tau H \overline{Y}$, where $\overline{Y}$ is average income. The effect on tax revenues of a marginal increase in G will be denoted by R_G. The government's budget constraint is $R(\tau, G) = C(G)$, where $C(G)$ is the cost of producing the public good. The marginal cost of producing G will be denoted by MC_G. For individual h, the optimal amount of the public good and the tax rate that is need to finance it are determined by the following first-order conditions:

$$\frac{\partial V^h}{\partial \tau} + \mu \left[H \overline{Y} + \tau H \frac{\partial \overline{Y}}{\partial \tau} \right] = 0, \tag{5.30}$$

$$\frac{\partial V^h}{\partial G} + \mu[R_G - MC_G] = 0, \tag{5.31}$$

where μ is the Lagrange multiplier on the government's budget constraint. In this context the marginal cost of public funds is equal to

$$MCF_\tau = \frac{\overline{Y}}{\overline{Y} + \tau(\partial \overline{Y}/\partial \tau)}. \tag{5.32}$$

It is assumed that the MCF_τ is increasing in τ. By Roy's theorem, $\partial V^h/\partial \tau = -\lambda_h Y_h$. We will also define $MB^h_G = \lambda_h^{-1} \partial V^h/\partial G$ as the marginal benefit that individual h derives from G. The optimal provision of the public good from this individual's perspective is described by the following condition:

$$\left(\frac{MB^h_G}{\overline{MB}_G}\right) \sum_{j=1}^H MB^j_G = \left(\frac{Y_h}{\overline{Y}}\right) MCF_\tau[MC_G - R_G], \tag{5.33}$$

where $\overline{MB}_G$ is the average marginal benefit that individuals place on the public good. Consequently an individual will want a relatively generous provision of the public good if his marginal benefit is above the average marginal benefit and if his earnings are below average earnings. If this preference for G is "single-peaked," the decisive voter will be the one who displays the median demand for G. If individuals' marginal benefits are monotonically increasing in income, monotonically decreasing in income, or constant, then the "median voter" will be the individual with the median income, $\tilde{Y}$. This form of the median voter model was first developed by Meltzer and Richard (1981, p. 914), who emphasized the following prediction of the model: "An increase in mean income relative to the income of the decisive [median] voter increases the size of government." In most societies the income distribution is skewed to the right and therefore $\tilde{Y} < \overline{Y}$.[12] An increase in income inequality, as measured by a reduction in the $\tilde{Y}/\overline{Y}$ ratio, would lead to an increase in the provision of the public good, because the median voter would bear a lower proportion of the total cost of providing an additional unit of G.[13] However, from our perspective, the most important thing to note is the central role that the MCF plays in the determination of public good provision and the level of taxation. The model predicts that an increase in the MCF_τ would lead to a reduction in the size of government. Thus the MCF concept is not simply a tool for determining what a government's fiscal policy "should be"; it also helps to explain why a government's fiscal policy "is what it is."

5.5.2   Probabilistic Voting Model

In the median voter model only one individual's preferences are decisive. In the simplest version of this model the decisive voter is the individual with the median income, and the political system caters to his preferences for the public good. However, this model does not capture full complexity of political behavior because it assumes that one type of public service is provided and only one tax base is used to finance it. In reality, most governments provide a range of public services financed through a variety of taxes and other sources of revenue. Nonfiscal issues, such as a party's position on abortion, may be very important for at least some voters. Political campaigns require resources and politicians need money and labor inputs if they are to be successful. Consequently all voters have at least some impact on the outcome of an election and the determination of a government's fiscal policy. In order to capture the inherent complexity of political equilibria, a probabilistic voting framework has been developed (see Hettich and Winer 1999, ch. 4). We will describe a simple version of this model in order to contrast it with the median voter model and to show the role that the MCF concept plays in this model.

The model is based on the assumption that a political party selects a tax rate, τ, and level of the public service, G, to maximize a political support function:

$$S = \sum_{h=1}^{H} \rho_h V^h, \tag{5.34}$$

where the voters' indirect utility function V^h and the government's budget constraint are the same as in section 5.5.1. The ρ_h parameter represents the sensitivity of the probability that individual h will vote for the political party with respect to changes in his utility level, and they have been normalized so that $\sum \rho_h = 1$. These parameters can be loosely interpreted as representing voters' political influence. For example, an individual who is a "swing voter" would have a higher p value than an individual who is strongly attracted to a party's nonfiscal policies because the latter is unlikely to defect in response to an unwelcome change in the party's fiscal policy. (The p parameters might also be interpreted as the weight that is placed on the preferences of individuals who contribute time and money to the party's campaign, although such contributions are not explicitly modelled here.) The first-order conditions for the political party's optimal fiscal package can be described by the following condition:

$$\left(\frac{\mathrm{Cov}(\rho_h, MB_G^h)}{\overline{MB}_G} + \frac{1}{H}\right) \sum_{j=1}^{H} MB_G^j = \left(\frac{\mathrm{Cov}(\rho_h, Y_h)}{\overline{Y}} + \frac{1}{H}\right) MCF_\tau [MC_G - R_G], \tag{5.35}$$

where the MCF_τ is the same as in (5.32), $\mathrm{Cov}(\rho_h, MB_G^h)$ is the covariance between voters' political influence and the marginal benefit that they derive from the public service, and $\mathrm{Cov}(\rho_h, Y_h)$ is the covariance between individuals' political influence and their income. Note that if these covariance terms were zero, then (5.35) would be equivalent to the Atkinson-Stern (1974) condition for the optimal provision of a public good in the absence of distributional considerations. Note that if the rich tend to have more political influence than the poor and marginal benefits from the public service are the same for all voters, such that $\text{Cov}(\rho_h, MB_G^h) = 0$ and $\text{Cov}(\rho_h, Y_h) > 0$, then the probabilistic voting model predicts that the political party will offer a lower level of public services and lower tax rates than the median voter model with $\tilde{Y} < \overline{Y}$. (See Tridimas and Winer 2005 for a proof of this result.) Again, the important result from our perspective is that while the terms containing the covariances reflect the importance of political influence in fiscal decision making, the political equilibrium also depends on the MCF. Political parties in a jurisdiction with a higher MCF_τ will tend to offer lower public services at lower tax rates.

5.5.3 Leviathan Model

Brennan and Buchanan (1980) developed a model of self-serving government in which the party in power attempts to maximize its tax revenues. Presumably these revenues go directly into the pockets of politicians and bureaucrats or they are spent on projects that mainly benefit these groups. However, it is unlikely that even the most secure dictatorship can completely ignore the impact of its policies on its citizens. In the model that we have presented in this chapter, it is useful to think of the Leviathan as maximizing $R(\tau, G) - C(G)$ subject to the constraint that a representative taxpayer's utility exceeds some minimal level, that is, $V((1 - \tau)w, G) \geq V$. The first-order conditions for the Leviathan's problem are given below; we are assuming that the utility constraint for the representative taxpayer is binding:

$$\frac{\partial R}{\partial \tau} + v \frac{\partial V}{\partial \tau} = 0, \tag{5.36}$$

$$R_G - C_G + v \frac{\partial V}{\partial G} = 0, \tag{5.37}$$

where v is the Lagrange multiplier on the utility constraint for the representative taxpayer. From (5.37) it can be seen that $MCF_\tau = -v^{-1}$ and that the two first-order conditions can be combined to yield $MB_G = MCF_\tau[MC_G - R_G]$. This is, of course, equivalent to the Atkinson-Stern condition, but now the second equation of the model is $V((1 - \tau)w, G) = \bar{V}$. Thus even though the Leviathan is not interested in maximizing the utility of the representative taxpayer, it will determine the optimal tax rate and expenditure level using the MCF to calculate the harm done to the taxpayer in raising an additional dollar of tax revenue. Note that if the utility constraint is not binding, the Leviathan would choose the tax and expenditure levels where $\partial R/\partial \tau = 0$ and $MC_G = R_G$ (assuming R_G is positive). In this case the marginal cost of public funds would be infinite because the Leviathan would be operating at the peak of its Laffer curve. Even in this case the MCF still plays an indirect role because the shape of the Laffer curve determines how quickly the MCF increases and what the revenue maximizing tax rate is.

Obviously these three models of political economy are highly simplistic, but they do show the importance of the MCF concept for studies determining a government's fiscal policies.

5.6   Studies of the Marginal Distortionary Cost of Taxing Labor Income

For general surveys of the literature on the MCF for taxes on labor income, see Ruggeri (1999) and Creedy (2000). Table 5.3 summarizes the previous studies of the marginal distortionary cost of taxing labor income. These studies have used a variety of frameworks and concepts—marginal cost of public funds (MCF), marginal excess burden (MEB), marginal efficiency cost (MEC)—to measure the marginal distortionary costs, making it very difficult to summarize and compare their results.

Further Reading for Chapter 5

Tuomala (1990) provides an overview of the optimal income tax literature. Diamond (1998) investigated the conditions under which optimal marginal tax rates may be U shaped, and Saez (2001) developed formulas for the optimal income tax using an elasticities approach. Gruber and Saez (2000) have computed the optimal income rates for various social welfare functions using estimates of the elasticity of taxable income. Tanzi and Shome (1993) survey of the literature on tax evasion. Slemrod and Yitzhaki (1987) and Fortin and Lacroix (1994) have made contributions to economics of tax enforcement. Saez (2004) contains is a detailed investigation of the linkage between variations in taxpayers marginal tax rates and their reported incomes in the United States from 1960 to 2000.

Exercises for Chapter 5

5.1 Suppose that all of the individuals in a society have the following utility function:

$$U = C^{\alpha} \cdot (T - L)^{1-\alpha},$$

where C is consumption, T is total amount of time available, L is the number of hours worked by the individual each week, α is a positive parameter with $0 < \alpha < 1$. In the absence of taxes, the individuals' budget constraint is

Table 5.3
Studies of the marginal distortionary cost of taxes on labor income

Author	Data	Results	Comments
Ahmad and Croushore (1994)	United States, 1976	MCFs were in the range 1.121 to 1.167.	Their measure incorporated nonseparable public goods in the MCFs.
Ballard, Shoven and Whalley (1985)	United States, 1973	MEBs for labor taxes at the industry level ranged from 0.112 to 0.234, depending on labor supply and savings elasticities. The MEBs for income taxes ranged from 0.163 to 0.314.	A large scale CGE model of the US economy was used for calculations.
Baylor and Beausejour (2004)	Canada, 1996–1998	Welfare gain per dollar of reduction in the present value of payroll tax revenue was 0.15. For a personal income tax cut, it was 0.32.	A dynamic CGE model of the Canadian economy was used for calculations.
Browning (1987)	United States, 1984	MWC of between 0.318 and 0.469.	Calculations were based on an increase in a progressive income tax where $dm/dt = 1.39$.
Campbell and Bond (1997)	Australia, 1988–1989	MCFs were between 1.19 and 1.24.	Calculations were based on simulations of labor supply responses in 10 deciles.
Dahlby (1994)	Canada, 1993	The MCF for an increase in the federal personal income tax rates was 1.38. For provincial governments, the MCF ranged from 1.40 in Alberta to 1.99 in Quebec.	Biases were computed in the provincial MCFs if the provinces ignore the impact of their tax increases on federal tax revenues.
Diewert and Lawrence (1996)	New Zealand, 1971–1991	MEBs ranged from 0.053 in 1972 to 0.183 in 1991, with an average value of 0.095.	Calculations were for a proportional wage tax increase, based on an econometric model of demand and supply elasticities of seven goods including labor demand and supply.
Feldstein (1999)	United States, 1993	The MCF of 3.00 was based on an elasticity of taxable income with respect to the after tax share of 1.04.	Calculation was based on estimates of taxpayer responses to tax rate changes using the NBER's TAXSIM model.
Findlay and Jones (1982)	Australia, 1978–1979	MWCs were between 0.111 with $\eta^c = 0.10$ and 0.485 with $\eta^c = 0.40$ for a proportional tax rate change.	MWCs were between 0.298 with $\eta^c = 0.10$ and 1.596 with $\eta^c = 0.40$ for a progressive tax rate increase.
Fortin and Lacroix (1994)	Canada (Quebec only), 1985	MCFs were in the range of 1.39 to 1.53.	Calculations were based on labor supply estimates of Quebec workers in the regular and irregular sectors of the economy. Inclusion of the irregular sector added 0.02 to 0.05 to the MCFs.

Table 5.3
(continued)

Author	Data	Results	Comments
Fullerton and Henderson (1989)	United States, 1984	MEBs for a tax on labor at the industry level ranged from 0.137 to 0.258, and their base case estimate was 0.169 compared to 0.247 for a personal income tax.	MEBs for labor taxes were lower than for corporate income taxes or capital gains taxes.
Gruber and Saez (2002)	United States, 1988	The implied MCF of 1.285 was based on an elasticity of taxable income with an after-tax share of 0.40.	Calculation was based on econometric estimates of taxpayer responses to federal and state tax rate changes from 1979 to 1990. An elasticity of 0.57 was found for taxpayers with incomes over $100,000. The elasticity with respect to a state's net of tax share was 0.63.
Hansson and Stuart (1985)	Sweden, 1969	The MCF was 1.69 for their base case estimate ($\eta = 0.10$, $\theta = -0.15$). With $\eta = -0.07$ and $\theta = -0.15$, the MCF was 0.95.	Result was computed for a one percentage point increase in the marginal tax rate, at the existing 70 percent level, and a 0.77 percentage point increase in the average tax rate. The authors estimated that the peak of the Laffer curve occurred at marginal tax rate of 81 percent.
Jorgenson and Yun (1991)	United States, 1986	MEC of a labor income tax increase was 0.376 and 0.520 for an individual income tax increase.	Calculations were based on a dynamic general equilibrium model. The rankings of the labor income tax and the individual income tax were reversed in the two studies.
Jorgenson and Yun (2001)	United States, 1996	MEC of a labor income tax increase was 0.404 and 0.352 for an individual income tax increase.	
Judd (1987)	Proto-type of the US economy	MDWLs for a wage tax ranged from 0.02 to 0.50, depending on the parameters of the model, but it was usually less than 0.15.	Calculations were based on a dynamic representative agent model. MDWLs calculated along the transition path to the new steady state equilibrium. MDWLs for labor taxes where generally lower than for capital taxes.
Kleven, and Kreiner (2006)	Five EU countries, 1998	MCFs for a proportional tax rate increase were 1.26 for the UK, 1.52 for Italy, 1.72 for France, 1.85 for Germany, and 2.20 for Denmark.	Computations included a participation effect as well as the standard labor supply response of employed workers (see table 5.2 for more details).

Table 5.3
(continued)

Author	Data	Results	Comments
Poapongsakorn et al. (2000)	Thailand, 1992	MCFs ranged from 1.01 to 1.11 for a one percentage point increase the marginal tax rates in each tax bracket.	A progressive tax rate structure showed marginal tax rates ranging from zero to 0.37.
Ruggeri (1999)	Canada, 1992	MCFs for an increase in a proportional tax increase on labor income were 1.18 and 1.13 for an income tax increase.	Calculations were based on a CGE model of the Canadian economy.
Stuart (1984)	United States, 1976	The MEB was 0.072 for an equi-proportional increase in marginal and average tax rates. The marginal tax rate was 0.427 and the average tax rate was 0.273.	A simple CGE model was used for calculations. The base case calculations assumed spending on a separable public good, $\eta = 0$, $\eta^c = 0.20$, and $\theta = -0.20$.
Thirsk and Moore (1991)	Canada, 1987	MWC ranged from 0.18 for a proportional tax rate increase with a low (0.2) compensated labor supply elasticity to 0.66 for $\eta^c = 0.3$ and $dm/dt = 2.46$. For intermediate parameter values; 0.30 to 0.45.	The methodology used was similar to that of Browning (1987).

Abbreviations: MCF is marginal cost of public funds, SMCF is social marginal cost of public funds, MWC is marginal welfare cost; MDWL is marginal deadweight loss, MEC is marginal efficiency cost, MEB is marginal excess burden; CGE is computable general equilibrium model; η is uncompensated labor supply elasticity, η^c is the compensated labor supply elasticity, and θ is the income elasticity for labor supply.

$$C = wL + M,$$

where w is a fixed hourly wage rate and M is the individuals' nonlabor income which is assumed to be constant.

(a) Show that in the absence of taxation the individual's labor supply function, consumption level, and marginal utility of income, λ, are equal to the following:

$$L = \alpha T - (1 - \alpha)\frac{M}{w},$$

$$C = \alpha(wT + M),$$

$$\lambda = \alpha^\alpha(1 - \alpha)^{1-\alpha}w^{\alpha-1}.$$

(b) Suppose that the government levies a tax of τ_L on labor market earnings and τ_K on nonlabor income. Show that the MCFs for the two types of taxes are

$$MCF_{\tau_L} = \frac{\alpha \cdot (1 - \tau_L)^2 \cdot w \cdot T - (1 - \alpha) \cdot (1 - \tau_L) \cdot (1 - \tau_K) \cdot M}{\alpha \cdot (1 - \tau_L)^2 \cdot w \cdot T - (1 - \alpha) \cdot (1 - \tau_K) \cdot M},$$

$$MCF_{\tau_K} = \frac{1}{1 + [\tau_L/(1 - \tau_L)] \cdot (1 - \alpha)}.$$

(c) Explain why the MCF_{τ_K} is less than one.

(d) Explain why the MCF_{τ_L} declines as τ_K increases.

5.2 Consider the special case of exercise 5.1 where $M = 0$ and the individual only has labor income.

(a) Derive an expression for EB_{EV}, the equivalent variation-based measure of the excess burden of the tax on labor income, in terms of the parameters α, τ_L, w, and T.

(b) Derive an expression for the marginal excess burden of the tax on labor income, MEB_{EV}, using equivalent variation based measure of excess burden, in terms of the parameters of the model.

(c) Verify that the relationship between the MCF_{τ_L} and MEB_{EV} given by equation (2.32) holds.

5.3 Suppose that the individuals in society have the following utility function:

$$U = \ln C - QL,$$

where C is consumption, Q is a positive parameter, and L is the number of hours worked by the individual each week. If an individual faces the budget constraint $C = (1 - \tau)wL + M$, where w is the hourly wage rate, τ is the tax rate on wage income, and M is nonlabor income, show that his labor supply function is

$$L = \frac{1}{Q} - \frac{M}{(1 - \tau)w},$$

that his indirect utility function is

$$V = \ln\left[\frac{(1 - \tau)w}{Q}\right] + \frac{QM}{(1 - \tau)w} - 1,$$

and that his expenditure function is

$$e = \frac{\left[V - \ln\left(\frac{(1 - m)w}{\theta}\right) + 1\right](1 - m)w}{\theta}.$$

Suppose that there are two types of individuals in the economy—high-wage earners who receive a wage rate of w_H and low-wage earners who receive w_L, where

$w_H > w_L$. Let n be proportion of low-wage individual. The average wage rate is $w_{ave} = n w_L + (1 - n) w_H$. With a linear income tax system all labor income is taxed at the rate τ and all individuals receive a lump-sum transfer of M from the government. In the absence of transfers from the government, all individual only receive labor income.

(a) Show that the optimal linear income tax system *from the perspective of a low wage individual* has the following characteristics:

$$\tau = \frac{w_{ave} - w_L}{w_{ave}},$$

$$M = \frac{w_L}{Q} \left(\frac{w_{ave} - w_L}{w_{ave}} \right).$$

(b) If $n = 0.75$, $Q = 0.025$, $w_L = 10$, and $w_H = 30$, calculate the optimal tax rate, and lump-sum income transfer under the optimal linear income tax.

(c) Calculate the net tax payment $(\tau w L - M)$ for each type of individual.

5.4 Suppose the individuals in society have the same utility functions as in exercise 5.3. Type 1 individuals earn a wage equal to $w_1 = 10$ and type 2 individuals earn a wage equal to $w_2 = 30$. The value of Q is 0.025. Neither group receives nonlabor income. That is, their consumption is entirely financed by their labor income. Both groups are of equal size. For simplicity, let the total population of the society equal one. Therefore the population of each group is 0.5.

(a) Suppose that the government introduces a 20 percent proportional tax on labor income. (The government uses the revenue to finance foreign aid.) Calculate the average excess burden per dollar of tax revenue using the equivalent variation based measure of excess burden.

(b) Suppose the government replaces the 20 percent proportion wage tax with the following progressive tax structure: individuals are taxed at a 15 percent rate on the first 500 of income. On income in excess of 500, the tax rate is 32.4 percent. Show that this tax raises (approximately) the same tax revenue as the 20 percent proportional wage tax (i.e., show that the difference in the total revenue raised by the two tax systems is less than one dollar).

(c) Calculate the average tax rates paid by the two groups of individuals.

(d) Calculate the average excess burden per dollar of tax revenue using equivalent variation based measure of the excess burden.

(e) Which tax system is more distortionary, and why is it more distortionary?

(f) Derive expressions for the MCFs for the marginal tax rates in the two brackets, and calculate their MCFs.

6 Applications of the MCF from Taxing Labor Income

Three applications of the MCF concept to the taxation of labor income are considered in this chapter. Section 6.1 incorporates one of the most important labor market distortions—involuntary unemployment—in the measurement of the MCF. The Shapiro and Stiglitz (1982) efficiency wage model is used to explain the existence of involuntary unemployment. The analysis uses numerical values based on the Canadian labor market and shows that incorporating involuntary unemployment significantly increases the MCF for an employer payroll tax.

Section 6.2 uses the MCF concept to evaluate a tax enforcement program in Thailand, based on a case study by Poapangsakorn et al. (2000). Tax evasion reduces the ability of governments to raise tax revenues and may exacerbate horizontal and vertical inequities in the tax system. Devoting more resources to tax enforcement activities, such as special audits for sectors with low tax compliance rates, can boost revenue collection and is an alternative to a direct tax rate increase. The analysis shows that more resources should be devoted to tax enforcement if (and only if) the marginal social cost of raising revenue from increased tax enforcement activity, $SMCF_p$, is lower than the social marginal cost of raising revenue by increasing tax rates, $SMCF_t$. Thus a methodology is outlined for measuring the $SMCF_p$ for a tax enforcement program. The Poapangsakorn et al. study found that the $SMCF_p$ was quite high for the Thai tax enforcement program, indicating that it was a high-cost source of additional tax revenue for the government of Thailand.

Section 6.3 analyzes the optimal "flat tax," which is a tax where all earnings above a given exemption level, X, are taxed a constant marginal tax rate, m. The flat tax is a progressive tax because the average tax rate increases with the taxpayer's income if they earn more than the basic exemption level. The flat tax can be made more progressive, for a given tax yield, by increasing X and m. One reason for focusing on the flat tax is that it has received a lot of public attention in recent years because tax reformers such as Steve Forbes have advocated its adoption in the United States. Although flat tax advocates include a number of elements in their proposals, including a form of consumption tax, the basic analytics of an optimal flat tax have not been fully articulated. In this section we derive expressions for the distributionally weighted marginal cost of funds from increasing the basic exemption level, $SMCF_X$, and for an increase in the marginal tax rate, $SMCF_m$. The optimal flat tax is characterized by the condition that $SMCF_X = SMCF_m$, and this condition is used to provide some insights into the structure of an optimal flat tax. However, like most optimal income tax problems, the optimality conditions are sufficiently complex that we need to simulate the model in order to fully appreciate their implications. In this section we use the model to compute the optimal flat tax for a government that needs to raise the same revenues as a 20 percent proportional tax on earnings. Our computations indicate that the optimal exemption level would be relatively high (43 percent of earners would not pay the tax) and the optimal marginal tax rate would be over 40 percent even with relatively modest distributional objectives. It is may be that research will some day show how this approach can be generalized and used to evaluate multi-bracket optimal tax systems.

6.1   Involuntary Unemployment and the MCF for a Payroll Tax

As was argued in chapter 3, it is important to incorporate market distortions in measuring the MCFs for commodity taxes. Likewise it is important to incorporate labor market distortions in measuring the MCF for taxing labor income. A major labor market distortion is involuntary unemployment. In this section we use a simple efficiency wage model, based on Shapiro and Stiglitz (1984), to incorporate the distortion caused by unemployment in the MCF. The efficiency wage model is a good framework because it provides a relatively simple explanation for the existence of unemployment. Other explanations for unemployment—wage rigidities caused by nominal wage contracts or minimum wage laws—would likely produce expressions for the MCF that are similar to the ones derived in below.[1]

Suppose that there are N identical workers in the labor market and each worker, if employed, supplies one unit of time. The work effort that is expended by an employed worker can take on two values—0 and $e > 0$. The production function is $x = F(L)$ if the L employed workers supply e units of effort. If workers shirk and their effort level is zero, nothing can be produced. An employed worker, who does not shirk, has a utility level of $(w - e)$, where w is the worker's wage rate and e is the money measure of the disutility of effort. An employed worker who "shirks" and supplies no effort has a utility level of w.

Employers observe only imperfectly the effort that a worker applies on the job. Let $0 < \chi < 1$ be the exogenously determined probability that a shirking worker is detected and fired from his job. A fired worker joins a pool of unemployed workers and receives unemployment benefits equal to B. Let $U = N - L$ be the number of unemployed workers, and $ur = U/N$ be the unemployment rate in the economy. Each period, an exogenously determined fraction of the employed workers, l, is laid off because of firm turnover. Also each period, a fraction of the pool of unemployed workers, h, are hired by firms. An equilibrium unemployment rate implies that $hU = lL$ or $h = l(1 - ur)/ur$.

The utility level of an individual who is employed and not shirking is given by

$$pV_E^N = w - e + l(V_U - V_E^N), \tag{6.1}$$

where ρ is the individual's discount rate, and V_U is the present value of the utility of an unemployed worker. Expressed in the equation is the notion that the value of an asset (in this case a job) times the market interest rate equals the flow of income plus the expected capital gain or loss on the asset. The utility level of a "nonshirking" worker can be expressed as

$$V_E^N = \left(\frac{\rho}{\rho + l}\right)\left[\frac{w - e}{\rho}\right] + \left(\frac{l}{\rho + l}\right)V_U. \tag{6.2}$$

The first term in this expression can be thought of as the present value of the net income from employment multiplied by the fraction of time that the worker can expect to be employed, and the second term is the fraction of time that the worker will be laid off multiplied by the utility level of an unemployed worker. The utility level of an employed worker who shirks will be

$$pV_E^S = w + (l + \chi)(V_U - V_E^S), \quad \text{or}$$

$$V_E^S = \left(\frac{\rho}{\rho + l + \chi}\right)\frac{w}{\rho} + \left(\frac{l + \chi}{\rho + l + \chi}\right)V_U. \tag{6.3}$$

Finally the utility level of an unemployed worker will be

$$pV_U = B + h(V_E - V_U), \quad \text{or}$$

$$V_U = \frac{\rho}{\rho + h}\left(\frac{B}{\rho}\right) + \frac{h}{\rho + h}V_E. \tag{6.4}$$

Since nothing is produced when workers shirk, it must be the case that $V_E^N \geq V_E^S$ and that employed workers do not have the incentive to shirk. According to (6.2), (6.3), and (6.4), this nonshirk constraint (NSC) imposes the following condition on the equilibrium wage rate and unemployment rate:

$$w \geq B + e + \frac{e}{\chi}\left(\frac{l}{ur} + \rho\right). \tag{6.5}$$

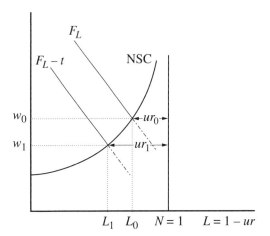

Figure 6.1
Effect of an employment tax in an efficiency wage model

The model predicts that the market wage rate will be higher when unemployment benefits, the cost of effort, the layoff rate, or the discount rate are higher. A higher detection rate or a higher unemployment rate will reduce the wage rate that employers need to offer in order to prevent shirking. In equilibrium the wage rate will satisfy the NSC and equal the value of the marginal product of labor F_L.

Figure 6.1 shows the equilibrium wage and unemployment rate if the total labor force is normalized to equal one and therefore $L = 1 - ur$. The NSC has a positive slope because as employment increases and the unemployment rate declines, the wage rate that employers have to pay in order to prevent shirking increases. The equilibrium wage rate w_0 occurs where the F_L curve intersects the NSC curve. The equilibrium unemployment rate is ur_0. In contrast with the conventional competitive labor market model, unemployment is not eliminated through a reduction in the wage rate that would increase the number of workers employed. At a lower wage rate, the opportunity cost of shirking would be too low, and all workers would shirk. Thus the model provides an explanation for the existence of involuntary unemployment that does not rely on government-imposed minimum wages or union wage determination that prevents wage rates from adjusting to eliminate unemployment.

We want to use this framework to investigate how unemployment could affect the MCF from taxing labor income. It will be assumed that a per worker payroll tax is imposed on employers, and therefore the profit-maximizing employment level is $w + t = F_L$. As shown in figure 6.1, the net marginal product of labor declines by the tax per worker, and a new equilibrium will be established with a lower wage rate and a higher unemployment rate. Part of the burden of the employer payroll tax is shifted to employed workers through a lower wage rate. Their expected utility is also reduced because of the increase in the unemployment rate, given the positive layoff rate. Taking the total differentials of the NSC and the profit-maximizing employment condition, the following comparative static results can be obtained:

$$\frac{dw}{dt} = \frac{(1 - ur)z\varepsilon_{Lw}}{(w + t) - (1 - ur)z\varepsilon_{Lw}}, \tag{6.6}$$

$$\frac{dur}{dt} = \frac{(1 - ur)\varepsilon_{Lw}}{(1 - ur)z\varepsilon_{Lw} - (w + t)}, \tag{6.7}$$

where $\varepsilon_{Lw} = (w + t)(L \cdot F_{LL})^{-1} < 0$ is the elasticity of demand for labor and $z = (e \cdot l)/(\chi \cdot ur^2)$ is the slope of the NSC. When the unemployment rate is low and the NSC is steeper, more of the tax burden is shifted to workers through lower wages. Note, however, that $-1 < dw/dt < 0$. Therefore some of the burden of the employer payroll tax is shifted to the owners of the other inputs used in production even though the total potential supply of labor is fixed.

An increase in an employer payroll tax adversely affects three groups in this economy. First, the unemployed are worse off because the unemployment rate increases, and they can expect to spend a longer time unemployed before being re-hired. Second, employed workers bear part of the burden through a lower wage rate. Third, firms receive lower after-tax profits because the wage rate does not fall by the full amount of the tax. Using the envelope theorem, we can show that the firms' burden is

$$\frac{d\Pi}{dt} = -L\left(1 + \frac{dw}{dt}\right), \tag{6.8}$$

where $\Pi = x - (w + t)L$ is the after-profit earned by firms. It will be assumed that the social welfare function that is used to evaluate the losses imposed by taxation has the following modified utilitarian form:

$$S = ur \cdot \rho \cdot V_U + (1 - ur) \cdot \rho \cdot V_E^N + \beta \cdot \Pi, \tag{6.9}$$

where β is a distributional weight that is applied to profit income. It will be assumed that $0 \leq \beta \leq 1$, perhaps because profits accrue to a small group of individuals in the economy who are relatively well off. From the equilibrium values for V_U and V_E^N in (6.2) and (6.3), this social welfare function has the following simple form:

$$S = ur \cdot B + (1 - ur) \cdot (w - e) + \beta \cdot \Pi. \tag{6.10}$$

That is, social welfare is equal to (1) the unemployment rate multiplied by the "surplus" that is received by the unemployed (for example their unemployment benefits) plus (2) the employment rate $(1 - ur)$ multiplied by the surplus that the employed receive, which is the difference between their wage rate and the cost of effort, plus (3) the distributionally weighted profit that accrues to the owners of firms.

Taking the total differential of the social welfare function in (6.10) gives the following expression for the marginal social impact of an increase in the employer payroll tax:

$$\frac{-dS}{dt} = \beta \cdot (1 - ur) + (w - (e + B)) \cdot \frac{dur}{dt} + (\beta - 1)(1 - ur) \cdot \frac{dw}{dt}. \tag{6.11}$$

This expression shows that there are three components to the social cost of an employer payroll tax increase. The first term is the distributionally weighted direct impact of the tax increase on employers, which is proportional to the level of employment. The second component is the net loss $(w - (e + B))$ that is sustained by a worker if unemployment increases due to a tax rate increase. The third component is the net social impact of the reduction in the wage rate caused by the tax increase. Note that this term vanishes, if $\beta = 1$ and profit income has the same social marginal utility as employment income, because the loss sustained by employees from a decline in the wage rate just offsets the increase in profits that arises because of the wage rate reduction.

To compute the MCF for the payroll tax increase, we need to divide (6.11) by the rate at which the government's net revenues increase when it increases its tax rate. It will be assumed that unemployment benefits are financed by the public sector and therefore

$$\frac{dR}{dt} = (1 - ur) - (t + B)\frac{dur}{dt}. \tag{6.12}$$

The first term reflects the size of the tax base while the second term reflects the reduction in net tax revenues because few workers are employed and more workers are drawing unemployment benefits. Combining (6.11) and (6.12), we obtain the following general expression for the MCF for an employer payroll tax in this efficiency wage model:

$$MCF_t = \frac{\left[\beta\left(1 + \frac{dw}{dt}\right) - \frac{dw}{dt}\right] + \delta_U \frac{w}{(1 - ur)} \frac{dur}{dt}}{1 - \left(\frac{t + B}{w}\right)\frac{w}{(1 - ur)} \frac{dur}{dt}}, \tag{6.13}$$

where $\delta_U = (w - e - B)/w$ is the labor market distortion caused by involuntary unemployment expressed as a percentage of the market wage rate. Note that this measure of the labor market distortion has the same general form as the environmental and market power distortions, δ_E and δ_M, that were discussed in chapter 3. This distortion arises from an asymmetric information problem. It is multiplied by the loss of labor income arising from the increase in unemployment caused by the tax increase. The term in square brackets in the numerator of (6.13) measures the distributionally weighted effect of the tax increase on employers and employees. In the denominator of (6.13), the rate of change in the payroll tax base per dollar is multiplied by the payroll tax rate and the unemployment benefit rate, expressed as a percentage of the market wage rate. In this model, B/w reflects the public expenditure externality, δ_G, that was discussed in section 3.4.2.

In order to calculate dw/dt and dur/dt using (6.6) and (6.7), we need to specify values for χ and e, and these parameters are not directly observable. Our strategy in selecting values for these parameters is to choose values for the other parameters of the model and then use to the model to calculate the values of χ and e that are consistent with that equilibrium. It is assumed that the production function is Cobb-Douglas with $x = (1 - ur)^\alpha$, where $0 < \alpha < 1$. The marginal product of labor is equal to $\alpha(1 - ur)^{\alpha-1}$. The wage rate, in the absence of unemployment and payroll taxes, would be α. In our calculations it will be assumed that $\alpha = 2/3$. This implies that the elasticity of demand for labor is $\varepsilon_{Lw} = -(1 - \alpha)^{-1} = -3$. The other labor market parameters were chosen to roughly approximate the Canadian labor market in the 1976 to 1991 period based on the labor market flows analyzed by Jones (1993). The average unemployment rate over this period was 8.9 percent, and the average layoff rate was 1.9 percent. It was assumed that the average tax rate was 30 percent of α and the average unemployment insurance benefit was 25 percent of α. It was also assumed that the discount rate is 0.05. Based on these parameters and values of χ from 0.10 to 0.90, the model was solved for the value of the effort parameter that would be consistent with the specified labor market equilibrium.

Table 6.1 shows that at the detection rate of 0.90 the corresponding cost of effort would have to be 57.9 percent of the wage rate to generate the observed labor market equilibrium. With these values about three-quarters of the wage tax would be borne by employees through a lower wage rate. The MCF would be 1.56 if profit income has the same distributional weight as labor income. Since the MCF in a competitive labor market with full employment and a fixed labor supply is 1.00, we can see that the distortion caused by unemployment adds 0.56 to the MCF if the detection rate is high. However, the table shows that with lower values for χ, and correspondingly lower values for the cost of effort, the MCF would be lower. With $\chi = 0.10$, unemployment adds "only" 0.25 to the MCF. So while the effect of incorporating unemployment in the calculation of the MCF is quite sensitive to the chosen values of the χ and e, it increases the measured MCF by a significant amount even when the χ is low. The reason for the decline in the MCF as the χ and e values decline is that although the distortion from unemployment, δ_U, increases, more of the tax burden is

Table 6.1
Computation of the MCF in a efficiency wage model

χ	e	δ_U	$\dfrac{w}{(1-ur)}\dfrac{dur}{dt}$	$\delta_U\dfrac{w}{(1-ur)}\dfrac{dur}{dt}$	$\dfrac{dw}{dt}$	MCF $\beta=0$	MCF $\beta=1$
0.9	0.306	0.170	0.543	0.092	−0.765	1.222	1.557
0.8	0.298	0.186	0.506	0.094	−0.781	1.213	1.517
0.7	0.288	0.206	0.468	0.096	−0.797	1.203	1.477
0.6	0.275	0.230	0.428	0.098	−0.814	1.194	1.437
0.5	0.259	0.260	0.387	0.100	−0.832	1.185	1.398
0.4	0.239	0.299	0.344	0.103	−0.851	1.176	1.360
0.3	0.211	0.352	0.299	0.105	−0.871	1.167	1.322
0.2	0.171	0.427	0.251	0.107	−0.891	1.159	1.285
0.1	0.109	0.544	0.202	0.110	−0.912	1.150	1.249

Notes: Computations based on the following parameters: $x = (1 - ur)^x$, $\alpha = 0.667$, $\varepsilon_{Lw} = -(1-\alpha)^{-1} = -3$, $ur = 0.089$, $l = 0.019$, $t = 0.3\alpha$, $B = 0.25\alpha$, and $\rho = 0.05$.

shifted to workers and therefore the tax increase has a smaller effect on the overall level of unemployment. In other words, the unemployment distortion per dollar of tax revenue is relatively constant, at around 0.10, when χ varies from 0.9 to 0.1 and the MCF declines because the loss of labor income per dollar of additional tax revenue declines.

Table 6.1 also shows the calculated values of the MCF when the distributional weight on profit is zero. These MCFs are, not surprisingly, lower because the costs of tax increases that are borne by firms are "ignored" in these calculations. These values for the MCF also declined as χ and e decline, but within a narrower range from 1.15 to 1.22.

The model indicates that it may be important to incorporate the distortion caused by unemployment in the calculation of the MCF. Although we used the framework of the Shapiro-Stiglitz model to calculate δ_U, dur/dt, and dw/dt terms, we could have used instead the results from econometric studies on the impact of payroll taxes on labor markets. This procedure could potentially narrow the range of values for the estimated MCF.

6.2 A Cost–Benefit Analysis of the Taxpayer Survey in Thailand

We now learn how the SMCF concept can be used in the evaluation of a government expenditure program, specifically a tax enforcement program in Thailand.[2] We find that the appropriate criteria for determining whether to devote more resources to tax enforcement is the Atkinson-Stern condition for the optimal provision of a publicly provided good, where the additional revenues are valued at the $SMCF_t$. We see that in evaluating a tax enforcement program, it is useful to derive the marginal cost of funds obtained through additional tax enforcement, $SMCF_p$, especially when there is some uncertainty regarding the shadow price of additional revenues for a government.

The cost–benefit analysis of the Thai taxpayer survey was conducted in 1994 at the request of the Internal Revenue Department of the Kingdom of Thailand. The goals of the taxpayer survey were to update information on existing taxpaying firms, and to contact firms that were not registered with the Internal Revenue Department, in order to get them started in paying corporate and personal income taxes and VAT. The target group was the small business sector in Thailand. Large established businesses, such as banks and hotels, and farmers were excluded. In 1993, 1,019 man-years, approximately 6.7 percent of the Internal Revenue Department's total manpower, were devoted to the survey, 377,674 firms were contacted, and 45,448 firms were added to the total number registered with the Internal Revenue Department. Given the considerable resources and the widespread feeling that a large numbers of small businesses operate outside the Thai tax system, it was natural to ask whether more resources, or fewer resources, should be devoted to the taxpayer survey.

6.2.1 A Framework for Evaluating a Tax Enforcement Program

Suppose that there are two groups of individuals in a society—the owners of small businesses who are currently evading taxes, but who can be identified through the taxpayer survey, and other individuals who are currently paying taxes. The evaders are contacted through the survey with probability p, in which case they incur some compliance costs and have to pay tax at the rate t. If they are not contacted by the survey, they do not pay tax or incur the compliance cost. The expected utility of the tax evaders will be represented as the function $W(t, p)$ which is decreasing in the tax rate, $W_t < 0$, and the probability of being contacted by the survey, $W_p < 0$. The expected utility of the individuals who are currently paying tax is represented by $V(t, p)$, where $V_t < 0$. It is assumed the existing taxpayers who are contacted by the survey also incur some compliance costs and therefore $V_p < 0$. Policy decisions are based on the social welfare function, $S(V(t, p), W(t, p))$, where $S_1 > 0$ and $S_2 \geq 0$. It is assumed that an increase in the well-being of the regular taxpayers always increases social welfare. An increase in the well-being of the tax evaders may, or may not, have a positive social value because they achieve their well-being as a result of an illegal activity—tax evasion. It is assumed that the social welfare preferences are not vindictive, meaning S_2 cannot be negative. Increasing the tax rate creates a direct social burden of $SML_t \equiv -(S_1 V_t + S_2 W_t)$ and an indirect cost through the distortion of economic decisions. Increased tax enforcement imposes an additional direct burden on tax evaders (and on some taxpayers through additional compliance costs), which has a social valuation of $SML_p \equiv -(S_1 V_p + S_2 W_p)$, and an indirect cost because more resources are diverted from productive uses.

Aggregate tax revenue, $R(t, p)$, is a function of the tax rate and the number of taxpayers. It is assumed that a higher tax rate will increase tax revenues, $R_t > 0$— the economy is not on the "wrong" side of the Laffer curve—and that an increase in the size of the survey increases the probability that a small business is contacted and contributes additional tax revenue. The size of the survey can be characterized by the probability of contacting a small business, and therefore it is assumed that $MR \equiv R_p > 0$. It is possible to increase p by devoting more resources to the survey. The total cost of the survey is $C(p)$, and the marginal cost of expanding the survey will be denoted by $MC \equiv C_p > 0$.

As in section 5.2, the social marginal cost of raising additional tax revenue through a tax rate increase is $SMCF_t = -SML_t / R_t$, while the social marginal cost of raising revenue through increased tax enforcement can be defined as

$$SMCF_p = \frac{-SML_p}{MR - MC}. \tag{6.14}$$

There is a net social gain from devoting more resources to tax enforcement if $SMCF_t > SMCF_p$. An alternative way of expressing the net social gain from a marginal expansion in tax enforcement is

$$NSG = SMCF_t \cdot (MR - MC) - SML_p > 0. \tag{6.15}$$

In other words, the net social gain (NSG) from increasing the size of the survey is equal to the increase in net revenue, $MR - MC$, valued at the social marginal cost of public funds, $SMCF_t$, minus the social marginal loss caused by increased tax enforcement, SML_p. Equation (6.15) is another way of writing the Atkinson and Stern (1974) condition for provision of a public good financed by distortionary taxation. See equation (2.18). In terms of the notation used in section 2.2, $SMB_G = -SML_p$, $R_G = MR$, and $MC_G = MC$, and the optimal level of tax enforcement would occur where $-SML_p = SMCF_t(MC - MR)$. (Note that in this case we are dealing with a "public bad," from the perspective of tax evaders, and the program generates net tax revenue if $MR > MC$, rather than utilizing revenues.) We will find it useful to use either criterion—$SMCF_t > SMCF_p$ or $NSG > 0$—in evaluating the gains from expanding the taxpayer survey.

Note that a *necessary* condition for an increase in tax enforcement activity to improve social welfare is $MR > MC$ if society places a positive value on the well-being of tax evaders, meaning S_2 is positive. If net revenue were maximized by expanding the survey until $MR = MC$, then too many resources would be devoted to the survey in the positive S_2 case. However, if the well-being of the tax evaders has no weight in social decision making ($S_2 = 0$), then more resources should be devoted to tax enforcement until the $MR = MC$ condition is satisfied.

A key component in the measurement of the $SMCF_p$ is the social cost imposed by increased tax enforcement, SML_p. To derive an expression for the SML_p, we can assume that the expected utility of tax evader i is equal to the following:

$$W^i = (1 - p)U(y_i) + pU(y_i - \tau(y_i)), \tag{6.16}$$

where $U(\cdot)$ is a von Neumann-Morganstern utility function, y_i is income if the individual is not contacted by the survey, and $\tau(y_i)$ is the tax payment and compliance cost imposed on the individual who is contacted by the survey. The private loss from increasing the probability of detection, ML_p^i, is equal to $U(y_i) - U(y_i - \tau(y_i))$ and this loss can be approximated as

$$ML_p^i \approx U'(y_i - \tau(y_i))\tau(y_i)\left[1 - \frac{1}{2}A_i\tau(y_i)\right], \tag{6.17}$$

where A_i is individual i's coefficient of absolute risk aversion, evaluated at $(y_i - \tau(y_i))$. In order for this approximation to be valid, the expression in square brackets in (6.17) must be positive and therefore the degree of risk aversion cannot be "too large" if this approximation is to be used. Note that the ML_p^i will be smaller the greater the degree of risk aversion displayed by the owner of the firm because a more risk averse individual places a lower value on the gain from tax evasion. For taxpayers, the expression for ML_p^i is equivalent to (6.17) except that the $\tau(y)$ is interpreted as compliance cost imposed on the taxpayer when contacted by the survey. The final step is to sum the marginal social losses over all the individuals who are affected by the survey, including taxpayers who incur compliance costs when they are contacted by the survey:

$$SML_p = \sum_{i=1}^{N} \beta_i \tau(y_i)\left[1 - \frac{1}{2}p\right], \tag{6.18}$$

where $\beta_i = S_j U'(y_i - \tau(y_i))$ is the distributional weight that is attached to income received by individual i, p is the partial risk aversion coefficient (the gamble multiplied by the coefficient of absolute risk aversion or $p = A\tau(y)$), and N is the total number of individuals (or businesses) subject to the survey. It is assumed that the coefficient of partial risk aversion is the same for all individuals. In general, the social marginal loss from increased tax enforcement will depend on the distributional weights applied to tax evaders and regular taxpayers, the degree of risk aversion displayed by the tax evaders and taxpayers, and their tax payments and compliance costs.

Table 6.2
Cost–benefit analysis of the Thai taxpayer survey in 1993 (in millions of Baht)

	Base case	Optimistic case	Pessimistic case
MR	582.451	917.04	349.18
MC	552.935	552.935	552.935
$MR - MC$	29.517	364.106	−203.751
$SMCF_t$[a]	1.043	1.043	1.043
Intermediate risk aversion, $\rho = 1.276$			
SML_ρ	342.337	508.471	226.512
NSG	−311.551	−128.709	−439.025
$SMCF_\rho$	11.60	1.40	na
Moderate risk aversion, $\rho = 0.564$			
SML_ρ	679.000	1,008.51	449.27
NSG	−648.214	−628.752	−661.783
$SMCF_\rho$	23.00	2.77	na

Source: Poapangsakorn et al. (2000).
a. See table 6.4. All distributional weights were set equal to 1.00.

6.2.2 Key Components of the Analysis

The MR was calculated using three alternative estimates of the present value of the tax revenues that would be obtained if the survey contacted a firm that was not currently paying taxes. One of the main issues in the measurement of these additional revenues is the "survival" rate of the small businesses. In Thailand, as in North America, the small business failure rate is high, and the majority of new small businesses fail in their first five years of operation. In table 6.2, the base case estimates are derived from the actual survival rates of firms in 1993 and 1994. (Data for earlier years were not available.) The other estimates, labeled "optimistic" and "pessimistic" in the table, were obtained from questionnaires that were sent to the Thai tax collection officials regarding the average number of years that a firm would continue to pay tax once it was contacted by the survey. Our base case estimate for MR was 582.451 million Baht (US$23.022 million at the 1994 exchange rate). In the optimistic case, the MR is 1.57 times as high as in the base case scenario, and in the pessimistic case, the MR was 59 percent of the base case MR.

It is assumed here that the cost of the survey was proportional to the size of the survey, such that $C(p) = pMC$. The MC can be interpreted as the estimated cost of contacting all firms in the target population, and this was estimated by dividing the total cost of the 1993 taxpayer survey by the estimated size of the survey. The total cost of the 1993 taxpayer survey included the salaries, fringe benefits, and lump-sum payments for the tax survey officers. (They were paid 50 Baht—or US$1.98—for contacting six firms per day.) Also included in the total cost were the implicit rental cost of equipment and land, office rental, supervision and administration, and materials and utilities. The total cost of the 1993 taxpayer survey was 144.768 million Baht (US$5.722 million), and labor costs were 76 percent of total cost. Given our assumption that the taxpayer survey was a random sample of the target group of small firms, the estimate of p for the 1993 taxpayer survey was 0.262. Assuming constant returns to scale, this implies that the MC was equal to 552.935 million Baht. The computations in table 6.2 imply that expanding the size of the taxpayer survey can generate additional net revenues under the base and optimistic cases, but that marginal costs can exceed marginal revenues in the pessimistic case.

The computation of the $SMCF_t$ was based on equation (5.18). From data on 23 groups of taxpayers who received only labor income in 1992, we have in table 6.3 the average income, average deduction, average expense allowance claimed, and average taxable income for each group. The calculations in this table indicate that the first six income groups did not earn enough to pay personal income tax, and the next five groups, earning between 64,833 Baht and 172,535 Baht, had taxable incomes that put them in the 5 percent tax rate bracket. The marginal PIT tax rates for the remaining groups were assigned in a similar fashion. The total marginal tax rate on labor income included both the MTR under the personal income tax and an implicit MTR of approximately 20 percent from the indirect taxes that are levied in Thailand. The table also shows the percentage shares of gross income for each group. In 1992, 43.32 percent of gross income was earned in the 5 percent tax bracket, 35.26 percent was earned in the 10 percent bracket, 3.47 percent was earned in the 20 percent bracket, 8.88 percent was earned in the 30 percent bracket, and 2.01 percent was earned in the 37 percent bracket.

The estimates of the labor supply elasticities were based on a study by Poapongsakorn (1979) where the compensated labor supply elasticity, η_j^c, was estimated to be 0.191 for males and 0.203 for females and the income elasticity, θ_j, was estimated to be -0.232 for males and -0.133 for females. The average of the male and female labor supply elasticities, $\eta_j^c = 0.20$ and $\theta_j = -0.18$ was used in calculated the $SMCF_t$. Note that this implies that the aggregate labor supply curve has a (slight) positive slope. We also calculated the $SMCF_t$ using $\eta_j^c = 0.30$ and $\theta_j = -0.20$ in order to compare the results with the calculations of the $SMCF_t$ in North America and other western countries.

In the absence of other information on how tax rates in Thailand would change in response to an increase in tax revenues, we decided to calculate the $SMCF_t$ for a one percentage point cut in the marginal tax rate in each personal income tax bracket. Given these assumed marginal tax rate changes, we calculated the average tax rate change for each of the income groups in table 6.3.

Table 6.3
Data used in computing the $SMCF_t$ for Thailand

Average income	Computed taxable income	MTR under the PIT	Percentage of gross income	Distributional weights $\beta_1 = 5$	$\beta_1 = 20$
6,059	0	0.00	0.02	5.000	20.000
15,354	0	0.00	0.08	4.124	13.989
25,522	0	0.00	0.21	3.711	11.495
35,793	0	0.00	0.60	3.461	10.086
45,348	0	0.00	1.57	3.294	9.210
55,054	0	0.00	4.57	3.165	8.543
64,833	1,940	0.05	4.26	3.061	8.021
74,735	5,952	0.05	4.12	2.973	7.608
85,061	9,569	0.05	3.86	2.898	7.247
94,871	14,432	0.05	3.48	2.835	6.957
121,295	25,726	0.05	16.92	2.697	6.344
172,535	61,953	0.05	10.68	2.517	5.581
242,620	128,536	0.10	13.82	2.352	4.919
378,127	260,966	0.10	14.26	2.158	4.194
598,759	478,228	0.10	7.18	1.971	3.532
859,183	732,965	0.20	3.47	1.847	3.134
1,342,858	1,209,811	0.30	5.29	1.709	2.710
2,701,893	2,555,713	0.30	3.59	1.515	2.167
4,780,061	4,625,666	0.37	1.24	1.364	1.785
6,744,516	6,579,110	0.37	0.44	1.286	1.597
8,670,407	8,487,815	0.37	0.17	1.228	1.468
11,887,231	11,745,231	0.37	0.11	1.158	1.317
25,279,333	25,104,000	0.37	0.05	1.000	1.000

Source: Poapangskorn et al. (2000).

The distributional weights were based on the following formula:

$$\frac{\beta_i}{\beta_{23}} = \left(\frac{(1 - t_{23}) y_{23}}{(1 - t_i) y_i} \right)^\xi, \tag{6.19}$$

where y_i is the average income for group i, t_i is the average tax rate, β_i is group i's distributional weight, the parameter ξ measures reflects the strength of the concern for distributional equity, and the index i is equal to 23 for the highest income class. The distributional weights were normalized so that β_{23} was always equal to one. Three sets of distributional weights were used in calculating the $SMCF_t$. The first set, with $\beta_i = 1$ for all i, indicates the private marginal cost of public funds. With the other two sets of distributional weights, β_1 was either 5 or 20. The distributional

Table 6.4
The $SMCF_t$ for the Thai income tax

	Distributional weights		
	$\beta_1 = 1$	$\beta_1 = 5$	$\beta_1 = 20$
$\eta^c = 0.20$, $\theta = -0.18$, $\eta = 0.02$	1.043	2.249	4.468
$\eta^c = 0.30$, $\theta = -0.20$, $\eta = 0.10$	1.110	2.393	4.754
Distributional weight at the 100,000 Baht annual income level	1	2.81	6.84

Source: Poapangskorn et al. (2000).

weights for the other intermediate income groups were calculated using values for ξ from the following formula:

$$\xi = \frac{\ln(\beta_1/\beta_{23})}{\ln(1 - t_{23})y_{23} - \ln(1 - t_1)y_1}.$$ (6.20)

The distributional weights at the various income levels for β_1 equal to 5 and 20 are shown in table 6.3. When all of the distributional weights are equal to 1, the $SMCF_t$ was 1.043 using the base case labor supply elasticities. Note that when the higher compensated labor supply elasticity was used, the $SMCF_t$ was only somewhat higher at 1.110. Table 6.4 also shows the calculated $SMCF_t$ with the distributional weights of $\beta_1 = 5$ and $\beta_1 = 20$.

The SML_p was calculated using the data on expected tax payments (previously discussed), compliance costs, and estimates of the degree of risk aversion. In a survey of experimental studies of risk aversion, Binswanger and Sillers (1983) concluded that farmers in developing countries display intermediate to moderate risk aversion, where risk aversion was classified as "intermediate" if the partial risk aversion coefficient was in the range 0.812 to 1.74 and "moderate" if it was in the range 0.316 to 0.812. Binswanger and Sillers noted that the behavior of between 92 and 97 percent of the Thai farmers who participated in a study of risk aversion by Grisley (1980) were in the intermediate to moderate range. We assumed that the Thai small businessmen displayed the same degree of risk aversion as farmers in Thailand and other developing countries. Two values for ρ were used in computing the SML_p—1.276, which is the midpoint of the range for intermediate risk aversion, and 0.564, which is the midpoint of the range for moderate risk aversion.

Compliance costs are imposed on tax evaders as well as on the firms that are currently paying taxes, and these costs are included in the computation of the SML_p. Based on information concerning the length of the initial interview with the owner of a firm, the time and travel costs of attending a subsequent meeting with the tax officials, and estimates of the entrepreneurs' opportunity cost of time, we calculated that the average compliance cost in 1993 was 70 Baht (US$2.77) for taxpaying firms and 262 Baht (US$10.36) for tax evading firms. Although the compliance cost imposed on the taxpaying firms was relatively low, they represent 84 percent of the firms contacted and account for 65 percent of the total compliance costs. The compliance costs for tax evaders were 7.8 percent of their expected tax payment in the base case. Total compliance cost were estimated to be 34.003 million Baht (US$1.344 million), which was about 23 percent of the total administration cost incurred the Internal Revenue Department.

The calculated SML_p with $\beta_i = 1$ are shown in table 6.2. In the base case, the SML_p was 342.337 million Baht (US$13.531 million) with intermediate risk aversion and 679 million Baht (US$26.482 million) with moderate risk aversion. Relative to the base case, the SML_p was about 50 percent higher in the optimistic case because of the higher expected tax payments by tax evaders and about 33 percent lower in the pessimistic case.

6.2.3 Net Social Gain and the SMCF for the Taxpayer Survey

Having computed $SMCF_t$, MR, MC, and SML_p, the net social gain and the social marginal cost of funds from expanding the taxpayer survey can be calculated. Table 6.2 shows that the NSG, with the $SMCF_t = 1.043$ and the $\beta_i = 1$, is negative in all six cases under consideration. These calculations indicate the taxpayer survey should not have been expanded; indeed our model implied, given our assumption of constant returns to scale, that the taxpayer survey should have been eliminated. However, these conclusions are probably not warranted on the basis of these results because the shadow price of revenue to the Kingdom of Thailand may have been significantly greater than 1.043 and the concern for distributional equity may be important in evaluating the benefits and costs of tax enforcement.

As previously noted, we did not know how the Kingdom of Thailand would use any additional tax revenue that an expansion of the taxpayer survey would generate. The shadow price of a Baht spent on some expenditure projects, such as education or health care, or the $SMCF_t$ from cutting some particularly distorting taxes, may be high enough to justify the expansion of the survey in the base or the optimistic cases. Given this ambiguity, we have calculated the $SMCF_p$ for the base and optimistic cases. If the shadow price of additional revenue to the Kingdom of Thailand exceeds these critical values, then the expansion of the taxpayer survey would be warranted. The $SMCF_p$ is 11.60 and 1.40 under these two scenarios with intermediate risk aversion and 23.00 and 2.77 with moderate risk aversion. Thus, in the base case, the shadow price of revenue to the Kingdom of Thailand must be very high in order to justify the expansion of the survey, but the $SMCF_p$ in the optimistic scenario is much lower in the intermediate risk aversion case and is similar to the figure derived by Fortin and Lacroix (1994) in their study of tax evasion in Quebec.[3] It should also be noted that as more resources are devoted to the survey, the "survival rate" of small businesses in the tax system may increase. This effect on MR has not been included in our calculations (because we were unable to measure this effect given our limited data on survival rates) and therefore the $SMCF_p$ may be underestimated.

It was assumed that the distributional weights for the owners of the small businesses in Thailand are based on the same formula, and reflected the same preference for vertical equity, as was used in determining the $SMCF_t$ from raising tax revenues from wage earners. Data from the taxpayer survey indicated that the average annual income of owners of tax paying firms was 100,000 Baht in 1993. As shown in table 6.4, when $\beta_1 = 5$ the distributional weight for the owner of a tax paying firm was 2.81, and when $\beta_1 = 20$, it was 6.84. Pro-poor distributional weights made expansion of the survey less attractive, given our assumption that the additional revenue would be used to finance an across-the-board cut in income tax rates for wage earners, because when β_1 increased from 1 to 5, the $SMCF_t$ increases by a factor of 2.16 whereas the distributional weight for small businesses increases by a factor of 2.81. Thus the use of pro-poor distributional weights increased the SML_p term more than the $SMCF_t(MR - MC)$ term, and therefore a stronger preference for vertical equity weakened the case for expanding the taxpayer survey. This result is contingent on the assumed tax cut. A more pro-poor tax cut or expenditure increase would strengthen the case for expanding the survey.

If tax policy in Thailand reflects an ethical aversion to tax evasion, then we should use a lower distributional weight in evaluating a loss sustained by a tax evader than we use in evaluating a loss sustained by a taxpaying individual. However, our analysis indicated that the ethical aversion to tax evasion must be very strong in the base case to justify an expansion of the survey.

Our overall conclusion was that the taxpayer survey likely generated additional revenues in excess of its cost, but that the losses imposed on the small business sector exceeded the social value of the marginal net revenue unless the shadow marginal cost of funds to the Thai government was very high or there was a strong ethical aversion to tax evasion. A greater concern for vertical equity diminished the attractiveness of the survey if the additional net revenue generated by the survey would have be used to finance an across-the-board cut in personal income tax rates for wage earners.

6.3   Optimal Flat Tax

Einstein is reputed to have said "Nothing is as complicated as income tax." From this remark we may speculate that Einstein tried to solve the optimal income tax problem, found it too difficult, and went back to his research on relativity. The solution to the optimal income tax developed by Mirrlees (1971) is very complicated because Mirrlees imposed very few restrictions on the structure of the income tax. Few predictions come out of the general optimal income tax model, other than that the marginal tax rate should be zero for the taxpayer with the highest wage rate and positive for other taxpayers.[4] We will focus our attention on more restricted versions of the optimal income tax problem such as Slemrod et al. (1994) who restricted the government's choices to two tax brackets and a demogrant: that is, the government's policy variables are m_1, m_2, X_1, and G, a universal lump-sum transfer. The authors investigated, using a numerical simulation model, whether the optimal m_2 was higher or lower than m_1. They found, for a wide variety of parameter values, that the optimal two bracket income tax has a lower marginal tax rate in the higher income tax bracket. However, this result might be specific to the type of utility function that they used to model individuals' labor leisure decisions. Furthermore they did not derive any analytical expressions describing the properties of the optimal two bracket income tax. Hence the relationship between the optimal income tax and the concept of the SMCF is not well articulated in the literature, except in the work of Saez (2001).

In this section we will impose even more structure on the optimal income tax problem than Slemrod et al. (1994) by focusing on the SMCF for a "flat tax," which is defined as an income tax in which the marginal income tax rate in the first tax bracket is zero and the marginal income tax rate in the second bracket is positive. The government's only policy variables are X_1, which determines the size of the first bracket, and m_2, the marginal tax rate on income in excess of X_1. We take the government's expenditures (including income transfer programs) as given. In other words, we do not include a lump-sum transfer to all individuals as policy variable of the government. Imposing this structure on the optimal income tax problem has two advantages. First, it allows us to develop tractable expressions for the SMCFs for the two policy instruments, X_1, and m_2. This should give some insights into the nature of the solution to the more general income tax design problem. Second, the optimal design of a flat tax is an interesting policy question in its own right because some economists (e.g., Hall and Rabushka 1995) have advocated the adoption of a flat tax for the United States. Since 1994 Estonia, Georgia, Latvia, Lithuania, Romania, Russia, Serbia, Slovakia, and Ukraine have adopted flat taxes with rates ranging from 12 percent to 19 percent. Belarus, Guatemala, the Kyrgyz Republic, Paraguay, and Poland have considered similar reforms (Ivanov, Keen, and Klemm 2005, p. 400). In addition the province of Alberta in Canada and several US states have adopted flat taxes.

6.3.1 Deriving the Conditions for the Optimal Flat Tax

We use the same framework as in section 5.2, except that we now assume that there is a continuous distribution of wage rates among the taxpayers. Suppose that the wage rate varies between 0 and w_{top}. Let $F(w)$ be the cumulative distribution function for wage rates, with $F(0) = 0$ and $F(w_{top}) = 1$. The density function will be denoted by $f(w)$. The total population of individuals will be normalized to equal one.

Individuals have an identical utility function $U(C, L)$, with $U_C > 0$ and $U_L < 0$. Let $Y = wL$ be the individual's income. (Nonlabor market income is assumed to be zero.) The individual's consumption opportunities are given by

$$C = Y \qquad \text{for } Y \le X_1$$
$$C = Y - m_2(Y - X_1) \quad \text{for } Y > X_1. \qquad (6.21)$$

The individual's preferences over consumption and income are determined by $U(C, Y/w)$, and the slope of an individual's indifference curves in (C, Y) space is $-(U_L/U_C)(1/w)$. This implies that individuals with higher wage rates have less steeply sloped indifference curves. Intuitively, for any (C, Y) combination, a high-wage person needs to work fewer hours to earn an additional dollar of income, and therefore he needs less additional consumption to compensate for the additional effort required to earn that additional dollar of income. We can also represent individuals' preferences using the indirect utility function $V((1 - m)w, Z)$, where m is zero if $Y \le X_1$ and $m = m_2$ if $Y > X_1$. The individual's virtual income is $Z = mX_1$, with $Z = 0$ if $Y \le X_1$ and $Z = m_2X_1$ if $Y > X_1$. The assumption of a continuous distribution of wage rates across taxpayers introduces a complication that was ignored in section 5.2 where it was assumed that all of the taxpayers in each bracket were concentrated at one income level in the interior of the tax bracket. Now we have to consider the possibility that some taxpayers will find it optimal to earn X_1 where there is a kink in the income–consumption opportunity locus. This possibility is illustrated in figure 6.2 where there is a "bunching" of individuals, with wage rates ranging from w_1 to w_2, at the kink in their consumption-income opportunity curve at X_1.[5] These wage rates are defined by the following equations:

$$w_1 = -\frac{U_L(X_1, X_1/w_1)}{U_C(X_1, X_1/w_1)}, \qquad (6.22)$$

$$w_2 = -\frac{U_L(X_1, X_1/w_2)}{U_C(X_1, X_1/w_2)} \frac{1}{(1 - m_2)}. \qquad (6.23)$$

The total number of individuals who earn exactly X_1 is $F(w_2) - F(w_1)$, and the total number of taxpaying individuals is $1 - F(w_2)$. An increase in X_1 (holding m_2 constant) will increase w_1 and w_2 because individuals with higher wage rates have less steeply sloped indifferences curves, and similarly an increase in m_2 will increase w_2.

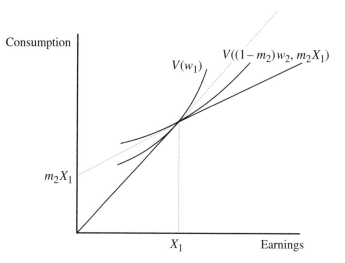

Figure 6.2
Individuals at the kink in their consumption–earnings schedule

The government's total tax revenue is equal to

$$R = \int_{w_2(m_2, X_1)}^{W_{\text{top}}} m_2(wL[(1 - m_2)w, Z] - X_1)f(w)dw,$$ (6.24)

where $L[(1 - m_2)w, Z]$ is the labor supply function of a taxpayer who receives a wage rate of w. The government can increase revenue by raising m_2 or by decreasing X_1. We begin by developing a measure of the marginal social cost of raising revenue by decreasing X_1. We then develop an expression for the SMCF of increasing m_2, noting in particular how the expression is related to the SMCF measures derived in section 5.2.

Applying Leibnitz's rule, we can write the derivative of (6.24) with respect to X_1 as

$$\frac{dR}{dX_1} = m_2 \int_{w_2}^{W_{\text{top}}} w \frac{dL}{dZ} \frac{dZ}{dX_1} f(w)dw - m_2 \int_{w_2}^{W_{\text{top}}} f(w)dw$$

$$- \frac{dw_2}{dX_1} m_2(w_2 L[(1 - m_2)w_2, Z] - X_1)f(w_2).$$ (6.25)

For taxpayers, an increase in X_1 is equivalent to a lump-sum tax cut of $m_2 dX_1$, and the first term reflects the income effect of this tax cut on the individuals' supply of labor. The second term is the decline in revenues from an increase in X_1, given the number of individuals in tax bracket two. The last term is the effect of an increase in X_1 on w_2, but this effect is zero because an individual with a wage rate of w_2 earns

X_1. We will denote the income effect for an individual earning a wage rate w by $\theta(w) = (1 - m_2)wdL/dZ$, and the effect of an increase in X_1 on revenues can be written as

$$\frac{dR}{dX_1} = -m_2[1 - F(w_2)] + m_2 \int_{w_2}^{w_{\text{top}}} \frac{m_2}{1 - m_2} \theta(w) f(w) dw. \tag{6.26}$$

The average income effect for taxpayers will be defined as

$$\bar{\theta}(w_2) = \frac{1}{1 - F(w_2)} \int_{w_2}^{w_{\text{top}}} \theta(w) f(w) dw. \tag{6.27}$$

Consequently the effect on tax revenues of an increase in X_1 can be expressed in terms of the average income effect among individuals earning more than w_2 as

$$\frac{dR}{dX_1} = -m_2[1 - F(w_2)]\left(1 - \frac{m_2}{1 - m_2} \bar{\theta}(w_2)\right). \tag{6.28}$$

As before we will use the general social welfare function $S(V(w, Z))$ to reflect a government's distributional preferences. It will be assumed that the distributional weights that are implicit in the social welfare function, $\beta(w) = S_V V_Z(w, Z)$, reflect pro-poor preferences. Otherwise, the government would want to set $X_1 < 0$ (see Zeckhauser 1971). It will be convenient to decompose social welfare as

$$S = \int_0^{w_1} S(V(w))f(w)dw + \int_{w_1}^{w_2} S\left(U\left(X_1, \frac{X_1}{w}\right)\right)f(w)dw$$

$$+ \int_{w_2}^{w_{\text{top}}} S(V((1 - m_2)w, Z))f(w)dw, \tag{6.29}$$

where the first term reflects the well-being of individuals who do not pay the tax, the second term reflects the well-being of individuals who are the kink in the income-consumption curve, and the third term reflects the well-being of taxpayers. Applying Leibnitz's rule, we can write the effect of an increase in X_1 as

$$\frac{dS}{dX_1} = \frac{dw_1}{dX_1} S_V \left[V(w_1) - U\left(X_1, \frac{X_1}{w_1}\right)\right]f(w_1)$$

$$+ \frac{dw_2}{dX_1} S_V \left[U\left(X_1, \frac{X_1}{w_1}\right) - V((1 - m_2)w_2, m_2 X_1)\right]f(w_2)$$

$$+ \int_{w_1}^{w_2} S_V \frac{dU(X_1, X_1/w)}{dX_1} f(w)dw + \int_{w_2}^{w_{\text{top}}} S_V \frac{dV((1 - m_2)w, Z)}{dX_1} f(w). \tag{6.30}$$

The first two terms in this expression are equal to zero and therefore the effect of an increase in X_1 on social welfare is measured by the third term—the effect of an increase in X_1 on the well-being of individuals at the kink—and fourth term—the effect on the tax paying individuals. For the taxpaying individuals, the marginal benefit from an increase in X_1 is simply m_2. For the individuals who are at the kink, the marginal benefit from an increase in X_1, mb_X, can be expressed as

$$\frac{dU}{dX_1} = U_C\left[1 - \frac{(-U_L/U_C)}{w}\right] = U_C mb_X(w). \tag{6.31}$$

Note that the mb_X will vary from zero, for individuals earning w_1, to m_2 for individuals earning w_2. The mb_X for individuals who earn between w_1 and w_2 is less than m_2 because these individuals are "off their labor supply curves" and consuming too much leisure. We will define the $smb_X(w_1, w_2)$ as the distributionally weight average mb_X for individuals at the kink where

$$smb_X(w_1, w_2) = \frac{1}{F(w_2) - F(w_1)} \int_{w_1}^{w_2} \beta(w) mb_X(w) f(x) dw. \tag{6.32}$$

Therefore the effect of an increase in X_1 on social welfare can be written as

$$\frac{dS}{dX_1} = smb_{X_1}[F(w_2) - F(w_1)] + \bar{\beta}(w_2)m_2[1 - F(w_2)], \tag{6.33}$$

where $\bar{\beta}(w_2)$ is the average distributional weight among individuals earning more than w_2:

$$\bar{\beta}(w_2) = \frac{1}{1 - F(w_2)} \int_{w_2}^{W_{top}} \beta(w) f(w) dw. \tag{6.34}$$

Combining (6.28) with (6.33), we obtain the following expression for the social marginal cost of raising revenue through a reduction in X_1:

$$SMCF_{X_1} = -\frac{dS/dX_1}{dR/dX_1} = \frac{smb_{X_1}[F(w_2) - F(w_1)] + \bar{\beta}(w_2)m_2[1 - F(w_2)]}{m_2[1 - F(w_2)](1 - (m_2/(1 - m_2))\bar{\theta}(w_2))}. \tag{6.35}$$

Note that the first term in the numerator of this expression is the distributionally weighted measure of the harm done to individuals who are at the kink in the income–consumption curve. The smb_{X_1} may be greater than $\bar{\beta}(w_2)m_2$ if the distributional preferences implicit in the social welfare function are sufficiently pro-poor. Therefore, even though the number of individuals who are at the kink will likely be much smaller than the number of taxpayers, this first term may be important in the measuring the $SMCF_{X_1}$ if preferences are sufficiently pro-poor. Note that in the absence of this term, the expression for the $SMCF_{X_1}$ would be very similar to the expression for the MCF for a lump-sum tax increase in the presence of a proportional wage tax that was derived in section 5.2—the only differences being the distributional weight $\bar{\beta}(w_2)$ and the definition of the income effect as $\bar{\theta}(w_2)$. Equation (6.35) indicates, not surprisingly, that the social marginal cost of raising revenue through lowering X_1 and imposing taxes on a larger percentage of the population will be lower the stronger the average income effect.

The derivation of the $SMCF_{m_2}$ proceeds in a similar fashion. First, taking the derivative of tax revenue with respect to m_2, we obtain

$$\frac{dR}{dm_2} = \int_{w_2}^{W_{\text{top}}} (wL - X_1)f(w)dw$$

$$+ \int_{w_2}^{W_{\text{top}}} m_2 w \left[\frac{dL}{d((1-m_2)w)}(-w) + \frac{dL}{dZ}X_1 \right] f(w)dw$$

$$= \bar{Y}(w_2)[1 - F(w_2)]\left(1 - \zeta - \frac{m_2}{1-m_2}[\hat{\eta}(w_2) - \zeta\bar{\theta}(w_2)] \right), \qquad (6.36)$$

where $\bar{Y}(w_2)$ is the average income of the taxpayers defined as

$$\bar{Y}(w_2) = \frac{1}{1 - F(w_2)} \int_{w_2}^{W_{\text{top}}} wL(w, Z)f(w)dw; \qquad (6.37)$$

ζ is the ratio of X_1 to $\bar{Y}(w_2)$; and $\hat{\eta}(w_2)$ is the (uncompensated) income-weighted average labor supply elasticity for taxpayers defined as

$$\hat{\eta}(w_2) = \frac{1}{1 - F(w_2)} \int_{w_2}^{W_{\text{top}}} \frac{wL}{\bar{Y}(w_2)} \eta(w)f(w)dw. \qquad (6.38)$$

Taking the derivative of the social welfare function, we obtain

$$-\frac{dS}{dm_2} = \int_{w_2}^{W_{\text{top}}} S_V \lambda(w)[wL(w, Z) - X_1]f(w)dw$$

$$= \bar{Y}(w_2)[1 - F(w_2)](\hat{\beta}(w_2) - \bar{\beta}(w_2)\zeta), \qquad (6.39)$$

where $\hat{\beta}(w_2)$ is the income-weighted average distributional weight for the taxpayers defined as

$$\hat{\beta}(w_2) = \frac{1}{1 - F(w_2)} \int_{w_2}^{W_{\text{top}}} \frac{wL}{\bar{Y}(w_2)} \beta(w)f(w)dw. \qquad (6.40)$$

Combining (6.36) with (6.39), we obtain the following expression for the $SMCF_{m_2}$:

$$SMCF_{m_2} = \frac{\hat{\beta}(w_2) - \bar{\beta}(w_2)\zeta}{1 - \zeta - (m_2/(1 - m_2))[\hat{\eta}(w_2) - \zeta\bar{\theta}(w_2)]}. \tag{6.41}$$

The roles played by each component of the SMCF can be easily identified. In the numerator, the two β reflect the social cost of the tax rate increase. The first β is an income-weighted average value because individuals with higher incomes will have higher tax increases. The second β enters the formula with a negative sign because it reflects the offsetting increase in virtual income that occurs when m_2 increases. Since the increase in virtual income is the same for each taxpayer, this β is an unweighted average. It is multiplied by ζ because the increase in virtual income is larger when X_1 is higher. In the denominator, the $(1 - \zeta)$ component reflects the proportion of income, on average, that is subject to the tax rate increase. The term in square brackets indicates the labor supply responses, where $\hat{\eta}(w_2)$ reflects the income-weighted average response to the decline in taxpayers' net wage rates. It is an income-weighted average because the labor supply changes by high-income taxpayers have a proportionately larger effect on tax revenues. The $\zeta\bar{\theta}(w_2)$ term in square brackets reflects the reduction in labor supplies because of the increase in virtual income. The reduction in labor supply will be larger when X_1 is relatively high and when the average income effect among taxpayers is relatively strong. Note that the formula in (6.41) would be equivalent to the formula for $SMCF_{m_2}$ in (5.20) if $\hat{\beta}(w_2) = \bar{\beta}(w_2)$, since $\chi_{22} = 1 - \zeta$.

The optimal flat tax can be defined as the (m_2, X_1) combination that, for a given level of tax revenue, maximizes the social welfare function. The optimal (m_2, X_1) combination will be found by equating the $SMCF_{m_2}$ in (6.41) with the $SMCF_{X_1}$ in (6.35). Note that this solution involves various parameters, such as $\hat{\eta}(w_2)$, $\bar{\theta}(w_2)$, $\hat{\beta}(w_2)$, and $\bar{\beta}(w_2)$, which are functions of w_2 and therefore functions of m_2 and X_1. So it is not possible to derive simple reduced-form equations for m_2 and X_1 for the most general case where the labor supply responses and distributional weights vary with the individuals' wage rates. However, some insights can be gleaned by equating (6.35) with (6.41), and solving for the $m_2/(1 - m_2)$ ratio:

$$\frac{m_2}{1 - m_2} = \frac{(1 - \zeta)[F(w_2) - F(w_1)]\beta_{\text{kink}} + (\bar{\beta} - \hat{\beta})(1 - F(w_2))}{[F(w_2) - F(w_1)]\beta_{\text{kink}}(\hat{\eta} - \zeta\bar{\theta}) + (1 - F(w_2))(\bar{\beta}\hat{\eta} - \hat{\beta}\bar{\theta})}, \tag{6.42}$$

where $\beta_{\text{kink}} = smb_x/m_2$, can be interpreted as the average effective distributional weight that is applied to the individuals who are at the kink in the income–consumption curve. The numerator in (6.42) can be interpreted as the marginal social gain from a lump-sum transfer financed by a marginal tax rate increase, β_{MTT}. To provide an intuitive interpretation of the denominator, we make the simplifying assumption that η and θ are constants, and using the Slutsky decomposition $\eta = \eta^c + \theta$ to eliminate η, we obtain the following:

$$\frac{m_2}{1 - m_2} = \frac{\beta_{MTT}}{\beta_{LST}\eta^c + \beta_{MTT}\theta}. \tag{6.43}$$

β_{LST} is the marginal social gain from a pure lump-sum transfer, or

$$\beta_{LST} = [F(w_2) - F(w_1)]\beta_{kink} + (1 - F(w_2))\bar{\beta}. \tag{6.44}$$

Since the left-hand side of (6.43) is increasing in m_2, we can interpret this relation as indicating that the optimal marginal tax rate will be higher when (1) the marginal social gain from a marginal tax rate financed transfer is higher relative to a pure lump-sum transfer, (2) the income effect on earnings of a lump-sum transfer is large (in absolute value), and (3) the substitution effect of a wage rate increase is low. All these factors accord well with our intuition, but unfortunately, (6.43) does not allow us to solve for m_2 because β_{MTT} and β_{LST} both depend on m_2 and X_1.

6.3.2 Computing the Optimal Flat Tax

To gain more insight into the nature of the optimal flat tax, we have used the model developed above to compute the optimal m_2 and X_1. Suppose that individuals have the following CES utility function:

$$U = [(1 - \alpha) \cdot C^{(\sigma-1)/\sigma} + \alpha \cdot (T - L)^{(\sigma-1)/\sigma}]^{\sigma/(\sigma-1)}, \tag{6.45}$$

where $T - L$ is the total amount of time available for leisure, σ is the elasticity of substitution between consumption of goods, C, and leisure, and α is a positive parameter determining strength of the preference for leisure. Following Stern (1976), we set the individual's labor supply function to be equal to

$$L = \frac{T - Z \cdot \left[\dfrac{\alpha}{(1 - \alpha) \cdot [(1 - m) \cdot w]}\right]^{\sigma}}{1 + (1 - m) \cdot w \cdot \left[\dfrac{\alpha}{(1 - \alpha) \cdot [(1 - m) \cdot w]}\right]^{\sigma}}. \tag{6.46}$$

This expression implies that the income effect for earnings will depend on the after-tax wage rate:

$$\theta = \frac{-[(1 - m) \cdot w] \cdot \left[\dfrac{\alpha}{(1 - \alpha) \cdot [(1 - m) \cdot w]}\right]^{\sigma}}{1 + (1 - m) \cdot w \cdot \left[\dfrac{\alpha}{(1 - \alpha) \cdot [(1 - m) \cdot w]}\right]^{\sigma}}. \tag{6.47}$$

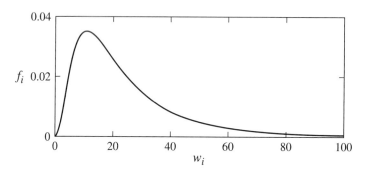

Figure 6.3
Distribution of wage rates

It also implies that the individuals at the kink in the income–consumption locus will have wage rates between

$$w_1 = \left(\frac{\alpha}{1-\alpha}\right)\left[\frac{X_1}{T-(X_1/w_1)}\right]^{1/\sigma} \tag{6.48}$$

and

$$w_2 = \left(\frac{\alpha}{1-\alpha}\right)\left\{\frac{X_1}{T-[X_1/((1-m_2)w_2)]}\right\}^{1/\sigma}\left(\frac{1}{1-m_2}\right). \tag{6.49}$$

Let us assume here that hourly wage rates follow a log normal distribution, where the mean wage rate is $\bar{w} = 20$. Therefore $\mu_w = \ln(\bar{w}) = 2.99573$. Let us also assume the standard deviation of the ln w to be $\sigma_w = 0.75$. Let us further assume the highest hourly wage rate to be 400. The corresponding distribution of wage rates across the population is shown in figure 6.3.

The preference parameters were selected based on the assumptions that an individual earning the average hourly wage rate will choose to earn \$36,000 a year in the absence of taxation, that the income effect at the average wage rate is equal to -0.15, and that $\alpha = 0.5$. These assumptions imply that $T = 2117.65$ and $\sigma = 1.579$. This elasticity of substitution is considerably higher than the elasticities that are conventionally used in the literature, so it might be expected that we would have relatively low values for the optimal marginal tax rate in our calculations. As we will see, this is not the case. The social welfare function used to calculate the distributional weights in the figure is $S = \int(1-\xi)^{-1}(V(w))^{1-\xi}f(w)dw$ (see section 2.7; Stern 1976 used this type of social welfare function to derive the optimal linear tax system). The distributional weights have been normalized so that $\beta(\bar{w}) = 1$. The optimal flat

Table 6.5
Optimal flat tax

	$\xi = 0.5$	$\xi = 1.5$
m_2	0.40958	0.5039
X_1	25,661	30,940
w_1	14.68	17.41
w_2	17.44	22.00
$\bar{Y}(w_2)$	67,089	73,799
$\zeta = X_1/\bar{Y}(w_2)$	0.38249	0.41925
$F(w_2) - F(w_1)$	0.08757	0.12388
$1 - F(w_2)$	0.57252	0.44962
smb_x	0.25563	0.29738
$\eta(w_2)$	0.34468	0.43891
$\eta(\bar{w})$	0.28854	0.50917
$\eta(2\bar{w})$	0.13502	0.19879
$\hat{\eta}(w_2)$	0.14169	0.18453
$\theta(w_2)$	−0.20585	−0.20041
$\theta(\bar{w})$	−0.19318	−0.20937
$\theta(2\bar{w})$	−0.13814	−0.15058
$\bar{\theta}(w_2)$	−0.15425	−0.15579
$\beta(w_2)$	1.0628	0.92908
$\beta(\bar{w})$	1.000	1.000
$\beta(2\bar{w})$	0.72362	0.5392
$\beta(w_{top})$	0.15953	0.01057
$\hat{\beta}(w_2)$	0.69741	0.46532
$\bar{\beta}(w_2)$	0.80432	0.59132

tax has been calculated such that it will yield the same revenue as a 20 percent proportional tax on earnings.

Table 6.5 shows the results for $\xi = 0.5$ and $\xi = 1.5$. With $\xi = 0.5$, the optimal marginal tax rate is close to 41 percent, with an exemption level of $25,661 such that only 57 percent of the population pay the tax. However, 8.8 percent of the population are at the kink in the income consumption curve. The average income of a taxpayer is $67,089. The uncompensated labor supply elasticities are positive, but decline as wage rates rise. The income-weighted average labor supply elasticity is 0.14169, which is within the usual range of values used in simulating the labor supply effects of tax policies. Similarly the income effect of a lump-sum transfer on earnings declines (in absolute value) at higher income levels with the average value for the income effect equal to −0.15425. The distributional weights that underlie these computations range from 1.0628 at the bottom of the tax bracket to 0.15953 at the highest income level. The model implies that even with "relatively moderate" distributional preferences and labor supply elasticities that are in the normal range of values used in applied tax policies studies, the marginal tax rate under the optimal flat tax will be significantly higher than the flat tax rates proposed for the US economy. In other words, the optimal flat tax may be considerably more progressive than either its critics or its proponents have supposed. Table 6.5 also shows that the optimal flat tax rate is over 50 percent if $\xi = 1.5$ such that the distributional weights range from 0.929 at the bottom of the tax bracket to 0.1057 at the top.

Of course, these computations are based on a simple model that uses a rather arbitrary distribution function for wage rates and ignores other features of taxpayer behavior, such as the ability of taxpayers, especially at high-income levels, to receive income in nontaxable, or low tax, forms such as fringe benefits. It has also ignores the potential for underreporting of earnings or tax evasion by working in the underground economy. All these factors are relevant in designing the optimal income tax. See section 5.4 on the incorporation of these widely ranging aspects of taxpayer behavior in the computation of the MCF for income taxes.

7 The MCF from Taxing the Return to Capital

In this chapter we investigate the optimal taxation treatment of the return to capital in a small open economy using the marginal cost of public funds concept. We begin with a simple two-period life cycle model to examine one of the most hotly contested tax policy issues—whether governments should levy income taxes or consumption taxes. We show how the Corlett and Hague optimal commodity tax model described in section 3.3 can provide insights into this issue. The Corlett and Hague rule—tax at a higher rate the good that is most complementary with leisure—implies that there should be a tax on the return to savings if future consumption is more complementary with leisure than current consumption. This insight, stemming from the work of Feldstein (1978) and Atkinson and Sandmo (1980), is a standard reference point in the literature. However, our model allows us to provide an alternative intuitive explanation of the optimal tax treatment of savings. By deriving formulas for the MCFs for taxes on current and future consumption, we obtain a simple expression for the optimal tax rate on the return to savings, which can be interpreted as implementing the Ramsey rule, that the compensated demands of all of the taxed commodities are reduced in the same proportion with the optimal tax system. In lowering the opportunity cost of leisure, a consumption tax will increase the ratio of future consumption to current consumption if future consumption is more complementary with leisure than current consumption. Under these conditions the return to savings should be taxed in order to offset the intertemporal consumption distortion caused by consumption taxation. On the other hand, if current consumption is more complementary with leisure than future consumption, consumption taxes will reduce the ratio of future to current consumption, and the rate of return on savings should be subsidized in order to eliminate this intertemporal consumption distortion.

Section 7.1.1 presents some numerical calculations that show how sensitive the optimal tax (or subsidy) on the return on savings is to the compensated cross-price elasticity of demand between future consumption and leisure, the elasticity of the supply of savings, and the labor supply elasticity. Overall, this type of model indicates that wage and investment income should be taxed at different rates and that neither a pure income tax nor a pure consumption is likely to be an optimal.

Nonetheless, many economists are in favor of a consumption tax system. In section 7.1.2 the procedure developed in section 2.3 is used to calculate the gain or loss in moving from a proportional income tax to an equal yield (in present value terms) consumption tax system. In keeping with the previous results, these calculations indicate that shifting to a consumption tax may entail either a large gain or a large loss depending on the value of the compensated cross-price elasticity of demand between future consumption and leisure, the elasticity of the supply of savings, and the labor supply elasticity.

Section 7.2 turns our attention from a residence-based tax on the return to savings to a source-based tax on the return to capital. The MCF framework is used to consider whether capital mobility will lead to a "race to the bottom," resulting in very low capital taxes and relatively high tax rates on the relatively immobile input, labor. First, expressions are derived for the MCFs of capital and labor taxes in a small open economy where there are pure profits because a third input (interpreted as land or natural resources) is in fixed supply. These expressions are used to derive a formula for the optimal tax rate on capital. For the special case where the government can levy a 100 percent tax on pure profits, the model yields the standard result—the optimal tax rate on capital should be zero. A zero tax rate on capital is optimal because any source-based capital tax will increase the cost of capital to the small open economy by the full amount of the tax, shifting part of the burden to labor through lower wage rates, and reducing tax revenues from pure profits. The increase in the gross return to capital means that less capital will be invested, total output will decline, and input decisions will be distorted. Since the same effective tax burden could be achieved by taxing labor, without distorting production decisions, it is more efficient to tax labor directly and to eliminate the source-based tax on capital.

However, levying a 100 percent tax rate on pure profits is not generally feasible because pure profits can be converted into other forms of income that are taxed at lower rates. When the profit tax rate is less than 100 percent, the optimal tax rate on capital should be positive, as Huizinga and Nielsen (1996) and Keen and Marchand (1997) have shown. The closed form expression for the optimal tax rate on capital derived in this section contributes to this literature, and our model shows that it depends on the own- and cross-price elasticities of demand for labor and capital, the labor supply elasticity, the tax rates on labor income and pure profits, and on distributional preferences. Indeed it shows that if the government only cares about the tax burden on labor and the production function is Cobb-Douglas, then the optimal tax rate on capital is the after-tax share of profits in total income. The model suggests that a small open economy should levy a source-based capital tax if full taxation of pure profits is not feasible, but the optimal capital tax rate tends to be quite low because pure profits are usually a relatively small component of total domestic income. The optimal capital tax rates based on this model are much lower than the actual tax rates that are observed in Canada and other OECD countries. One reason why the actual effective tax rates on capital may be higher than those predicted by this model is that the most important form of capital taxation in most countries is the corporate income tax (CIT), a form of taxation that combines a tax on pure profits with a tax on the return to shareholders' equity.

Section 7.3 focuses on the MCF for a CIT in a small open economy. One of the most important factors affecting the MCF_{CIT} is how a capital-importing country's tax system interacts with the tax regime of the capital-exporting country. An increase in a host country's CIT rate will, in general, affect the gross rate of return that capital has to earn in order to attract foreign investors. The increase in the gross rate of return will depend on the way the home country treats the taxes that are levied by the host country. In this section we analyze the MCF_{CIT} for a small capital-importing country when the home country adopts (1) a foreign tax credit system, (2) an exemption system, or (3) a deduction system. Under a foreign tax credit system, the home country provides a tax credit for foreign taxes paid on foreign source income, up to the level of the home country's tax rate. Under an exemption system, the home country does not tax income generated by its residents' foreign investments. Under a deduction system, the home country allows the deduction of the foreign income taxes paid by its residents on their foreign source income. The MCF_{CIT} for a host country can be very low under the foreign tax credit regime if its CIT rate is below the home country CIT rate because the CIT burden is effectively transferred to the home country through an increase in the foreign tax credit. If the host country rate exceeds the home country rate, a CIT rate increase raises the required before-tax rate of return on capital, and the MCF_{CIT} for the host country is the identical to that under an exemption system. If the home country adopted a deduction system, a marginal investment has to earn an after-tax rate of return equal to the gross rate of return on investment in the home country. Consequently, under a deduction system, an increase in the host country's CIT rate increase has a bigger impact on the required rate of return on capital than under the exemption system, and therefore the MCF_{CIT} is also higher.

In section 7.3.2 we use the expressions for the MCFs to calculate the optimal CIT rate and wage tax rate for a small capital-importing economy under the three international tax regimes. If the home country has a foreign tax credit system and the host country places the same distributional weight on labor income and economic profits, then its optimal corporate tax rate is the same as the home country tax rate for a wide range of parameter values; it may be higher than the home country rate if the distributional weight applied to economic profits is zero and the share of economic profits in domestic income is sufficiently high. Under the exemption system, the host country's optimal CIT rate is much lower than under the foreign tax credit system, indicating that the international taxation regime of the home country can have a dramatic effect on the tax rates of other countries. However, our calculations also indicate that if a low distributional weight is applied to profit income and if the share of profits in total income is sufficiently high, then a host country's optimal CIT rate can exceed the home country's CIT rate even if the home country adopts the exemption system. Finally, the optimal CIT rates under the deduction system are lower than under the exemption and foreign tax credit systems, but they can also exceed the home country rates if economic profits are sufficiently high and no social value is attached to profit income. Our overall conclusion is that although, in general, capital mobility puts downward pressure on CIT rates, especially if capital-exporting countries adopt the exemption or deduction system, relatively high rates could be chosen by a small capital-importing country if pure profits are a relatively large share of domestic income and low distributional weights are applied to profits.

7.1   The MCF from Taxing the Return to Savings in a Small Open Economy

We will begin by examining the taxation of the return to savings in the context of a small open economy, where the prices of all goods and services, including the before-tax rate of return on capital, are determined on world markets and are not affected by changes in output, saving, or investment in this economy. The wage rate is fixed because, as noted in chapter 4, the demand for labor will be perfectly elastic if output prices are fixed and the supply of capital to the economy is perfectly elastic. Let the before-tax rate of return on capital be r and the wage rate equal w. The government levies a residence-based tax on individuals' incomes; that is, individuals are taxed on the labor and capital income that they receive, regardless of whether it is earned in the domestic economy or abroad. Let τ_L be the ad valorem tax rate on wage income and τ_r be the ad valorem tax rate on investment income. Under a proportional income tax, $\tau_L = \tau_r$, but we will consider the general case where the two types of income may be taxed at different rates. The government also levies a destination-based consumption or sales tax at the rate τ_c. Finally, it is assumed that the government does not levy a source-based tax on the return to capital in the economy. Source-based capital taxes, such as the corporate income tax, are investigated in sections 7.2 and 7.3.

Our analysis is based on a simple life cycle model of savings. A representative individual lives for two periods, consuming C_1 units of goods and X_0 units of leisure in the first period. We will refer to C_1 as "current consumption." The total amount of time spent working is $L = T - X_0$. Total net labor income in the first period is $(1 - \tau_L)wL$. In the second period the individual consumes C_2, and all of the individual's time is devoted to leisure. (It is useful to think of the second period as the individual's retirement period.) It is assumed that the individual does not inherit any wealth, make any bequests, nor receive any transfers from the government. Therefore C_2, which we will also call "future consumption," is equal to the savings, S, from the net labor income in the first period plus the net rate of return on savings, $(1 - \tau_r)rS$. The budget constraints for the individual have the following forms:

$$S = (1 - \tau_L)wL - (1 + \tau_c)C_1, \tag{7.1}$$

$$(1 + \tau_c)C_2 = (1 + (1 - \tau_r)r)S. \tag{7.2}$$

Combining the two budget constraints by eliminating S, we obtain the individual's intertemporal budget constraint:

$$q_0 X_0 + q_1 C_1 + q_2 C_2 = q_0 T, \tag{7.3}$$

where

$$q_0 = \frac{(1 - \tau_L)w}{1 + \tau_c}, \tag{7.4}$$

$$q_1 = 1, \tag{7.5}$$

$$q_2 = \frac{1}{1 + (1 - \tau_r)r}. \tag{7.6}$$

The individual's real after-tax wage rate, q_0, can be interpreted as the opportunity cost or price of leisure. Consumption in the first period is the numéraire ($q_1 = 1$) and q_2 is the present value of a dollar received in the second period discounted at the after-tax rate of return. It can be interpreted as the price of future consumption for the individual, that is, the amount of current consumption that the individual has to sacrifice in order to obtain a dollar of consumption in the future period.

The individual's well-being is given by the intertemporal direct utility function $U = U(X_0, C_1, C_2)$ or equivalently by the indirect utility function $V = V(q_0, q_1, q_2, I)$, where $I = q_0 T$. It will be assumed that leisure, current consumption, and future consumption are all "normal goods," and therefore an increase in I, with the q_0, q_1, and q_2 held constant, will increase X_0, C_1, and C_2. The "producer" prices of leisure, current consumption, and future consumption are $p_0 = w$, $p_1 = 1$, and $p_2 = (1 + r)^{-1}$, and the tax system distorts the price of leisure and the price of future consumption, with $q_0 < p_0$ and $q_2 > p_2$. The wage and consumption taxes distort q_0, while the tax on interest income distorts q_2.

Another difference between the taxes is the timing of the tax revenues. The wage tax revenue is received in the first period, whereas revenue from the tax on interest income is received in the second period. The consumption tax revenue is spread over the two periods according to the pattern of consumption over time. It will be assumed that the government of this small open economy can borrow or lend at the before-tax rate of return, r, and that in order to finance its expenditures it has to raise a certain amount of revenue in present value terms. The present value of the government tax revenues are therefore given by

$$PVR = \tau_L wL + \tau_c C_1 + p_2 \tau_c C_2 + p_2 \tau_r rS. \tag{7.7a}$$

We will define the tax rate on savings as $\tau_s = \tau_r r p_2$. Note that $\tau_s = (q_2 - p_2)/q_2$ represents the rate of increase in the price of future consumption caused by the interest income tax. Since savings are equal to the present value of future consumption expenditure, or $S = q_2(1 + \tau_c)C_2$, the present value of the government's tax revenues can also be written as

$$PVR = \tau_L wL + \tau_c C_1 + (\tau_c + \tau_s)q_2 C_2. \tag{7.7b}$$

Finally, noting that $q_0 L = C_1 + q_2 C_2$, we can rewrite the present value of the government's tax revenues as

$$PVR = \tau_{ec} C_1 + (\tau_{ec} + \tau_s)q_2 C_2, \tag{7.7c}$$

In this expression τ_{ec} is the effective consumption tax rate from the combination of sales and wage taxes imposed by the government:

$$\tau_{ec} = \frac{\tau_c + \tau_L}{1 - \tau_L}. \tag{7.8}$$

Note that $(q_0 - p_0)/q_0 = -\tau_{ec}$, and therefore τ_{ec} represents the effective reduction in the real after-tax wage rate caused by the consumption and wage taxes.

7.1.1 Optimal Tax Rate on Savings

Equation (7.7c) indicates that the present value of the government's tax revenue from its sales, wage, and interest income taxes is equivalent to taxing first-period consumption at the rate $\tau_1 = \tau_{ec}$, and to taxing second-period consumption at the rate $\tau_2 = \tau_{ec} + \tau_s$. The advantage in writing the government's budget constraint in this way is that it allows us to apply, in a straight-forward manner, the results of the optimal tax theory from section 3.3. Recall that the Corlett and Hague model derives the optimal tax rates on two goods given that the tax rate on a third good, usually interpreted as leisure, is constrained to be zero.[1] The intertemporal consumption model outlined above is equivalent to the Corlett and Hague model, and therefore the optimal taxation of savings can be based on the Corlett and Hague rule—tax at a higher rate the commodity that is more complementary with leisure. In the context of the current model this implies that $\tau_2 \gtreqless \tau_1$ and therefore $\tau_s \gtreqless 0$ as $\varepsilon_{20}^c \lesseqgtr \varepsilon_{10}^c$, where ε_{i0}^c is the compensated elasticity of demand for consumption in period i with respect to the price of leisure, the real after-tax wage rate.

We can use equations (3.11) and (3.12), which describe the MCFs for the two taxes in the Corlett and Hague model, to derive an expression for the optimal tax rate on savings. Substituting $\tau_1 = \tau_{ec}$ and $\tau_2 = \tau_{ec} + \tau_s$ into these equations, we obtain

$$MCF_{\tau_1} = \frac{1}{P^{-1} - \tau_s\varepsilon_{11}^c - (\tau_{ec} + \tau_s)\varepsilon_{10}^c} \tag{7.9a}$$

and

$$MCF_{\tau_2} = \frac{1}{P^{-1} + \tau_s\varepsilon_{22}^c - \tau_{ec}\varepsilon_{20}^c}, \tag{7.9b}$$

where ε_{ij}^c is the compensated elasticity of demand for consumption in period i with respect to price of consumption in period j and P is a price index that converts welfare changes measured at the undistorted prices (p_0, p_1, p_2) to money measures of the welfare changes at the current tax-distorted prices (q_0, q_1, q_2). From the condition $MCF_{\tau_1} = MCF_{\tau_2}$ we derive can derive the following expression for the optimal tax rate on savings for any given effective tax rate on consumption:

$$\tau_s = \left(\frac{\varepsilon_{20}^c - \varepsilon_{10}^c}{\varepsilon_{22}^c - \varepsilon_{12}^c}\right)\tau_{ec}. \tag{7.10}$$

The condition above can be explained intuitively. Recall that the general principle of optimal commodity taxation—the Ramsey rule—indicates that the compensated demands for all taxed commodities should be reduced in the same proportion. In the current context this implies that the C_2/C_1 ratio should remain constant with the optimal values for τ_{ec} and τ_s. We can think of τ_{ec} as positive and largely determined by the size of the government's revenue requirement. The effective consumption tax rate, by lowering the real after-tax wage rate, will increase or reduce the C_2/C_1 ratio by $(\varepsilon_{20}^c - \varepsilon_{10}^c)(-\tau_{ec})$. The optimal τ_s offsets the change in the C_2/C_1 that is induced by τ_{ec}. If $\varepsilon_{20}^c > \varepsilon_{10}^c$, consumption taxation lowers q_0 and causes the C_2/C_1 ratio to fall. Therefore savings should be subsidized, $\tau_s < 0$, in order produce an offsetting increase in the C_2/C_1 ratio equal to $(\varepsilon_{22}^c - \varepsilon_{12}^c)\tau_s$.[2] This situation is shown in figure 7.1, where the two curves show the reductions in the C_2/C_1 ratio as τ_{ec} and τ_s increase. For any given effective rate of consumption taxation, such as τ_{ec}^1, there is an offsetting subsidy rate for saving τ_s^1. Figure 7.2 shows the opposite situation, where $\varepsilon_{20}^c < \varepsilon_{10}^c$. If the tax rate on consumption is τ_{ec}^1, causing the C_2/C_1 ratio to increase, savings should be taxed at the rate τ_s^1 in order to restore the C_2/C_1 value.

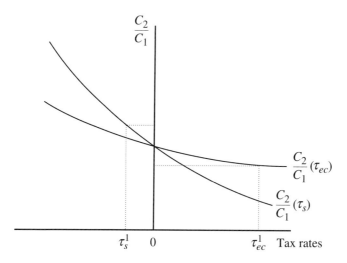

Figure 7.1
Optimal subsidy rate on savings when $\varepsilon_{20}^c > \varepsilon_{10}^c$

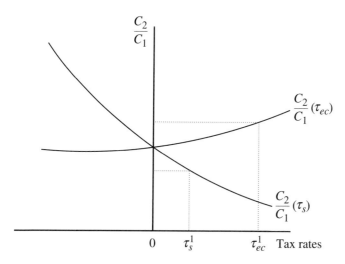

Figure 7.2
Optimal tax rate on savings when $\varepsilon_{20}^c < \varepsilon_{10}^c$

The preceding analysis has shown that whether savings should be taxed or subsidized depends on the relative magnitudes of two compensated price elasticities, ε_{20}^c and ε_{10}^c. Using the symmetry conditions ($\varepsilon_{ij}^c = (b_j/b_i)\varepsilon_{ji}^c$, where b_j is the budget share of j and the homogeneity condition ($\varepsilon_{02}^c + \varepsilon_{01}^c + \varepsilon_{00}^c = 0$), this differential can be expressed as

$$\varepsilon_{20}^c - \varepsilon_{10}^c = \frac{b_0}{b_1 b_2} [\varepsilon_{02}^c + b_2 \varepsilon_{00}^c]. \tag{7.11}$$

Since $\varepsilon_{00}^c < 0$, a sufficient condition for the optimal τ_s to be positive is $\varepsilon_{02}^c < 0$. In other words, if a reduction in the after-tax rate of return on savings increases the compensated supply of labor, then a positive tax rate should be imposed on the return on savings because this helps to correct the labor supply distortion caused by the sales and wage taxes. The optimal τ_s also depends on the labor supply and savings elasticities. The labor supply elasticity is $\eta_L = -b_0 \varepsilon_{00} + \theta_L$, where $\theta_L = q_0(dL/dI) < 0$ is the income effect on labor earnings. The elasticity of savings with respect to the real after-tax rate of return is $\eta_s = (1 + \varepsilon_{22}) = (1 + \varepsilon_{22}^c - \theta_2)$, where $\theta_2 = q_2(dC_2/dI)$ is the marginal propensity to spend on future consumption.

As Atkinson and Sandmo (1980, p. 539) pointed out over twenty-five years ago, the problem with using this model to calculate the optimal tax treatment of savings is that while we have econometric estimates of η_L and η_S, "very little is known . . . about the elasticity of labor supply with respect to the interest rate." This statement still characterizes our knowledge about labor supply responses to interest rates. We do not know whether an increase in the real after-tax rate of return on savings increases or reduces the (compensated) labor supply because empirical studies of labor supply have not included this variable in the estimated econometric equations. Given this lacunae in our knowledge about labor supply responses, we cannot use the theory to derive "precise" estimates of the optimal tax rate on savings.

Still the theory can be used to see how sensitive the optimal tax rate on savings is to the values of ε_{20}^c, η_L, and η_S and whether, over a "reasonable" range of values for these parameters, the model justifies either positive or negative tax rates on savings. To carry out these computations, we need to specify a consistent set of compensated demand elasticity parameters. In this model, there are three compensated own-price elasticities and six compensated cross-price elasticities. We can use the three homogeneity conditions and the symmetry conditions to determine six of the nine elasticities, for given values of ε_{20}^c, ε_{00}^c, and ε_{22}^c The latter two parameters can be in turn derived from values for η_L, η_S, θ_L, and θ_2.

In our base case calculations, it is assumed that $\varepsilon_{20}^c = 0$, $\eta_L = 0$, and $\eta_S = 0$. It is assumed that $\tau_L = 1/3$ which implies that $\tau_{ec} = 0.5$. The before-tax rate of return is assumed to be 3 (roughly the rate of return implied by a 7 percent annual rate of

Table 7.1
Optimal tax rate on the return to savings if $\tau_L = 0.333$

ε_{20}^c	$\eta_S = 0, \eta_L = 0$	$\eta_S = 0.2, \eta_L = 0$	$\eta_S = 0, \eta_L = 0.2$
0.50	−0.519	−0.311	−0.222
0.25	−0.130	−0.082	0.130
0.00	0.174	0.114	0.406
−0.25	0.418	0.284	0.627
−0.50	0.619	0.433	0.810

interest if the first period is thirty years long). The C_2/C_1 ratio is equal to one, and this implies that the savings rate is $b_2 = q_2 C_2/q_0 L_0 = 0.25$ and therefore $b_1 = 0.75$. As in section 4.2, leisure is assumed to represent half of the individual's lifetime resources and therefore $b_0 = q_0 X_0/(q_0 L) = 1.$[3] It was also assumed that the marginal propensity to spend on current and future consumption is the same. With $\theta_0 = -\theta_L = 0.15$, this implies that $\theta_1 = \theta_2 = 0.425$. Therefore the matrix of compensated price elasticities is

$$
\varepsilon_{ij}^c = \begin{pmatrix} -0.15 & 0.15 & 0 \\ 0.2 & -0.392 & 0.192 \\ 0 & 0.575 & -0.575 \end{pmatrix}.
$$

Table 7.1 indicates that with these baseline parameter values, the optimal tax rate on the return to savings is $\tau_r = 0.174$, roughly half the tax rate that is imposed on wage income. Savings should be taxed in the base case scenario because with $\varepsilon_{20}^c = 0$ and $\varepsilon_{10}^c = 0.20$ the wage tax causes the C_2/C_1 ratio to increase as in figure 7.2. The table also shows that the optimal tax rate on the return to savings is very sensitive to the value of ε_{20}^c. If $\varepsilon_{20}^c = 0.5$, a 50 percent subsidy on the rate of return on saving would be optimal. On the other hand, if $\varepsilon_{20}^c = -0.5$, the tax rate on the return to savings should be almost twice as high as the tax rate on the labor income. The extreme sensitivity of the optimal τ_r to values of ε_{20}^c, a parameter for which we have very little information, means that this model provides little support for either a consumption tax or a general income tax, a conclusion that Atkinson and Sandmo reached in their classic 1980 paper on the welfare effects of taxing savings. The calculations in table 7.1 also indicate that the optimal τ_r is quite sensitive to the values of the labor supply and savings elasticities. The third column in the table shows that if $\eta_S = 0.2$ both the optimal subsidy rates for $\varepsilon_{20}^c > 0$ and the optimal tax rates for $\varepsilon_{20}^c < 0$ would be significantly reduced compared to the base case calculations. On the other hand, if $\eta_L = 0.2$, the subsidy rates would be reduced and very high tax rates on the return to savings would be optimal if $\varepsilon_{20}^c < -0.25$.

7.1.2   Application: Gain from Switching to a Consumption Tax

While the preceding analysis indicates that the optimal tax treatment of the return on savings is highly uncertain, some authors have argued that the gains from moving from an income tax to a consumption tax are likely to be substantial even if the optimal tax rate on savings is not zero. Thus Feldstein (1978, p. S49) argued that "the efficiency gain from switching completely to a progressive consumption tax may ... be large even if a consumption tax is not itself the optimum optimorum." In this section we will build on the numerical computations in the preceding section by showing how the MCFs can be used to calculate the gain (or loss) from replacing an income tax with a consumption tax.

Suppose the government is initially levying a proportional income tax with $\tau_y = \tau_L = \tau_r = 1/3$, and the sales tax rate is zero. Given the parameter values used in section 7.1.1, the effective tax rates on consumption and savings in the initial situation are $\tau_{ec}^1 = 0.50$ and $\tau_s^1 = 0.25$. If there is a revenue-neutral tax reform, and the income tax is replaced by a consumption tax, then in the post–tax reform situation $\tau_s^2 = 0$ and $\tau_{ec}^2 > \tau_{ec}^1 + b_2\tau_s^1 = 0.562$. The increase in the effective tax rate on consumption that is required to replace the income tax revenues will exceed the savings rate multiplied by the tax rate on savings, $b_2\tau_s^1$, because both q_0 and q_2 will decline as τ_s is reduced and τ_{ec} increases. As a result individuals may supply less labor, which reduces the consumption tax base, and they may shift consumption to the future, which reduces the present value of the government's tax revenues. For these reasons the revenue-neutral consumption tax rate will depend on the labor supply and savings elasticities as well as their cross-price elasticities. In the computations presented below, we use these elasticities to estimate the revenue-neutral increase in τ_{ec}.

Using the framework developed in section 2.3, we can approximate the gain per dollar of tax revenue from switching from an income tax to a consumption tax by calculating the MCFs with the pre-reform and post-reform taxes by the formula

$$\Gamma = 0.5[(MCF_{\tau_s}^1 - MCF_{\tau_{ec}}^1) + P^2(MCF_{\tau_s}^2 - MCF_{\tau_{ec}}^2)]. \tag{7.12}$$

In (7.12) the MCFs for the two forms of taxation are

$$MCF_{\tau_s} = \frac{1}{1 - \tau_s(-\varepsilon_{22}^c + \theta_2) - \tau_{ec}(\varepsilon_{20}^c + \theta_L)}, \tag{7.13}$$

$$MCF_{\tau_{ec}} = \frac{1}{1 - \tau_s(b_2\varepsilon_{20}^c + \theta_2) - \tau_{ec}(\eta_L)}, \tag{7.14}$$

and P^2 is a price index that converts the money measure of the welfare change from replacing the last dollar of income tax revenue with a dollar of consumption tax

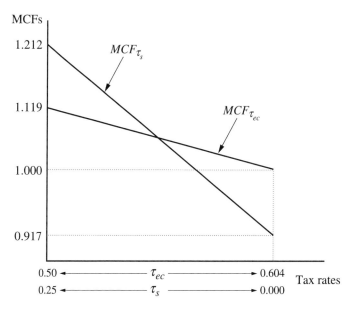

Figure 7.3
Gain from replacing an income tax with a consumption tax

revenue, measured at the post-reform prices, to a money measure of this welfare change at the pre-reform prices. As shown in section 2.5, this price index can be approximated by

$$P^2 = 1 - (b_2\rho + \theta_2)\frac{\Delta q_2}{q_2} + (\rho + \theta_L)\frac{\Delta q_0}{q_0}, \tag{7.15}$$

where p is the elasticity of the marginal utility of income. In our base case calculations, with $\varepsilon_{20}^c = 0$, $\eta_L = 0$, and $\eta_S = 0$, $MCF_{\tau_s}^1 = 1.212$ and $MCF_{\tau_{ec}}^1 = 1.119$; see figure 7.3. The $MCF_{\tau_s}^1$ exceeds $MCF_{\tau_{ec}}^1$ because in the pre-reform situation $\tau_r = 0.333$, whereas the optimal $\tau_r = 0.174$. Initially, replacing a dollar of income tax revenue with a dollar of consumption tax revenue yields a gain of $0.093. As τ_s declines and τ_{ec} increases, the MCFs for both taxes decline. The "last" dollar of income tax revenue only imposes a burden of $0.917 because taxing future consumption helps offset the increase in the C_2/C_1 ratio caused by consumption tax. (Even though $\varepsilon_{20}^c = 0$, the consumption tax increases the C_2/C_1 ratio because $\varepsilon_{10}^c > 0$, and therefore compensated demand for C_1 declines as q_0 falls.) The cost of replacing the last dollar of income tax revenue with a dollar of consumption tax revenue is 1.00 in our base case calculation because of the assumption that $\eta_L = 0$. Consequently there is a welfare loss equal to $0.083 in replacing the last dollar of income tax revenue with an additional dollar of consumption tax revenue. This welfare loss is measured at the post-

Table 7.2
Gain from replacing an income tax with a consumption tax

ε_{20}^c	$MCF_{\tau_s}^1$	$MCF_{\tau_{ec}}^1$	$MCF_{\tau_s}^2$	$MCF_{\tau_{ec}}^2$	P^2	τ_{ec}^2	G
Base case parameter values, $\eta_S = 0$ *and* $\eta_L = 0$							
0.50	1.739	1.159	1.159	1.000	1.093	0.577	0.428
0.25	1.429	1.139	1.063	1.000	1.106	0.590	0.180
0.00	1.212	1.119	0.917	1.000	1.12	0.602	+0.000
−0.25	1.053	1.100	0.801	1.00	1.134	0.62	−0.136
−0.50	0.930	1.081	0.708	1.000	1.15	0.636	−0.244
High savings elasticity case, $\eta_s = 0.20$ *and* $\eta_L = 0$							
0.50	2.000	1.159	1.255	1.000	1.097	0.56	0.560
0.25	1.600	1.139	1.063	1.000	1.110	0.594	0.266
0.00	1.333	1.119	0.916	1.000	1.124	0.609	0.060
−0.25	1.143	1.100	0.800	1.000	1.138	0.624	−0.092
−0.50	1.000	1.081	0.706	1.000	1.154	0.641	−0.210
High labor supply elasticity case, $\eta_L = 0.20$ *and* $\eta_s = 0$							
0.50	1.739	1.311	1.258	1.133	1.102	0.586	0.283
0.25	1.429	1.285	1.064	1.137	1.117	0.601	0.031
0.00	1.212	1.260	0.915	1.141	1.132	0.617	−0.152
−0.25	1.053	1.236	0.797	1.146	1.149	0.636	−0.292
−0.50	0.930	1.212	0.701	1.151	1.168	0.656	−0.403

reform prices. To make it comparable to the money measure of the welfare changes at the pre-reform prices, we have to multiply it by the price index P^2, which has a value of 1.12 if $p = -1.5$. (The value of P^2 is not very sensitive to the assumed value for p.) P^2 is greater than one because both q_0 and q_2 are lower in the post-reform situation, and therefore a dollar of "loss" represents a larger utility loss than a dollar of loss measured at the pre-reform prices.

Table 7.2 shows that there is virtually no gain from this tax reform with the base case parameter values since $\Gamma = 7.568 \times 10^{-5}$. The gain from replacing an income tax with a consumption tax is very sensitive to the value of ε_{20}^c because, as table 7.1 has indicated, the optimal tax rate on the return savings is very sensitive to the value of this parameter. Table 7.2 also shows, as might be expected, that the gains from replacing an income tax with a consumption tax are higher (or the losses are smaller) when the savings elasticity is 0.20. Conversely, the gains from replacing an income tax with a consumption tax are lower (or the losses are greater) when the labor supply elasticity is 0.20. Consequently, if the values of the parameters fall within the range of values that we have used in these calculations, there may be either large gains or large welfare losses in switching from an income tax to a consumption tax. This, of course, does not mean that income taxes are preferred to consumption taxes. Half of the optimal τ_r values in table 7.1 are less than τ_y. On the other hand, half of the optimal τ_r values exceed τ_y. Therefore this framework provides little support for either pure consumption or pure income taxation. We have to look to other models to provide clues as which type of taxation is preferred. Further discussion of these issues occurs in the Further Reading section of this chapter as well as in section 6.5 of the next chapter.

7.2 The MCF from Taxing the Return to Capital in a Small Open Economy

In the preceding section we were concerned with the MCF from a residence-based tax, and now we turn our attention to the MCF for source-based taxes, namely taxes on the return to capital that is earned in the economy whether or not the income accrues to residents. We begin by considering a basic question: What tax rate should a small open economy impose on the return to capital?

There is a well-known proposition concerning a country's optimal tax structure

Proposition 1 The government of a small open economy should not impose a source-based tax on the return to capital if it can set other taxes (e.g., destination-based consumption taxes, wage taxes, and profits taxes) at their optimal values.[4]

This proposition is based on the argument that if capital is perfectly mobile, any source-based capital tax will increase the cost of capital to the economy by the full amount of the tax. This means that the burden of source-based capital taxes will be shifted to the relatively immobile inputs—labor and resources that are in fixed supply (land)—because investors will have to be compensated for any tax that is imposed on the return to capital by the small open economy. Otherwise, they will not invest in the economy. The increase in the gross return to capital means that less capital will be invested, total output will decline, and input decisions will be distorted because there will be an increase in the cost of capital relative to prices of labor and land. Since the same effective tax burden could be achieved by directly taxing labor and land, without distorting production decisions, it is more efficient to tax labor and land and eliminate source-based taxes on capital.

This is a very strong proposition that seems to suggest that the continued existence of source-based capital taxes in many countries is a policy error. Alternatively, one might argue that the proposition is not relevant for most countries because, while capital is highly mobile, it is not perfectly mobile.[5] Still the proposition can be viewed as a prediction about the long-run trend in the tax mix as economic integration proceeds and a borderless capital market becomes a reality.

The existence of pure profits provides a reason why the governments of small open economies might levy source-based capital taxes. Proposition 1 only holds if a 100 percent tax rate is imposed on economic profits. However, there are limitations on the taxation of economic rents because these rents cannot be readily measured, and if the rate of tax on pure profits becomes too high, investors will find ways of characterizing pure profits as other forms of income that are taxed at lower rates. For example, Gordon and MacKie-Mason (1994) have argued that if the tax rate on pure profits exceeds the tax rate on wage income, recorded economic profits will quickly "disappear" because the owners of firms would pay themselves very high wages and salaries that would be taxed at the lower rates. Thus, information problems prevent governments from imposing 100 percent taxes on pure profits.

What is the implication of a government's inability to completely tax away pure profits? A second proposition addresses this question.

Proposition 2   If the government of a small open economy cannot impose a 100 percent tax on pure profits, then it should impose positive tax rates on labor income and a source-based tax on capital.[6]

This proposition explains why a small open economy should tax capital—to get at the economic rents that are otherwise incompletely taxed. The question is: Do the limitations on the taxation of pure profits justify high source-based capital taxes in small open economies?

To answer this question, the optimal tax rates on labor income and capital will be derived for a small open economy where the tax rate on pure profits is constrained to be less than 100 percent. The model is based on Keen and Marchand (1997). Output is produced using labor, L, and capital, K, according to the production function $F(L, K)$, which exhibits decreasing returns to scale because of a fixed input. The supply of labor by residents of the economy is $L(w_n)$, where w_n is the net wage rate and the labor supply elasticity is $\eta_{Lw} \geq 0$. For simplicity the tax rates imposed on labor and capital are modeled as per unit taxes, t_L and t_K respectively. Output is the numéraire. The net wage is $w_n = w - t_L$ and the gross rate of return to capital is c. In a small open economy, $dc/dt_K = 1$. Gross economic profit is equal to $\Pi = F(L, K) - wL - cK$. The ad valorem tax rate on economic profit is $0 \leq \tau_\pi \leq 1$. The total tax revenue obtained by the government is $R = t_L L + t_K K + \tau_\pi \Pi$. For simplicity it is assumed that the government does not levy a residence-based tax on the capital incomes of its residents.

Tax policy is determined according to the following social welfare function, which is based on the indirect utility functions of the residents of the economy, $S = S(w_n, \Pi_n)$, where $\Pi_n = (1 - \tau_\pi)\Pi$ and $S_{w_n} > 0$, and $S_{\Pi_n} \geq 0$ are the marginal social valuations of an increase in the after-tax wage income and net economic profit respectively. We will adopt a normalization of the social welfare function such that the distributional weight that the government applies to after-tax wage income, S_{w_n}, is equal to one. Let $\beta = S_{\pi_n}/S_{w_n}$ denote the relative social valuation of a dollar of after-tax economic profit. A society may place a lower value on a dollar of income from pure profits than on a dollar of labor income if profits accrue disproportionately to the rich or to foreigners, or if it is felt that individuals are not "entitled" to profits. Consequently it is assumed that $0 \leq \beta \leq 1$.

We now proceed to derive expressions for the marginal cost of funds derived from taxing labor and capital. The social valuation of an increase in the tax rate on labor is equal to

$$\frac{dS}{dt_L} = S_{w_n} L\left(\frac{dw}{dt_L} - 1\right) + S_{\pi_n}(1 - \tau_\pi)\frac{d\Pi}{dt_L}. \tag{7.16}$$

By the envelope theorem, $d\Pi/dt_L = -L(dw/dt_L)$. Consequently the marginal social cost of an increase in the tax rate on labor is

$$\frac{-1}{S_{w_n}}\frac{dS}{dt_L} = L\left(\left(1 - \frac{dw}{dt_L}\right) + \beta(1 - \tau_\pi)\frac{dw}{dt_L}\right), \tag{7.17}$$

where the first term in brackets is the net reduction in labor income and the second term is the social value of the reduction in after-tax profit. A competitive labor market is assumed and therefore

$$\frac{dw}{dt_L} = \frac{\eta_{Lw}}{\eta_{Lw} - (1 - \tau_L)\varepsilon_{Lw}}, \tag{7.18}$$

where τ_L is the equivalent ad valorem tax rate on labor, t_L/w, and $\varepsilon_{Lw} < 0$ is the elasticity of demand for labor.

The effect on tax revenues of an increase in the tax rate on labor is

$$\frac{dR}{dt_L} = L + t_L\frac{dL}{dw}\frac{dw}{dt_L} + t_K\frac{dK}{dw}\frac{dw}{dt_L} + \tau_\pi\frac{d\Pi}{dt_L}$$

$$= L\left(1 + \left(\tau_L\varepsilon_{Lw} + \tau_K\frac{\alpha_K}{\alpha_L}\varepsilon_{Kw} - \tau_\pi\right)\frac{dw}{dt_L}\right), \tag{7.19}$$

where τ_K is the equivalent ad valorem tax rate on capital, t_K/c, α_L is labor's share of the value of total output, α_K is capital's share of the value of total output, and ε_{Kw} is the elasticity of demand for capital with respect to the wage rate.[7]

Using (7.17), (7.18), (7.19), and the fact that $\varepsilon_{Lc} = (\alpha_K/\alpha_L)\varepsilon_{Kw}$, where ε_{Lc} is the elasticity of demand for labor with respect to the cost to capital, we can write the marginal cost of public funds from taxing labor as

$$MCF_{t_L} = \frac{(-1/S_{w_n})dS/dt_L}{dR/dt_L}$$

$$= \frac{\beta(1 - \tau_\pi)\eta_{Lw} - (1 - \tau_L)\varepsilon_{Lw}}{(1 - \tau_\pi)\eta_{Lw} - (1 - \tau_L)\varepsilon_{Lw} + \tau_L\eta_{Lw}\varepsilon_{Lw} + \tau_K\varepsilon_{Lc}\eta_{Lw}}. \tag{7.20}$$

Note that in the special case where $\tau_\pi = \tau_K = 0$ and $\beta = 1$, (7.20) is equivalent to the formula for the MCF for a tax on labor in equation (5.5).

The marginal cost of public funds from a tax on capital is derived in the same way. The effect on social welfare of an increase in the tax rate on capital is

$$\frac{dS}{dt_K} = S_{w_n} L \frac{dw}{dt_K} + S_{\pi_n} (1 - \tau_\pi) \frac{d\Pi}{dt_K} = S_{w_n} L \frac{dw}{dt_K} - S_{\pi_n} (1 - \tau_\pi) \left[K + L \frac{dw}{dt_K} \right], \qquad (7.21)$$

where the right-hand-side of (7.21) is based on the envelope theorem, $d\Pi/dt_K = -(K + Ldw/dt_K)$, and the assumption that for a small open economy $dc/dt_K = 1$. The effect of an increase in the capital tax on total tax revenues is given by

$$\frac{dR}{dt_K} = K + t_K \frac{dK}{dt_K} + t_L \frac{dL}{dt_K} + t_L \frac{dL}{dw} \frac{dw}{dt_K} + t_k \frac{dK}{dw} \frac{dw}{dt_L} + \tau_\pi \frac{d\Pi}{dt_K}$$

$$= K \left((1 - \tau_\pi) + \tau_K \varepsilon_{Kc} + \tau_L \frac{\alpha_L}{\alpha_K} \varepsilon_{Lc} + \left(\tau_L \varepsilon_{Lw} + \tau_K \frac{\alpha_K}{a_L} \varepsilon_{Kw} - \tau_\pi \right) \frac{L}{K} \frac{dw}{dt_K} \right). \qquad (7.22)$$

Let the share of the capital tax burden that is shifted to labor be

$$\Omega_{Lc} = \frac{-L}{K} \frac{dw}{dt_K} = \frac{(\alpha_L / \alpha_K) \varepsilon_{Lc}}{\varepsilon_{Lw} - \eta_{Lw}} = \frac{\varepsilon_{Kw}}{\varepsilon_{Lw} - \eta_{Lw}} > 0 \qquad (7.23)$$

and $(1 - \Omega_{Lc})$ be the share of the capital tax burden that is borne by the recipients of profits. (None of the burden is borne by the recipients of capital income because of our assumption that the supply of capital to the economy is perfectly elastic.) Note that even if the supply of labor is completely inelastic, part of the capital tax burden is borne by the recipients of profits because $0 < \Omega_{Lc} = \varepsilon_{Kw}/\varepsilon_{Lw} < 1$. Intuitively an increase in a capital tax leads to a reduction in the demand for capital and labor, and the wage rate initially declines by the full amount of the tax. However, the decline in the wage rate causes an offsetting increase in the demand for capital, thereby increasing the demand for labor, which results in an offsetting wage rate increase and a decline in economic profits. The marginal cost of public funds from taxing capital is therefore equal to

$$MCF_{t_K} = \frac{(-1/S_{wn})dS/dt_K}{dR/dt_K}$$

$$= \frac{\Omega_{Lc} + \beta(1 - \tau_\pi)(1 - \Omega_{Lc})}{1 - \tau_\pi(1 - \Omega_{Lc}) + \tau_K(\varepsilon_{Kc} - \varepsilon_{Lc}\Omega_{Lc}) + \tau_L(\varepsilon_{Kw} - \varepsilon_{Lw}\Omega_{Lc})}. \qquad (7.24)$$

The numerator shows the social cost of a capital tax rate increase and the denominator shows the increase in total tax revenues. The first term in the numerator shows the burden of the capital tax rate increase on labor, and the second term is the (distributionally weighted) burden of the capital tax that is borne by the recipients of profits. The second term in the denominator is the loss of profit tax revenues as a result of the decline in profits. The third term is the decline in capital tax revenues as a result of the decline in the demand for capital. The fourth term is the change in payroll tax revenues as a result of the change in the demand for labor. This term will be negative if the labor supply elasticity is positive.

The optimal tax rates on labor and capital are found by equating the marginal cost of public funds from the two sources of tax revenue given in (7.20a) and (7.24). The optimal tax rate on capital is given by the following expression:[8]

$$\tau_K = \frac{(1-\tau_\pi)(\varepsilon_{Kw}-\varepsilon_{Lw})[1-\beta(1-\tau_L\eta_{Lw})]}{\beta(\varepsilon_{Lc}-\varepsilon_{Kc})(1-\tau_\pi)\eta_{Lw}+\varepsilon_{Lw}\varepsilon_{Kc}-\varepsilon_{Kw}\varepsilon_{Lc}}. \tag{7.25}$$

This formula for the optimal tax rate on capital is consistent with propositions 1 and 2—the optimal tax rate on the return to capital invested in the economy is zero if the tax rate on pure profits is one, and a positive tax rate should be imposed if $0 \le \tau_\pi < 1$. Furthermore the tax rate on capital will tend to be higher when the optimal tax rate on labor is higher and when the distributional weight on profit income is lower. Note that the optimal tax rate on capital is independent of the labor supply elasticity if $\beta = 0$. Otherwise, the effect of the labor supply elasticity on the optimal τ_K is equal to

$$\frac{\partial\tau_K}{\partial\eta_{Lw}} \gtrless 0 \quad \text{as} \quad (\varepsilon_{Kw}-\varepsilon_{Lw})\tau_L \gtrless (\varepsilon_{Lc}-\varepsilon_{Kc})\tau_K. \tag{7.26}$$

This condition implies that if a change in the capital–labor ratio from the wage tax is greater than the change in the capital–labor ratio from the capital tax, an increase in the labor supply elasticity will induce greater reliance on capital taxation.

For the remainder of this section we focus on an economy with a Cobb-Douglas production function:

$$X = AL^{\alpha_L}K^{\alpha_K}, \tag{7.27}$$

where $\alpha_\pi = 1-\alpha_L-\alpha_K$ is the share of economic profit in total output, the elasticities of demand for labor and capital are equal to $\varepsilon_{Lw}=(\alpha_K-1)/\alpha_\pi$, $\varepsilon_{Lc}=-\alpha_K/\alpha_\pi$, $\varepsilon_{Kc}=(\alpha_L-1)/\alpha_\pi$, and $\varepsilon_{Kw}=-\alpha_K/\alpha_\pi$. Substituting these values for the own- and cross-price elasticities of demand for labor and capital into (7.25), we obtain the following expression for the optimal tax rate on capital:

$$\tau_K = \frac{(1-\tau_\pi)\alpha_\pi[1-\beta(1-\tau_L\eta_{Lw})]}{1+(1-\tau_\pi)\alpha_\pi\beta\eta_{Lw}}. \tag{7.28}$$

If the government only cares about the tax burden on labor ($\beta = 0$), the optimal tax rate on capital is $\tau_K = (1 - \tau_\pi)\alpha_\pi$, which is the after-tax share of profits in total income. With a Cobb-Douglas production function and $\beta > 0$, the optimal τ_K will be increasing in α_π if $\tau_L \geq \tau_K$.

The optimal tax rates on labor and capital have been calculated for an economy with a Cobb-Douglas production function where the income shares of labor and capital are 75 percent and 20 percent, respectively. This implies that pure profit represents 5 percent of total income or 20 percent of nonlabor income. The labor supply elasticity is assumed to be 0.15. The tax rates on profits and wages are constrained to be the same rate, that is $\tau_\pi = \tau_L$, and the tax system is required to generate revenues equal to 29.4 percent of total output. If profits and labor income have equal social value ($\beta = 1$), the optimal tax rates are $\tau_K = 0.00345$, and $\tau_L = \tau_\pi = 0.367$. If policy makers are only concerned about the burden on labor ($\beta = 0$), the optimal tax rates are $\tau_K = 0.065$ and $\tau_L = \tau_\pi = 0.351$. By way of comparison, McKenzie, Mansour, and Brule (1997, p. 27) calculated that the average marginal effective tax rate (METR) in Canada is in the 22 to 27 percent range. Many other countries impose similar marginal effective tax rates on capital (see Chennells and Griffith 1997). Obviously other parameter values would generate somewhat different values, but these calculations suggest that the optimal tax rates on capital income are much lower than the rates of taxation on capital that are currently imposed in Canada and other countries.

However, this model does not reflect some important aspects of the taxation of capital in small open economies. First, the corporate income tax (CIT) is the main component of the taxation of capital in most countries, and the CIT taxes both economic profits and the return on equity-financed capital. An increase in the corporate income tax rate increases both the rate of taxation of economic profit and the marginal effective tax rate on capital in the economy. The model described above does not link the rate of taxation on profits to the rate of taxation on capital, and this linkage may be important in explaining the current rate of taxation of capital. Second, the model does not incorporate the foreign tax credits systems that the United States, United Kingdom, Japan, and other countries use to reduce the "double taxation" of dividend income from foreign investments. It is often argued that the foreign tax credit system means that if the host country's CIT is fully credited by a foreign government, an increase in the CIT rate is effectively borne by the treasury of the foreign government. This means that a significant share of the CIT burden may be exported to foreigners, which greatly enhances its attractiveness. In the following section we outline a simple model of the MCF for a corporate income tax, and we use it to calculate the optimal CIT rate under alternative assumptions regarding the taxation regimes by foreign governments.

7.3   The MCF for the Corporate Income Tax in a Small Open Economy

We begin by outlining a simple model of a foreign-owned firm's cost of capital. The firm's economic profits are equal to

$$\Pi = X - wL - (r + \delta)K, \tag{7.29}$$

where r is the opportunity cost of funds invested in the firm and δ is the economic rate of depreciation. The opportunity cost of funds is $r = bi + (1 - b)\rho$, where b is the proportion of the firm's investment that is financed by debt, i is the interest rate on the firm's debt, and ρ is the required after-host-country tax rate of return on equity invested in the firm. Corporate profits differ from economic profits because the required return on equity is not deductible, and capital can be depreciated for tax purposes at the rate a that may or may not equal δ. Hence corporate profits are given by

$$\Pi_{corp} = X - wL - (bi + a)K. \tag{7.30}$$

The firm seeks to maximize the present value of its after-tax profits $(\Pi - u\Pi_{corp})/r$, where u is the statutory corporate income tax rate. The first-order conditions for the maximization of after-tax profits are

$$F_L = w,$$

$$F_K = c = \frac{(1 - u)bi + (1 - b)\rho}{1 - u} + \frac{\delta - au}{1 - u}, \tag{7.31}$$

where c is the user cost of capital.[9]

In a small open economy, the rate of return on equity and debt are determined on world capital markets. The return on equity has to compensate investors in a capital-exporting country for the source-based CIT levied by the host country, plus any additional tax levied by the investor's home country. Let u_h be the tax rate in the home country and ρ_h be the gross rate of return on an investment in the home country. A capital market equilibrium requires that the after-tax return on an investment in the home country, $(1 - u_h)\rho_h$, equals the after-tax return on an investment in the host country, ρ.

7.3.1   The MCF for the CIT under Alternative Foreign Income Tax Systems

In this section we analyze the MCF_{CIT} for a small capital-importing country when the home country adopts (1) a foreign tax credit system, (2) the exemption system, and (3) the deduction system. Table 7.3 shows the required after-host-country tax rate of return for three alternative foreign tax regimes under the assumption that the

Table 7.3
Required rate of return under alternative tax regimes

Foreign tax credit system	
Capital market equilibrium condition	$(1 - u_h)\rho_h = \rho - u_h \dfrac{\rho}{1-u} + Iu \dfrac{\rho}{1-u} + (1-I)u_h \dfrac{\rho}{1-u}$
	$I = 1$ if $u \le u_h$ (excess limit case) or
	$I = 0$ if $u > u_h$ (excess tax credit case)
	$\rho = \dfrac{(1-u)(1-u_h)\rho_h}{1 - Iu_h - (1-I)u}$
User cost of capital	$c = bi + \dfrac{(1-b)(1-u_h)\rho_h}{1 - Iu_h - (1-I)u} + \dfrac{\delta - au}{1-u}$
	$\dfrac{dc}{du} \equiv \dfrac{dt_K}{du} \equiv \phi = \dfrac{(1-b)(1-u_h)(1-I)\rho_h}{(1 - Iu_h - (1-I)u)^2} + \dfrac{\delta - a}{(1-u)^2}$
Exemption system	
Capital market equilibrium condition	$(1 - u_h)\rho_h = \rho$
User cost of capital	$c = bi + \dfrac{(1-b)(1-u_h)\rho_h}{1-u} + \dfrac{\delta - au}{1-u}$
	$\dfrac{dc}{du} \equiv \dfrac{dt_K}{du} \equiv \phi = \dfrac{(1-b)(1-u_h)\rho_h}{(1-u)^2} + \dfrac{\delta - a}{(1-u)^2}$
Deduction system	
Capital market equilibrium condition	$(1 - u_h)\rho_h = \rho - u_h\left(\dfrac{\rho}{1-u} - u\dfrac{\rho}{1-u}\right)$
	$\rho_h = \rho$
User cost of capital	$c = bi + \dfrac{(1-b)\rho_h}{1-u} + \dfrac{\delta - au}{1-u}$
	$\dfrac{dc}{du} \equiv \dfrac{dt_K}{du} \equiv \phi = \dfrac{(1-b)\rho_h}{(1-u)^2} + \dfrac{\delta - a}{(1-u)^2}$

foreign earnings are taxed on an accrual basis. Later in this section we will consider the implications of the deferral of the tax on earnings until dividend payments are made to the home country's shareholders.

The Foreign Tax Credit System
Under a foreign tax credit system the home country imposes a tax on the gross return on the investment in the host country, $\rho/(1-u)$ and provides a tax credit for the foreign taxes paid up to the maximum tax that would apply in the home country. If $u \le u_h$, the firm is in an "excess limit" position (the indicator variable I equals 1) and $\rho/(1-u)$ is equal to ρ_h. In other words, in the excess limit case the before-tax rate of return in the host country has to equal the before-tax rate of return in the home country because domestic and foreign investments are effectively taxed at the home country tax rate u_h. In the "excess credit" case where $u > u_h$ and $I = 0$, the foreign tax credit only covers the home country's tax, and therefore $\rho = (1-u_h)\rho_h$. In other words, in the excess credit case the after-host-country tax rate has to equal the post-tax rate of return on equity in the home country, and therefore the pre-tax rate

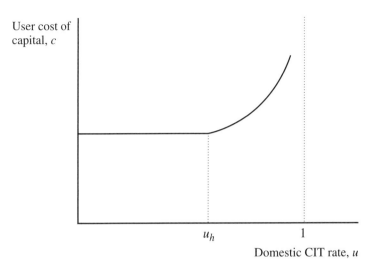

Figure 7.4
The CIT rate and the user cost of capital with a foreign tax credit

of return on investment in the host country, $\rho/(1-u)$, is equal to $(1-u_h)\rho_h/(1-u)$, which exceeds ρ_h.

The host country user cost of capital, c, and the rate of increase in the user cost of capital with respect to u are also shown in table 7.3. If the firm is in an excess limit position $(I = 1)$, then the user cost of capital is independent of the host country's CIT rate if $a = \delta$. If the government of the host country sets its CIT rate above u_h and the firm is in an excess credit position $(I = 0)$, foreign investors will require a higher rate of return and the cost of capital in the host country will increase. The relationship between the host country's CIT rate and the user cost of capital is illustrated in figure 7.4 for the case where the capital cost allowance equals the true economic rate of depreciation. If the capital cost allowance is less than the economic rate of depreciation, then the user cost of capital will also increase as the CIT rate increases below u_h, but there will be a "kink" in the cost of capital schedule at u_h when the maximum foreign tax credit is reached. This kink in the cost of capital schedule means that there will be a vertical discontinuity or "jump" in the MCF for the CIT when the CIT rate equals u_h.

We now derive the host country's MCF for the CIT under the foreign tax credit system. Tax policy is based on the social welfare function $S(w_n, \Pi_n)$, where Π_n is after-tax economic profits $(1-u)(X - wL - cK)$. The direct effect of an increase in the corporate tax rate on social welfare is

$$\frac{dS}{du} = S_{w_n} L \frac{dw}{dt_K} \phi + S_{\pi_n} \frac{d\Pi_n}{du} = -S_{w_n} \Omega_{LC} \phi K - S_{\pi_n} [\Pi + (1-u)(1 - \Omega_{LC})\phi K]. \quad (7.32)$$

Total tax revenues are equal to

$$R = t_L L + u \Pi_{corp}. \tag{7.33}$$

The effect of an increase in the corporate tax rate on tax revenues is equal to

$$\frac{dR}{du} = t_L \left(\frac{dL}{dw} \frac{dw}{dt_K} + \frac{dL}{dc} \right) \phi + \Pi_{corp} + u \frac{d\Pi_{corp}}{du}. \tag{7.34}$$

It can be shown that

$$\frac{d\Pi_{corp}}{du} = \left[\left(\frac{(1-b)\rho + \delta - a}{1-u} \right) \left(\frac{dK}{dc} + \frac{dK}{dw} \frac{dw}{dt_K} \right) - L \frac{dw}{dt_K} \right] \phi, \tag{7.35}$$

where $\phi = dc/du$. If we define the effective tax rate on capital under the CIT as

$$\tau_K = u \left(\frac{c - (bi + a)}{c} \right), \tag{7.36}$$

then the effect of an increase in the CIT rate on total tax revenues can be expressed as the following:

$$\frac{dR}{du} = \Pi_{corp} + [u\Omega_{Lc} + \tau_K(\varepsilon_{Kc} - \varepsilon_{Lc}\Omega_{Lc}) + \tau_L(\varepsilon_{Kw} - \varepsilon_{Lw}\Omega_{Lc})]\phi K. \tag{7.37}$$

Consequently the marginal cost of public funds from increasing the corporate income tax rate is equal to

$$MCF_u = \frac{(-1/S_{w_n})dS/du}{dR/du}$$

$$= \frac{\Omega_{Lc}\phi K + \beta[\Pi + (1-u)(1-\Omega_{Lc})\phi K]}{\Pi_{corp} + [u\Omega_{Lc} + \tau_K(\varepsilon_{Kc} - \varepsilon_{Lc}\Omega_{Lc}) + \tau_L(\varepsilon_{Kw} - \varepsilon_{Lw}\Omega_{Lc})]\phi K}. \tag{7.38}$$

As in all formulas for the marginal cost of public funds, the numerator reflects the (distributionally weighted) burden of a tax rate increase, and the denominator reflects the rate of increase in total tax revenues from a tax rate increase. Note that $\Omega_{Lc}\phi K$ is the reduction in labor income that arises from a CIT rate increase, and therefore the first term in the numerator is the burden that falls on labor. The second term is the distributionally weighted burden of an increase in the CIT rate that falls on the recipients of pure profits. (The first term in square brackets is the direct effect of a CIT rate increase on after-tax profits, and the second term is the net reduction in after-tax economic profits resulting from the increase in the cost of capital that is not offset by a reduction in wage payments.) The first term in the denominator is the increase in tax revenues, given the corporate tax base. The terms in the square brackets are the change in tax revenues that occur as a result of the increase in the cost of capital. The first term in square brackets is the increase in corporate tax revenues as a result of the reduction in wage payments. The second term is the reduction in corporate tax revenues as a result of the reduction in the capital stock and the third term is the change in payroll taxes as a result of the reduction in employment.

The general formula for the MCF_u is rather complex, but some insights can be gained from considering the case where $u < u_h$ and the user cost of capital is independent of the host country's CIT rate, that is $\phi = dc/du = 0$. If all economic profits accrue to domestic residents and if $\beta = 1$, the MCF_u is equal to

$$MCF_u = \frac{\Pi}{\Pi_{\text{corp}}}, \tag{7.39}$$

or the ratio of pure profit to corporate profit. Since corporate profits include the return on shareholders' equity, corporate profits exceed pure profit and therefore the MCF_u is less than one.[10] The underlying reason why the MCF_u is less than one is that the CIT burden on the return to shareholders' equity is exported to foreign governments when $u < u_h$. The ratio, Π/Π_{corp} is the fraction of the tax burden that is not exported. The notion that the MCF_u can be less than one because part of the tax burden is borne by foreign governments' treasuries is not new. The Carter Commission, which proposed tax reform in Canada in the 1960s, justified the retention of the corporate income tax on the basis of the tax exporting through the foreign tax credit. More recently Thirsk (1986) and Damus, Hobson, and Thirsk (1991) used a computable general equilibrium model for the Canadian economy to show that the marginal excess burden from the CIT might be relatively low due to tax exporting.[11]

With a CIT, the formula for the $MCF_{\tau L}$ is the same as in (7.20), except with u substituted for τ_π. The MCFs for the CIT and the payroll tax are shown in figure 7.5 using parameter values that have been chosen to roughly reflect the tax rates in the nonmanufacturing sector of the Canadian economy in the late 1990s. In particular, the parameters reflect an average METR of 22.8 percent when the average statutory tax rate is 44.3 percent. It has been assumed that the average capital cost allowance rate is 8 percent, which is less than the economic depreciation rate of 10 percent in order to illustrate the effect of this additional distortion. (This assumption might be rationalized by noting that capital cost allowances are not indexed and therefore decline in value with the rate of inflation.) The simulation model implies that the elasticity of demand for capital with respect to the CIT rate ($u = 0.433$) is -0.67, which is very close to the estimated elasticity of foreign direct investment (FDI) with respect to the host country tax rates in a number of econometric studies (see Hines 1999). Economic profits are 2.5 percent of total income and represent one-third of total corporate profits. The ad valorem payroll tax rate is 35 percent and the

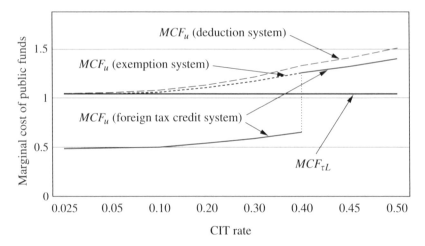

Figure 7.5
Marginal cost of public funds for a CIT and a payroll tax

capital-exporting country's tax rate, u_h, is 0.40. As expected, the MCF_u is less than one when $u < u_h$. When u hits u_h, an increase in the host country's CIT rate pushes the user cost of capital up at a faster rate because the marginal tax rate increases are no longer credited against foreign taxes, and the MCF_u jumps from 0.654 to 1.259. When the u increases to 50 percent, the MCF_u has increased to 1.399. Note that the $MCF_{\tau L}$ for $\tau_L = 0.35$ increases only slightly as u increases and is equal to 1.040 for $0.025 < u < 0.5$. (Both the MCF_u and the $MCF_{\tau L}$ are smaller than in some other studies because this model does not take into account all of the distortions created by these taxes.) These calculations suggest that there is a wide range of tax rates on labor such that the optimal corporate income tax rate is equal to the capital exporting country's tax rate, u_h. The model does not imply that the optimal CIT rate is always equal to u_h, but u_h is the optimal CIT rate for a wide range of parameter values because it maximizes tax exporting with a minimal distortion to the allocation of resources in the economy.

The Exemption System
If the home country adopts the exemption system (also known as the territorial system), it does not impose any tax on (active business) income from foreign investments. Therefore the after-host-country tax rate of return must equal the after-home-country tax rate of return, $\rho = (1 - u_h)\rho_h$, and the user cost of capital has the same form as in the excess foreign tax credit case. Under the exemption system an increase in the host country's CIT rate always increases the user cost of capital. Figure 7.5 shows the MCF_u for a small open economy if the capital exporting country adopts

the exemption system. It exceeds the MCF_u under the foreign tax credit system for $u \leq u_h$ and coincides with it for $u_h \leq u$.

The Deduction System

Under the deduction system the capital market equilibrium condition implies that $\rho = \rho_h$ (see table 7.3). In other words, an investment in the host country must earn an after-host-country tax rate of return equal to the before-tax rate of return on investments in the home country. The user cost of capital is higher under the deduction system than under the exemption and foreign tax credit systems. The rate of increase in the user cost of capital, ϕ, is also higher. Figure 7.5 shows that the MCF_u is higher deduction system than under the exemption system.

The foreign tax credit model outlined above assumed that foreign earnings were taxed on an accrual basis. However, under the foreign tax credit systems used by Japan, the United States, and the United Kingdom, the active business income of a foreign subsidiary is only taxed when a dividend payment is made to the parent corporation in the home country. Consequently a multinational can defer or postpone the residual home country tax liability that arises when the host country's tax rate is less than the home country rate by retaining the profits in the foreign subsidiary. Hartman (1985) and Leechor and Mintz (1993) have shown that the deferral system implies that the residual home country tax is an "unavoidable fixed cost" for a firm with a mature subsidiary that can finance its investments out of retained earnings. Consequently the home country tax rate should not affect the investment decisions made by mature subsidiaries, and the capital market equilibrium condition under the deferral system is the same as under the exemption system. Therefore the deferral system effectively converts the foreign tax credit system, or the deduction system, into an exemption system. With deferral, the subsidiary's cost of capital will be an increasing function of the host country's tax rate under the foreign tax credit system, even if its tax rate is less than the home country rate. A higher host country CIT rate will therefore tend to discourage investment.

For an "immature" foreign subsidiary, which requires equity investments from the parent, the home country tax rate will affect the required return on the investment and the capital market equilibrium condition is given by $(1 - u_h)\rho_h = (1 - Iu_h - (1 - I)u)\rho$, where I is now interpreted as the projected dividend payout rate for the subsidiary. Therefore an increase in the home country rate will affect an immature foreign subsidiary's cost of capital and its level of investment.

Another aspect of international taxation that is neglected in this model is the provision for worldwide averaging of foreign taxes under US tax law. In calculating its foreign tax credits, a US multinational is able to use the low tax burdens in some countries to offset its excess tax credits on investments in other high tax countries (with some restrictions on averaging across different types of income). By averaging taxes from high and low tax sources, a multinational can avoid being in an excess tax credit position, such that its foreign tax credits exceed its overall US tax liability.[12] Therefore it is possible that an increase in the CIT rate in a low tax country may push up the MNE's overall tax rate and therefore may not be fully credited at the margin. In that case an increase in the host country's CIT rate increases its user cost of capital, even though its rate is below the US rate. Indeed, Gordon (2000, p. 30) has concluded "it does not appear that the use of tax credits can explain the survival of taxes on capital income, given that profits from foreign subsidiaries are taxed only at repatriation and with world-wide averaging."

The extent to which deferral and worldwide averaging have effectively converted the US credit system into an exemption system is basically an empirical question. Slemrod (1990) analyzed FDI in the United States from countries using the exemption system and the foreign tax credit system over the period 1962 to 1987, and concluded that FDI from exemption countries was not more sensitive to US tax rate changes than FDI from the countries providing foreign tax credits. Auerbach and Hassett (1993) also found no difference in the tax responsiveness of FDI in the United States from countries using the exemption or the foreign tax credit systems. However, Hines (1996) found that FDI from countries with exemption systems was much more sensitive to the state CIT rates than FDI from countries with foreign tax credit systems. He found that a 1 percent increase in a state's tax rate reduced the share of manufacturing capital by exemption countries from 9 to 11 percent compared to foreign tax credit counties and that foreign investors from exemption countries were much more likely to invest in states with zero CIT rates than were the investors from the foreign tax credit countries. Finally, Shah and Slemrod (1991) examined the FDI flows into Mexico over the period 1965 to 1987 and tested whether a measure of US multinationals' foreign tax credit status affected FDI from the United States to Mexico. They found that in the deficit tax credit case the US tax rate, not the Mexican tax rate, affected FDI to Mexico. However, in general, both the United States and the Mexican tax rates affected FDI to Mexico. Finally, a recent study by Desai, Foley, and Hines (2001) has found that the dividend payout rate of the foreign subsidiaries of US corporations is inversely related to the residual US tax on dividends, with an estimated elasticity of -1.0. Their results seem to be inconsistent with Hartman's prediction that a mature subsidiary's dividends should be independent of the home country tax rate.

Overall, the empirical results indicate that neither view of the foreign tax system— as a de facto exemption system because of deferral and worldwide averaging or as a pure foreign tax credit system—provides an adequate description of the impact of a host country's CIT tax rates on foreign direct investment, and therefore the cost of capital will be affected by both the host and home country tax rates.

Table 7.4
Optimal host-country tax rates

		Case 1: $\alpha_K = 0.125$, $\alpha_\pi = 0.025$		Case 2: $\alpha_K = 0.135$, $\alpha_\pi = 0.015$		Case 3: $\alpha_K = 0.100$, $\alpha_\pi = 0.050$	
		$\beta = 0$	$\beta = 1$	$\beta = 0$	$\beta = 1$	$\beta = 0$	$\beta = 1$
Foreign tax credit	τ_L	0.350	0.353	0.353	0.353	0.333	0.353
	u	0.436	0.400	0.400	0.400	0.593	0.400
	τ_K	0.215	0.190	0.190	0.190	0.340	0.190
Exemption	τ_L	0.350	0.378	0.357	0.376	0.333	0.381
	u	0.436	0.050	0.336	0.029	0.593	0.111
	τ_K	0.215	0.018	0.151	0.010	0.340	0.042
Deduction	τ_L	0.361	0.388	0.369	0.386	0.344	0.391
	u	0.377	0.035	0.277	0.020	0.545	0.080
	τ_K	0.211	0.016	0.144	0.009	0.346	0.037

Notes: Computations based on $u_h = 0.40$, $p_h = 0.10$, $\alpha_L = 0.85$, $b = 0.35$, $\delta = 0.10$, $a = 0.08$, $i = 0.08$, and $\eta_{Lw} = 0.10$.

7.3.2 Application: The Optimal CIT and Wage Tax Rates

Table 7.4 shows the optimal CIT and payroll tax rates for various values of α_K, α_π, and β under the three international tax regimes. The computations indicate that if the society places an equal value on labor income and economic profits, then the optimal corporate tax rate is 0.40, the assumed value of the home country tax rate, for a wide range of values for α_K and α_π, and the implied optimal effective tax rate on capital is 0.190. The optimal corporate tax rate exceeds 0.40 if the distributional weight is applied to economic profits is zero, and the share of economic profits in domestic income is sufficiently high.

Table 7.4 also shows the host country's optimal CIT and payroll tax rates if the home country adopts the exemption system. If equal distributional weights apply to labor income and economic profits, then the optimal CIT rates are much lower under the exemption system than under the foreign tax credit system. For example, in case 1 the optimal CIT rate would decline from 40 to 5 percent and the optimal effective tax rate on capital would decline from 19 to 1.8 percent if the home country switched from a foreign tax credit system to an exemption system. Thus the international taxation regime of the home country can have a dramatic effect on the optimal CIT rate of a small open economy.[13] However, the model also indicates that if very low distributional weights are attached to profit income and if the share of profits in total income is sufficiently high (as in cases 1 and 3), then the optimal CIT rate for a small open economy can exceed the home country's CIT rate even if the home country adopts the exemption system.

Finally, table 7.4 shows that the optimal CIT rates are lower under the deduction system than under the exemption and foreign tax credit systems. In case 1 the optimal CIT rate is only 3.5 percent and the optimal effective tax rate on capital is only 1.6 percent if $\beta = 1$. However, the computations also suggest that a CIT rate of over 50 percent is optimal, given u_h is 40 percent, even under the deduction system if economic profits are sufficiently high and no social value is attached to profit income.

7.4 Studies of the Marginal Distortionary Cost from Taxing the Return to Capital

There have been a number of studies of the distortionary effects of taxes on the return to capital. See Baylor (2006) for a survey of the literature on the distortionary effects of taxes in dynamic models. Table 7.5 summarizes some of the key results of the key studies, but the warnings issued in previous chapters about the lack of comparability of the results apply here as well. The authors of these studies have used different measures of the marginal distortionary cost of taxing capital, using different frameworks, and therefore it is not possible to compare the magnitudes of their results.

Further Reading for Chapter 7

Bernheim (2002) and Auerbach and Hines (2002) examine the optimal taxation of the return to savings, drawing on the principles of optimal commodity taxation. Judd (1999) and others have pointed out that a constant tax rate on the return to savings implies that the implicit tax rate on future consumption increases over time. For example, if the annual rate of interest is 5.0 percent and the tax rate on the return to savings is 40 percent, then there is an implicit tax rate of 1.9 percent on consumption one year from today, 9.2 percent on consumption five years from today, and 17.5 percent on consumption ten years from today. The implicit tax rate approaches 100 percent over an infinite time horizon. It is unlikely that a tax rate pattern such as this would be optimal even in a model that requires positive tax rates on future consumption. Furthermore, since the excess burden of taxation increases with the square of the tax rate, the deadweight loss caused by even small taxes on the return to savings becomes very large over time. Therefore many models indicate that the optimal tax rate on the return to savings should decline over time and approach zero in the long-run. However, as Auerbach and Hines (2001, p. 81) point out:

The time-varying nature of optimal capital taxation makes such a policy time-inconsistent, in that whatever profile of future taxes that is optimal as of year t would not be optimal as of year $t + 1$, and optimizing governments might therefore be tempted not to follow through on previously announced tax plans. Private agents, anticipating such behavior by governments, could not then be expected to respond to announced tax plans in the same way that they would if the government could commit reliably to the taxes that it announces.

Table 7.5
Studies of the marginal distortionary cost of taxes on the return to capital

Author	Data	Results	Comments
Ballard, Shoven and Whalley (1985)	United States, 1973	MEBs for capital taxes at the industry level ranged from 0.181 to 0.463 depending on labor supply and savings elasticities.	A large scale CGE model of the US economy was used for calculations.
Baylor and Beausejour (2004)	Canada, 1996–1998	Welfare gains per dollar of reduction in the present value government tax revenues were corporate income tax, 0.37; sales taxes on capital goods, 1.29; personal capital income, 1.30; capital cost allowances on new capital, 1.35.	A dynamic CGE model of the Canadian economy was used for calculations.
Diewert and Lawrence (1998)	Australia, 1966–1967 to 1993–1994	MEBs for a tax on the return to capital rose from 0.21 in 1967, when the tax rate on capital was 0.29, to 0.48 in 1993, when the tax rate on capital was 0.43.	Calculations were based on an econometric model with 12 goods including labor and four types of capital.
Diewert and Lawrence (2000)	Canada, 1974–1998	MEB for an increase in the business tax rate varied from 0.467 in 1974 to 0.018 in 1986, with an average value of 0.093. The average MEB was 0.135 for a property tax and −0.63 for a sales tax on machinery and equipment.	Calculations were based on an econometric model with 8 goods including labor and three types of reproducible capital.
Fullerton and Henderson (1989)	United States, 1984	MEBs were 0.310 for a corporate income tax, 0.202 for a capital gains tax, 0.036 for a dividend tax, and 0.028 for interest income taxation.	Computations were based on a model with 38 types of capital employed in three sectors: corporate, noncorporate, and housing. In contrast to Judd (1987), they found that reducing ITCs was the most efficiency-enhancing tax policy change. Lowering the ITCs reduced the dispersion in tax rates among assets leading to an improvement in the allocation of capital.
Jorgenson and Yun (1991)	United States, 1986	MECs of a corporate tax were 0.448 and 1.1017 for an individual capital income tax.	Calculations were based on a dynamic general equilibrium model. There were substantial reductions in the calculated MEC of capital taxes between the 1991 study and the 2001 study. Labor income taxes had a lower MEC than capital taxes in 1991, but not in 2001.
Jorgenson and Yun (2001)	United States, 1996	MECs of a corporate tax were 0.279 and 0.257 for an individual capital income tax.	

Table 7.5
(continued)

Author	Data	Results	Comments
Judd (1987)	Proto-type of the US economy	MDWLs for a tax on the return to capital ranged from 0.15 to 1.31, depending on the parameters of the model, but it was usually more than 0.40.	Calculations were based on a dynamic representative agent model. MDWLs calculated along the transition path to the new steady state equilibrium. There would be efficiency gains from reducing capital income taxation and imposing higher labor taxation and more investment subsidies.

Abbreviations: MDWL is marginal deadweight loss, MEC is marginal efficiency cost, MEB is marginal excess burden, CGE is computable general equilibrium model, and ITC is investment tax credit.

Thus the problem of time inconsistency thwarts the implementation of optimal taxes on the return to savings.

There is a large literature attempting to measure the gains from moving from an income tax to a consumption tax in the context of a closed economy, specifically the US economy. Summers (1981) claimed that there would be very large gains from a switch to a consumption tax, but his model assumed that labor supply was fixed and therefore a consumption tax is equivalent to a lump-sum tax in his model, whereas the income tax distorted intertemporal consumption decisions. In addition he only considered the welfare gains by future generations in the new long-run equilibrium, and therefore his measure ignored the welfare losses of generations that are alive at the time the switch to a consumption tax occurs. Older workers at the time of the tax reform would lose in switching to a consumption tax because an increase in a consumption tax is equivalent to a lump-sum tax on assets that they have accumulated to finance their consumption in retirement. Auerbach and Kotlikoff (1987) addressed these problems with the Summers model by using an overlapping generations model where taxes distort both labor supply and savings decisions. They also properly accounted for the intergenerational effects of a switch to a consumption tax. They found that there were net social gains, but much smaller than those claimed by Summers. Their model, updated to reflect the structure of the US economy in 1996, has been used to simulate of the impact fundamental tax reforms (see Altig et al. 2001). Switching to a consumption tax is predicted to increase national output by 10.9 percent in the long-run, but older workers would be worse off, as would low wage workers in future cohorts. Mankiw and Weinzierl (2006) analyze the effects of reductions in taxes on wages and the return to capital in the context of a Ramsey growth model.

Gordon and Hines (2002) provide an overview of international taxation issues. Wilson (1999) and Fuest, Huber, and Mintz (2003) survey the tax competition literature. Thirsk (1986) and Damus, Hobson, and Thirsk (1991) used a computable general equilibrium model for the Canadian economy to show that the MEB from the CIT might be relatively low due because of the foreign tax credit mechanism. Keuschnigg (2007) has developed a model of the MCF from the CIT in a monopolistically competitive industry.

Exercises for Chapter 7

7.1 In the two-period life cycle model, an individual's intertemporal budget constraint can be written as follows if the government only levies a proportional consumption tax τ_c:

$$C_1 + p_2 C_2 = q_0 L + \frac{A}{1 + \tau_c},$$

where C_1 is first period consumption, C_2 is second period consumption, $p_2 = (1+r)^{-1}$, r is the rate of return on savings, $q_0 = w/(1+\tau_c)$, w is the wage rate, L is the labor supplied in period 1, and A is the individual's financial assets at the beginning of period 1. The individual's labor supply function can be written as $L = L(q_0, F)$, where F is equal $A/(1 + \tau_c)$. Let $PVC = C_1 + p_2 C_2$ be the present value of the individual's consumption. Show that the marginal cost of public funds for the consumption tax can be written as follows:

$$MCF_{\tau_c} = \frac{1}{1 - \dfrac{\tau_c}{1 + \tau_c}\left[1 + \dfrac{q_0 L}{PVC}\eta^c + \theta\right]},$$

where η^c is the compensated labor supply elasticity, and θ is the income or wealth effect on labor supply. Why does the substitution effect have less weight than the income effect in this expression for the MCF?

7.2 Suppose that the aggregate production function for an economy is

$$X = a_0 K - \frac{a_1}{2} K^2 + b_0 L - \frac{b_1}{2} L^2,$$

where the a_0, a_1, b_0, and b_1 are positive constants, K is the capital input, and L is the labor input. Suppose that the economy faces a perfectly elastic supply of capital at the after-tax rate of return of r and that the supply of labor to the economy is

$$L = z_0 + z_1(1 - \tau_L)w,$$

where z_0 and z_1 are positive constants, w is the wage rate, and τ_L is the tax rate on labor. The government also imposes ad valorem taxes of τ_K on the return on capital and τ_π on profits. All of the profits accrue to residents of the country.

Calculate the marginal cost of public funds for the tax on labor income and for the tax on the return to capital for the following parameter values if the government applies the same distributional weight to labor income and profits, and

$$a_0 = 1.1, \quad a_1 = 0.1, \quad b_0 = 15, \quad b_1 = 1.0, \quad z_0 = 1.0, \quad z_1 = 0.01,$$

and $\tau_L = \tau_K = \tau_\pi = 0.20$.

8 The MCF from Public Sector Borrowing

This chapter begins with a brief overview of the postwar literature on the burden of the public debt. This historical background helps put into context the models of the public debt that are considered in this chapter. The postwar debates over the burden of the public debt identified two main mechanisms by which the public debt can impose a burden on the economy—through a wealth effect and through a distortionary tax effect. In section 8.2 we use Diamond's overlapping generations model to analyze the wealth effect of the public debt and to derive a measure of the marginal cost of funds from public sector borrowing. In the Diamond model the public debt lowers private sector savings and the capital stock in the long run, resulting in potential large welfare loss to future generations. However, the generations that are alive when the debt is issued may benefit from the debt, regardless of how the proceeds are spent, and from their perspective MCF from public debt may be negative.

In section 8.3 we use a simple model, originally developed by Elmendorf and Mankiw, to analyze the MCF from public sector debt when interest payments on the debt are financed by a distortionary tax on total output. This framework is used in section 8.4 to derive a rule for the optimal financing of lumpy expenditure projects: use debt financing to equalize the marginal cost of public funds over time. A numerical example shows that there can be significant welfare gains from debt-financing lumpy expenditures. Finally, in section 8.5 we use a simple endogenous growth model, which incorporates the Ricardian equivalence effect and the distortionary tax effect, to derive a measure of the marginal cost of funds from public sector borrowing and to explore the connection between the level of public debt and the rate of economic growth. With this model we compute the marginal cost of public funds from public sector borrowing in Canada and the United States and consider the effect of higher public debt on the optimal level of public expenditures.

8.1   Postwar Debates on the Burden of the Public Debt

In the late 1950s and early 1960s a major battle broke out among economists when four future Nobel laureates—James Buchanan, James Meade, Franco Modigliani, and William Vickrey—challenged the prevailing Keynesian orthodoxy that the public debt does not impose a burden on future generations.[1] The main proponent of the Keynesian orthodoxy was Abba Lerner (1948) who argued that the public debt could not impose a burden on future generations because the "real" burden occurs at the time that a government uses the resources that are financed by borrowing. When a government fights a war or builds a highway, it uses resources that could have been used by the private sector. According to the Keynesian orthodoxy, it is this reallocation of resources from the private to the public sector that constitutes the burden of the government expenditure, and this burden is independent of whether the expenditure is financed by taxation or borrowing. In either case the burden occurs at the time the resources are used by the public sector, and therefore it cannot be "transferred" to future generations. The Keynesian orthodoxy acknowledged that interest payments on the public debt have to be financed by higher taxes on future generations, but pointed out that interest payments on the public debt also represent income for the future generation. The Keynesian orthodoxy viewed interest payments as merely a transfer from future taxpayers to future bondholders, and therefore it did not represent a net loss to the future generation. The public debt does not constitute a burden because "we owe it to ourselves." According to the Keynesian orthodoxy, the method of financing public expenditure—taxation or borrowing—should be determined by macroeconomic considerations, namely the size of the deficit or surplus required to keep the economy at full employment with a low rate of inflation.

Buchanan (1958) is generally credited with launching the assault on the Keynesian orthodoxy. A key element of his argument was the distinction between coercive and voluntary payments. Taxes are coercive payments. The element of coercion means the taxpayer is worse off for having to make the payment. Otherwise, coercion would not be necessary. On the other hand, borrowing by government is based on the voluntary agreement of individuals to purchase government debt in exchange for claims on future resources. By definition, its voluntary purchase of the debt cannot make the current generation worse off. Thus the burden of government spending financed by debt must be borne by future generations.

How is this burden shifted to the future generation? In attempting to clarify the Buchanan position, Bowen, Davis, and Kopf (1960, p. 703), argued

[T]he issuance of government bonds permits the generations alive at the time the public project is undertaken [Generation I] to be compensated in the future for their initial sacrifice. Generation I merely makes a loan of its reduced consumption, and the real reduction of consumption is borne by the generation(s) alive at the time this loan is extinguished. Consequently, even though the real private consumption of the community as a whole need not be altered by the growth of the public debt, it is still possible for the distribution of the community's private consumption *between generations* to depend on whether or not public projects are debt-financed. (Italics in the original)

The Bowen et al. thesis is that the public debt is a burden because it is a claim on the resources of future generations. Some orthodox Keynesians challenged this thesis by arguing that the public debt might be constantly rolled over and never repaid. Future generations do not bear a burden because the debt is never "extinguished." Some even suggested that the interest payments on the debt could be infinitely postponed by further borrowing. Obviously, if government debt is a "pyramid scheme," then the Bowen et al. mechanism never comes into play.

The grounds of the debate then shifted to the effect that the method of government finance has on the resources available to future generations. As Modigliani (1961, p. 736) succinctly noted:

[T]he way we use today's resources can affect in three major ways the output that will result from tomorrow's labor input: (i) by affecting the natural resources available to the future; (ii) by improving technological knowledge; and (iii) by affecting the stock of man-made means of production, or capital, available to future generations. Hence government expenditure, and the way it is financed, *can* affect the economy in the future if it affects any of the above three items. (Italics in the original)

Vickrey (1961, p. 133) provided a concise description of the way in which the method of financing the government expenditures affects the stock of capital available to future generations. He noted:

[I]f we assume a "public debt illusion" under which individuals pay no attention to their share in the liability represented by the public debt in determining how much of their income they will spend, we can expect consumer demand to be higher when the project is debt-financed than when it is tax-financed; ... the increased demand for borrowed funds represented by the debt financing must be allowed to tighten the money market ... drive interest rates up and generally increase the difficulties of financing to the point where private investment is curtailed sufficiently to remove inflationary pressure[2].... The shifting of the burden to the future that is produced by debt financing is then essentially the shifting of resources out of private investment and into consumption that is induced by the change in the method of financing.

A formal model of the burden of the public debt caused by the "crowding out" of private investment was provided by Modigliani (1961). His model is portrayed in figure 8.1. Individuals want to hold a certain amount of wealth based on their disposable incomes. Because initially there is no public debt, aggregate wealth is equal to the private stock of capital K. At time t_0 the government temporarily increases government spending on goods and services by dG (perhaps to fight a war), and it finances this increase in spending by issuing bonds equal to B. Borrowing by the government crowds out private investment, in the manner described by Vickrey, and the

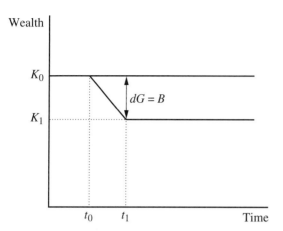

Figure 8.1
Effect of public debt in the Modigliani model

capital stock declines to K_1. The reduction in the capital stock, $K_0 - K_1$, is equal to B. This decline in the capital stock is permanent because individuals treat the bonds as part of their wealth, and $B + K_1 = K_0$. In other words, $dK/dB = -1$. A dollar of debt displaces a dollar of capital in the Modigliani model. Aggregate output and consumption are lower in every subsequent year. Future generations bear the burden of the public debt because they have a smaller capital stock, leading to lower output, lower wages, and lower consumption.

The burden of the public debt can be measured by the reduction in annual output that occurs because of the reduction in the capital stock. The reduction in output from a one dollar reduction in the capital stock is the marginal product of capital, r, which will also be equal the rate of return on government bonds because investors will require the same before-tax rate of return on private capital and government debt (ignoring for simplicity differences in their risk characteristics). Therefore the annual loss of output from an additional dollar of public debt is r. Since this annual output is lost forever, the present value of the lost output from one dollar of debt, calculated using the market interest rate, is equal to one dollar. In other words, in the Modigliani model the annual interest payment on the public debt measures the annual lost output caused by the public debt, and the value of the public debt measures the present value of current and future lost output. Diamond (1965) developed a more elaborate model of the wealth effect of public debt, and this model will be described in more detail in section 8.2.

Most of the "heavy hitters" in this debate were highly critical of the Keynesian orthodoxy, and it might be supposed that their side won. In fact the Keynesian orthodoxy is no longer prevalent among economists, although it still has its adherents.[3]

The view that the "public debt is a burden" emerged from the debate as a generally accepted proposition among academic economists until it was in turn challenged in the 1970s by Barro (1974). He noted that government debt has an effect on savings behavior in the Modigliani and Diamond models because individuals do not fully take into account the future taxes that have to be paid to finance the interest payments on the public debt. Hence government debt represents net wealth for the private sector. However, Barro showed that if the current generation is concerned about the well-being of the next generation and makes positive bequests to them, then an increase in the public debt, *financed by lump-sum taxes*, will not affect the net savings rate because individuals will offset the future tax needed to finance the public debt by increasing bequests to the next generation. In other words, the current generation will save more to pay for the future tax increase, and the net savings rate, public and private, will be unaffected by a public sector deficit, which increases the public debt. Under these conditions what has become known as the Ricardian equivalence effect would prevail, and the "fiscal effects involving changes in the relative amounts of tax and debt finance for a given amount of public expenditure would have no effect on aggregate demand, interest rates, and capital formation" (Barro 1974, p. 1116).

Over the last thirty years the theoretical validity and the empirical relevance of Ricardian equivalence has been actively debated within the economics profession and no general consensus has emerged. (Some further references to the theoretical and empirical literature on Ricardian equivalence are contained in the Further Reading section of this chapter.) Barro (1979) himself showed that if we relax one assumption in his Ricardian equivalence proposition and admit that governments levy distortionary taxes to finance their expenditures, then an increase in the public debt can have a real effect on the economy. If the additional efficiency loss from a higher distortionary tax increases as the tax rate increases, then the optimal fiscal policy is to "smooth" the tax rate, rather than to vary the tax rate in response to fluctuations in government expenditures. In other words, a constant tax rate could lower the efficiency cost of taxation compared to the fluctuating tax rates that would be required under the policy of balancing the budget each period and raising the same amount of tax revenue in present value terms.

8.2   The MCF from Public Debt in an Overlapping Generations Model

Diamond (1965) showed that the crowding-out effect of the public debt, based on the wealth effect, could be much greater than one. In Diamond's model individuals live for two periods, receiving wage income in the first period and saving to provide for their consumption in their retirement in the second period. We will focus on a simple version of the Diamond model in which there is no population growth and labor supply is completely inelastic (and normalized to equal one). Aggregate production is based on a Cobb-Douglas production function, $Y = K^\alpha$, and the rate of return on capital, which equals the interest rate on the public debt, is equal to $r = \alpha K^{\alpha-1}$. This implies that wage income is $(1 - \alpha)K^\alpha$. Interest payments on the public debt, rB, are financed by lump-sum taxes on workers. For simplicity it will be assumed that there are no other public expenditures. Individuals have Cobb-Douglas utility functions defined over consumption in the two periods of their lives, $U_t = (1 - s) \ln C_{w_t} + s \ln C_{o_{t+1}}$, where $0 < s < 1$ and C_{w_t} is the individual's consumption at time t while he is working and $C_{o_{t+1}}$ is his consumption in the next period when he is retired. It is assumed that there are no inheritances or bequests. Given the assumption of a Cobb-Douglas utility function, workers' savings rate is a constant proportion, s, of their disposable income in the first period. Workers' savings finance the public debt and the stock of capital that is available for production in the next period:

$$K_{t+1} + B = s((1 - \alpha)K_t^\alpha - \alpha K_t^{\alpha-1}B). \tag{8.1}$$

In the long-run equilibrium, $K_{t+1} = K_t$ and the rate of return on capital will be equal to

$$r = \left(\frac{\alpha}{s}\right)\left(\frac{1 + \kappa}{1 - \alpha(1 + \kappa)}\right), \tag{8.2}$$

where $\kappa = B/K$ is the public debt to capital ratio. A higher debt to capital ratio increases the equilibrium rate of return because public debt displaces capital in workers' portfolios. A higher savings rate, or a larger share of income going to workers, reduces the equilibrium rate of return. If the initial capital stock is too low (or equivalently if the initial debt to capital ratio is too high), workers will not be able to save enough to maintain the capital stock and the stock of capital will shrink indefinitely. The stability condition, which can be written as $r < s(1 - \alpha)(1 + \kappa)$, imposes an upper bound on the rate of return in the economy. This stability condition places an upper bound of the debt to capital ratio:

$$\kappa < \kappa_{\max} = \frac{2\alpha^2 - 3\alpha + (4\alpha - 3\alpha^2)^{1/2}}{2\alpha(1 - \alpha)}. \tag{8.3}$$

Note that $\kappa_{\max}$, the maximum sustainable debt to capital ratio, is independent of the savings rate, and it is decreasing in capital's share of output.[4] The stability condition can also be expressed in terms of the maximum sustainable interest payments on the public debt as a percentage of total output. Define $b = B/Y$ as the debt to output ratio. The maximum interest payments ratio is $(rb)_{\max} = \alpha\kappa_{\max}$. If $\alpha = 1/3$, then $\kappa_{\max} = 0.5$ and $(rb)_{\max} = 0.167$. Rankin and Roffia (2003) have noted that in 1994 the debt to capital ratios of G7 countries ranged from 0.24 for Germany to 0.52 for

Canada. However, it would be unwarranted to conclude from this simple model that Canada exceeded its maximum sustainable debt in 1994, especially since the condition on the maximum sustainable interest payments was satisfied.[5]

In the long-run the crowding-out effect of the public debt is equal to

$$\frac{dK}{dB} = \frac{1 + s \cdot r}{s(1 - \alpha)(1 + \kappa)r - 1} = \frac{1}{\alpha(1 - \alpha)\kappa^2 + \alpha(3 - 2\alpha)\kappa - (\alpha - 1)^2} < -1. \qquad (8.4)$$

The first dollar of public debt reduces the long-run capital stock by $1/(1 - \alpha)^2 > 1$ dollars, and the crowding-out effect increases as the debt to capital ratio increases. Therefore, in contrast to Modigliani's model, the wealth effect in Diamond's model reduces the capital stock by more than the public debt. The reason why public debt crowds out capital by more than one for one in Diamond's model can be explained as follows: If an extra dollar of debt is issued in period 1, workers buy the government debt instead of capital for their portfolios, and the capital stock is reduced by one dollar in period 2. As a result of the reduction in the capital stock, workers' net incomes in period 2 are reduced for two reasons. First, they have to pay higher taxes to finance the additional interest payments on the public debt, and second, they receive lower wage incomes because of the decline in the capital stock. As a consequence their savings are lower, resulting in a further reduction in the capital stock in period 3. This process continues until a new long-run equilibrium capital stock is achieved. From (8.4) note that the long-run crowding-out effect is independent of the savings rate and is larger in absolute value when the debt to capital ratio is larger or when production is more capital intensive. If $\alpha = 1/3$ and $\kappa = 0$, $dK/dB = -2.25$. If $\kappa = 0.24$ or equivalently $rb = 0.08$, $dK/dB = -4.08$. In other words, this simple version of Diamond's model predicts that at Germany's 1994 debt to capital ratio, an additional euro of public debt would reduce the private capital stock by just over four euros.

Macroeconomists have focused on the crowding-out effects of taxes and government debt, but the linkage between the MCF from public debt and the crowding-out effect has not been articulated in the literature. Below we will see how the MCF from public sector borrowing, MCF_B, is related to the crowding-out effect. The MCF_B is the welfare loss sustained by individuals when the government issues another dollar of debt. Alternatively, the MCF_B could consider the gain from eliminating a dollar of public debt (perhaps through an unanticipated inflation), and it could be used to determine the optimal provision of "lumpy" infrastructure where financing by debt is optimal from a "tax-smoothing" perspective. This topic is covered in section 8.4.

Defining the MCF_B is problematic in the context of Diamond's overlapping generations model because it is not clear how the welfare losses of future generations should be treated. At one extreme, it can be argued that in a model where individuals do not care about future generations, only the welfare effects of those who are alive at the time the debt is issued should be counted because only their preferences will determine the government's debt policy. (Future generations have no say on current policy, and those who are currently alive do care about the impact of fiscal policies upon future generations.) Ignoring the impact on future generations' welfare would be consistent with economists' general practice of respecting individuals' preferences and not imposing "correct" preferences on them.

Suppose that we only consider the effects of an increase in the public debt on the two generations that are alive when the debt is issued. Initially the economy is in long-run equilibrium with each generation achieving a utility level U_0. An increase in the debt by ΔB in period 1 has no direct effect on the well-being of the retired generation because their consumption is determined by the existing capital stock, K_1, and the existing debt level, B_1, that is, $(1 + r_1)(K_1 + B_1)$. (Of course, the retired generation could be made better off if the debt finances higher transfers to them or more public goods, but here we are only interested in the welfare effects of issuing more public debt, not the welfare effects of the expenditures that it finances.) Similarly workers' net incomes and consumption levels in period 1 are unaffected by the increase in the debt in period 1, since their wage income is $(1 - \alpha)K_1^\alpha$ and their tax payment is $T_1 = r_1 B_1$. In period 2 the capital stock will have fallen by ΔB, and therefore the consumption of the workers when they are "old" in period 2 will increase because $C_{o2} = (1 + r_2)(K_2 + B_1 + \Delta B) = (1 + r_2)(K_1 + B_1)$ and $r_2 > r_1$ because $K_2 < K_1$. Therefore workers in period 1 enjoy higher consumption in their old age in period 2 as a result of the increase in the rate of return on their savings. The present value of the gain to this generation of workers per dollar of additional debt is

$$\frac{1}{\lambda}\frac{dU_1}{dB} = \left[\frac{r}{1+r}\right]\left(\frac{1+\kappa}{-\varepsilon}\right), \tag{8.5}$$

where λ is the marginal utility of income and ε is the elasticity of demand for capital. (It should be emphasized that this measure does not include the gains that workers' may have received if the additional debt is used to finance higher public expenditures or to lower their tax burden.) The gain to the current generation of workers is increasing in the debt to capital ratio and is lower when the demand for capital is more elastic. Consequently in a two-period overlapping generations model everyone who is alive at the time the debt is issued is better off, or at least not worse off, as a result of an addition to the public debt.

These gains come at the expense of future generations because of the decline in savings and the reduction in the capital stock. Diamond (1965, eq. 29) derived the following measure of the present value of the welfare losses to future generations in the new long-run equilibrium:

$$\frac{1}{r}\left(\frac{1}{\lambda}\right)\frac{dU_\infty}{dB} = -1 - \frac{K+B}{1+r}\frac{dr}{dB} = -1 - \left(\frac{1+\kappa}{1+r}\right)\cdot\left(\frac{r}{\varepsilon}\right)\cdot\frac{dK}{dB}$$

$$= -1 + \left(\frac{1}{\lambda}\frac{dU_1}{dB}\right)\frac{dK}{dB}. \tag{8.6}$$

The welfare loss incurred by future generations in the new long-run equilibrium results from the increase in the rate of return on capital because this takes the economy further from the "Golden Rule" capital stock where the rate of return equals the growth rate of the labor force, which is zero in the model under consideration. Equation (8.6) can be interpreted as indicating that the "excess burden" of an additional dollar of debt on future generations is equal to the gain obtained by the generation of workers who were alive when the debt was issued multiplied by the reduction in the long-run capital stock.

Diamond's measure of the welfare loss is not a good measure of the marginal cost of funds from public sector borrowing because it does not include the welfare losses incurred by the generations that are alive during the transition path to the new equilibrium. As we have seen, the first generation benefits from the debt and the welfare losses of the immediately following generations will generally be smaller than the welfare losses sustained by the generation alive in the new long-run equilibrium. If we value future welfare losses at current prices (i.e., use the current marginal utility of income to calculate the monetary value of the utility changes and the current rate of interest to discount them), the marginal cost of funds from public sector borrowing can be defined as

$$MCF_B = \frac{\sum_{t=1}^\infty [(U_0 - U_t)/\lambda_0]/(1+r_0)^{t-1}}{\Delta B}. \tag{8.7}$$

Table 8.1 shows the MCF_B calculated using (8.7) to generate the sequence of K_t and C_t for a small increase in the debt. For $\alpha = 1/3$ and $s = 0.15$, the MCF_B is 1.50 when the economy is initially debt free. Workers who are alive when the debt is issued gain 0.51 from the first dollar of debt (even if the debt does not finance any public expenditure increase, or tax cut, that benefits them) while future generations lose 2.15. If interest payments on the public debt are 10 percent of output (or equivalently if $\kappa = 0.30$), the MCF_B is 1.76. Workers who are alive at the time the debt is issued gain 0.72 from an additional dollar of debt, while future generations in the new long-run equilibrium will lose 4.79.

Thus the Diamond model indicates that the wealth effect can generate a potentially large crowding-out effect. The large crowding-out effect implies that the MCF_B is quite high, if we include the losses sustained by future generations. The model also indicates that issuing debt benefits workers who are alive at the time the debt is

Table 8.1
MCF_B in the overlapping generations model

Interest payments on the public debt as a percentage of output, rb	0.00	0.10
dK/dB	-2.25	-5.23
$(1/\lambda)(dU_1/dB)$	0.51	0.72
$(1/\lambda)(1/r)(dU_\infty/dB)$	-2.15	-4.79
MCF_B	1.50	1.76

Notes: Calculations based on $\alpha = 1/3$, $s = 0.85$, and $g = 0$.

issued. In the absence of a default risk, there is a strong incentive for governments to increase the public debt because all the costs are incurred by future generations who, of course, cannot vote and have no influence on the decision. If the "real world" were like this, the public debt would be quickly pushed to the maximum sustainable level. While the governments of most developed countries have significant levels of debts, it is difficult to argue that they have been pushed to unsustainable levels (except perhaps in some European countries if one counts unfunded public pension liabilities as part of the public debt). This might suggest that the absence of a debt explosion is evidence of intergenerational altruism, by at least some workers. However, before we consider the implications of intergenerational altruism and Ricardian equivalence effects, we will explore the crowding-out effects of public debt when the interest payments on the public debt are financed by distortionary taxation.

8.3   The MCF from Debt Financed by Distortionary Taxation

We will use a simple model developed by Elmendorf and Mankiw (1999) and Mankiw (2000)[6] to derive (1) the condition under which a one dollar increase in the public debt crowds out more than one dollar of capital, (2) an expression for the maximum sustainable public debt, and (3) an expression for the marginal cost of funds obtained from public sector borrowing when interest payments on the debt are financed by distortionary taxes.

The model consists of four equations:

$$Y = f(K), \tag{8.8}$$

$$\tau Y = \rho B + G, \tag{8.9}$$

$$r = f'(K), \tag{8.10}$$

$$(1 - \tau)r = \rho, \tag{8.11}$$

where Y is the aggregate output produced by the capital stock K, τ is the proportional income tax rate, B is the public debt, G is the government's program spending, and p is the savers' rate of time preference, which is assumed to be constant. Equation (8.8) is the economy's aggregate production function, and equation (8.9) is the government's budget constraint. It has been assumed that interest payments on the government debt are not taxed, and therefore the government's tax revenues are τY. Arbitrage in the capital market reduces the interest rate on government bonds to $(1 - \tau)r = p$, and therefore the government's annual expenditures are $pB + G$.[7] Equation (8.10) is the marginal productivity condition for investment. This condition determines the capital stock given the before-tax rate of return that investors require on capital, and equation (8.11) determines this before-tax rate of return. We can interpret the model either as a closed economy, where the supply of savings is perfectly elastic at the after-tax rate of return p, or as a small open economy where the residents can borrow on world capital markets at the constant after-tax rate of return of p.

Taking the total differential of this system of equations, we obtain the impact of an increase in the public debt on the aggregate capital stock as equal to

$$\frac{dK}{dB} = \frac{(1 - \tau)\alpha\varepsilon}{(1 - \tau) + \tau\alpha\varepsilon}, \tag{8.12a}$$

where $\alpha = rK/Y$ is capital's share of output and $\varepsilon = f'/(Kf'') < 0$ is the elasticity of demand for capital. Note that $\tau = g + pb$, where $g = G/Y$ is the program spending ratio, and $b = B/Y$ is the government's debt to GDP ratio. Therefore the crowding-out effect can also be expressed in terms of g, p, and b:

$$\frac{dK}{dB} = \frac{\alpha\varepsilon[1 - (g + pb)]}{1 - (1 - \alpha\varepsilon)(g + pb)}. \tag{8.12b}$$

If the production function is Cobb-Douglas, with $Y = K^\alpha$ and $\varepsilon = -(1 - \alpha)^{-1}$, the crowding-out effect is equal to

$$\frac{dK}{dB} = -\frac{\alpha(1 - \tau)}{1 - \alpha - \tau} = -\frac{\alpha(1 - g - pb)}{1 - \alpha - g - pb}. \tag{8.12c}$$

Under what conditions does a one dollar increase in the public debt reduce the aggregate capital stock by more than one dollar? From (8.12a) it can be shown that $dK/dB \gtrless -1$ as $\tau \lessgtr 1 + \alpha\varepsilon$. With a Cobb-Douglas production function, this condition becomes $dK/dB \gtrless -1$ as $\tau \lessgtr (1 - 2\alpha)(1 - \alpha)^{-1}$. With $\alpha = 1/3$, $dK/dB \gtrless -1$ as $\tau \lessgtr 0.5$. In other words, if capital's share of output is one-third and the tax rate is less than 50 percent, the crowding-out effect of the public debt is less than one for one. Consequently the distortionary taxes used to finance an increase in the public debt may induce a smaller crowding-out effect than the wealth effect in Diamond's overlapping generations model.

This model can also be used to derive the maximum debt ratio that a government can finance. From (8.12a), note that $dK/dB \rightarrow -\infty$ as $\tau \rightarrow (1 - \alpha\varepsilon)^{-1}$, or as $\tau \rightarrow (1 - \alpha)$ if the production function is Cobb-Douglas. At this tax rate the government is at the peak of its Laffer curve. That is, tax revenue, $R = \tau Y$, is a maximum since $dR/d\tau = Y(1 + \tau(1 - \tau)^{-1}\alpha\varepsilon) = 0$ when $\tau = (1 - \alpha\varepsilon)^{-1}$. The peak of the Laffer curve determines the maximum debt to GDP ratio that a government can finance. Since $b = (\tau - g)/p$, the maximum debt to GDP ratio is

$$b_{\max} \equiv \frac{1 - (1 - \alpha\varepsilon)g}{(1 - \alpha\varepsilon)\rho}. \tag{8.13}$$

With a Cobb-Douglas production function, $b_{\max} = (1 - \alpha - g)\rho^{-1}$, which indicates that at $b_{\max}$ interest payments on the public debt, program expenditures, and payments to the owners of capital equal total output, meaning nothing is left over to pay the fixed factor of production (presumably labor). If we interpret the model as a small open economy that can borrow at a fixed real rate of $p = 0.08$ and $\alpha = 1/3$, then $b_{\max} = 5.83$ if $g = 0.20$ and $b_{\max} = 2.08$ if $g = 0.50$, a range of g values that brackets the fiscal positions of most OECD countries. Thus the model predicts that the maximum debt ratio that a country can finance with distortionary taxation is much higher than the 60 percent debt to GDP ceiling imposed on EU countries under the Maastricht Treaty and the Stability and Growth Pact, or the debt ratios at which most countries fall into a debt crisis. This suggests that it is not the inability to raise more revenue to finance a high debt level that leads to a debt "crisis," but rather the unwillingness of government to impose high tax rates. In other words, the marginal cost of public funds for a heavily indebted country that falls into a debt crisis is high, but finite.

We can also use this model to derive an expression for the marginal cost of funds from public sector borrowing. Private consumption is $C = Y - G - \Delta K$. Given full employment of resources, a small increase in the debt will reduce private consumption in the initial period by $(1 + dK/dB)$, and it will reduce future consumption by $dY/dB = rdK/dB$, provided that G is held constant. Therefore the marginal cost of public funds obtained through public sector borrowing can be measured by

$$MCF_B = \left[1 + \frac{dK}{dB}\right] - \left[\frac{1 - \rho}{\rho}r\frac{dK}{dB}\right] = 1 - \frac{1}{\rho}(r - \rho(1 + r))\frac{dK}{dB}, \tag{8.14a}$$

where the first term in square brackets is the immediate effect on consumption of an increase in the public debt and the second term in square brackets is the present value of the change in future consumption due to the crowding out effect. Note that if individuals increased their savings by the amount of the increase in the public debt, $dK/dB = 0$ and $MCF_B = 1.00$. If there is a crowding-out effect, then the MCF_B depends on the difference between the rate of return on capital and savers' marginal rate of time preference. In this model, taxes create the wedge between r and p, and the MCF_B can approximated, given that rp is small, as

$$MCF_B = 1 - \left(\frac{\tau}{1-\tau}\right)\frac{dK}{dB}. \tag{8.14b}$$

If $\alpha = 1/3$ and $\tau = 1/3$, $dK/dB = -2/3$ and $MCF_B = 1.33$. In other words, an additional dollar of public debt imposes a burden of \$1.33 through the crowding-out effect caused by distortionary taxes.

8.4 Tax Smoothing and Optimal Debt Financing of Public Expenditures

As noted at the start of this chapter, Barro (1979) argued that when a government has to finance its expenditures with distortionary taxes, it should "smooth" its tax rates in the face of fluctuating expenditure requirements. Barro did not model the distortionary effects of taxation explicitly. Instead he assumed that output in each period was a decreasing convex function of the tax rate in that period. In this section we will use a simple model to show that the optimal debt policy allows the government to equalize the marginal cost of public funds in the current and future time periods. This is the intertemporal equivalent of the rule for optimal commodity taxation—equalize the marginal cost of public funds from each tax base—that was analyzed in section 3.2.

The framework that we will use is also very simple. Suppose that there is a single representative individual who lives forever. The government spends M dollars on project in period 1, which will yield benefits of $W(M)$ in each future period. During the "construction" phase in period 1 there are no benefits from the project, and in the future periods there are no operating costs associated with the project. Building on the framework in section 8.3, we will assume that the government can borrow at a fixed rate of return of p and that it finances its expenditures by taxing output at the rate τ_j in period j. In period 1 the government's budget constraint is

$$\tau_1 Y_1 = G + \delta M + (1-\delta)M, \tag{8.15}$$

where Y_1 is output in period 1, δ is the fraction of the project expenditure that the government finances by issuing debt in period 1, and G is other program expenditures (assumed to be constant over time). Interest payments on the public debt are equal to $\delta p M$ in each period. Therefore the government's budget constraint in each future period $t = 2 \ldots \infty$, is

$$\tau_t Y_t = G + \delta \rho M, \tag{8.16}$$

where τ_t and Y_t is the constant tax rate and output level in each future period. The present value of the government's expenditures is

$$PVE = [G + \delta \rho M + (1 - \delta)M] + \frac{(1 - \rho)}{\rho}[G + \delta \rho M] = \frac{G}{\rho} + M. \tag{8.17}$$

The government's intertemporal budget constraint will be satisfied if the present value of its tax revenues, PVR, is equal to the present value of its expenditures where

$$PVR = \tau_1 Y_1 + \frac{1 - \rho}{\rho}\tau_t Y_t. \tag{8.18}$$

To keep the model as simple as possible, let us assume that the marginal utility from consumption of the private good is a constant and equal to one. The utility obtained by the individual from the government's program expenditures and the project are separable and equal to $B(G) + W(M)$. The optimal level of spending on the project, the degree of debt financing, and the tax rates are obtained by maximizing the following Lagrangian:

$$\Lambda = C_1 + B(G) + \frac{1 - \rho}{\rho}[C_2 + B(G) + W(M)] + \mu_1[\tau_1 Y_1 - G - \delta \rho M - (1 - \delta)M]$$

$$+ \mu_t[\tau_t Y_t - G - \delta \rho M], \tag{8.19}$$

where μ_1 is the Lagrange multiplier associated with the first-period budget constraint and μ_t is the Lagrange multiplier associated with the budget constraint in each of the following t periods. Note that $dC_j/d\tau_j = -Y_j$, so the first-order conditions for the maximum for each of the four choice variables, τ_1, τ_t, δ, and M are given as

$$\frac{Y_1}{Y_1 + \tau_1(dY_1/d\tau_1)} \equiv MCF_1 = \mu_1, \tag{8.20}$$

$$\frac{1 - \rho}{\rho}\frac{Y_t}{Y_t + \tau_t(dY_t/d\tau_t)} \equiv \frac{1 - \rho}{\rho} MCF_t = \mu_t, \tag{8.21}$$

$$\mu_1 = \frac{\rho}{1 - \rho}\mu_t, \tag{8.22}$$

$$\frac{1 - \rho}{\rho} W'(M) = [1 - (1 - \rho)\delta]\mu_1 + \delta \rho \mu_t = (1 - \delta)MCF_1 + \delta MCF_B. \tag{8.23}$$

Equation (8.20) indicates, in the usual way, that the Lagrange multiplier on the government's first-period budget constraint can be interpreted as the marginal cost of public funds in the first period. Equation (8.21) indicates that the Lagrange multiplier on the future budget constraints is equal to the present value of raising an additional dollar of revenue in each of the future periods. Equation (8.22) determines the optimal degree of debt financing, δ. Using (8.21) and (8.22), we find that optimal debt financing occurs when $MCF_1 = MCF_t$. In other words, with the optimal debt policy the government shifts the tax burden between the current and future periods so as to equalize the marginal cost of public funds over time and to achieve the optimal tax rate in each period. If the MCFs are not constant over time, then it is possible to achieve a gain through an intertemporal shift in the tax burden, either by incurring additional debt or by running a surplus and acquiring assets that will provide the government with investment income in future periods. Suppose that given the current expenditure commitments and level of borrowing, $MCF_t < MCF_1$. In this case an additional dollar of debt will produce a gain because it will allow the government to reduce its tax burden in the current period by $(1 - p)$ dollars in the current period, and this yields a social gain of $(1 - p)MCF_1$. However, the interest payments on debt will impose an additional social burden of $pMCF_t$ in each future period. The present value of this loss is $(1 - p)MCF_t$. Consequently the gain from an additional dollar of debt is simply equal to $(1 - p)[MCF_1 - MCF_t]$. In other words, the marginal cost of public sector debt is equal to $MCF_B = pMCF_1 + (1 - p)MCF_t$.

Equation (8.23) indicates that with the optimal investment in infrastructure the present value of the marginal benefit from an additional dollar spent on infrastructure should be equal to the marginal cost of funds in the current period plus the marginal cost of funds from debt financing, with each term multiplied by the proportion of the funds that come from current tax revenues and public sector borrowing. Of course, if the government has adopted the optimal debt policy and $MCF_1 = MCF_t = MCF_B$, then the optimal level of infrastructure equates the present value of the marginal benefit from infrastructure spending with the marginal cost of public funds which is constant overtime. However, if the government is not be able to adopt the optimal debt policy, perhaps because there are legislative constraints on its ability to finance infrastructure spending by debt, then the optimal provision of infrastructure will be determined by the weight average of MCF_1 and MCF_B.

Using the framework developed in section 2.3, we can approximate the gain from the optimal debt policy as a proportion of the expenditure on the project:

$$\Gamma \approx \frac{1}{2}(1 - p)[MCF_1 - MCF_t], \tag{8.24}$$

where the MCFs are based on the tax rates that would apply if $\delta = 0$ and the entire project is funded from tax revenues in period 1. If it is assumed that the production function for the economy is Cobb-Douglas, we can express the gain from debt financing in terms of the tax rates that would apply if the entire project were financed out of tax revenues in the first period:

$$\Gamma = 0.5(1-p)\left[\left(1 - \frac{\tau_1}{1-\tau_1}\frac{\alpha}{1-\alpha}\right)^{-1} - \left(1 - \frac{\tau_t}{1-\tau_t}\frac{\alpha}{1-\alpha}\right)^{-1}\right]$$

$$= \frac{0.5(1-p)\alpha(1-\alpha)(\tau_1 - \tau_t)}{(1-\alpha-\tau_1)(1-\alpha-\tau_t)}. \tag{8.25}$$

This equation indicates that the gain from debt financing is proportional to the tax rate increase that is required in the current period in order to finance the project and that the gain from debt financing is higher when the tax rates are higher because the excess burden of taxation is proportional to the square of the tax rates. A further approximation of the gain from debt financing can be made if we assume that $\tau_1 = g + m$ and $\tau_t = g$, where $g = G/Y_1$ and $m = M/Y_1$, that is,

$$\Gamma = \frac{0.5(1-p)\alpha(1-\alpha)(m)}{(1-\alpha-g-m)(1-\alpha-g)}. \tag{8.26}$$

Figure 8.2 shows the gain from debt financing, calculated using (8.26), for $p = 0.08$ and $p = 0.25$ when $\alpha = 1/3$. (In the latter case the high discount rate would be justified if the "construction" period is three or four years in duration.) These calculations indicate that if the project is more than 5 percent of total output, then the gain from debt financing is more than 2 percent of the cost of the project. So the restrictions on government's ability to borrow to finance large "lumpy" projects may be quite high.

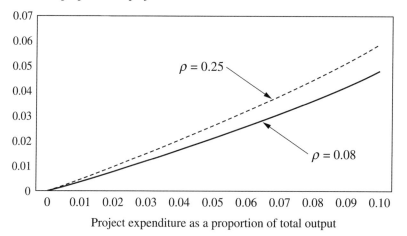

Figure 8.2
Gain from debt financing "lumpy" expenditures

As previously noted, most of the literature refers to the optimal debt policy as a "tax-smoothing" policy, in which tax rates are constant (or at least relatively stable) overtime, rather than as a "equate the marginal cost of public funds over time" policy. The two policies are equivalent in the simple framework that we have adopted because the MCF in period j only depends on the tax rate in period j, and the MCF is increasing in the tax rate. However, in a more general model, MCF_j may depend on the current as well as future tax rates if, for example, there are adjustment costs in changing the capital stock and these adjustment costs are deductible from taxable income. Under these conditions, equating the marginal cost of public funds in all time periods will generally imply a nonconstant tax rate over time, just as optimal commodity taxation generally involves a non-uniform tax rate for all taxed commodities. Therefore we should only consider "tax smoothing" to be a special case of the optimal debt policy. The problem of optimal taxation over time, with time-varying tax rates, gives rise to the problem of time-inconsistent policies because, the optimal τ_j from the perspective of period 1 will be different from the optimal τ_j in period j because the MCF_j will be different when period j arrives. This problem was first fully articulated by Kydland and Prescott (1977) who received the Nobel prize in economics for this contribution in 2004.

8.5   The MCF from Public Sector Borrowing in an Endogenous Growth Model

In this section a simple AK endogenous growth model is used to explore the connections among the public debt, distortionary taxation, and the rate of economic growth and to develop a measure of the MCF for public sector borrowing. It is a model of a closed economy where the net savings rate (the difference between the private sector savings rate and the public sector's deficit ratio) is equal to the investment rate. Even though individuals' savings behavior has the Ricardian equivalence property in this model, the net saving rate declines with an increase in the public debt because the increase in the tax rate that is required to finance the higher interest payments on public debt reduces the net rate of return on saving, making savings less attractive. This distortionary tax effect causes the investment rate, and hence the rate of economic growth, to decline.

8.5.1   A Simple Endogenous Growth Model with Public Debt

Total output at time t is equal to

$$Y_t = AK_t, \tag{8.27}$$

where K_t is the accumulated factor of production (physical and human capital) and A is the constant rate of return on this input. We will restrict our attention to the balanced growth path for this economy, where total output is growing at a constant rate γ. The capital stock also grows at the constant rate γ because it is assumed that there is no technological change and no depreciation. This implies that the annual rate of net investment is $I_t = \gamma K_t$. Substituting back into (8.27), we obtain

$$\gamma = Ai, \tag{8.28}$$

where i is the investment rate, I/Y. In other words, the growth rate is proportional to the investment rate in the economy. This simple relationship between the growth rate of the economy and the investment rate is the key feature of this endogenous growth model, and there is considerable empirical evidence indicating that countries with higher investment rates also have higher growth rates.[8]

The population is normalized to equal one, so all of the stocks and flows can be interpreted as per capita variables. Individuals are identical and are represented by a single individual whose utility at time t is

$$U_t = \left(\frac{\sigma}{\sigma-1}\right)C_t^{(\sigma-1)/\sigma} + \beta\left(\frac{\sigma}{\sigma-1}\right)G_t^{(\sigma-1)/\sigma}, \tag{8.29}$$

where C_t is private consumption, G_t is consumption of a publicly provided good, which we will refer to as the government's program spending, $\sigma > 0$ is the intertemporal elasticity of substitution, and $\beta > 0$ is a parameter that reflects the relative valuation of private and public consumption goods. The representative individual takes as given the level of the public good, and the tax rate, τ, used to finance it. Each period the individual chooses his level of consumption and allocates his savings between investment in new capital and purchases of government bonds, B_t. The individual's budget constraint in each time period is

$$C_t + \dot{K}_t + \dot{B}_t = (1-\tau)AK_t + (1-\tau)AB_t, \tag{8.30}$$

where $\dot{K}_t$ and $\dot{B}_t$ are the rates of change in capital and government bonds. The right-hand side of (8.30) shows the individual's current after-tax income from production and interest payments on government bonds. This is a closed economy, and there is no external debt, meaning the individuals owe the public debt to themselves. The representative individual discounts future utility at the rate $\rho > 0$ and makes consumption–savings decisions to maximize his well-being V, where

$$V = \int_0^\infty U_t e^{-\rho t}\, dt. \tag{8.31}$$

To simplify the notation, we will omit the time subscript unless it is necessary for the interpretation of the variables.

With the optimal consumption plan, private consumption grows at the rate, γ, where

$$\frac{\dot{C}}{C} = \sigma((1 - \tau)A - \rho) = \gamma. \tag{8.32}$$

An increase in the tax rate will slow the growth rate of consumption because it reduces the net rate of return on savings. The reduction in the growth rate caused by an increase in the tax rate, $\partial\gamma/\partial\tau = -\sigma A$, is proportional to the intertemporal elasticity of substitution, σ, the key behavioral parameter in the model.

The growth of the public debt is equal to the public sector's budget deficit, which is given by the right-hand side of (8.33):

$$\dot{B}_t = (1 - \tau)AB_t + G_t - \tau Y_t. \tag{8.33}$$

Along the balanced growth path of the economy, C, B, K, G, and Y all grow at the rate γ, and the public sector's debt ratio, $b = B/Y$, its program expenditure ratio, $g = G/Y$, and the tax rate, τ, remain constant. Therefore the deficit ratio is equal to γb, where

$$\gamma b = (1 - \tau)Ab + g - \tau. \tag{8.34}$$

This intertemporal budget constraint can also be written as

$$\tau - g = [(1 - \tau)A - \gamma]b = \theta b. \tag{8.35}$$

The government's primary surplus ratio, which is the left-hand side of (8.35) where we assume for simplicity that interest on the government's debt is not taxed, has to equal the equilibrium debt ratio multiplied by θ, the difference between the after-tax rate of return on capital and the growth rate of the economy, if the debt ratio is to remain constant.

The government's intertemporal budget constraint does not depend on whether interest payments on government debt are taxed. If interest on the public debt is not taxed, the interest rate on government bonds would be equal to the after-tax return on capital, $(1 - \tau)A$. If interest on the public debt is taxed, the interest rate on the public debt is before-tax return on capital, and the right-hand side of the (8.35) would be $(A - \gamma)b$. However, the left-hand side would be equal to $\tau(1 + Ab) - g$, and therefore the government's intertemporal budget constraint is the same as in the case where interest on the public debt is not taxed. It will be convenient to assume that interest on the public debt is not taxed because this implies that the public sector and the private sector will discount future income streams using the same discount rate. Thus the present values of tax revenues and program expenditures are based on the after-tax rate of interest, $(1 - \tau)A$, and not the before-tax rate of return on capital. In section 8.5.3 we show how the definition of the MCF changes when the government uses the before-tax rate of return on capital to discount future revenue streams and costs.

Using the expression for the equilibrium growth rate of the economy in (8.32), we have θ equal to

$$\theta = (1 - \sigma)(1 - \tau)A + \sigma\rho. \tag{8.36}$$

A condition for dynamic stability is that $\theta > 0$, which implies that the after-tax rate of return on capital must exceed the growth rate of the economy. Since $\tau < 1$, this condition will be satisfied if $\sigma < 1$, which is the relevant range of values for σ based on econometric studies of savings behavior.[9] Note that $\partial\theta/\partial\tau < 0$ if $\sigma < 1$, which implies that, with the debt ratio held constant, the primary surplus that the government has to run in order to have a sustainable fiscal policy decreases as the tax rate increases. As we will see, this effect tends to ease the government's fiscal burden when its debt increases, thereby helping moderate the MCF from public sector borrowing.

To derive the consumption ratio along the balanced growth path, we divide both sides of (8.30) by K:

$$\frac{C}{K} + \frac{\dot{K}}{K} + \frac{\dot{B}}{B}\left(\frac{B}{K}\right) = (1 - \tau)A\left(1 + \frac{B}{K}\right). \tag{8.37}$$

Substituting γ for $\dot{K}/K$ and $\dot{B}/B$ in (8.37), and noting that B/K is equal to Ab, we obtain

$$c = \frac{C}{Y} = \frac{\theta(1 + Ab)}{A}. \tag{8.38}$$

The model predicts that an increase in debt ratio, if the tax rate is held constant, will increase the consumption ratio and that an increase in the tax rate, if the debt ratio is held constant, will reduce the consumption ratio provided that $\sigma < 1$ because $\partial\theta/\partial\tau < 0$.

The growth rate of the economy is proportional to the investment rate, which in this closed economy is equal to the net savings rate—the difference between the private sector savings rate and the public sector's deficit ratio. Therefore $i = s - \gamma b$, where s represents the private sector's savings ratio, S/Y.

Given g, b, A, ρ, and σ, the model yields the following closed form solutions for the key endogenous variables:

$$\gamma = \sigma\frac{(1 - g - \rho b)A - \rho}{1 + (1 - \sigma)Ab}, \tag{8.39}$$

$$\tau = \frac{g + [(1 - \sigma)A + \sigma\rho]b}{1 + (1 - \sigma)Ab}, \tag{8.40}$$

$$s = \sigma\left(\frac{1 + Ab}{A}\right)\left(\frac{(1 - g - pb)A - p}{1 + (1 - \sigma)Ab}\right), \tag{8.41}$$

$$c = \left(\frac{1 + Ab}{A}\right)\left[\frac{(1 - g)(1 - \sigma)A + \sigma p}{1 + (1 - \sigma)Ab}\right], \tag{8.42}$$

and $i = s - \gamma b$.

Below we will consider an intuitive explanation of the effect of an increase in the debt ratio on the growth rate of the economy. Here we note that an increase in the debt ratio, with the expenditure rate held constant, leads to an increase in the tax rate, provided that the condition for dynamic stability is satisfied:

$$\frac{d\tau}{db} = \frac{(1 - g)(1 - \sigma)A + \sigma p}{(1 + (1 - \sigma)Ab)^2} > 0. \tag{8.43}$$

The effect of an increase in the debt ratio on the private sector savings rate can be decomposed as follows:

$$\frac{ds}{db} = \gamma - \sigma(1 + Ab)\frac{d\tau}{db}. \tag{8.44}$$

The first term on the right-hand side of (8.44) is the *Ricardian equivalence effect*. An increase in b will increase the deficit ratio, γb, and this prompts an individual to increase his savings rate to offset the decline in the public sector savings rate. This forward-looking response arises from our assumption that the economy is composed of infinitely lived individuals. The second term on the right-hand side of (8.44) is the *distortionary tax effect*, which arises because the higher tax rate that is required to finance additional debt reduces the net rate of return on saving. These effects push the private sector savings rate in opposite directions, and therefore an increase in the debt ratio has an ambiguous effect on the private sector savings rate.

The overall effect of an increase in b on the growth rate depends on its effect on the investment rate, which in turn depends on the change in the net savings rate $s - \gamma b$, as shown below:

$$\frac{d\gamma}{db} = A\frac{di}{db} = A\left[\frac{ds}{db} - \left(\gamma + b\frac{d\gamma}{db}\right)\right]. \tag{8.45}$$

The first term in square brackets is the effect of an increase in b on the private sector savings rate, and the second term is the effect on the deficit ratio. Substituting (8.44) into (8.45) yields

$$\frac{d\gamma}{db} = -A\sigma\frac{d\tau}{db} < 0. \tag{8.46}$$

An increase in b causes γ to decline, even though an increase in b has an ambiguous effect on the private sector savings rate, since the Ricardian equivalence effect from the private sector savings response exactly offsets the increase in the deficit ratio. Therefore the total net savings rate declines by the distortionary tax effect, leading to declines in the investment rate and the equilibrium growth rate. In section 8.5.4 the model is used to calculate the impact on the growth rate of an increase in the public debt, based on parameter values that allow the model to replicate γ and c, given g and b for the Canadian and US economies in the 1990s.

8.5.2 The MCF in an Endogenous Growth Model

We begin by deriving an expression for the equilibrium level of welfare in the economy. Along the balanced growth path, $C_t = zK_0e^{\gamma t}$ and $G_t = gAK_0e^{\gamma t}$ where K_0 is the economy's capital stock at time 0 and $z = \theta(1 + Ab)$. Substituting these values into (8.29) and (8.31), we write the discounted value of the representative individual's utility stream as

$$V(\tau, g) = \left(\frac{\sigma}{\sigma - 1}\right) \int_0^\infty ((zK_0e^{\gamma t})^{(\sigma-1)/\sigma} + \beta(gAK_0e^{\gamma t})^{(\sigma-1)/\sigma})e^{-\rho t}\, dt$$

$$= \left(\frac{\sigma}{\sigma - 1}\right) \left[\frac{(zK_0)^{(\sigma-1)/\sigma}}{\theta} + \frac{\beta(gAK_0)^{(\sigma-1)/\sigma}}{\theta}\right]$$

$$= \left(\frac{\sigma}{\sigma - 1}\right) \left(\frac{(AK_0)^{(\sigma-1)/\sigma}}{\theta}\right) [c^{(\sigma-1)/\sigma} + \beta g^{(\sigma-1)/\sigma}], \tag{8.47}$$

since $\gamma((\sigma - 1)/\sigma) - p = -\theta$. This expression indicates that the representative individual's welfare depends on the shares of income devoted to private consumption and government services and the present value of the stream of "potential utility" $(AK_0)^{(\sigma-1)/\sigma}$, calculated at the "implicit" discount rate, θ, which is the same implicit discount rate used to calculate the present value of the government's tax revenues and program expenditures. Welfare also depends on τ because θ and c are functions of the tax rate. In other words, the implicit discount rate used to calculate the representative individual's welfare level depends on the rate of taxation because it reduces the after-tax rate of return on savings and because it lowers the rate of economic growth.

For future reference, the marginal benefit from an increase in the program expenditure ratio, MB_g will be defined as

$$MB_g = \frac{1}{\lambda_0} \frac{\partial V}{\partial g} = \beta \left(\frac{AK_0}{\theta}\right) \left(\frac{c}{g}\right)^{1/\sigma}, \tag{8.48}$$

where $\lambda_0 = (cAK_0)^{-1/\sigma}$ is the marginal utility of consumption at time 0. MB_g is a money measure of the gain from a permanent increase in the proportion of output devoted to public program expenditures, measured at the initial marginal utility of income.

The marginal cost of public funds is the cost to a society in raising an additional dollar of tax revenue. In static models, the MCF is usually defined as $(-1/\lambda)(\partial V/\partial \tau)/(\partial R/\partial \tau)$, where R is annual tax revenue. However, Liu (2002) has shown that when the cost of government programs is affected by the tax rate, it is more appropriate to define the MCF as $(-1/\lambda)(\partial V/\partial \tau)/(\partial NR/\partial \tau)$, where $\partial NR/\partial \tau$ is the rate of change in the government's net revenues, the difference between its tax revenues and program expenditures. In a dynamic model, the most useful definition of the MCF is one based on the rate of change in the present value of the government's net revenue stream.

The present value of the government's net revenue stream is equal to

$$PVNR = (\tau - g)\left(\frac{AK}{\theta}\right). \tag{8.49}$$

An increase in the tax rate has two offsetting effects on the present value of the tax/expenditure base, AK/θ. On the one hand, an increase in the tax rate reduces the growth rate of the economy, which lowers the present value of the tax/expenditure base. On the other hand, a higher tax rate lowers the after-tax rate of return on government debt, which increases the present value of the tax/expenditure base. Taking the partial derivative of PVNR in (8.49) with respect to τ, we obtain

$$\frac{\partial PVNR}{\partial \tau} = \frac{AK_0}{\theta} - (\tau - g)\left(\frac{AK_0}{\theta^2}\right)\frac{\partial \theta}{\partial \tau}$$

$$= \frac{AK_0}{\theta}\left[1 - b\frac{\partial \theta}{\partial \tau}\right] = \frac{AK_0}{\theta}[1 + (1 - \sigma)Ab], \tag{8.50}$$

since $\tau - g = \theta b$ along the balanced growth path and $\partial \theta/\partial \tau = -(1 - \sigma)A$. Consequently the government's PVNR Laffer curve has a positive slope for $\sigma < 1 + (Ab)^{-1}$, which is the empirically relevant case, and therefore it is not possible to increase the present value of the government's net revenues by lowering the tax rate.[10] In fact, as shown in figure 8.3, the slope of this Laffer curve increases with the tax rate when $\sigma < 1$. The implications of the shape of the PVNR Laffer curve for the MCF are noted below.

The marginal cost of public funds for a tax rate increase is defined as follows:

$$MCF_\tau = \left(\frac{-1}{\lambda}\right)\left(\frac{\partial V/\partial \tau}{\partial PVNR/\partial \tau}\right). \tag{8.51}$$

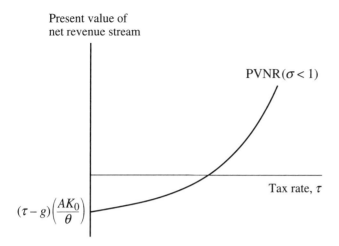

Present value of
net revenue stream

$$\text{PVNR}(\sigma < 1)$$

Tax rate, τ

$(\tau - g)\left(\dfrac{AK_0}{\theta}\right)$

Figure 8.3
The PVNR Laffer curve for $\sigma < 1$

Taking the partial derivative of (8.47) with respect to τ, we obtain the following expression for the social cost of a tax increase:

$$\frac{-1}{\lambda_0}\frac{\partial V}{\partial \tau} = \frac{AK_0}{\theta}\left[1 + \sigma\beta\left(\frac{c}{g}\right)^{(1-\sigma)/\sigma}\right](1 + Ab). \tag{8.52}$$

Then, combining (8.50) and (8.52), we obtain the formula for the MCF_τ:

$$MCF_\tau = \frac{(-1/\lambda_0)\partial V/\partial \tau}{\partial PVNR/\partial \tau} = \left[\left(1 + \sigma\beta\left(\frac{c}{g}\right)^{(1-\sigma)/\sigma}\right)(1 + Ab)\right]\left(\frac{1}{1 + (1-\sigma)Ab}\right). \tag{8.53}$$

This formula indicates that the MCF has two components. The component in round brackets is the inverse of the elasticity of the PVNR with respect to $(\tau - g)$. The greater the distortionary effect of a tax increase, the lower is the elasticity of the PVNR, and the higher is the MCF for debt financing. This component of the MCF will be higher the greater the debt to capital ratio, and the greater the intertemporal elasticity of the substitution.

The other component in square brackets is the social loss caused by the reduction in private and public service consumption. In particular, public program expenditures are assumed to be a constant proportion of output, and therefore a slower rate of economic growth, caused by a tax rate increase, means the level of public services is lower than it otherwise would be. This loss depends on the strength of the preference for the public services, β, and the (c/g) ratio. One of the key insights from this derivation of the MCF is the importance of accounting for the value of the forgone public consumption in calculating the MCF for a tax increase. As we will see in section 8.5.4, incorporating this component of the welfare loss from taxation has an important impact on the measured MCF.

Note also that the MCF approaches 1.00 as σ approaches 0 and the tax becomes nondistortionary. For $0 < \sigma \leq 1$, the MCF is greater than one but decreasing in τ. Normally we expect the MCF to be increasing in the tax rate because the deadweight loss from tax distortions increases with the square of the tax rate. One way of explaining this anomalous feature of the MCF in this model is that the slope of the PVNR Laffer curve is increasing in the tax rate for $0 < \sigma < 1$, and therefore marginal tax revenues (in present value terms) are increasing as the tax rate increases, thereby lowering the cost of raising additional revenues. Finally, note that the MCF is increasing in b when the (c/g) ratio is held constant.

We have derived this expression for the MCF for a tax rate increase, but it can also be interpreted as the marginal cost of public funds from public sector borrowing as is shown below:

$$
MCF_b = \frac{\dfrac{-1}{\lambda_0}\dfrac{\partial V}{\partial b}\,db}{(AK_0)\,db} = \frac{\dfrac{-1}{\lambda_0}\dfrac{\partial V}{\partial \tau}\dfrac{d\tau}{db}}{AK_0} = \frac{\left(\dfrac{-1}{\lambda_0}\dfrac{\partial V}{\partial \tau}\right)\dfrac{\theta}{1+(1-\sigma)Ab}}{AK_0}
$$

$$
= \left[1 + \sigma\beta\left(\frac{c}{g}\right)^{(1-\sigma)/\sigma}\right]\left(\frac{1+Ab}{1+Ab-\sigma Ab}\right). \tag{8.54}
$$

Intuitively the MCF_b is the same as the MCF_τ because, if the government borrows an extra dollar, the present value of its net revenue stream must also increase by one dollar. In the remainder of this section we will simply refer to this common value as the MCF.

8.5.3   Effect of the Public Debt on Optimal Public Expenditures

To this point it has been assumed that the government's program expenditure ratio, g, remains constant when the debt ratio increases and that all of the fiscal adjustment to an increase in the debt occurs on the tax side of the budget. However, some observers feel that an increase in interest payments on the public debt crowds out program spending. In this section the condition determining the optimal level of public program spending is derived in order to analyze the cost–benefit criterion in this economy and to analyze the effects of an increase in the public debt on the program expenditure ratio.

To determine the government's optimal tax and expenditure program (with the government's debt ratio held constant), we maximize (8.47) with respect to τ and g subject to the government's intertemporal budget constraint in (8.35). The Lagrangian for this problem is

$$\Lambda = V(\tau, g) + \mu[\tau - g - \theta b], \tag{8.55}$$

where μ is the Lagrange multiplier on the government's intertemporal budget constraint. The first-order conditions for this problem are

$$\frac{\partial V}{\partial \tau} + \mu\left[1 - b\frac{\partial \theta}{\partial \tau}\right] = 0,$$

$$\frac{\partial V}{\partial g} - \mu = 0. \tag{8.56}$$

Using (8.48), (8.50), and (8.52), we find that the condition for optimal program expenditures has the form

$$\frac{MB_g}{MC_g} \equiv \beta\left(\frac{c}{g}\right)^{1/\sigma} = \left[1 + \sigma\beta\left(\frac{c}{g}\right)^{(1-\sigma)/\sigma}\right]\frac{(1 + Ab)}{1 + (1 - \sigma)Ab} \equiv MCF, \tag{8.57}$$

where $MC_g = (AK_0)/\theta$ is the marginal cost of an increase in the program expenditure ratio and the value of c is determined by (8.42). Equation (8.57) is the equivalent of the static Atkinson-Stern condition for optimal public expenditures financed by distortionary taxation for a public good that does not affect tax revenues.

The optimal (g, τ) combination satisfies (8.43) and (8.57). It is not possible to obtain a general closed form solution for τ and g, but some insights can be gained from examining the solution for $\sigma = 1$:

$$g = \left(\frac{\beta}{1 + \beta}\right)\frac{\rho}{A}, \tag{8.58}$$

$$\tau = \left(\frac{\beta}{1 + \beta}\right)\frac{\rho}{A} + \rho b, \tag{8.59}$$

$$c = \frac{\rho(1 + Ab)}{A}, \tag{8.60}$$

$$\gamma = (1 - \rho b)A - \left[1 + \frac{\beta}{1 + \beta}\right]\rho. \tag{8.61}$$

The reason why the optimal program expenditure ratio is independent of the public debt ratio when $\sigma = 1$ is shown in figure 8.4. For a given level of the public debt b_0, the MCF is $(1 + \beta)(1 + Ab_0)$ and therefore independent of the program expenditure ratio and the tax rate, while the ratio MB_g/MC_g is decreasing in g and independent of the tax rate. The optimal public expenditure ratio is g_0 when the debt level is b_0. An increase in the debt ratio, increases both the MCF and the MB_g/MC_g ratio in the same proportion, and therefore has no effect on the optimal level of g. Thus the key

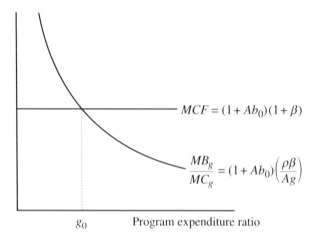

Figure 8.4
Optimal program spending ratio when $\sigma = 1$

reason why the optimal g is independent of b is that a higher debt ratio raises the marginal benefit from g in the same proportion as it increases the MCF. This effect arises with the preferences specified in (8.29) because private consumption and public consumption are complementary, and a higher debt ratio leads to a higher consumption ratio.

The sign dg/db is ambiguous when $0 < \sigma < 1$. However, calculations using a wide range of parameter values indicate that the optimal g is (slightly) increasing in b when $\sigma < 1$. (The calculations in the next section will illustrate this effect.) Figure 8.5 shows why the optimal g is increasing in b for $\sigma < 1$. The optimal (g, τ) combination is the solution to equation (8.57), which we will label the optimization condition (OC), and equation (8.35), which is the government's intertemporal budget constraint (BC). In the absence of the public debt, BC is a 45 degree line from the origin. OC has a negative slope in (g, τ) for $0 < \sigma < 1$.[11] Initially there is no public debt, and the optimal expenditure and tax rates are g_0 and τ_0. An increase in the public debt to $b_1 > 0$, shifts the intercept of BC to τ_L and the maximum program expenditure ratio that can be financed is g_u. The slope of BC, which is equal to $[1 + (1 - \sigma)Ab]^{-1}$, declines when the public debt increases because the tax rate needed to finance an increase in g causes the after-tax interest rate to decrease, thereby reducing the amount of tax revenue needed to finance the public debt when $0 < \sigma < 1$. Therefore the required $\Delta\tau$ is less than Δg. An increase in the public debt also causes OC to shift up because an increase in b increases the MB_g/MC_g ratio (through its effect on c) more than the MCF. To restore equality, holding τ constant, g must increase because an increase in g reduces the MB_g/MC_g ratio proportionately more than it reduces the MCF. The upward shift in OC and the reduction in the slope of BC offset the

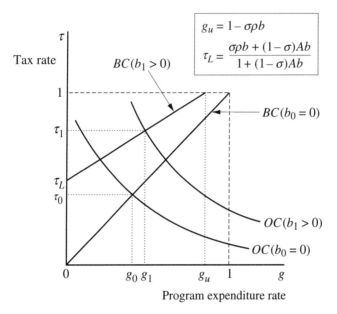

$$g_u = 1 - \sigma \rho b$$

$$\tau_L = \frac{\sigma \rho b + (1-\sigma)Ab}{1 + (1-\sigma)Ab}$$

Figure 8.5
Optimal program expenditure ratio and tax rate when $0 < \sigma < 1$

upward shift in the BC, and the optimal g remains virtually constant. Therefore almost all of the adjustment to the higher debt ratio occurs on the tax side of the budget.

While the model predicts that public debt does not crowd out spending on government services as a proportion of GDP, it can be shown that an increase in the public debt will crowd out program spending in the sense that the (c/g) ratio is increasing in b if $\sigma \leq 1$. In other words, the model predicts that a higher public debt will reduce public service consumption relative to private consumption.

As was noted in section 8.5.1, the government's intertemporal budget constraint is the same whether or not interest on the public debt is taxed, and therefore the optimal level of public expenditure is independent of whether interest on the public debt is taxed. It has been convenient to assume that interest on the public debt is not taxed, in deriving the formula for the MCF and the optimal program expenditure rate, since in this case both the private and public sectors use the after-tax rate of return on assets to discount future benefits, tax revenue, and costs. If the interest on the public debt is taxed and the government uses the before-tax interest rate to discount future tax revenues and costs, the marginal cost of funds formula would be amended to equal $MCF' = ((A - \gamma)/\theta) \cdot MCF$. Since $(A - \gamma)/\theta > 1$, the $MCF' > MCF$. However, the definition of the marginal cost of increasing the program expenditure

Table 8.2
MCF_B based on Canadian parameter values

Debt ratios	$b = 0$	$b = 0.728$	$b = 1.456$
Base case: Parameter values are $A = 0.081$, $\rho = 0.02$, $\sigma = 0.391$, $\beta = 0.088$			
γ	0.017	0.016	0.015
g	0.211	0.213	0.215
τ	0.211	0.246	0.278
c	0.578	0.589	0.600
c/g	2.739	2.765	2.789
MCF^a	1.166	1.195	1.221
$\dfrac{1 + Ab}{1 + (1 - \sigma)Ab}$	1.000	1.022	1.043
MCF'^b	1.426	1.516	1.607
High elasticity of substitution case: Parameter values are $A = 0.081$, $\rho = 0.0396$, $\sigma = 0.75$, $\beta = 0.375$			
γ	0.018	0.016	0.014
g	0.211	0.213	0.214
τ	0.211	0.246	0.279
C	0.565	0.589	0.612
c/g	2.672	2.765	2.855
MCF^a	1.390	1.455	1.519
$\dfrac{1 + Ab}{1 + (1 - \sigma)Ab}$	1.000	1.043	1.086
MCF'^b	1.520	1.616	1.712

a. MCF calculated using the after-tax rate of return on government bonds to discount net revenues and costs.
b. MCF' calculated using the before-tax rate of return on government bonds to discount net revenues and costs.

ratio would also change if the government uses the before-tax rate of return to discount future costs, and it would equal $MC'_g \equiv AK_0/(A - \gamma) < MC_g \equiv AK_0/\theta$. Therefore $MCF' \cdot MC'_g = MCF \cdot MC_g$, and the optimal g is independent of whether or not the interest payments on the public debt are taxed, and whether the government uses the before-tax or the after-tax rate of return to calculate the present value of future tax revenues and costs. Note, however, that the MB_g would be calculated using the after-tax rate of return that the private sector receives on savings in either case.

8.5.4   Application: The MCF from Public Sector Borrowing in Canada and the United States

Table 8.2 shows the calculation of the marginal cost of public funds using parameter values that replicate the average values of the key variables for the Canadian economy in the 1990s. In particular, for Canada in the 1990s, the average growth rate was $\gamma = 0.016$, the debt to GDP ration was $b = 0.728$, the consumption ratio was $c = 0.589$, and the government expenditure ratio was $g = 0.213$.[12] Given these values, $A = \gamma/(1 - c - g) = 0.081$. That leaves the preference parameters—ρ, σ, and β—to be determined. In the base case scenario we have used a conventional value for the personal rate of time preference, $\rho = 0.02$. We then computed the values of $\sigma = 0.391$ and $\beta = 0.088$ that generate values of $c = 0.589$ and $g = 0.213$ from equations (8.42) and (8.57). All these parameter values are plausible. (One of the attractive features of this simple model is that it can replicate key features of the Canadian economy in the 1990s with a few "reasonable" parameter values.)

With these base case parameters the MCF is 1.195. In other words, the "hurdle benefit–cost ratio" that a debt-financed public project needs in order to generate a net social gain is about 1.2. Alternatively, these calculations indicate that reducing the public debt by \$1.00 has a long-term payoff, through lower taxes and slightly higher rates of economic growth, of \$1.20.

As noted above, one of the most important features of our derivation of the formula for the MCF was showing that its value depends on the strength of the preference for the public good. If the private sector did not value the public good and $\beta = 0$, then the $MCF = (1 + Ab)/[1 + (1 - \sigma)Ab] = 1.022$. This shows that the MCF would be significantly underestimated if we ignored the social loss that arises from the reduction in public good consumption as a result of a slower rate of economic growth. Finally, the table shows that MCF', the marginal cost of public funds when tax revenues and program costs are discounted using the before-tax rate of return, is significantly higher than the MCF value based on the after-tax rate of return. We want to stress, however, that either value of the MCF can be used as long as the marginal cost of g is defined in a consistent manner.

Table 8.2 also shows how the growth rate, the MCF, and the optimal program expenditure ratio vary with the public debt ratio. If the public debt were eliminated, the model predicts that the growth rate of the Canadian economy would increase by a tenth of a percentage point. If the debt ratio doubled to 1.456, the growth rate of the economy would decline by a tenth of a percentage point. The relatively modest impact of the public debt on the growth rate in this model occurs because, as noted earlier, the Ricardian equivalence effect offsets the increase in the deficit ratio and therefore the reduction in the net savings rate from a major increase in the debt ratio is modest.

The MCF would decline only modestly from 1.195 to 1.166 if the public debt was eliminated, and it would increase to 1.221 if the public debt ratio doubled. The reason why the MCF is so unresponsive to the debt ratio is that the tax rate only falls by 3.5 percentage points with the elimination of the public debt, and therefore a fairly large distortionary tax remains even if the debt is eliminated. Thus the social cost of the first dollar of public debt is almost as high as an additional dollar of debt when the debt ratio is over 100 percent.

Finally, the model predicts that with the elimination of the public debt, the optimal program expenditure ratio would decrease very slightly to 0.211. Doubling the public debt would increase the program expenditure ratio slightly to 0.215. Thus the calculations confirm the analysis in figure 8.5, which shows that an increase in the public debt can increase the optimal program expenditure ratio if $0 < \sigma < 1$.

These calculations are based on the parameter values $\rho = 0.02$ and $\sigma = 0.391$. While the value for $\rho = 0.02$ is commonly used in simulations of endogenous growth models, the value for σ is lower than the values used in calculating the effects of tax policies in endogenous growth models. For example, in the four endogenous growth models surveyed by McGrattan and Schmitz (1999), the elasticity of substitution varied between 0.5 and 1.0. In order to see how sensitive the predictions of this model are to the value of σ, we can perform a second set of calculations using $\sigma = 0.75$. We then compute the values of $\rho = 0.0396$ and $\beta = 0.375$, which generate values of $c = 0.589$ and $g = 0.213$. With the higher values for ρ, σ, and β, the two alternative measures of the marginal cost of public funds are higher—$MCF = 1.455$ and the $MCF' = 1.616$—which is not surprising, since this makes the growth rate more sensitive to increases in the tax rate and the social loss from reduced program expenditures is also higher. These calculations indicate that the MCF is somewhat sensitive to the assumed value of the elasticity of substitution and the implied values of the other parameters.

Table 8.3 shows the same set of calculations using parameter values that replicate the average values of key variables for the US economy in the 1990s, with $\gamma = 0.021$, $b = 0.47$, $c = 0.668$, and $g = 0.190$.[13] Given these values for the United States, $A = \gamma/(1 - c - g) = 0.148$. Assuming $\rho = 0.02$, we calculate the values of $\sigma = 0.225$ and $\beta = 0.00405$ using equations (8.42) and (8.57). The results using these US parameter values are qualitatively similar to the calculations using Canadian parameters, but the MCFs are significantly lower because the value for σ that is used in these calculations is substantially lower. When a value of $\sigma = 0.75$ is adopted (along with the implied values $p = 0.085$ and $\beta = 0.253$), the MCF for the US economy is 1.355 for $b = 0.47$, and the economic growth rate is much more sensitive to the level of the public debt.

The theoretical model and the calculations suggest that the optimal g and (c/g) ratios will be relatively insensitive to variations in the debt ratio. To my knowledge, there are no empirical studies of the extent to which public debt crowds out government spending on goods and services. Some evidence concerning the impact of public debt on the size of the public sector are contained in figures 8.6 and 8.7, which plot the average ratio of consumptive government spending to GDP and the average ratio

Table 8.3
MCF_B based on US parameter values

Debt ratios	$b = 0$	$b = 0.47$	$b = 0.94$
Base case: Parameter values are $A = 0.148$, $\rho = 0.02$, $\sigma = 0.225$, $\beta = 0.004054$			
γ	0.023	0.021	0.020
g	0.188	0.190	0.192
τ	0.188	0.233	0.274
c	0.660	0.668	0.676
c/g	3.504	3.516	3.527
MCF^a	1.069	1.085	1.100
$\dfrac{1 + Ab}{1 + (1 - \sigma)Ab}$	1.000	1.015	1.028
MCF'^b	1.305	1.400	1.494
High elasticity of substitution case: Parameter values are $A = 0.148$, $\rho = 0.085$, $\sigma = 0.75$, $\beta = 0.253$			
γ	0.026	0.021	0.016
g	0.188	0.190	0.192
τ	0.188	0.233	0.277
c	0.636	0.688	0.699
c/g	3.379	3.516	3.647
MCF^a	1.285	1.355	1.423
$\dfrac{1 + Ab}{1 + (1 - \sigma)Ab}$	1.000	1.051	1.101
MCF'^b	1.380	1.482	1.583

a. MCF calculated using the after-tax rate of return on government bonds to discount net revenues and costs.
b. MCF' calculated using the before-tax rate of return on government bonds to discount net revenues and costs.

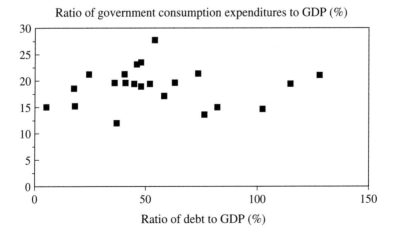

Ratio of government consumption expenditures to GDP (%)

Ratio of debt to GDP (%)

Figure 8.6
Government consumption spending ratios

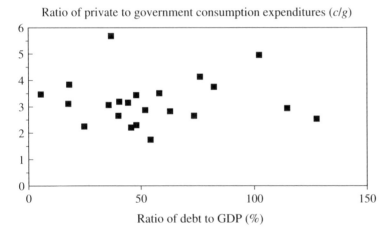

Figure 8.7
Public to private consumption spending ratios

of public to private consumption spending to the average debt ratio for twenty-two industrialized countries over the period 1990 to 1998. In either case a country's debt ratio does not have a statistically significant effect on its g or g/c, results that are broadly consistent with the prediction of this model. Of course, this is only a superficial analysis, and a more detailed empirically analysis is required to test the hypotheses regarding the effect of debt on government spending.

Further Reading for Chapter 8

For a general survey of the economic literature on government debt, see Elmendorf and Mankiw (1999). Lucas and Stokey (1983) investigated the optimal fiscal policy when public expenditures are stochastic and the government can issue debt with state contingent payoffs. The returns to bondholders are higher when government expenditures are higher because this reduces the real value of the public debt and therefore insures the government against the high expenditure state. This state contingent payoff on government debt could be interpreted as an unanticipated inflation that reduces the real value of the public debt. Cooley and Ohanian (1997) have used the "tax-smoothing" framework to analyze the fiscal policies of the US and British governments during World War II. They concluded that the British government's decision to finance a good part of its wartime expenditures with high taxes, especially on capital income, generated slower economic growth in the postwar period than would have been the case if their policy had relied more on debt. Hall and Krieger (2000) used the Lucas and Stokey framework to evaluate changes in the US public debt. Aiyagari et al. (2002) analyzed optimal fiscal policy where program expenditures are stochastic and public debt is not state contingent. They show that the optimal fiscal policy has the tax-smoothing characteristic, but that the optimal fiscal policy may involve the government acquiring enough assets so that it can finance its expenditures from investment income and therefore eliminate distortionary taxes.

Van der Ploeg (1996) and Turnovsky (1997) developed open economy endogenous growth models with foreign borrowing. In these models a higher level of foreign indebtedness increases the interest rate charged by foreign lenders, and this reduces investment and the rate of economic growth. Saint-Paul (1992) and Scarth (2004) analyzed the burden of the debt in non-Ricardian models. Other dynamic model of the effects of public debt on economic growth include Lin (2000), who analyzed the effects of an increase in the public debt in an overlapping generations model, and Hayakawa and Zak (2002) who used a two-country open economy CGE model to evaluate the gains from reducing the public debt and concluded that the gains were small. Calvo (2003) developed a model of the debt crises when governments finance their expenditures with distortionary taxes.

Hubbard and Engen (2004) and Ardagna, Caselli, and Lane (2004) are econometric studies of the effect of government deficits and debt on interest rates.

Exercises for Chapter 8

8.1 Suppose that an individual lives for two periods and his utility function is

$$U = C_1 + \alpha \cdot \ln(1 - L_1) + \frac{1}{1 + \rho} \cdot (C_2 + \alpha \cdot \ln(1 - L_2)),$$

where C_t is consumption in period t, L_t is labor supplied in period t, ρ is the individual's rate of time preference, and α is a positive constant. The individual will earn a wage rate of w_t in period t and $w_2 > w_1$. Suppose that the government has to incur G_1 dollars of program expenditures in period one and that G_2 is zero. Assume that both the government and the individual can borrow or lend at a fixed interest rate of r and that $p = r$. Finally, assume that the government finances its expenditures by imposing an ad valorem tax rate τ_i on wage income in period i and that at the start of the first period it has no debt.

(a) Show that the optimal fiscal policy requires $0 < \tau_1 < \tau_2$.

(b) Explain why the optimal debt policy does not involve "tax smoothing," that is, why $\tau_1 \neq \tau_2$ with the optimal fiscal policy.

(c) Explain why the optimal fiscal policy is not a balanced budget policy.

(d) Calculate the gain in moving from a balanced budget policy to the optimal debt policy as a percentage of the government's first-period expenditure if $\alpha = 20$, $r = 0.15$, $w_1 = 200$, $w_2 = 300$, $G_1 = 75$, and $G_2 = 0$.

8.2 Suppose that the aggregate production function for an economy is $X = K(1 + K)^{-1}$. The government and the private sector borrow on world capital markets at an after-tax rate of return of 0.08. Capital's share of output is one-third. The government's program spending is 25 percent of total output, and the debt to output ratio is 0.375. Calculate the crowding-out effect of the debt on the capital stock and the marginal cost of public funds from public sector borrowing.

9 The MCF in a Federal System of Government

In most countries taxes are levied by more than one level of government, and intergovernmental grants are an important part of the national fiscal architecture. It is therefore important to consider the MCF in a federation where different levels of government impose taxes on the same, or interdependent, tax bases and where intergovernmental grants may affect the fiscal capacities and the fiscal incentives of recipient governments. It is also widely recognized that governments' tax and expenditure decisions may be distorted by horizontal fiscal externalities, which occur among jurisdictions at the same level of government, and vertical fiscal externalities, which occur between different levels of government.

This chapter begins with a brief discussion of the nature of the tax externalities that arise in a federation and the associated problem of fiscal imbalance—misallocations of the tax burden and the provision of public services among subnational governments and between different levels of government. The conventional definitions of fiscal imbalance are not very helpful for policy purposes, and defining fiscal imbalance in terms of differences in the marginal cost of public funds between governments is a useful way of thinking about horizontal and vertical imbalances.

Section 9.2 develops a simple model of horizontal tax externalities in which subnational governments levy taxes on a mobile tax base. Higher tax rates by one government cause tax base flight, which increases the tax bases and revenues of other subnational governments.[1] Each government's perceived MCF is biased upward because it does not take into account the positive fiscal externality that its taxes create for other subnational governments. This can lead to underprovision of public services, as shown by Wilson (1986) and Zodrow and Mieszkowski (1986).

Intergovernmental grants can be used to correct the biases caused by horizontal fiscal externalities as Wildasin (1989) and others have pointed out. Section 9.3.1 considers how intergovernmental grants can be structured to correct the fiscal distortions caused by horizontal tax and expenditure externalities. However, correcting horizontal externalities is not the only rationale for intergovernmental grants. Many countries, such as Australia, Canada, and Germany provide equalization grants because of variations in fiscal capacity among subnational governments (for surveys of equalization systems, see Ma 1997 and Martinez-Vazquez and Searle 2007). Section 9.3.2 uses the framework in Dahlby and Wilson (1994) to develop a rationale for equalization grants. In that framework, equalization grants help achieve an optimal allocation of the tax burden across the federation by equalizing the MCFs across subnational governments. This way equalization grants achieve one of the conditions characterizing an optimal tax system—the equalization of the MCFs across tax bases. The section shows that the optimal equalization grants will depend on the relative sizes of the tax bases of the subnational governments as well as on the relative tax sensitivity of their tax bases. This approach also provides a better understanding and measure of that elusive concept—fiscal capacity. The section then compares and contrasts the "optimal equalization grant" formula with the representative tax system (RTS) formula that serves as the basis for equalization in Australia and Canada.

Section 9.4 examines the vertical fiscal externalities that can occur in a federal state because of the interdependence of the central and subnational governments' tax bases. The framework developed in Dahlby and Wilson (2003), where both central and subnational governments levy taxes on labor income and profits, is used to show that the subnational governments' MCFs can be biased either up or down because of the vertical tax externality.

Section 9.5 uses a model developed by Keen and Kotsogiannis (2002) to describe the conditions under which either the vertical or the horizontal tax externalities dominate and subnational governments' spending is too low or too high. This framework is also used to illustrate situations where there is a vertical fiscal imbalance, in the sense that the MCFs of the federal and state governments are not equal, and state spending is either too little or too much relative to federal spending.

9.1 Fiscal Externalities and Fiscal Imbalances

Interjurisdictional tax externalities occur when a government's taxes affect the residents of other jurisdictions within the federation either (1) directly by changing their consumer prices or the returns from the inputs that they provide in factor markets or (2) indirectly by altering their governments' tax revenues.[2] The direct fiscal externalities are always *horizontal*, meaning they affect individuals in other jurisdictions, whereas the indirect externalities can be either horizontal or *vertical*, meaning they affect the budget constraints of another level of government. Tax externalities may have positive or negative effects on the well-being of residents of other jurisdictions. An example of a direct tax externality is a hotel tax levied by a state government that is largely borne by out-of-state visitors through higher prices for hotel rooms.[3] A state's taxes on mobile tax bases may increase the other states' tax bases because they may induce cross-border shopping or capital flight.[4] A vertical tax externality can also arise when subnational governments' taxes are deductible in computing a federal income tax because an increase in a state's tax reduces the federal government's net revenues, and this affects taxpayers in all states. A vertical tax externality can also arise when two levels of government tax the same base, such as cigarettes or alcohol, or two interrelated tax bases such as sales taxes and payroll taxes.[5]

We focus on the tax externalities in this chapter because we expect that subnational governments will only consider the effects of their tax policies on their own residents, and not take into account the full effects of their policies on nonresidents. Tax externalities will distort subnational governments' fiscal decision-making by altering the subnational governments' perceived MCFs. That is, the tax externalities may cause a state government's MCF to diverge from its true or social MCF, which is the MCF includes the effects of raising additional tax revenue on all of the residents of a federation.

Another reason for focusing on fiscal externalities is that they can cause vertical fiscal imbalances to emerge between the tiers of government. In the following section we see that the vertical fiscal imbalances—the misallocation of taxation and spending between levels of government—can be defined as the inequality of the MCFs between levels of government. Horizontal fiscal imbalances, which can be viewed as an inequality in the MCFs among governments in the same tier, are discussed in section 9.1.3.

9.1.1   Conventional Definition of Vertical Fiscal Imbalance[6]

The existence of a fiscal imbalance between the federal and provincial governments has been a hotly contested issue in Canada in recent years.[7] Provincial politicians in Quebec and Ontario have argued that the federal government "appears to have more money than it knows what to do with," but the federal government under Prime Minister Paul Martin denied the existence of a vertical fiscal imbalance because the Canadian provinces have a broad range of tax powers and could raise more tax revenues by increasing their tax rates. Some commentators, such as Andrew Coyne (2005), have argued that the notion of fiscal imbalance is one of those ephemeral concepts "like dark matter or quantum uncertainty that defy comprehension by ordinary layman." Unlike Coyne, I think that fiscal imbalance is a meaningful concept, capable of being understood by laymen, but that the conventional definition of vertical fiscal imbalance is almost totally useless as a guide for public policy.

Much of the confusion and debate over fiscal imbalances can be attributed to a faulty conception of what constitutes a vertical fiscal imbalance. The conventional definition focuses on a mismatch between the spending responsibilities and access to tax revenues by an entire tier of government, especially subnational governments (e.g., see Breton 1996, p. 197; Webb 2002, p. 1). This way of defining vertical fiscal imbalance has the ephemeral quality referred to by Coyne. An entire tier government would be unable to fund its spending responsibilities from its own revenue sources only in situations where all of the governments are at the top of their Laffer curves and cannot raise any more revenues by raising tax rates. While this might occur in some rare situations, it is surely not a generic problem. Subnational governments almost always can raise more tax revenue by increasing their tax rates, but they do not want to because the cost of raising additional revenue is high. Furthermore, defining a vertical fiscal imbalance as a gap between revenue and spending responsibilities is unsatisfactory because, while constitutions usually specify the spending responsibilities of the subnational governments, the level of spending and the quality of these services are not specified. Consequently we can never really determine whether governments have met their spending responsibilities. Confronted with these shaky conceptual foundations, empirical studies of vertical fiscal imbalance have resorted to measuring the extent to which subnational government spending is financed by central government transfers.[8]

Measuring the gap between spending and own-revenues for any particular level of government is an accounting measure of fiscal imbalance. To determine whether taxes and spending are too high or too low for any particular level of government, we have to rely on economic concepts. In any economic model of resource allocation whether something is too high or too low depends on the gap between marginal costs and marginal benefits, and not on the gap between revenue and expenditure. For example, the fact that a firm's revenue exceeds its expenditure by $1 million does not tell us whether the firm's output is too high or too low, given its goal of maximizing profit. To determine whether the firm should produce more output or less, we need to know its marginal revenue and its marginal cost of production. Similar principles apply in evaluating fiscal policy in the public sector. From an economist's perspective, balance does not mean that revenues equal expenditures for a particular government at a particular point in time or for a particular level of government. We do not know whether taxes or expenditures are "too high" or "too low" unless we have some measures of the additional benefit from increased spending and the additional burden from tax rate increases.

The main problem with the accounting definition of vertical fiscal imbalance is that it lacks any grounding or basis in the normative theory of fiscal federalism—there are no theorems in public economics which indicate that own-revenues should equal own-expenditures at each level of government. Yet use of the word "imbalance," as Breton (1997, pp. 197–98) has noted, evokes the words:

[D]istortion, irresponsibility, illusion, and manipulation, [which] if they do not speak of intrinsic evil, do not signal much that should be encouraged and nurtured, either.... those who focus on the effects of vertical fiscal imbalance and on the money flows among governments... almost invariably decry vertical fiscal imbalance and the consequent flows of intergovernmental funds.

The conventional definition seems to suggest that federations should be "in balance" with each level of government raising sufficient revenues to cover its own expenditures and no intergovernmental transfers. However, this accounting approach to fiscal imbalance does not provide any guidance as to how the burden of raising tax revenue should be allocated between levels of government in a federation.

9.1.2   Alternative Definition of Vertical Fiscal Imbalance

There is a vertical fiscal imbalance in a federation if the marginal cost of raising tax revenue differs between the levels of government.

This definition provides a basis for determining whether taxes are too high or too low across the various levels of government. For example, if the MCF is 1.20 for the federal government and 1.40 for the state governments, then a small increase in taxation at the federal level that financed a transfer to the state governments, allowing them to reduce their taxes by the same amount, would result in a net social gain of 0.20. With this interpretation there is a "vertical fiscal balance" when the MCF is the same at both the federal and the state level because this will minimize the cost of raising a given amount of tax revenues.

Defining vertical fiscal balance as the equality of the MCFs across levels of government integrates the concept of vertical fiscal balance with the theory of optimal taxation, which is the backbone of normative public finance. An optimal tax system is one that minimizes the total deadweight cost of raising a given amount of tax revenue. This can be achieved if a government sets its tax rates so as to equalize the MCFs across its various tax bases. Defined in this manner, vertical fiscal balance in a federation is simply an application of the principle of optimal taxation to a multi-tiered system of governments.

The idea that efficiency in the allocation of resources in a federation requires the equalization of the marginal cost of public funds across levels of government is implicitly assumed (or explicitly discussed) in papers on fiscal federalism by Gordon (1983), Wildasin (1984), and Ahmad and Stern (1987). The first analytic model of vertical fiscal imbalance was developed by Hettich and Winer (1986). They argued that because taxpayers are more mobile at the provincial level compared to the federal level, the relative tax price of federal public services would be lower than the provincial tax price, and there would be an inherent "long-run bias towards centralization of the public sector" (p. 753). Hettich and Winer proposed that the resulting vertical fiscal imbalance be measured by the difference between the social welfare with the optimal allocation of federal and provincial spending (as defined by a Lindahl equilibrium where all taxpayers contribute their marginal benefit to pay for public services) and the actual allocation. In a footnote they pointed out that grants from the federal government to provinces would reduce the vertical fiscal imbalance.

Dahlby and Wilson (1994) and Dahlby (1996) took the next step in defining fiscal balance in a federation in terms of the equality of the MCFs between governments at the same level and across levels of government. In their view, a fiscal gap—the difference between a subnational government's tax revenues and its expenditures—is not an indication of fiscal imbalance. Quite the opposite. Fiscal transfers from a central government to subnational governments will often be required to equalize the MCFs across levels of government. The most recent contribution to this approach to defining fiscal balance is by Boadway and Tremblay (2006) who examine the emergence of fiscal imbalances when regions are subject to shocks and the federal government cannot commit to a particular level of transfers.

In the absence of intergovernmental transfers, why would the MCFs differ between levels of government? In particular, why would the MCF be higher at the subnational level than at the federal level if both levels of government can tax the same tax bases? One reason is that almost all tax bases are more mobile at the subnational level, and therefore subnational tax rate increases are more distortionary than a federal, nationwide, tax increases. For example, a state government's sales tax increase may induce its residents to shop in other states and bordering countries to avoid a tax increase, while a similar federal sales tax increase would create an incentive for international cross-bordering shopping, but not inter-state cross-border shopping. (A model of cross-border shopping in a federation in section 10.3 illustrates these effects.) Similarly the personal and corporate income tax bases are usually more tax sensitive at the subnational level than at the national level because some individuals and firms may relocate within a country in response to higher state tax rates, but a federal tax rate increase does not alter location decisions within a country. There is some empirical evidence that subnational governments' tax bases are more tax sensitive than federal tax bases. For the United States, Gruber and Saez (2002) found that the elasticity of taxable income with respect to a tax rate increase was 50 percent higher at the state level than at the federal level, although their estimates of the elasticities were not statistically different. For Canada, Mintz and Smart (2004) found that the provincial corporate income tax revenues were very tax sensitive, implying that the provincial MCFs for a corporate income tax increase may be substantially higher than at the federal level.

Because tax bases are generally more mobile at the state level than at the federal level, a state government's MCF may be significantly higher than the federal government's MCF. This is one reason why central governments in most federations raise more in taxes than they spend on their own programs and why they make transfers to subnational governments. However, one should not jump to the conclusion that subnational governments' MCFs are always higher than the central government's because other vertical and horizontal tax externalities might have the opposite effect. For example, tax exporting—shifting the burden of a tax to the residents of other states—imparts a downward bias to a state's MCF. The deductibility of subnational governments' taxes from federal income taxes also shifts some of the burden to tax-payers in other states and lowers the MCF for the state government.[9] Smart (1998) and Dahlby (2002a) have argued that equalization grants reduce the MCFs of recipient states because the equalization formula shelters them from the full distortionary cost of a tax rate increase. More generally, the overlap of provincial and federal tax bases means that subnational governments may face an MCF which is biased, either up or down, as Dahlby and Wilson (2003) have shown.

It is difficult to determine whether a federation has achieved a fiscal balance because the MCFs of the federal and subnational governments are not directly observable. In this chapter we develop theoretical models of the biases in subnational governments' MCF caused by these vertical and horizontal fiscal externalities in order to try to clarify these issues. Obviously we need econometric studies of tax base sensitivities at the federal and subnational levels and economic models that allow us to calculate the MCFs for both levels of government and account for the interdependence of the tax bases of the two levels of government.

9.1.3 Horizontal Fiscal Imbalances in a Federation

Horizontal fiscal imbalances arise in a federation when subnational governments have different "fiscal capacities." This can give rise to large variations in the provision of public services and/or the level of taxation by subnational governments in the federation. However, the concept of fiscal capacity is almost as ephemeral as the concept of vertical fiscal imbalance. Again, the MCF concept can come to the rescue. An optimal allocation of the tax burden in a federation occurs when the MCF is the same for all subnational governments. If the MCF for state i was 1.40 and the MCF for state j was 1.20, then a transferring a dollar from state i to state j would reduce the total cost of raising a given amount of tax revenue in the federation. Of course, such a transfer would not be a Pareto improvement because the residents of state j would generally be worse off. However, most tax and expenditure policies adopted in a federation would not pass such a test, although we would hope that they would pass a less rigorous cost–benefit, namely that the total gains to citizens within the federation exceed the losses imposed on some citizens. Dahlby and Wilson (1994) used this idea as the basis for the equalization grants that are used in many federations to reduce fiscal disparities among state governments. Within this framework a natural way to define horizontal fiscal imbalances is in terms of the differences in state governments' MCFs. In addition the formulas that determine the optimal equalization grants contain a definition of fiscal capacity that reflects both the size of a government's tax bases and the tax sensitivity of those tax bases. These ideas about the nature of horizontal fiscal imbalances and the policies to ameliorate them are discussed in section 9.3.2.

9.2   Horizontal Fiscal Externalities and the MCF of a Subnational Government

We begin by focusing on how the horizontal fiscal externalities caused by tax base mobility affect subnational governments' MCFs. We will assume that the central government only levies lump-sum taxes, thereby eliminating any vertical fiscal externalities from changes in states' tax rates. In sections 9.5 and 10.3 we consider models where there are both vertical and horizontal tax externalities.

Consider a country where the total capital stock is fixed but capital is perfectly mobile between states within the country. Let p be the after-tax rate of return on capital. Initially we will assume that each state is small and treat p as exogenous. Let t_i be the per unit tax rate on capital levied by state i. The gross rate of return that is earned on capital in state i is $r_i = p + t_i$. Output in state i is determined by the production function $f(K_i)$, with $f'(K_i) > 0$ and $f''(K_i) < 0$. The demand for capital is determined by the marginal productivity condition:

$$f'(K_i) = p + t_i = r_i. \tag{9.1}$$

The demand for capital in state i is decreasing in t_i:

$$\frac{dK_i}{dt_i} = \frac{1}{f''(K_i)} < 0. \tag{9.2}$$

The residents of state i own the fixed factor of production (land or possibly inelastically supplied labor) and $\hat{K}_i$ units of capital. For simplicity we will assume that all of the residents of state i are identical. Consumption of the private good, x_i, is determined by the representative resident's budget constraint:

$$x_i = f(K_i) - (p + t_i)K_i + p\hat{K}_i. \tag{9.3}$$

The well-being of the representative individual in state i is $U(x_i, g_i)$, where g_i is the public service provided by state i. Note that g_i is a consumptive public good, and it does not enter the production function for output. The unit cost of producing g_i is constant and equal to one. It is assumed that capital is the only tax base that is used to finance state government spending. Therefore $R_i = t_i K_i = g_i$.

The marginal cost of public funds that is perceived by state i is defined by

$$MCF_i = \frac{-(1/\lambda_i)dU/dt_i}{dR_i/dt_i}. \tag{9.4}$$

Initially we will assume that state i is small compared to the rest of the federation and the perceived effect of its tax rate changes on the overall return to capital is negligible, such that $dp/dt_i = 0$ and $dr_i/dt_i = 1$. The formula for the MCF_i is derived in the usual way. In the denominator we have

$$\frac{dR_i}{dt_i} = K_i + t_i \frac{dK_i}{dr_i} = K_i(1 + \tau_i \varepsilon_i), \tag{9.5}$$

where $\tau_i = t_i/r_i$ is the ad valorem tax rate on capital in state i and $\varepsilon_i < 0$ is the elasticity of demand for capital in state i. An expression for the numerator of the MCF_i can be derived by substituting the representative individual's budget constraint into the utility function and noting that

$$\frac{dU^i}{dt_i} = \lambda_i \left(f' \frac{dK_i}{dr_i} - r_i \frac{dK_i}{dr_i} - K_i \right) = -\lambda_i K_i, \tag{9.6}$$

where λ_i is the dU^i/dx_i. Therefore the MCF_i can be written as

$$MCF_{t_i} = \frac{K_i}{K_i + t_i(dK_i/dr_i)} = \frac{1}{1 + \tau_i \varepsilon_i}. \tag{9.7}$$

The state government will provide the public service up to the point where

$$MB_{g_i} \equiv \frac{U_{G_i}}{\lambda_i} = MCF_{t_i}. \tag{9.8}$$

It is assumed that the marginal benefit from the public service, MB_{g_i}, is decreasing in g_i.

The potential bias in the state government's tax-expenditure decision arises from the fact that it does not take into account the impact of its fiscal decisions on the residents of other states. To keep the notation as simple as possible, we will denote the well-being of the residents in all other states by $U^j(x_j, g_j)$, where the arguments in this utility function are private consumption and public services provided in "state j." Note that this model assumes that there are no benefit spillovers from the provision of public services in state i.

The total social marginal cost of funds for state i will be defined as the total social cost of raising an additional dollar of tax revenue by the entire public sector or

$$SMCF_{t_i} = \frac{S_i(dU^i/dt_i) + S_j(dU^j/dt_i)}{(dR_i/dt_i) + (dR_j/dt_i)}, \tag{9.9}$$

where S_h is the marginal social welfare gain from an increase in well-being of state h's residents. Note that this is the SMCF that an omnipotent planner would use to maximize social welfare if the planner could set t_i, t_j, g_i, and g_j. Recall that the distributional weights are defined as $\beta_h = S_h \lambda_h$. Note that there is no direct fiscal impact of an increase in t_i on the residents of state j is zero, since

$$\frac{dU^j}{dt_i} = \lambda_j \left(f'(K_j) \frac{dK_j}{dt_i} - c_j \frac{dK_j}{dt_i} \right) = 0. \tag{9.10}$$

The fiscal externality from a tax rate increase by state i is realized through a change in the budget constraint of the government of state j, which is captured by the dR_j/dt_i term and equal to

$$\frac{dR_j}{dt_i} = t_j \frac{dK_j}{dt_i} = -t_j \frac{dK_i}{dt_i}, \tag{9.11}$$

since the total amount of capital in the economy is fixed and $dK_j = -dK_i$. Therefore the social marginal cost of funds is equal to

$$SMCF_{t_i} = \frac{\beta_i K_i}{K_i + (t_i - t_j)(dK_i/dr_i)} = \frac{\beta_i}{1 + [(t_i - t_j)/(p + t_i)]\varepsilon_i}. \tag{9.12}$$

If distributional concerns are not important and $\beta_i = 1$, the $MCF_i > SMCF_i$ if $t_j > 0$ because the government of state i fails to take into account the positive fiscal externality, $-t_j dK_i/dt_i$, that arises because the tax revenues of the other states will increase as a result of the exodus of capital from state i. Note that if all states are identical and $t_j = t_i$ in a symmetric fiscal equilibrium, then the $SMCF_{t_i} = 1$ and the optimal provision of the state provided public good would satisfy the condition $MB_{g_i} = 1$. In general, the upward bias in its perceived MCF_{t_i} causes state i to set a tax rate on capital that is too low, leading to underprovision of the public good. If, for example, $f(K) = K^\alpha$ with $\alpha = 1/3$, $p = 0.10$, and $t_i = t_j = 0.02$, then the $MCF_{t_i} = 1.33$ and $SMCF_{t_i} = 1$, indicating a significant upward bias in the states' perceived MCF and a potentially significant underprovision of the public good.[10]

The analysis above assumed that each state in the federation is small and that their individual tax rates have a negligible effect on the return to capital. However, in many federations there are large states (e.g., Ontario in Canada or California in the United States) that may affect the net rate of return on capital through their choice of the tax rate. This in turn may affect their taxation decisions and the fiscal externalities that they generate. Again, we will assume that capital is fixed for the entire economy and treat the rest of the economy as a single homogeneous region j that imposes a tax rate of t_j on capital. Now the effect of an increase in the tax rate on capital by state i is

$$\frac{dK_i}{dr_i}(dp + dt_i) + \frac{dK_j}{dr_j}(dp) = 0 \tag{9.13}$$

or

$$\frac{dp}{dt_i} = \frac{-\varepsilon_i(K_i/K_j)}{\varepsilon_i(K_i/K_j) + \varepsilon_j(r_i/r_j)} < 0, \tag{9.14}$$

where $\varepsilon_i < 0$ is the elasticity of demand for capital in state i and $\varepsilon_j < 0$ is the elasticity of demand for capital in state j (i.e., the rest of the economy). If the elasticities of demand for capital and the tax rates are the same in the capital-importing and exporting regions, then dp/dt_i is equal to minus the share of capital employed in state i. Therefore, if the share of capital employed in state i is small compared to the rest of the economy, dp/dt_i is close to zero, and the analysis in the previous section applies. If the (K_i/K_j) ratio is not "small," then dp/dt_i will be negative, and it will affect the state's perception of its MCF from taxing capital.

Taking into account dp/dt_i, the numerator of the MCF_{t_i} will now be equal to

$$-\frac{1}{\lambda_i}\frac{dU^i}{dt_i} = K_i\left[1 + \left(1 - \frac{\hat{K}_i}{K_i}\right)\frac{dp}{dt_i}\right]. \tag{9.15}$$

The second term in square brackets will be positive if state i is a capital-exporting state, that is $\hat{K}_i > K_i$, and negative if it is a capital-importing state. The marginal perceived cost of a tax rate increase will be higher for a large capital-exporting state compared to a small state because a tax rate increase will lower the net income of its residents through a reduction in the after-tax return on capital. Conversely, for a large capital-importing state with $K_i > \hat{K}_i$, the perceived cost of a capital tax rate increase will be reduced because some of the tax burden will be shifted to the residents of the capital-exporting states.

The effect on state i's tax revenues will also be modified as follows:

$$\frac{dR_i}{dt_i} = K_i + t_i\frac{dK_i}{dr_i}\left(1 + \frac{dp}{dt_i}\right). \tag{9.16}$$

State i's tax revenues will be more responsive to a tax rate increase than in the case of a small state because $(1 + dp/dt_i)$ is positive but less than one. This factor will reduce the MCF_i for both a large capital-exporting and capital-importing state compared to the small state that does not affect the rate of return on capital through its taxation decisions.

Combining (9.15) and (9.16), we obtain the following expression for the MCF_{t_i}:

$$MCF_{t_i} = \frac{K_i + (K_i - \hat{K}_i)\dfrac{dp}{dt_i}}{1 + t_i\dfrac{dK_i}{dr_i}\left(1 + \dfrac{dp}{dt_i}\right)} = \frac{1 + \left(1 - \dfrac{\hat{K}_i}{K_i}\right)\dfrac{dp}{dt_i}}{1 + \tau_i\varepsilon_i\left(1 + \dfrac{dp}{dt_i}\right)}. \tag{9.17}$$

Compared to a small state, the MCF_{t_i} will be reduced for a large capital-importing state because part of the tax burden will be shifted to the residents of the capital-exporting region. For the large capital-exporting state, the MCF_{t_i} may be higher or lower because while the terms of trade effect harms its residents, its tax revenues are now less sensitive to a tax rate increase.

The social marginal cost of funds from state i's taxing capital can now be written as

$$SMCF_{t_i} = \frac{\beta_i K_i + [\beta_i (K_i - \hat{K}_i) + \beta_j (K_j - \hat{K}_j)] \dfrac{d\rho}{dt_i}}{K_i + (t_i - t_j) \dfrac{dK_i}{dc_i} \left(1 + \dfrac{d\rho}{dt_i}\right)}. \tag{9.18}$$

The $SMCF_{t_i}$ will be higher if state i is a capital-exporting state and its distributional weight is relatively high. If the distributional weights that apply to the residents of the capital-importing and capital-exporting states are identical, then the term in square brackets in the numerator of (9.18) is zero and the terms-of-trade effect vanishes from the numerator (9.18). In this case, (9.17) compared with (9.18) shows that the $SMCF_{t_i}$ will be less than the MCF_{t_i} for a capital-exporting state because the numerator will be lower, and the denominator will be larger because it will incorporate the positive effect on state j's tax revenues from an increase in state i's tax rate. For example, if $f(K) = K^{\alpha}$ with $\alpha = 1/3$, $p = 0.10$, $t_i = t_j = 0.02$, and if the residents of state i own 20 percent of the total capital stock but only 10 percent of the total capital stock is invested in state i, then the $MCF_{t_i} = 1.419$ and $SMCF_{t_i} = 1$, indicating that there is an upward bias in the state's perceived MCF that is greater than in the case of a small state, where the $MCF_{t_i} = 1.33$. In general, the large capital-exporting state's MCF will be greater than that of a very small state if $\hat{K}_i / K_i > (1 + \tau_i \varepsilon_i)^{-1} > 1$, where $\tau_i = t_i / r_i$.

Whether the MCF_{t_i} for a capital-importing state is greater than or less than its $SMCF_{t_i}$ will depend on whether the revenue externality is greater than or less than the direct impact of the terms-of-trade effect on the residents of the other state. The latter effect can be thought of as a form of tax exporting that reduces the perceived MCF. In the case where the tax rates and elasticities of demand for capital are the same in the capital-exporting and capital-importing regions, the MCF_{t_i} for a capital-importing state will be less than the $SMCF_{t_i}$ if $\hat{K}_i / K_i < 1 + \tau_i \varepsilon_i (K_j / K_i)$. If $f(K) = K^{\alpha}$ with $\alpha = 1/3$, $p = 0.10$, $t_i = t_j = 0.02$, with 40 percent of the total capital stock employed in state i, $MCF_{t_i} < SMCF_{t_i}$ if $\hat{K}_i / K_i < 0.625$. In other words, if residents of the capital-importing region own less than 62.5 percent of the capital stock invested in the state, then the tax-exporting effect will outweigh the revenue externality and the state's perceived MCF will be too low, leading to excessive expenditures on public goods.

9.3 Intergovernmental Grants and Subnational Governments' MCFs

9.3.1 Correcting Horizontal Expenditure Externalities

It has long been recognized that matching grants from a central government can be used to correct the resource allocation problems associated with benefit spillovers between subnational governments, that is, a situation where the provision of a good or service by state i directly affects the residents of other states. Let g_i be a publicly provided good or service by state i at a constant marginal cost of production of MC. If the central government provides a matching grant at the rate m_g for expenditures on g_i, the optimal provision of this good by state i will be determined by the following version of the Atkinson-Stern condition:[11]

$$MB_i = MCF_i[(1 - m_g)MC - R^i_{g_i}], \tag{9.19}$$

where MB_i is the marginal consumption benefit that g_i provides to the residents of state i and $R^i_{g_i}$ is the effect that an additional unit of good i on state i's revenues. Recall that $R^i_{g_i}$ may be positive or negative, depending on how g_i affects the revenues generated by state i. For example, if the publicly provided good is a highway, MB_i would be the consumption benefits from a highway improvement and $R^i_{g_i}$ would be the change in government revenues because lower transportation costs for highway users may increase profits or wages, thereby affecting the government's tax bases. It will be assumed that the matching rate is set by the central government in order to maximize the net social gain, and therefore it will satisfy the condition

$$MB_i + MB_j = MCF[MC - R^i_{g_i} - R^j_{g_i}], \tag{9.20}$$

where MB_j is the direct marginal benefit from the spillover to residents of state j and $R^j_{g_i}$ is the effect on state j's revenues of an additional unit of g_i. Note that MB_j and $R^j_{g_i}$ could be positive or negative depending on whether they confer benefits or costs on state j or increase or reduce state j's tax bases. It is assumed that the fiscal system is optimal in the sense that marginal cost of funds has been equalized across the governments, possibly through a series of intergovernmental transfers, such that $MCF_i = MCF_j = MCF_0$, where MCF_0 is the marginal cost of funds for the federal government. (Grant mechanisms to equalize the marginal cost of funds across governments will be discussed below.) Under these conditions the optimal matching grant rate is the following:

$$m_g = \frac{MB_j + MCF \cdot R^j_{g_i}}{MB_i + MB_j + MCF(R^i_{g_i} + R^j_{g_i})}. \tag{9.21}$$

In other words, the matching rate should be the ratio of the total marginal spillover to the total social marginal benefit from the provision of g_i. This formula incorporates the standard result—that the matching rate should equal $MB_j/(MB_j + MB_i)$, the share of total direct marginal benefits that accrue outside state i—but it also includes the revenue effects of the public good, valued at the common MCF for the governments in the federation. Note that if the marginal spillovers are negative, perhaps because of adverse impacts on the environment in a neighboring state or because it lowers revenues generated in the other state, then m_g will be negative and the central government should tax g_i to discourage its provision by state i. However, in many countries it would be difficult to enforce a measure such as this. For example, in Canada the constitution prohibits one level of government from taxing another level of government.

9.3.2   Correcting Horizontal Tax Externalities

Matching grants could also be used to correct tax externalities. To keep the analysis as simple as possible, we will use the capital tax competition model in section 9.2 to illustrate the use of matching grants to correct tax externalities. Let m_R be the matching rate that applies to the tax revenues generated by state i. Assuming that all states are small, and ignoring distributional concerns, the MCF for state i will be equal to

$$MCF_i = \frac{K_i}{(1 + m_R)(dR_i/dt_i)}, \tag{9.22}$$

while the social marginal cost of funds, ignoring distributional concerns, will be equal to

$$SMCF_i = \frac{K_i}{(dR_i/dt_i) + (dR_j/dt_i)}, \tag{9.23}$$

where the dR_j/dt_i captures the revenue effect of the tax base flight for other states. The matching rate that equates MCF_i and $SMCF_i$ is

$$m_R = \frac{dR_j/dt_i}{dR_i/dt_i} = \frac{dR_j}{dR_i}. \tag{9.24}$$

In other words, the matching rate should be the rate at which revenue of other states increase when state i increases its tax revenues by one dollar. In the capital tax competition model this matching rate would be equal to

$$m_R = \frac{-\tau_i \varepsilon_{Kc_i}}{1 + \tau_i \varepsilon_{Kc_i}}. \tag{9.25}$$

If the same parameter values as in section 9.2 are used, if $f(K) = K^{\alpha}$ with $\alpha = 1/3$, $p = 0.10$, $t_i = t_j = 0.02$, then the optimal revenue matching rate would be $m_R = 1/3$. In other words, the central government should supplement the state governments' revenues by 33 cents for every dollar of tax revenue raised by the state governments in order to correctly align the state government's perceived MCF with the true MCF.

9.3.3 Optimal Equalization Grants

Many federal countries, such as Australia, Canada, and Germany, provide equalization grants to states with "deficient fiscal capacity." The rationale for such grants has been based on the need to correct incentives for fiscally-induced migration or to promote horizontal equity in the federation.[12] In this section we outline a different, but largely complementary, motivation for equalization grants—one that is based on the principles of optimal taxation and the desire to minimize the total cost of raising a given amount of tax revenue by equalizing the marginal cost of public funds across subnational governments. A more elaborate derivation and discussion of the theory of optimal equalization grants is contained in Dahlby and Wilson (1994).

Assume that there are only two states. Each state has the same population and only one tax base that is not mobile between the states. It is assumed that each state has to raise a fixed amount of revenue, R, to finance a given amount of the public good where $R = t_i B_i$ is the revenue raised in state i by taxing its base B_i at the tax rate t_i. The MCF for state i is

$$MCF_i = \frac{B_i}{B_i + t_i(dB_i/dt_i)} = \frac{1}{1 + (R/B_i)(d\ln B_i/dt_i)}, \tag{9.26}$$

where $d\ln B_i/dt_i < 0$ measures the tax sensitivity of state i's tax base. State i's MCF will higher the larger the amount of tax revenue to be raised, the greater the tax sensitivity of its tax base, and the smaller the size of the tax base.

Appealing to optimal tax theory and ignoring distributional issues, there will be an optimal allocation of the tax burden across the two states if the MCFs are the same in the two states. Suppose, for concreteness, that MCF_i exceeds MCF_j in the absence of intergovernmental transfers. The optimal allocation of the tax burden can be achieved if state j makes a transfer, E, to state i. This would shift the tax burden from a state i where the MCF is high to state j where the MCF is lower, thereby lowering the total burden of raising the given amount of tax revenue. The budget constraints of the two states will then become $R = t_i B_i + E$ in state i and $R = t_j B_j - E$ in state j. State i will be a recipient of equalization if $E > 0$ and a contributor if $E < 0$. (Here for simplicity we are assuming the equalization system is funded directly by the states and not by the central government.) The two state's MCFs will be

$$MCF_i = \frac{1}{1 + [(R - E)/B_i](d\ln B_i/dt_i)},$$ (9.27)

$$MCF_j = \frac{1}{1 + [(R + E)/B_j](d\ln B_j/dt_j)}.$$ (9.28)

The optimal equalization grant which equalizes the MCFs will be equal to the following:

$$E = \left(\frac{\dfrac{B_j}{-\xi_j} - \dfrac{B_j}{-\xi_i}}{\dfrac{B_j}{-\xi_j} + \dfrac{B_i}{-\xi_i}} \right) R = \left(\frac{FC_j - FC_i}{FC_j + FC_i} \right) R,$$ (9.29)

where $\xi_i = (d\ln B_i/dt_i)$ is the semielasticity of the tax base, a measure of the tax sensitivity of state i's tax base, and $FC_i = B_i/(-\xi_i)$ is a measure of the fiscal capacity of state i. This simple model points out an important concept that has been largely ignored in the literature on equalization grants—a state's fiscal capacity depends on the tax sensitivity of a state's tax base as well as the size of a state's tax base. The amount of equalization received or paid by a state will depend on its relative fiscal capacity, as defined above, and the amount of revenue that has to be raised to finance expenditures.

If the tax bases display the same degree of tax sensitivity in both states, then the equalization formula simply becomes

$$E = \left(\frac{B_j - B_i}{B_j + B_i} \right) R.$$ (9.30)

In other words, the equalization grant depends on the difference in the tax base shares of the two states and the total revenues to be raised by each state. This is the same equalization grant that would be provided under a representative tax system (RTS) equalization grant formula. For example, if $B_j = 120$, $B_i = 80$, and $R = 20$, then an equalization grant of 4 would be made to state i from state j under the RTS formula and the optimal equalization grant formula if the tax bases in both states were equally tax sensitive.

However, the amount of equalization and even the direction of the equalization payments would change if there are significant differences in the tax sensitivity of the tax bases between the states. For example, if $\xi_i = -0.4$ and $\xi_j = -0.5$, then the optimal equalization grant would be reduced from 4.00 to 1.818. Furthermore, if $\xi_j/\xi_i > B_j/B_i > 1$, state j would be the recipient of equalization even though its per capita tax base is larger than that of state i.

This presentation of the optimal equalization grant ignored two important effects that equalization grants can have on the behavior of state governments. First, total spending by the state government is not fixed and the presence of an equalization grant may cause the state to provide more services (increase expenditures) because its MCF is lower. Second, most states can tax more than one tax base and the equalization system may affect the tax rates that a state government imposes on its various tax bases to finance a given level of expenditures. These issues are considered in section 10.2.

9.4   Vertical Fiscal Externalities in a Federation

A vertical fiscal externality occurs in a federation when the taxes or expenditures of one level of government affect the budget constraint of another level of government. As Keen and Kotsogiannis (2002, p. 363) have noted "the vertical externalities that are...at the heart of federal tax architecture have—until recently—been largely neglected in the theory of fiscal federalism, which has focused instead on horizontal externalities arising from mobility of the tax base between the states." This branch of the fiscal federalism literature developed slowly. Early and somewhat neglected papers by Cassing and Hillman (1982) and Hansson and Stuart (1987) pointed out some of the implications that arise when federal and state governments impose taxes on the same tax base. Flowers (1988) then showed that a federation of Leviathan governments may end up on a downward-sloping sector of the Laffer curve if they ignore the impact of their tax rates on the revenues of the other level of government.[13] Papers by Johnson (1988, 1991) showed that tax base overlap may increase the incentive for benevolent state governments to redistribute income to their residents because some of the cost of the redistribution is borne by all federal taxpayers. Dahlby (1996), Boadway and Keen (1996), Keen (1998), and Boadway et al. (1998) analyzed the tax and expenditure decisions of benevolent governments where both levels tax wage income. They concluded that tax rates will be too high if, as seems likely, state governments ignore the reduction in federal tax revenue that occurs because the state's tax increase causes the shared tax base to shrink.

In all these papers, tax base overlap creates the public sector version of a common property resource problem. The overexploitation of shared tax bases is the public sector equivalent of the overexploitation of fishing grounds. The vertical fiscal externality caused by tax base overlap is illustrated in figure 9.1. Suppose that the federal and a state government impose per unit excise taxes of t_0 and t_i respectively on commodity X, which has a perfectly elastic supply curve S and downward-sloping supply curve D. Initially the state tax rate is t_i^0 and the price of the commodity is P^0. The federal government's tax revenue is equal to area c + area e. The state government's

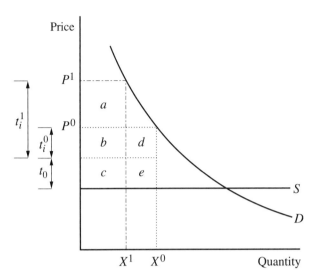

Figure 9.1
Vertical tax externality with tax base overlap

tax revenue is area b plus area d. If the state government increases its tax rate to t_i^1, the price of the commodity will increase to P^1, the state government's tax revenues will increase if area a is greater than area d. Federal tax revenue will decline by area e because the tax base has declined from X^0 to X^1. It is possible that the decline in federal tax revenue exceeds the increase in state tax revenue, and therefore the governments may be operating on the downward-sloping section of the Laffer curve for total federal and state tax revenues. Even if they are on the upward-sloping section of the total revenue Laffer curve, the state government will underestimate the marginal cost of public funds from this tax source because the state's perceived marginal cost of public funds is $MCF = X/(X + t_i dX/dt_i)$, whereas the true marginal cost of public funds is $X/(X + (t_i + t_0)dX/dt_i)$.

The preceding analysis reflects the general presumption in the literature, that the vertical tax externality is negative—an increase in taxes by one level of government results in a reduction in revenue to the other level. This implies that governments will underestimate the marginal cost of funds, leading to excessive taxation. However, Dahlby and Wilson (2003) show that the vertical tax externality can be positive when ad valorem taxes, rather than per unit taxes, are levied and the demand for the taxed good is price inelastic. Another interesting aspect of the vertical tax externality is that it can be positive or negative depending on which side of the market the tax is levied. These are unusual results because normally, in competitive markets, the distributional and efficiency effects of taxes do not depend on whether the tax is collected suppliers or consumers, and they do not depend on whether the tax is levied as an ad valorem or a per unit tax.

In this section we use the Dahlby and Wilson (2003) model to analyze the effects of vertical tax externalities on a state governments' MCF. Suppose that both the central government and the state governments tax wages and profits. The state governments are assumed to be identical and small relative to the entire federation. To simplify the notation, we focus on only one state government. Let τ_0 and τ_i be the ad valorem tax rates on employees' wage incomes, and let u_0 and u_i be the proportional tax rates on profits, levied by the federal and state governments respectively where $\tau = \tau_0 + \tau_i$ is the total tax rate by wage incomes by both levels of government. It is assumed that all economic profits are taxed away by the federal and state governments so that $u_0 + u_i = 1$. We assume that the profit tax rates are positive and exogenously determined, perhaps by the constitution.

The state government provides a purely consumptive public good, which is financed at least in part by a tax on the wage incomes earned in the state.[14] For simplicity, it is assumed that the state-provided public good does not affect labor supply decisions. Aggregate production is given by $X = f(L)$, where L is the amount of labor supplied by residents of the state at the net wage rate $w_n = (1 - \tau)w$, where $w = f'(L)$ and $f''(L) < 0$. (Note that it is assumed that the wage tax is collected from workers. Later we will consider the effect of an employer payroll tax.) Economic profit is equal to $\Pi = f(L) - wL$. It is assumed that labor is completely immobile between states, but that the supply of labor in a state is a nondecreasing function of the net wage rate where the labor supply elasticity is $\eta = (\partial L / \partial w_n)(w_n / L) \geq 0$. The assumption that labor is immobile between states allows us to focus on the vertical tax externality.

The effects of a wage rate tax increase on the wage rate paid by employers and their before-tax profits are given by

$$\frac{dw}{d\tau} = \frac{w}{1 - \tau} \cdot \frac{\eta}{\eta - \varepsilon} \geq 0, \tag{9.31}$$

$$\frac{d\Pi}{d\tau} = -L \frac{dw}{d\tau} \leq 0, \tag{9.32}$$

where $\varepsilon = f' / (Lf'') < 0$ is the elasticity of demand for labor. Equation (9.31) indicates that an increase in the wage tax rate will cause a larger increase in the gross wage rate the more elastic the supply of labor and the less elastic the demand for labor. As equation (9.32) indicates, the increase in the gross wage rate causes a decline in economic profit that is proportional to the amount of labor employed.

Each level of government sets its tax rates on wage income independently. The revenue raised by the state government is $R_i = \tau_i wL + u_i \Pi$, and the revenue raised by the federal government is $R_0 = \tau_0 wL + u_0 \Pi$. It is assumed that $\tau_0 > 0$ and $\tau_i > 0$, meaning both levels of government at the margin finance their expenditures by taxing employees' wage income.

Taking the total differential of R_0 with respect to τ_i and using equations (9.31) and (9.32) yields

$$\frac{dR_0}{d\tau_i} = \tau_0 L \frac{dw}{d\tau_i} + \tau_0 w \left(\frac{dL}{dw_n} \frac{dw_n}{d\tau_i} \right) + U \frac{d\Pi}{d\tau_i} = \frac{wL}{1-\tau} \cdot \frac{\eta}{\eta - \varepsilon} (\tau_0 (1 + \varepsilon) - u_0), \qquad (9.33)$$

where $dR_0/d\tau_i \gtreqless 0$ as $\tau_0 (1 + \varepsilon) \gtreqless u_0$. The vertical tax externality from an increase in the state government's wage tax can be positive or negative. In particular, if the demand for labor is inelastic, $-1 < \varepsilon < 0$, the wage tax base, wL, increases by $(1 + \varepsilon)L(dw/d\tau_i)$ while the profit tax base declines by $Ldw/d\tau_i$. If $\tau_0 (1 + \varepsilon)$ exceeds u_0, then the increase in federal wage tax revenue exceeds the decline in federal profit tax revenue, and total federal tax revenue increases when the state government increases its tax rate on wage income.

This situation is illustrated in figure 9.2 where, for convenience, it is assumed that the state tax rate on wage income is initially zero, and the wage tax base is initially $w^0 L^0$. When the state government introduces a wage tax of τ_i, the change in the wage tax base is area $w^1 \alpha \beta w^0$ minus area $L^1 \beta \gamma L^0$, whereas the profit tax base declines by area $w^1 \alpha \beta w^0$. Consequently total federal tax revenues will increase when the state government taxes employees' wages if the federal wage tax rate is relatively high compared to the federal profit tax rate and the demand for labor is quite inelastic.

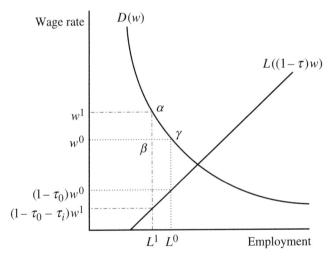

Figure 9.2
Effect of a state's tax on wage income on federal tax revenues

Note that if the federal government taxes wage and profit income at the same rate, then total federal tax revenues will increase if the demand for labor is inelastic and decrease if the demand for labor is elastic.

In the situation portrayed in figure 9.1 the vertical tax externality is always negative because it was assumed that the federal government levied a per unit tax, and therefore the federal tax base necessarily declines when the state government increases its tax rate. If the federal government levies an ad valorem tax rate on wage income, its tax revenue may increase because its wage tax base may increase when the state government levies tax on wage income.

Another interesting aspect of the vertical tax externality is that it depends on which side of the market the tax is levied. Figure 9.3 shows the vertical fiscal externality that arises when both levels of government levy ad valorem payroll taxes on employers. In the initial situation the federal government taxes employers' payrolls at the rate τ_0^*, and state employer payroll tax rate is zero. Federal wage tax revenue is $\tau_0^* w^0 L^0$. When the state government introduces an ad valorem employer payroll tax at the rate τ_i^*, employment declines to L^1 and the wage rate declines to w^1. Therefore federal tax revenue declines because $w^1 L^1 < w^0 L^0$, and economic profits are also reduced because $(1 + \tau_0^* + \tau_i^0)w^1 > (1 + \tau_0^*)w^0$.

Consequently the vertical tax externality depends on which side of the market the tax is levied. With an ad valorem employer payroll tax, the vertical tax externality is always negative, whereas it may be positive if an ad valorem tax is levied on employees wage incomes and the demand for labor is inelastic. The reason for the difference is that when the tax is levied on the employee the federal wage tax base

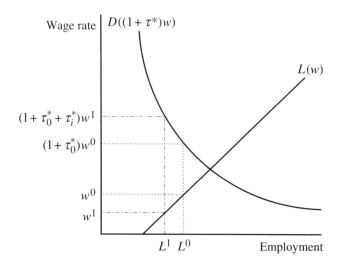

Figure 9.3
Effect of a state's employer payroll tax on federal tax revenues

includes the state government's wage tax. With the employer payroll tax, the federal wage tax base excludes the state's tax revenues.

As we have seen, the vertical tax externality from a state government's tax increase may be positive or negative depending on which side of the market the tax is levied, whether the tax is per unit or ad valorem, and whether the demand for labor is elastic or inelastic. It also depends on the federal government's relative tax rates on wages and profits. To determine the direction and extent of the bias, assume the both levels of government levy taxes on employees' wage incomes. It is assumed that the state government ignores the effect of its tax rate changes on federal revenues, and therefore the perceived MCF for the state government is

$$MCF_{\tau_i} = \frac{-L\dfrac{dw_n}{d\tau_i}}{\dfrac{dR_i}{d\tau_i}} = \frac{wL\left(\dfrac{-\varepsilon}{\eta - \varepsilon}\right)}{wL + \tau_i w \dfrac{dL}{dw}\dfrac{dw}{d\tau_i} + \tau_i L \dfrac{dw}{d\tau_i} + u_i \dfrac{d\Pi}{d\tau_i}}$$

$$= \frac{1}{1 - \dfrac{\tau_i}{1-\tau}\eta - \left[1 + \dfrac{\tau_i - u_i}{1-\tau}\right]\dfrac{\eta}{\varepsilon}}. \tag{9.34}$$

If the state's tax rates are low, the state's MCF_t is approximately equal to $\varepsilon/(\varepsilon - \eta) < 1$, which is the proportional reduction in worker's net wage rates from a tax rate increase. It is less than one because in this simple case the state only takes into account the impact of a tax increase on its residents' wage rate and does not take into account the decline in federal wage and profit taxes. The true or social marginal cost of funds can be obtained from the formula above for the special case where there is no vertical fiscal externality, namely when $u_i = 1$, $\tau_0 = 0$, and $\tau_i = \tau$, and it is equal to

$$SMCF_{\tau_i} = \frac{1}{1 - [\tau/(1-\tau)]\eta}. \tag{9.35}$$

The difference between the state's MCF in (9.34) and its true MCF in (9.35) will depend on whether the vertical tax externality is positive or negative. It can be shown that $MCF_{\tau_i} \gtreqqless SMCF_{\tau_i}$ as $dR_0/d\tau_i \gtreqqless 0$. In other words, a state will overestimate (underestimate) the marginal cost of public funds from its wage tax if an increase in wage tax increases (reduces) total federal tax revenues. Consequently a state government will underprovide (overprovide) a purely consumptive public good if $\tau_0(1 + \varepsilon)$ is greater than (less than) u_0.

Table 9.1 illustrates how the bias in the state's MCF varies with its tax rate on profits and the elasticity of demand for labor if $\tau_0 = \tau_i = 0.20$ and $\eta = 0.10$. Under these conditions the $SMCF_{\tau_i}$ is equal to 1.071. In cases 1 and 2, the state is assumed

Table 9.1
Bias in a state's MCF due to a vertical tax externality

	u_i	ε	$\tau_0(1+\varepsilon)-u_0$	MCF_{τ_i}	$SMCF_{\tau_i}$
Case 1	0.20	−0.50	−0.70	0.857	1.071
Case 2	0.20	−1.50	−0.90	0.968	1.071
Case 3	1.00	−0.50	0.10	1.111	1.071
Case 4	1.00	−1.50	−0.10	1.059	1.071
Case 5	0.00	−0.50	−0.90	0.811	1.071
Case 6	0.00	−1.50	−1.10	0.947	1.071

Notes: Other parameter values: $\tau_i = 0.20$, $\tau_0 = 0.20$, and $\eta = 0.10$.

to tax profits at the same rate as wage income. In case 1, the elasticity of demand for labor is inelastic (-0.50), but the vertical tax externality is negative because the federal tax rate on profit income (0.80) is high, and the MCF_{τ_i} is 0.857, significantly below the $SMCF_{\tau_i}$. In case 2, with an elastic demand for labor (-1.50), the state's MCF would be downward biased, but degree of bias would be reduced. In cases 3 and 4, all of the profits accrue to the state government. If labor demand is inelastic, a tax rate increase by the state government would increase federal government's wage tax revenues. The state's MCF would be upward biased, but the degree of bias is relatively small, 1.111 instead of 1.071. In case 4, with an elastic labor demand, the state's MCF is downward biased, but the extent of the bias is very small, 1.059 versus 1.071. In cases 5 and 6, it is assumed that all of the profits accrue to the federal government. In these cases there is a significant downward bias in the state's MCF, especially if demand for labor is relatively inelastic.

9.5 Vertical Fiscal Imbalance in a Federation

To this point we have only considered models in which there is either a horizontal tax externality or a vertical tax externality, but not both. This is unrealistic, since both types of externalities occur in most federations. As was argued in section 9.1, the existence of vertical and horizontal tax externalities means that the MCFs of the central and subnational governments may differ, and thus give rise to a vertical fiscal imbalance in the federation. In this section we use a model based on Keen and Kotsogiannis (2002) to determine whether there is a vertical fiscal imbalance in a federation when the state and federal governments' tax policies generate both vertical and horizontal tax externalities.[15]

We consider here a federation with N identical states. (The assumption of identical states means that there will not be any horizontal fiscal imbalances in this model. The model in section 10.3 will address that issue.) The population of each state is fixed and equal to one unit. The government of state i finances its expenditures with a per unit tax, t_i, on the capital invested in the state, K_i, $i = 1, 2, \ldots, N$. The federal government levies a per unit tax, t_0, on all capital employed in the country. Capital is perfectly mobile between the states, and total amount of capital in the country is determined by its citizens' savings. Let $f(K_i)$ be the total output of state i, with $f' > 0$ and $f'' < 0$. The total amount of capital employed in state i is determined by the marginal productivity condition:

$$f'(K_i) = r_i = p + t_i + t_0, \tag{9.36}$$

where p is the after-tax rate of return on capital that is received by savers throughout the country. The demand for capital in state i is a decreasing function of the total rate of return that has to be earned on capital, that is, $K'(r_i) = 1/f''(K_i) < 0$. The economic profit (or return to the fixed factor of production) generated by production in state i accrues only to the residents of state i and is equal to

$$\Pi_i = f(K_i) - r_i K_i. \tag{9.37}$$

Each individual in state i has the following two-period intertemporal consumption model:

$$W = U(Y - S) + \theta[(1 + p)S + \Pi] + G^f(g_0) + G^s(g_i), \tag{9.38}$$

where $U(\cdot)$, $G^f(\cdot)$, and $G^s(\cdot)$ are increasing concave functions, θ is a positive constant, Y is the representative individual's first period endowment, S is savings, g_0 is the public service provided by the federal government, and g_i is the public service provided by state i. An individual's savings is determined by the condition

$$U'(Y - S) = \theta(1 + p). \tag{9.39}$$

It is assumed that savings are an increasing function of the net rate of return, that is, $S'(p) > 0$. Equilibrium in the capital market is determined by the condition

$$\sum_{i=1}^{N} K_i(p + t_i + t_0) = N \cdot S(p). \tag{9.40}$$

To simplify the notation, we will assume that we are dealing with a symmetric equilibrium in which every state levies the same tax rate and provides the same level of public service. Taking the total differential of the capital market equilibrium condition, we have the effect of an increase in state i's tax rate on the economywide after-tax rate of return on capital as follows:

$$\frac{dp}{dt_i} = \left(\frac{1}{N}\right)\left(\frac{K'}{S' - K'}\right) = \left(\frac{1}{N}\right)\left(\frac{(1 - \tau_i)\varepsilon}{\eta_S - (1 - \tau_i)\varepsilon}\right) < 0, \tag{9.41}$$

where $\varepsilon = K'rK^{-1} < 0$ is the elasticity of demand for capital, $\eta_S = S'\rho S^{-1}$ is the elasticity of savings, and $\tau_i = (t_i + t_0)/r_i$ is the ad valorem equivalent of the total tax on the return to capital in state i. An increase in the federal tax rate has the following effect on the after-tax rate of return on capital:

$$\frac{d\rho}{dt_0} = \left(\frac{(1 - \tau_i)\varepsilon}{\eta_S - (1 - \tau_i)\varepsilon} \right) = N \frac{d\rho}{dt_i} < 0. \tag{9.42}$$

Equation (9.42) represents the usual tax-shifting result—the decline in the after-tax rate of return will be greater the more elastic the demand for capital and the less elastic the supply of savings—while (9.41) indicates that an individual state's impact on the net rate of return will be very small if there are a large number of states and an individual state's share of the total capital stock is small. Initially it will be assumed that there are no transfers between the two levels of government and that each government's budget constraint has the forms

$$R_0 \equiv t_0 \cdot \sum_{j=1}^{N} K_j = N \cdot g_0 \tag{9.43}$$

and

$$R_i \equiv t_i \cdot K_i = g_i, \tag{9.44}$$

where the unit cost of producing government services is assumed to be constant and equal to one. A state government's tax rate increase has the following effect on its tax revenues:

$$\frac{dR_i}{dt_i} = K_i \left[1 + \tau_i^s \varepsilon \left(1 + \frac{d\rho}{dt_i} \right) \right], \tag{9.45}$$

where $\tau_i^s = t_i/r_i$ is the ad valorem tax rate imposed by state i. It is assumed that the state government is operating on the upward sloping section of its Laffer curve and therefore $dR_i/dt_i > 0$.

9.5.1 The MCF for a State Government

Following Keen and Kotsogiannis (2002), we now assume that the state government takes into account the direct effects its tax increase on its residents as well as the indirect effect on its residents that occurs through its effect on the budget constraint of the federal government. The latter effect means that the state government takes into account the reduction in federal services in the state when the federal tax base is eroded by the state government's higher taxes. The impact of a state tax rate increase on its representative resident is

$$\frac{dW}{dt_i} = U' \cdot (-S')\frac{d\rho}{dt_i} + \theta S\frac{d\rho}{dt_i} + \theta(1+\rho)S'\frac{d\rho}{dt_i} + \theta\frac{d\Pi}{dr_i}\frac{dr_i}{dt_i} + \frac{dG^f}{dg_0}\left(\frac{1}{N}\right)\frac{dR_0}{dt_i}$$

$$= \theta S\frac{d\rho}{dt_i} - \theta K_i\left(1 + \frac{d\rho}{dt_i}\right) + \frac{dG^f}{dg_0}\left(\frac{1}{N}\right)\frac{dR_0}{dt_i}$$

$$= -\theta K_i + \frac{dG^f}{dg_0}\left(\frac{1}{N}\right)\frac{dR_0}{dt_i}, \tag{9.46}$$

since $d\Pi/dt_i = -K_i(1 + d\rho/dt_i)$, $S = K_i$, and

$$\frac{dR_0}{dt_i} = Nt_0 S'\frac{d\rho}{dt_i} = \frac{\tau_i^f}{1-\tau_i}NS\eta_S\frac{d\rho}{dt_i} < 0, \tag{9.47}$$

where $\tau_i^f = t_0/r_i$ is the federal ad valorem tax rate in state i. A state government's tax increase has a negative impact on federal revenues to the extent it reduces the net rate of return on savings because this reduces aggregate savings in the economy.

Using (9.46) and (9.47), we will find it convenient to define the state government's MCF_{t_i} as

$$MCF_{t_i} = \frac{K_i - MB_{g_0}\left(\frac{1}{N}\right)\frac{dR_0}{dt_i}}{\frac{dR_i}{dt_i}} = \frac{1 - MB_{g_0}\frac{\tau_i^f}{1-\tau_i}\eta_S\frac{d\rho}{dt_i}}{1 + \tau_i^s\varepsilon\left(1 + \frac{d\rho}{dt_i}\right)}, \tag{9.48}$$

where $MB_{g_0} = (dG^f/dg_0)(1/\theta)$ is the marginal benefit from the federal public service. There are two sources of bias in the state's MCF. First, it only takes into account a fraction $(1/N)$ of the reduction in federal revenues that is caused by its tax increase because the loss of federal revenue is spread across the entire country. This effect imparts a downward bias to the state government's MCF. On the other hand, the state also ignores the positive effect of its tax rate increase on the revenues of other states (as previously noted in section 9.2). The total effect on the other states tax revenues is given by

$$\sum_{\substack{j=1 \\ i \neq j}}^{N} \frac{dR_j}{dt_i} = (N-1)K\tau_i^s\varepsilon\frac{d\rho}{dt_i} > 0. \tag{9.49}$$

This effect is positive, and it imparts an upward bias to the state's MCF. To compare the magnitudes of these offsetting biases, we form the following expression for the social marginal cost of funds from a dollar of state government revenue:

$$SMCF_{t_i} = \frac{K_i - MB_{g_0}\dfrac{dR_0}{dt_i} - MB_{g_j}\sum_{\substack{j=1 \\ i \neq j}}^{N}\dfrac{dR_j}{dt_j}}{\dfrac{dR_i}{dt_i}}$$

$$= \frac{1 - MB_{g_0}\dfrac{\tau_i^f}{1 - \tau_i}N\eta_S\dfrac{dp}{dt_i} - MB_{g_i}(N-1)\tau_i\varepsilon\dfrac{dp}{dt_i}}{K_i^{-1}\dfrac{dR_i}{dt_i}}. \tag{9.50}$$

First, note that both the horizontal and vertical externalities would disappear if the demand for capital was completely inelastic and $dp/dt_i = 0$ with $MCF_{t_i} = SMCF_{t_i} = 1$.[16]

Let us assume that the demand for capital is not completely inelastic. It can then be shown that

$$MCF_{t_i} \gtreqless SMCF_{t_i} \quad \text{as} \quad MB_{g_i}\tau_i^s(1 - \tau_i)(-\varepsilon) \gtreqless MB_{g_0}\tau_i^f\eta_S. \tag{9.51}$$

This condition indicates that the state government will overestimate its marginal cost of public funds (and underprovide public services) to the extent that the product of the marginal benefit from the state's public services, the state's tax rate, and the elasticity of demand for capital is higher than the product of the marginal benefit from federal public services, federal tax rate, and the elasticity of savings.[17] This condition is consistent with the predictions about the direction of bias in proposition 1 in Keen and Kotsogiannis (2002, p. 367), which states that if economic rents are not taxed the "vertical externality dominates if the interest responsiveness of savings is sufficiently high relative to that of the demand for capital." One clear-cut case where a state government's MCFs are biased upward is when savings is completely inelastic ($\eta_S = 0$) because in that case there is no negative vertical tax externality. An interesting aspect of the condition in (9.51) is that it depends on both the marginal benefits and the tax rates of both levels of government; that is, it depends on how a state government's tax rate increase affects the relative amounts of tax revenue collected by the other states or the federal government (which varies with their relative tax rates) and with the relative marginal benefits from services provided by the two levels of government. Another interesting aspect of condition (9.51) is that it does not directly depend on the number of state governments.

While condition (9.51) accords well with our intuition concerning the conditions under which the vertical or the horizontal externalities dominate, it does not provide definitive answers because the MB_{g_i} and MB_{g_0} depend on the MCFs of the state and federal governments, as do the tax rates of the two levels of government. In order to get a deeper understanding of the conditions under which either the vertical or the horizontal externalities dominates, we need to solve the simultaneous equation model that determines g_i, g_0, τ_i^s, and τ_i^f. The complexity of the model precludes a simple reduced form solution, and instead we have resorted to a numerical simulation model to investigate which of the two externalities dominates. This simulation model is described below.

9.5.2   Simulation Model of Vertical Fiscal Imbalance

The extent of the vertical fiscal externality depends on the level of federal taxes and marginal benefit from federal services, and therefore we also have to model the behavior of the federal government. In the model outlined below, it is assumed that the federal government takes the tax rates of the state governments as given in making its tax and expenditure decisions.[18] However, the federal government recognizes that its tax rate affects the states' revenues and therefore the states' expenditure levels. Given this behavior, the MCF for the federal government would be equal to the following:

$$MCF_{t_0} = \frac{N \cdot S - N \cdot MB_{g_i} \cdot \dfrac{dR_i}{dt_0}}{\dfrac{dR_0}{dt_0}} = \frac{1 + MB_{g_i} \cdot \tau_i^s \cdot (-\varepsilon) \cdot \left(1 + \dfrac{d\rho}{dt_0}\right)}{1 + \dfrac{\tau_i^f}{1 - \tau_i} \cdot \eta_S \cdot \dfrac{d\rho}{dt_0}}. \tag{9.52}$$

It assumes that both levels of government choose g_0 and g_i to satisfy the conditions $MB_{g_j} = MCF_{t_j}$, $j = 0, 1, \ldots, N$.

To compute the solution to the model, we need to specify the individuals' utility function and the production function. The utility function that we have adopted is

$$W = \ln(Y - S) + \theta(1 + \rho)S + (\Gamma^f g_0 - 0.5\gamma^f g_0^2) + (\Gamma^s g_i - 0.5\gamma^s g_i^2), \tag{9.53}$$

where the Γ and γ are positive parameters. With this utility function the level of savings is

$$S = Y - \frac{1}{\theta(1 + \rho)}, \tag{9.54}$$

and the savings elasticity is

$$\eta_S = \frac{\rho}{\theta(1 + \rho)^2} \left(Y - \frac{1}{\theta(1 + \rho)}\right)^{-1}, \tag{9.55}$$

which is positive if the savings level is positive. In our calculations the initial endowment, Y, was set equal to one. For the low savings elasticity case, the θ parameter was set equal to 2.222 so that $\eta_S = 0.10$ if $p = 0.20$. For the high savings elasticity calculations, the θ parameter was set equal to 1.181 so that $\eta_S = 0.40$ if $p = 0.20$.

The marginal benefits from public services are given by

$$MB_{g_0} = \frac{1}{\theta}[\Gamma^f - \gamma^f g_0] \tag{9.56}$$

and

$$MB_{g_i} = \frac{1}{\theta}[\Gamma^s - \gamma^s g_i]. \tag{9.57}$$

The Γ^f and Γ^s parameters were chosen so that the price elasticity of demand for the public goods would be equal to -0.50 if the $MCF = 1$. The γ^f and γ^s parameters were chosen so that the first-best provision of the public good would represent a particular fraction of the first-period endowment. The choice of these parameters is described in more detail later in this section.

The key parameter on the production side of the model is the elasticity of demand for capital. We will utilize two alternative production functions so that we can use a "high" and a "low" elasticity of demand for capital. The high elasticity of demand calculations are based on the following production function:

$$x = AK^\alpha \qquad A > 0, 0 < \alpha < 1, \tag{9.58}$$

where $A > 0$, $0 < \alpha < 1$, capital's share of the cost of production is α, and the elasticity of demand for capital is $(\alpha - 1)^{-1}$. Alternatively, for the low elasticity of demand calculations, the following production function was used:

$$x = A \cdot \frac{a \cdot K}{a + K}, \tag{9.59}$$

where $A > 0$, $a > 0$, capital's share of the cost of production is $a/(a + K)$, and the elasticity of demand for capital is $-0.5(a + K)/K$. In either case the production parameters were chosen such that in the absence of taxation, the demand for capital would equal the supply of savings at a 0.20 rate of return and that capital would represent one-third of the cost of production. The values of all the parameters used in the calculations are given in the notes to table 9.2, which describes the simulation results.

As we saw in section 9.1.2, we can characterize a vertical fiscal imbalance in a federation as a situation where the federal and state governments have different MCFs, giving rise to a misallocation of the tax burden and public expenditures between the two levels of government. Accordingly we have adopted the following index of the degree of vertical fiscal imbalance:

Table 9.2
Vertical fiscal imbalances and optimal intergovernmental transfers

		Scenarios				
		1	2	3	4	5
	Savings elasticity	Low	High	Low	High	High
	Capital demand elasticity	High	High	Low	Low	High
	Optimal relative sizes of the federal and state sectors	Equal	Equal	Equal	Equal	Federal spending four times state spending
Number of states in the federation						
1 (unitary state)	MCF_f	1.047	1.566	1.043	1.37	1.566
	MCF_s	1.047	1.566	1.043	1.37	1.566
	VFI	0	0	0	0	0
	G/G^*	0.977	0.717	0.979	0.815	0.717
	g/g^*	0.977	0.717	0.979	0.815	0.717
	η	0.074	0.269	0.076	0.301	0.269
	ε	−1.50	−1.50	−0.76	−0.822	−1.50
2	MCF_f	1.048	1.548	1.043	1.370	1.573
	MCF_s	1.187	1.665	1.100	1.367	1.466
	VFI	0.140	0.117	0.057	−0.003	−0.127
	G/G^*	0.976	0.726	0.978	0.815	0.714
	g/g^*	0.906	0.668	0.95	0.817	0.777
	η	0.075	0.278	0.076	0.301	0.264
	ε	−1.50	−1.50	−0.76	−0.822	−1.50
	T/g	0.849	0.288	0.72	−0.017	−0.780
10	MCF_f	1.048	1.533	1.044	1.37	1.578
	MCF_s	1.307	1.744	1.148	1.364	1.342
	VFI	0.259	0.211	0.104	−0.006	−0.236
	G/G^*	0.976	0.734	0.978	0.815	0.711
	g/g^*	0.846	0.628	0.926	0.818	0.829
	η	0.076	0.284	0.077	0.301	0.260
	ε	−1.50	−1.50	−0.759	−0.822	−1.50
	T/g	0.849	0.288	0.72	−0.017	−0.781

Note: Parameter values:

$\Gamma^f = \Gamma^s = 6.167 \; \gamma^f = \gamma^s = 177.778$ scenarios 1 and 3

$\Gamma^f = \Gamma^s = 3.542 \; \gamma^f = \gamma^s = 94.444$ scenarios 2 and 4

$\Gamma^f = \Gamma^s = 3.542 \; \gamma^f = 59.028 \; \gamma^s = 236.111$ scenario 5

$\theta = 2.222$ scenarios 1 and 3

$\theta = 1.181$ scenarios 2, 4, and 5

$x = 0.439K^{1/3}$ scenario 1

$x = 0.265K^{1/3}$ scenarios 2 and 5

$x = 1.8 \dfrac{0.312K}{0.312 + K}$ scenario 3

$x = 1.8 \dfrac{0.147K}{0.147 + K}$ scenario 4

$$VFI_i = MCF_{t_i} - MCF_{t_0}. \tag{9.60}$$

It represents the net gain or loss that would occur if a dollar is transferred from the federal government to a state government.

Table 9.2 shows the vertical fiscal imbalance (VFI) under five different parameter configurations. In scenario 1, the parameters were chosen so that the savings elasticity is 0.10 in the no tax equilibrium and the elasticity of demand for capital is -1.50. The MB_gs were scaled so that the first-best levels of the public services for both the federal and state governments, denoted by g_0^* and g_i^*, would each be 2.5 percent of the initial endowment. The solution to the model was calculated for one, two, and ten state governments to see how an increase in the number of state governments affected the degree of vertical fiscal imbalance. The solution of the model with one state government can be interpreted as a unitary state, and this serves as a useful reference point. As table 9.2 shows, the MCFs of the "federal" and "state" governments would be the same in a unitary state and equal to 1.047. (The MCFs are relatively low in this scenario because the savings elasticity is only 0.074.) Both g_0 and g_i would be provided at the same level, 97.7 percent of the first-best level.

When the model was solved with two state governments, the MCFs of the two levels of government diverged. The MCF for the federal government rose slightly to 1.048, while the MCF for the state government increased to 1.187, because of tax competition, creating a vertical fiscal imbalance of 0.140. This fiscal imbalance is reflected in the relative underprovision of the state public service, 90.6 percent of the first-best level.

When the model was solved with ten state governments, the VFI index increased to 0.259, indicating that a dollar transferred from the federal government to the state government would generate a net social gain of 25.9 cents.[19] In summary, these calculations indicate that when the federal tax base is relatively inelastic and the state tax base is highly elastic, the horizontal externality dominates the vertical externality and a significant vertical fiscal imbalance can result.

The calculations in scenario 2 show how an increase in the elasticity of savings affects the degree of vertical fiscal imbalance. In these calculations, the savings elasticity is 0.40 in the no-tax equilibrium. The MCF in the unitary state jumps to 1.566 with the more elastic savings, and the government only provides 71.7 percent of the first-best levels of the public goods. With two state governments, a vertical fiscal imbalance would emerge that is only slightly lower than in scenario 1. With ten state governments, the VFI would be 0.211, again reflecting a very significant imbalance in the relative levels of federal and state spending. Therefore this scenario indicates that even with relatively high savings elasticities, the horizontal fiscal externality would still dominate if the capital demand elasticity is quite elastic.

In scenario 3, we adopt the lower elasticity of demand for capital model combined with a low savings elasticity. These calculations indicate that a VFI of 0.104 will emerge with ten state governments.

Scenario 4 illustrates a situation that is more likely to give rise to a negative VFI—high savings elasticity and low elasticity of demand for capital. However, these calculations indicate that the VFI is virtually zero. Despite the relatively high savings elasticity the vertical tax externality is almost exactly offset by the horizontal tax externality.

Scenario 5 indicates how a negative VFI can emerge if the federal government is responsible for a larger share of total spending and has to apply high tax rates to finance its spending. In these calculations the parameters of the MB_G and MB_g functions were chosen so that the federal spending in the first-best optimum is 4 percent of the initial endowment and state spending is 1 percent of the initial endowment. These calculation, for the same parameters as scenario 2, would cause the MCF for the federal government to increase slightly 1.578 and for the state governments' MCF to decline to 1.342, creating a negative fiscal imbalance of −0.236 for the ten-state case. In this case there will be an imbalance in the sense that there will be a relative overprovision of the state public service, and there will be a net gain if funds are transferred from the states to the central government.[20] These calculations indicate that it is not just the relative tax sensitivity of the tax bases that will determine whether there is a VFI in the federation. The relative responsibilities of the governments and the taxes that they have to levy to finance their expenditures will affect the size and direction of the VFI.

In an econometric study of tax setting by municipal governments in Switzerland, Brülhart, and Jametti (2006) found that smaller municipalities set higher tax rates, an outcome that is predicted by the Keen and Kotsogiannis model, when the vertical tax externality with the cantonal government dominates the horizontal tax externality with other municipalities. Our simulation results in table 9.2 also display this property. When the vertical fiscal externality dominates in scenario 5, subnational government spending is increasing in the number of governments; in the other cases where the horizontal externality dominates, subnational government spending is decreasing in the number of governments.

As noted above, when there is a vertical fiscal imbalance and the two levels of government do not have the same MCF, there is the potential for a net gain if funds are transferred between the two levels of government until the MCFs are equalized. The simulation model was expanded to allow for a transfer from the federal government to the states, $T > 0$, or from the states to the federal government, $T < 0$, such that $MCF_{t_0} = MCF_{t_i}$. This lump-sum transfer, which is expressed as a percentage of a state's expenditure on public services, is also shown for the various scenarios in table 9.2. In scenario 1, a transfer from the federal government to the state governments, equal to 84.9 percent of state government spending, would be required to equalize the MCFs of the two levels of government and allow them to achieve the same fiscal outcomes as a unitary state. Note that an interesting aspect of this lump-sum intergovernmental transfer is that it is independent of the number of state governments. In scenarios 2 and 3, federal transfers of 28.8 percent and 72 percent of state spending would be required to equalize the MCFs of the two levels of government. Note that the relative size of the transfer is not directly related to the vertical fiscal imbalance in the absence of a transfer. Scenarios 4 and 5 illustrate cases where a very small and a very large transfer from the state governments to the federal would be required to achieve a vertical fiscal balance.

The model justifies the use of intergovernmental lump-sum transfers to correct vertical fiscal imbalances in a federation. Using the welfare analysis developed in section 2.3, the net gain per dollar of transfer approximately is equal to 0.5 VFI. The simulations in table 9.2 indicate that there may be some very substantial welfare gains from transfers that help to equalize the MCFs between the two levels of government. The model indicates the urgent need for more empirical research on the MCFs of the federal and state governments in federations like Canada or Australia where the issue of vertical fiscal imbalance has been at the center many public policy debates.

Appendix to Chapter 9

Under the RTS equalization grant system, a state that receives equalization will be able to raise the standard amount of revenue if it imposes the standard tax rate on its tax base, or

$$E_i + t_s B_i = t_s B_s = R,$$

where E_i is the equalization entitlement of state i, B_i is state i's per capita tax base, t_s is the "standard" tax rate, and B_s is the "standard" per capita tax base. To keep the model simple, we will assume that there are only two states, i and j, and that they have the same population:

$$E_i = t_s[B_s - B_i].$$

Under the representative tax system (RTS),

$$t_s = \frac{R}{(B_i + B_j)/2}$$

and

$$B_s = \frac{B_i + B_j}{2}.$$

Consequently

$$E_i = \left[1 - \frac{B_i}{B_s}\right] R = \left[\frac{B_j - B_i}{B_j + B_i}\right] R = \left[\frac{1}{2} - \frac{B_i}{B_i + B_j}\right] 2R.$$

In the first formula, state i's per capita equalization grant depends on the ratio of its per capita tax base to the standard tax base. In the second formulation, state i's per capita equalization grant depends on the ratio of the difference in per capita tax bases to the total tax base. In the third formulation, state i's per capita equalization grant depends on the difference between its share of the population (one-half in our simple model) and its share of the tax base multiplied by total tax revenues in both states.

Exercises for Chapter 9

9.1 The residents of a state have the following utility function:

$$U = C + v \ln(G - \gamma),$$

where C is a private consumption good and G is a state-provided public good which has a constant marginal cost of one dollar. The state, which taxes capital employed in the state to finance expenditure on the public good, is small compared to the rest of the economy, and the elasticity of demand for capital in the state is $\varepsilon < 0$. Show that the underprovision of the public good compared to the first-best provision is $-\tau v \varepsilon$, where τ is the ad valorem tax rate imposed by the state.

9.2 The aggregate production function of a state is the following:

$$x = \frac{K}{1 + K},$$

where K is the amount of capital invested in the state. The state's per unit tax rate on capital is 0.02 and the after-tax return on capital is 0.10. The payments to capital represents one-third of total output. Capital is perfectly mobile within the federation but in fixed supply for the entire federation. All states have identical production functions, impose the same tax rates, and ignore the impact of their taxes on the federal government. Calculate the state's MCF under the following alternative conditions:

(a) The amount of capital invested in the state is very small compared to the federation.

(b) The state is a capital exporter with 20 percent of the total capital stock owned by the state's residents and only 10 percent of the total capital stock invested in the state.

(c) The state is a capital importer with 20 percent of the total capital stock owned by the state's residents and 30 percent of the total capital stock invested in the state.

10 Applications of the MCF in Federations

In this chapter we use the MCF to analyze three policy issues that arise in a federation. In section 10.1 we use the marginal cost of funds concept to analyze the provision of investment incentives by subnational governments, and we use this framework to evaluate the provision of R&D tax subsidies by provincial governments in Canada. Almost all previous studies of R&D tax policies have focused either on the tax sensitivity of R&D or on external rate of return from R&D. The main contribution of this section is to show how the tax sensitivity of R&D, its external rate of return, and the marginal cost of public funds can be combined in evaluating tax subsidies for R&D.

In most federations the federal and subnational governments have different "fiscal capacities" because either the sizes of their tax bases differ or the tax sensitivity of their tax bases differ. These differences in fiscal capacities can give rise to horizontal and vertical fiscal imbalances within a federation. Intergovernmental grants are part of the fiscal architecture of most federations in order to address these imbalances, but the intergovernmental grants can have unintended effects on the tax and expenditure decisions of national and subnational governments. In section 10.2, we see how the fiscal equalization grants can affect the MCFs of the recipient governments. We draw on the research in Dahlby and Warren (2003), which shows how equalization grants may influence the fiscal decisions of the state governments in Australia.

In the final section of this chapter, we use a modified version of the Kanbur and Keen (1993) cross-border shopping model to analyze the effects of an equalization grant system on the horizontal and vertical fiscal imbalances in a federation. We explore how the financing of equalization grants—either funding by the federal government out of general tax revenues or direct contributions by the state governments—affects the ability of equalization grants to address the vertical and horizontal fiscal imbalances that arise when subnational governments differ in the size or the tax sensitivity of their tax bases. We use a simulation model to find the efficient allocation of the tax burden in a federation that may require higher tax rates in regions with less sensitive tax bases. Differential tax rates are shown to implement the equivalent of the Ramsey rule for optimal taxation by shrinking the regional tax bases in the same proportion. Equalization grant systems can play an important role in helping to achieve an efficient allocation of the tax burden in a federation. The simulations show how an equalization grant system can improve welfare, as measured by a utilitarian social welfare function, if states vary in the size of their tax bases or the tax sensitivity of their tax bases.

10.1   Evaluating the Canadian Provinces' Tax Incentives for R&D

Governments around the world provide tax incentives for private sector R&D. The standard justification for this policy is that firms do not capture all of the benefits from their R&D spending because R&D may lead to innovations that cannot be patented, and even patent protection is of limited duration and scope. Other firms can often "free ride" on the R&D activity of another firm by imitating its productivity improvements or product innovations. Therefore the social rate of return from R&D activity exceeds the private rate of return, and private firms will underinvest in R&D because they ignore the spillover effects, or the external rate of return, r^e, from R&D. In the absence of other distortions, including distortionary taxes, the optimal corrective Pigouvian subsidy is equal to the external rate of return on R&D. But, as outlined in section 3.4, when the tax subsidies have to be financed by distortionary taxes, this simple rule for the optimal subsidy has to be modified.

In this section we use the marginal cost of public funds concept to evaluate the R&D tax policies of provincial governments in Canada.[1] A province's optimal tax rate (or subsidy) for R&D is derived, given the presence of a federal tax subsidy for R&D and federal taxes on the additional returns that are generated by the R&D spending. The Canadian federal government's tax treatment of R&D is among the most generous in the world, and all of the provinces except Alberta and Prince Edward Island also provide tax credits which effectively subsidize private sector R&D spending.[2] As a result of the federal and provincial tax incentives the effective subsidy rates range from 35 percent in Prince Edward Island to 200 percent in Quebec. The specific question that we address in this section is: Should a provincial government, Alberta in particular, provide tax subsidies for R&D? While the focus of the analysis is on Canadian provincial tax incentives, this framework can be applied to evaluating R&D incentives by other levels of governments in other countries.

Let t_{RD_i} be the tax rate on R&D spending in province i. Even though t_{RD_i} is typically negative because it represents a subsidy, we can consider the marginal cost of public funds for a provincial government from increasing t_{RD_i}, and it is given by the following formula:

$$MCF_{t_{RD_i}} = \frac{1 + (1 - \tau_0 - \tau_i)r^e \cdot \kappa}{1 - t_{RD_i} \cdot \kappa - \tau_i \left[r^e + \dfrac{\rho + t_{RD_0} + t_{RD_i}}{1 - \tau_0 - \tau_i} \right] \kappa}, \tag{10.1}$$

where τ_0 is the federal marginal income tax rate, τ_i is the provincial marginal income tax rate, t_{RD_i} is the provincial tax rate on R&D capital, t_{RD_0} is the federal tax rate on R&D capital, r^e is the external rate of return on R&D capital, ρ is the after-tax rate of return earned on R&D capital, and κ measures the tax sensitivity of R&D activity. Conventionally κ is defined as the increase in R&D capital in response to an additional dollar of R&D tax subsidy. In our notation, $\kappa = -dK_{RD}/(K_{RD}dt_{RD_i}) > 0$.

As with all expressions for the MCF, the numerator is the loss sustained by the private sector from a small increase in the tax rate, and the denominator is the rate of increase in provincial government revenues from a small tax rate increase. The resulting ratio is the loss sustained by the private sector from each additional dollar received by the provincial government as a result of a tax rate increase.

The expression for the $MCF_{t_{RD_i}}$ in (10.1) has the same general form as the expression for the MCF from taxing a commodity that generates a consumption externality in (3.14). In the current context, $\delta_E = (1 - \tau_0 - \tau_i)r^e$ and $\kappa = -\varepsilon_{ii}(dq_i/dt_i)$. The $(1 - \tau_0 - \tau_i)r^e\kappa$ term is the reduction in the after-tax incomes, generated by the external rate of return on R&D, because of the decline in R&D investment. In the denominator the increase in provincial tax revenues from a small increase in the tax rate on R&D consists of three components—the "one" is the direct effect of the tax increase; the "$-t_{RD_i}\kappa$" term is the change in revenue associated with the reduction in R&D activity caused by a tax increase on R&D. Note that since t_{RD_i} is negative, the reduction in R&D activity will cause tax revenues to increase. The third term is the loss of provincial tax revenues from the decline in provincial incomes due to the reduction in R&D. This income reduction is equal to the external rate of return, r^e, plus the gross private rate of return on R&D, $(\rho + t_{RD_0} + t_{RD_i})/(1 - \tau_0 - \tau_i)$. This decline in income will be greater when R&D investments exhibit greater tax sensitivity. It is assumed that the decline in output and incomes, caused by an increase in t_{RD_i}, reduces provincial tax revenues at the provincial marginal income tax rate.

The $MCF_{t_{RD_i}}$ can be viewed as the loss sustained by the private sector when the R&D subsidy is reduced by one dollar or alternatively as the gain to the private sector when the R&D tax subsidy is increased by one dollar. However, this gain comes with a cost because it has to be financed by an increase in some other distortionary tax or a reduction in provincial spending on goods and services. Let MCF represent the marginal cost of funds from the alternative tax bases (e.g., personal income tax or corporate income tax) that would have be raised if the government were to increase its tax subsidy for R&D. Under an optimal fiscal system the size of the tax subsidy for R&D would be adjusted until the $MCF_{t_{RD_i}}$ equaled the MCF from its alternative tax sources. From the condition $MCF_{t_{RD_i}} = MCF$, the following formula for the optimal tax rate on R&D activity can be derived:

$$t_{RD_i} = \frac{1 - \tau_0 - \tau_i}{1 - \tau_0} \left[\frac{1 - \tau_0 - \tau_i(1 - MCF)}{MCF} \right] (-r^e)$$

$$- \frac{\tau_i}{1 - \tau_0}(\rho + t_{RD_0}) + \frac{1 - \tau_0 - \tau_i}{1 - \tau_0} \frac{MCF - 1}{\kappa \cdot MCF}. \tag{10.2}$$

The optimal provincial tax rate on R&D has three components. The first term on the right-hand side of (10.2) is the component of the tax subsidy that corrects the resource allocation problem caused by the R&D externality. If both the federal and provincial governments imposed nondistortionary lump-sum taxes ($\tau_i = \tau_0 = t_{RD_0} = 0$) and $MCF = 1$, then the formula yields $t_{RD_i} = -r^e$. That is, a government should provide a tax subsidy equal to the external rate of return on R&D if it can finance its expenditures with nondistortionary lump-sum taxes. The formula in (10.2) indicates that when governments have to rely on distortionary taxes, the coefficient on the $(-r^e)$ component is positive, but less than one if $MCF > 1$ and $0 < \tau_i < 1$ and $0 < \tau_0 < 1$. The coefficient on the external rate of return component becomes smaller the higher the marginal cost of public funds for alternative sources of tax revenue. In other words, providing a tax subsidy based on the R&D externality becomes more costly when the opportunity cost of public funds to support R&D subsidies is higher, and therefore a smaller tax subsidy is optimal.[3]

The second component, which is the term in square brackets, represents the tax subsidy that should be provided because increasing R&D generates additional tax revenues for the provincial government. This component will be larger in absolute value the higher the provincial income tax rate and the higher the private before-tax rate of return on R&D.

The third component is the tax on the return to R&D that should be imposed in order to raise revenues at the lowest possible cost to the private sector. This component will be larger when the MCF from alternative tax sources is higher or when the tax sensitivity of R&D investment is low.

It should be stressed that the t_{RD_i} given in (10.2) is "optimal" from the perspective of a provincial government, but it is not necessarily the socially optimal tax rate because it ignores horizontal and vertical fiscal externalities. To the extent that a province's tax incentives shift the location of R&D from another province in Canada, a province will tend to overestimate the social return from the R&D subsidy. In addition the fact that the federal and provincial governments' tax bases overlap—both levels of government collect personal and corporate incomes taxes, sales taxes, payroll taxes, and excises taxes—means that a tax increase by one level of government will generally affect the tax revenues of the other level of government. As was indicated in section 9.4., this could bias the province's choice of tax rates either up or down. In the current context, these interactions might mean that the provinces may underprovide tax incentives for R&D because they ignore the increase in the federal income tax revenues. However, sorting out the potential biases in the provision of provincial tax incentives for R&D is beyond the scope of this analysis.

Three important parameters—r^e, κ, and MCF—are required to calculate the optimal provincial tax rate on R&D, given the tax rates imposed by the federal and provincial governments. Over the past fifty years economists have tried to measure the external rate of return on R&D. Early studies found very high social rates of return from the R&D that lead to particular innovations. For example, Griliches (1958) found that the public R&D expenditures that lead to hybrid corn had a social rate of return of 40 percent, and Mansfield et al. (1977) found that the median social rate of return from 17 private sector innovations in the US economy was 56 percent, while the median private rate of return was 25 percent. However, the high social rates of return measured in these studies may not reflect the average or expected rate of return for all R&D activity because they focused on successful innovations. In addition, the high rates of private rates of return may reflect the higher degree of risk, as well as higher implicit rates of "depreciation," for R&D investments.[4] In addition to the problem of depreciation Hall (1996) has noted that there are two other major problems in measuring the social rate of return from R&D. One is that price indexes may not adequately reflect changes in the quality of goods and therefore productivity improvements are underestimated. Second, it is difficult to measure the lags in the production and dissemination of new knowledge. It may take a number of years before research activity generates new products and production innovations, making it difficult to calculate the return on R&D in any one year. Given these problems in measuring the external rate of return from R&D, it is not surprising that a wide range of estimates has emerged from empirical studies in the United States, Canada, and other countries. Given this uncertainty, the best that an analyst can do is to use a broad range of estimates, as suggested by Nadiri (1993, p. 35), who concluded that "the spillover effects of R&D are often much larger than the effects of own R&D at the industry level. The indirect and social rates of return often vary from 20 percent to over 100 percent with an average close to 50 percent."

Before reviewing the literature on the tax sensitivity and the spillover effects of the R&D, we need to consider the applicability of these parameter estimates for evaluating provincial R&D tax policy. All the empirical studies have been for national economies and not for a provincial or regional economy, and a particular provinces' industrial structure may not generate the same external effects as a national economy. For example, R&D spending in manufacturing in Alberta, where the economy is reliant on the oil and natural gas, forestry, and agriculture sectors, may generate externalities that are quite different from those generated in Ontario where the economy is more reliant on manufacturing. Second, only the R&D spillovers that accrue within a province are relevant for provincial tax policy. The externalities from R&D in manufacturing will tend to be smaller at the provincial level than at the national level because more of the spillovers will occur outside the provincial boundaries. For example, Alberta, with about 10 percent of Canada's population and 15 percent of its GDP, might only expect to capture 10 to 15 percent of the external returns from R&D. These considerations suggest that the lower end of Nadiri's range of spillover effects—say 10 to 30 percent—is the relevant range of values for evaluating R&D tax incentives for a province such as Alberta.

The second parameter that plays a crucial role in determining the optimal tax treatment of R&D is the tax sensitivity of R&D. Public interest in the effectiveness of tax incentives for R&D has spawned a relatively large number of studies of this parameter in United States, Canada, and other countries.[5] Hall and Reenen (2000, p. 462) seem to reflect a consensus, based largely on US studies, that "the R&D tax credit produces roughly a dollar-for-dollar increase in reported R&D spending on the margin." In their study of R&D spending in nine OECD countries from 1979 to 1997, Bloom et al. (2002, p. 18) found that physical capital and R&D were complements. Lowering the marginal effective tax rate on physical capital, for example, by lowering the CIT rate, increased R&D spending. Canadian studies of the effectiveness of R&D subsidies indicate a somewhat larger stimulatory effect in the range of $1.00 to $1.38 per dollar of tax expenditure. Whether these estimates would apply to a provincial tax incentive program is an open question because there have not been, to my knowledge, any studies of the responsiveness of R&D to provincial tax incentives. Given that some R&D is potentially footloose and can be attracted from other parts of Canada by a provincial tax incentive, the stimulatory effect of provincial tax subsidies might be considerably higher than the $1.00 to $1.38 range that emerges from the national studies. However, the location of R&D activity within a country is not solely influenced by provincial tax incentives. Other factors, such as the access to key industry networks, the quality of university and government research facilities, and the overall personal and corporate tax burdens, are also likely to play important roles in determining the location of R&D activities.

The MCF reflects the opportunity cost of providing tax incentives for R&D. The only study of the marginal cost of public funds for provincial governments in Canada by Dahlby (1994) found that the MCF for a proportional personal income tax increase ranged from about 1.40 for Alberta to 2.00 for Quebec. The MCF for a provincial corporate tax rate would likely have an even larger MCF because a number of studies have found that taxes on corporate income are especially distortionary. In the computations to be reported below, we will use an MCF of 1.40 as a base case, although a higher MCF might be warranted.

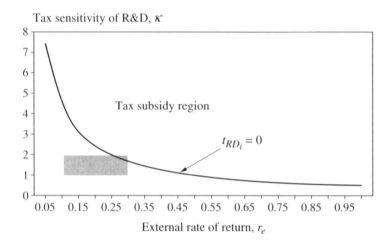

Figure 10.1
Optimal tax treatment of R&D when $MCF = 1.40$

Given the uncertainty about the appropriate values of the key parameters, especially r^e and κ, it seems that the best way to portray a government's policy choice is to calculate the critical values of r^e and κ such that the optimal tax rate on R&D investments is zero. To find these critical values, we set t_{RD_i} equal to zero in (10.2) and solve for κ:

$$\kappa = \frac{1 - MCF}{\tau_i(\rho + t_{RD_0})MCF + [1 - \tau_0 + (MCF - 1)\tau_i]r^e}. \tag{10.3}$$

In figure 10.1 the solid line represents the boundary between the values of κ and r^e where a tax subsidy is optimal and the values of these parameters where a positive tax rate on R&D is optimal if the $MCF = 1.40$, $\tau_0 = 0.29$, $\tau_i = 0.10$, and $t_{RD_0} = -0.029$.[6] The boundary has a negative slope because a higher external rate of return on R&D means that a lower tax incentive effect is required to justify a tax subsidy. Figure 10.1 shows, for example, that if an additional dollar of tax incentive generates an additional dollar of R&D, then the external rate of return on R&D must exceed 50 percent for a provincial tax subsidy to be warranted if the MCF is 1.40.

A reasonable range of values for κ is 1.00 to 2.00, given that R&D may be more tax sensitive at the provincial level than at the national level. A reasonable range of values for r^e is 0.10 and 0.30, which is the lower end of Nadiri's range of values because spillovers are likely to be lower at the provincial level than at the national level. The shaded rectangle in Figure 10.1 indicates this "reasonable" range of parameter values. Note that only a small corner of the shaded rectangle is above the boundary. In other words, the tax incentive effect has to be very close to 2.00 and the external rate of return has to be more than 30 percent in order to justify a provincial tax subsidy for R&D when the marginal cost of funds from alternative tax sources is 1.40. If the MCF were higher, then the boundary would shift up, the reasonable range of values for κ and r^e would be entirely below the boundary, and a provincial tax subsidy for R&D would not be justified.

The computations above indicate that a provincial tax subsidy is not warranted in Alberta, given our best guesses concerning the magnitudes of the tax incentive effect and the external rate of return on R&D. However, further research at the provincial level may reveal larger values for the key parameters, and therefore we do not want to emphasize any particular policy conclusion. Instead we would like to stress the usefulness of the framework, which takes into account the tax sensitivity of R&D, its external rate of return, and the marginal cost of public funds in evaluating tax subsidies for R&D. Almost all previous studies of R&D tax policies have focused either on the tax sensitivity of R&D or on its external rate of return. While the magnitudes of these parameters are extremely important for evaluating R&D subsidies, knowledge of either parameter is not sufficient to answer the question—Should the government provide a more generous tax incentive for R&D?—given that we live in a world where governments impose distortionary taxes to finance their activities.

10.2   Incentive Effects of the Australian Equalization Grant System

Concerns about the incentive effects of the equalization systems in Australia and Canada have been expressed by economists over a number of years.[7] The following section, which is based on the Dahlby and Warren (2003), analyzes the incentive effects of the Australian equalization system.

Let the per capita revenue received by state i equal

$$R_i = \sum_{j=1}^{n} t_{ij} B_{ij} + A_i + E_i, \tag{10.4}$$

where A_i is state i's per capita autonomous revenues (including lump-sum grants the central government), t_{ij} is the tax rate imposed by state i on tax base j, B_{ij} is the per capita tax base j in state i, and E_i is the "revenue needs" component of the central government's grants to state i. This equalization component is given by

$$E_i = \sum_{j=1}^{n} t_{sj}(B_{sj} - B_{ij}), \tag{10.5}$$

where t_{sj} is the standard tax rate for tax base j, and B_{sj} is the per capita standard tax base for tax base j used to calculate equalization grants. The Australian equalization system is based on a representative tax system (RTS), and the standard tax rate for any tax base is the average tax rate imposed by the six states and two territories:[8]

$$t_{sj} = \frac{\sum_{i=1}^{8} t_{ij} p_i B_{ij}}{\sum_{i=1}^{8} p_i B_{ij}} = \sum_{i=1}^{8} b_{ij} t_{ij}, \tag{10.6}$$

where p_i is state i's share of the population and b_{ij} is the state i's share of the total tax base j. The standard tax base j is the average per capita tax base j:

$$B_{sj} = \sum_{i=1}^{8} p_i B_{ij}. \tag{10.7}$$

In modeling a state government's fiscal decisions, we have assumed that the state's politicians choose the tax rates and public expenditures to maximize the well-being of their voters. (Alternatively, the model could be interpreted as one in which the politicians try to maximize their probability of re-election.) To minimize the social cost of the taxes that are imposed on the state's population, tax rates are set so as to equalize the marginal cost of funds (the MCFs) across the various tax bases that are available to a state government. The marginal cost of public funds for state i with respect to tax base j is given by

$$MCF_{ij} = \frac{\omega_{ij} B_{ij}}{dR_i/dt_{ij}}, \tag{10.8}$$

where ω_{ij} is the distributional characteristic for tax base j in state i. It measures the perceived social cost of increasing the tax on this particular tax base. For example, taxes that fall on goods that are disproportionately consumed by low-income individuals will have a high value for ω_{ij} if the society places a higher valuation on a dollar of income received by individuals with lower incomes. Alternatively, ω_{ij} could be interpreted as the marginal reduction in the probability of re-election by taxing base j.[9]

Taxpayers respond in various ways to an increase in a tax rate in order to avoid, or at least reduce, the amount of additional tax to be paid. Therefore, in general, tax bases shrink as tax rates increase, and dB_{ij}/dt_{ij} will usually be negative. For example, a higher payroll tax in state i increases the cost of employing workers in that state, leading to a reduction in employment and/or wage rates over time. Tax bases are also interrelated, so an increase in the tax rate on one base will either increase or reduce the size of the other tax bases.

The equalization system may alter a state's MCFs because its choice of tax rates may affect the three sets of parameters in the equalization grant formula—the t_s, B_s, and B_{ij}. Differentiating (10.4) with respect to t_{ij} and substituting in (10.8), state i's MCF from taxing base j will be equal to the following:

MCF_{ij}

$$= \frac{\omega_{ij} B_{ij}}{B_{ij} + \sum_{h=1}^{n} t_{ij}(dB_{ih}/dt_{ij}) + \sum_{h=1}^{n}(B_{sh} - B_{ih})(dt_{sh}/dt_{ij}) + \sum_{h=1}^{n} t_{sh}(dB_{sh}/dt_{ij} - dB_{ih}/dt_{ij})}.$$

$$(10.9)$$

The first two sets of terms in the denominator of (10.9) show how a tax rate change affects the state's own-source tax revenues. The third set of terms shows how its tax rate change affects its tax revenues through changes in its federal grants as a result of induced changes in the standard tax rates. We will refer to this as the *equalization rate effect*. The fourth set of terms shows how the tax rate changes its grant through induced changes in its differential fiscal capacity. We will refer to this as the *equalization base effect*.

For simplicity it will be assumed that the interactions between a state's tax bases are small, such that $dB_{ih}/dt_{ij} = 0$ and $dt_{sh}/dt_{ij} = 0$ for $h \neq j$. Noting from (10.9) that $dt_{sj}/dt_{ij} \approx b_{ij}$ if db_{ij}/dt_{ij} is small, and that $dB_{sj}/dt_{ij} = p_i dB_{ij}/dt_{ij}$, the MCF can be rewritten as follows:

$$MCF_{ij} = \frac{\omega_{ij}}{1 + \dfrac{t_{ij}}{B_{ij}} \dfrac{dB_{ij}}{dt_{ij}} + b_{ij}\left(\dfrac{B_{sj}}{B_{ij}} - 1\right) + \dfrac{t_{sj}}{B_{ij}}\left(p_i \dfrac{dB_{ij}}{dt_{ij}} - \dfrac{dB_{ij}}{dt_{ij}}\right)}. \qquad (10.10)$$

As in section 9.3.2 we will define the tax sensitivity of a state's tax base with respect to its tax rate as $\xi_{ij} = (d\ln B_{ij}/dt_i)$. We assume here that $-1 < t_{ij}\xi_{ij} < 0$. If $t_{ij}\xi_{ij} < -1$, the state is on the downward-sloping section of its Laffer curve for revenues from this tax base, and ignoring interactions with other tax bases and the equalization system, the state can increase its tax revenues by lowering its tax rate on this tax base.

By this definition of the tax base elasticity, the formula for the MCFs can be written as

$$MCF_{ij} = \frac{\omega_{ij}}{1 + t_{ij}\xi_{ij} + \rho_{ij} + \beta_{ij}}, \qquad (10.11)$$

where

$$\rho_{ij} = b_{ij}\left(\frac{B_{sj}}{B_{ij}} - 1\right), \qquad (10.12)$$

$$\beta_{ij} = (1 - p_i)t_{sj}(-\xi_{ij}). \qquad (10.13)$$

The marginal cost of raising revenue from tax base j for state i will depend on four factors:

• The distributional characteristic, ω_{ij}. This reflects the distributional effects of the tax increase in the state's residents.

• The tax sensitivity of the tax base, ξ_{ij}. This affects the rate at which a state government's own-source tax revenues increase when it increases its tax rates.

• The equalization rate effect, ρ_{ij}. This measures the change in a state's grant from the central government caused by the increase in the standard tax rate for tax base j when it raises its own-source tax revenue by one dollar from that base.

• The equalization base effect, β_{ij}. This measures the increase in a state's grant caused by the reduction in the state's relative fiscal capacity when it raises an additional dollar of tax revenue from tax base j through a tax rate increase.

The equalization rate effect will be negligible for small states because their shares of the total tax base (the b_{ij}) are usually small. However, for a large state such as New South Wales, the b_{ij} may be relatively large, and the ρ_{ij} will be negative (positive) if the state's relative fiscal capacity (B_{ij}/B_{sj}) is greater than (less than) one. A negative ρ_{ij} means that the state loses grants when it raises its tax rate on that tax base, and this will increase the perceived marginal cost of raising tax revenues from that base.

Figure 10.2 shows the equalization rate effects for the major sources of tax revenues for the state governments in Australia in 2000 and 2001. We will (somewhat arbitrarily) define a significant equalization rate effect as one that is greater than 0.05 in absolute value. The figure shows that for most taxes and for the four smallest states the equalization rate effects are not very large. The most significant equalization rate effects are as follows:

• Mining taxes for New South Wales (0.21), Victoria (0.23), Queensland (−0.15) and Western Australia (−0.32).

• Stamp duties on conveyances for New South Wales (−0.12) and Victoria (0.05).

• Financial transactions taxes for New South Wales (−0.07).

• Insurance taxes for New South Wales (−0.07).

• Heavy vehicle registration fees and taxes for New South Wales (0.07).

The equalization base effect will be larger the smaller the state's population, the more responsive its tax base is to tax rate increases, and the lower its tax rate compared to the average or standard tax rate. Consequently, as a state's share of the population and the tax base becomes larger, equalization rate effect and the equalization base effect will tend to move in opposite directions. The rate effect will become larger (in absolute value) because a larger state's tax rate will have a larger effect on the standard tax rate that is used to calculate the equalization grants. On the other hand, the basc effect will become smaller because the increase in a state's entitlement,

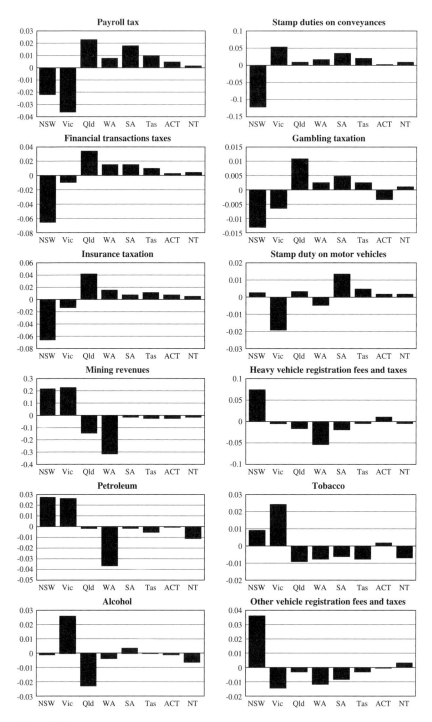

Figure 10.2
Equalization rate effects for the Australian states in 2000 and 2001

caused by the reduction in its tax base, will be offset by the reduction in the standard tax base for a larger state. Thus the equalization formula can affect the perceived marginal cost of imposing taxes for large and small states, but the sources and magnitudes of these distortions will generally be different for large and small states.

While it is difficult to measure the equalization base effect for most tax bases, it can be measured reasonably accurately for land taxes in Australia. As noted by Warren (2002), the Australian equalization system uses the market value of land in determining the fiscal capacity of a state, and this measure is negatively related to a state's tax rate if land taxes are fully capitalized in land values.

The elasticity of a state's land tax base can be easily calculated under the assumption that the supply of land is completely inelastic, and that current and future land taxes are capitalized in the value of the land. Let B_{i1} be the per capita value of land in state i. Let N_i be the annual rents that accrue to the owners of the land, and let r be the discount rate that is used to determine the value of the land. Because the land tax is imposed on the market value of the property, the value of the land is equal to

$$B_{i1} = \frac{N_i - t_{i1} B_{i1}}{r} = \frac{N_i}{r + t_{i1}}. \tag{10.14}$$

In other words, if land taxes are fully capitalized in land values, the annual rental income from a property is capitalized using the effective discount rate $r + t_{i1}$. Given the relationship between the tax base and the tax rate for land in (10.14), the tax sensitivity of the land tax base is $\xi_{il} = -(r + t_{il})^{-1}$.

It will be convenient to normalize the distributional characteristics for the tax bases such that $\omega_{i1} = 1$.[10] All of the other ω_{ij}s measure the social or political cost of imposing a dollar of tax from tax base j relative to a dollar raised through the land tax. In deriving the MCF for the land tax, other special features of the land tax are also utilized. First, the burden of a tax rate increase on land is $(B_{i1} + t_{i1} dB_{i1}/dt_{i1}) = r/(r + t_{i1})B_{i1}$ because the value of the property declines when the tax is imposed. In addition it can be shown that

$$\frac{dt_{s1}}{dt_{i1}} = b_{i1}\left(\frac{r + t_{s1}}{r + t_{i1}}\right). \tag{10.15}$$

Using the features above for the land tax, the MCF for the land tax is equal to

$$MCF_{i1} = \frac{r}{r + (r + t_{s1})b_{i1}[(B_{s1}/B_{i1}) - 1] + (1 - p_i)t_{s1}}. \tag{10.16}$$

In the absence of equalization ($b_{i1} = t_{s1} = 0$), the MCF for the land tax would simply be 1.00 because the supply of land is completely inelastic. In analyzing the effects of the equalization system on the MCF, first consider the case of a small state

Table 10.1
Australian equalization system and the MCF for state land taxes

	Tax rates t_{i1}	Shares of the land tax base b_{i1}	Relative fiscal capacity B_{i1}/B_{s1}	Equalization effects		MCF for the land tax MCF_{i1}
				Rate effect, ρ_{i1}	Base effect, β_{i1}	
New South Wales	0.0168	0.4917	1.46	−0.163	0.229	0.915
Victoria	0.0232	0.2279	0.92	0.019	0.233	0.716
Queensland	0.0164	0.1247	0.67	0.065	0.282	0.672
Western Australia	0.0221	0.1033	1.05	−0.005	0.285	0.698
South Australia	0.0434	0.0287	0.37	0.035	0.285	0.656
Tasmania	0.0590	0.0004	0.16	0.013	0.242	0.662
Australian Capital Territory	0.0254	0.0111	0.69	0.005	0.295	0.672
Northern Territory	0.0000	0.0085	0.84	0.002	0.485	0.672

Notes: The standard tax rate, t_{s1}, in 2000 and 2001 was 0.0196. Equalization rate and base effects and the MCF_{il} were calculated using a discount rate, r, of 0.04 and the formulas

$$\rho_{i1} = b_{i1} \left(\frac{r + t_{s1}}{r + t_{i1}} \right) \left(\frac{B_{s1}}{B_{i1}} - 1 \right),$$

$$\beta_{i1} = \frac{(1 - p_i)t_{s1}}{r + t_{i1}}.$$

($b_{i1} \approx 0$ and $p_i \approx 0$). Its MCF_{i1} is equal to $r/(r + t_{s1}) < 1$. The equalization system reduces the perceived cost of raising tax revenues from raising land taxes rates because it compensates the state for the reduction in its tax base due to tax capitalization. In the case of a large state, such as New South Wales, which has above average fiscal capacity with respect to land taxes, the equalization rate effect is negative and nontrivial, and this tends to raise its MCF for the land tax. Indeed it is possible for the MCF_{i1} for a large state to be greater than 1.00 if it has a relatively large fiscal capacity.

In table 10.1 the 2000 and 2001 Commonwealth Grants Commission data were used to compute the equalization rate and base effects and the MCFs for the land tax for the various state governments in Australia. The equalization rate effect for New South Wales (NSW) was quite significant because New South Wales had a large share of the land tax base (0.4917), and the state's relative fiscal capacity was high (1.46). Because of the equalization rate effect, New South Wales lost grants at a rate of 16.5 cents for every dollar of additional land tax revenue that it raised. However, NSW got 22.9 cents in additional grants for every dollar of land tax revenue that it raised through the equalization base effect. Consequently New South Wales gets approximately $1 - 0.163 + 0.229 = 1.066$ in revenues for every additional dollar of land tax revenue imposed by the state, and this is why land taxes MCF for New South Wales is approximately equal to 1/1.066. Each additional dollar of land tax revenue collected by the state only appeared to cost the NSW's taxpayers 91.5 cents. (Of course, the additional grants from the federal government have to come from higher federal taxes, and the taxpayers of New South Wales will bear a significant portion of those higher taxes, but we assume that the state government ignores this "second-round effect" when it evaluates the merits of a land tax increase.)

Table 10.1 also shows that the equalization rate effects were generally quite small for the other states, except for Queensland, which received 6.5 cents in additional grants through the equalization rate effect when it imposed an additional dollar of land tax revenue. On the other hand, the equalization base effects are quite large for the smaller states and lower the MCFs for their land tax. In particular, the calculations indicate that the Northern Territory would receive 48.5 cents in additional grants with the first dollar of land tax revenue that it imposed. From the perspective of the Northern Territory, the land tax would be a "cheap" source of tax revenue. However, there are fixed administration costs in levying a tax, and the land tax base in the Northern Territory is small, so there may be little net gain in levying a land tax even though the marginal cost of land tax revenue is low for the Northern Territory.

Hence we have shown how a fiscal equalization system may affect the taxation and expenditure decisions of recipient governments by modifying their perceived MCFs. A more detailed empirical analysis of the effects of equalization systems on the behavior of subnational governments is beyond the scope of this chapter. However, econometric studies of the incentive effects of the equalization system have been conducted by Snoddon (2003) and Smart (2006) for Canada, Buettner (2006) for Germany, and Dahlby and Warren (2003) for Australia, and they generally indicate that the equalization systems affect the fiscal decisions of recipient governments.

10.3 Equalization Grants and Vertical and Horizontal Fiscal Imbalances

In section 9.5 a model of vertical fiscal imbalance was presented. One limitation of that model was the assumption that all subnational governments are identical. This simplifying assumption is troubling because federations exist, at least in part because regions have different economic, cultural, or linguistic characteristics. Given these differences, a country's political and economic institutions have to be decentralized in order to tailor economic and cultural policies to local conditions. Federations exist because of regional heterogeneity, and if we ignore heterogeneity in our models of fiscal federalism, we may be overlooking important aspects of tax policy and intergovernmental finance. In this section we develop a model of a federation with heterogeneous states based on the cross-border shopping of Kanbur and Keen (1993). We use this model to analyze fiscal externalities and intergovernmental transfers when regions differ with respect to either the size of their tax bases or the tax sensitivity of their tax base. Vertical tax externalities arise in the model because the tax bases of the federal and state governments overlap. Horizontal tax externalities also occur because of tax base flight and tax exporting can occur when cross-border shopping is possible. Bucovetsky and Smart (2006) have shown that equalization grants can offset the distortions caused by horizontal fiscal externalities arising from capital tax competition. Specifically, they show that if the total supply of capital is fixed for the economy as a whole and states face the same elasticity of demand for capital and have the same demand for public goods, then the equalization grants induce the states to provide the same level of public services as would be provided in a unitary state. In essence, the incentive effects of the equalization formula reduce the states' perceived MCFs so that it coincides with the true or social MCF. (See section 10.2 on the incentive effects of equalization grants.) One significant limitation of the Bucovetsky and Smart result is the absence of vertical fiscal externalities because the federal government does not play a role in their model—the equalization grants are financed by contributions from states with above average fiscal capacity. Therefore it is interesting to consider the ability of the equalization grants to offset the distortions in state governments' decisions when there are both horizontal and vertical tax externalities.

We have developed a relatively simple model that incorporates both vertical and horizontal tax externalities. Unfortunately, even though we have tried to keep the model as simple as possible, it is not possible to obtain analytical results. We have to rely on numerical simulations to obtain some insights into the effects of the equalization grants on fiscal imbalances.

The basic model is described with reference to figure 10.3. There are two regions. Each has one unit of population and is one unit of distance in width. The population is uniformly distributed across each region. In region i individuals consume a product (e.g., cigarettes) at the rate b_i. The demand for the product is completely price inelastic. Individuals can purchase this product in the location where they live at a price $p + t_0 + t_i$, where p is the producer price, t_0 is a federal excise tax on the product, and t_i is the excise tax levied in region i where they live. Alternatively, they can travel to the border of either the neighboring region or the neighboring country to purchase the good. For concreteness, suppose that the tax rate in region 2, t_2, is higher than the tax rate in region 1, t_1. A resident of region 2 is better off if she travels to region 1 to purchase the commodity if $p + t_0 + t_1 + \delta m < p + t_0 + t_2$, where δ is the cost per unit of distance of a round trip to region 1 to acquire the commodity and m is the distance that the individual lives from the border with region 1. Note that we are assuming that transportation costs are proportional to the distance traveled and the

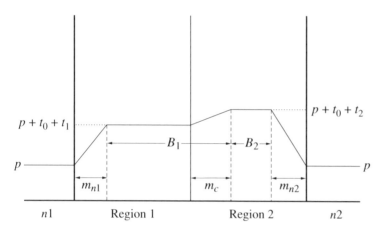

Figure 10.3
Model of cross-border shopping in a federation

volume of goods purchased. From this condition we can define the critical distance m_c such that all residents of region 2 who live closer to the border with region 1 than m_c purchase the commodity in region 1:

$$m_c = \frac{t_2 - t_1}{\delta}. \tag{10.17}$$

Note also that m_c can be interpreted as the proportion of the residents of region 2 who buy the commodity in region 1. Alternatively, residents of region 2 who live near the border with the foreign country to the "east" of region 2 will shop in the neighboring foreign country if $p + \delta_{n2} m < p + t_0 + t_1$, where δ_{n2} is the per mile cost of a return trip to the neighboring country. To simplify the model, we assume that the individual is able to buy the product tax free in the neighboring country. Therefore all individuals who live within the distance m_{n2} of the border with the neighboring country to the east of region 2 engage in cross-border shopping where

$$m_{n2} = \frac{t_0 + t_2}{\delta_{n2}}. \tag{10.18}$$

Similarly, in region 1, individuals who live within m_{n1} miles of the neighboring country $n1$ will engage in cross-border shopping where

$$m_{n1} = \frac{t_0 + t_1}{\delta_{n1}}. \tag{10.19}$$

We will assume that δ is less than either δ_{n1} or δ_{n2} because travel to a foreign country may be more expensive, per unit of distance, than travel within a country. For example, individuals may have to fly to the foreign country, whereas they can use cheaper ground transport for within country cross-border shopping. Of course, some of the additional costs of going to a foreign country to shop are fixed costs that do not vary with the distance traveled. However, we will ignore this complication in order to simplify the model.

The tax bases in regions 1 and 2 are

$$B_1 = (1 - m_{n1})b_1 + [Ib_2 + (1 - I)b_1]m_c, \tag{10.20}$$

$$B_2 = (1 - m_{n2})b_2 - [Ib_2 + (1 - I)b_1]m_c, \tag{10.21}$$

where I is an indicator variable with $I = 1$ when $t_2 > t_1$ and $I = 0$ when $t_2 < t_1$. The federal tax base is

$$B_0 = B_1 + B_2 = b_1(1 - m_{n1}) + b_2(1 - m_{n2}). \tag{10.22}$$

Substituting the expressions for m_c, m_{n1}, and m_{n2} in the equations for the tax bases, we obtain the following system of equations:

$$B_0 = (b_1 + b_2) - \alpha_{00}t_0 - \alpha_{01}t_1 - \alpha_{02}t_2, \tag{10.23}$$

$$B_1 = b_1 - \alpha_{10}t_0 - \alpha_{11}t_1 + \alpha_{12}t_2, \tag{10.24}$$

$$B_2 = b_2 - \alpha_{20}t_0 + \alpha_{21}t_1 - \alpha_{22}t_2, \tag{10.25}$$

where

$$\alpha_{00} = \frac{b_1}{\delta_{n1}} + \frac{b_2}{\delta_{n2}}, \quad \alpha_{01} = \frac{b_1}{\delta_{n1}}, \quad \alpha_{02} = \frac{b_2}{\delta_{n2}},$$

$$\alpha_{10} = \frac{b_1}{\delta_{n1}}, \quad \alpha_{11} = \frac{I \cdot b_2 + (1 - I) \cdot b_1}{\delta} + \frac{b_1}{\delta_{n1}}, \quad \alpha_{12} = \frac{I \cdot b_2 + (1 - I) \cdot b_1}{\delta},$$

$$\alpha_{20} = \frac{b_2}{\delta_{n2}}, \quad \alpha_{21} = \frac{I \cdot b_2 + (1 - I) \cdot b_1}{\delta}, \quad \alpha_{22} = \frac{I \cdot b_2 + (1 - I) \cdot b_1}{\delta} + \frac{b_2}{\delta_{n2}}.$$

In the special case where $t_2 = t_1$, we have $\alpha_{11} = b_1(1/\delta + 1/\delta_{n1})$, $\alpha_{12} = b_2/\delta$, $\alpha_{21} = b_1/\delta$, and $\alpha_{22} = b_2(1/\delta + 1/\delta_{n2})$.

We now use this framework to compare the fiscal outcomes of a unitary state, where the central government sets t_1 and t_2 (t_0 being redundant) with a federal state where the central government sets t_0 to finance a federal public service g_0, and the state governments independently set t_1 and t_2 to finance state public services g_1 and g_2. We can assume that the fiscal outcomes are evaluated based on a utilitarian social welfare function:

$$S = m_{n1}\left[b_1 + Y - b_1\left(p + \frac{\delta_{n1}m_{n1}}{2}\right)\right] + (1 - m_{n1})[b_1 + Y - b_1(p + t_0 + t_1)]$$

$$+ m_c\left[b_2 + Y - b_2\left(p + t_0 + t_1 + \frac{\delta m_c}{\delta}\right)\right]$$

$$+ (1 - m_{n2} - m_c)[b_2 + Y - b_2(p + t_0 + t_2)]$$

$$+ m_{n2}\left[b_2 + Y - b_2\left(p + \frac{\delta_{n2}m_{n2}}{2}\right)\right]$$

$$+ 2[\Gamma g_0 - 0.5\gamma g_0^2] + (\Gamma g_1 - 0.5\gamma g_1^2) + (\Gamma g_2 - 0.5\gamma g_2^2), \tag{10.26}$$

where Y is the individuals' exogenous income and m_c is assumed to be positive. The first five terms are the average real incomes of the five groups of consumers in this economy, starting with the group that purchases the good in neighboring country $n1$. The three terms in the last line represent the total benefits that the individuals in the two states receive from the public services provided by the federal and state governments. To simplify the notation, we have assumed that the benefits from the three public services have the same functional form and parameter values $\Gamma > 0$ and $\gamma > 0$. Note that individuals benefit from the public services whether or not they engage in cross-border shopping, and there are no spillovers of benefits from one state to another.

10.3.1 A Unitary State

A convenient reference point for evaluating the fiscal outcomes under federalism are the policies that would be adopted by a unitary state government that would set t_1 and t_2 to finance g_0, g_1, and g_2. The budget constraint of a unitary government is

$$t_1 B_1 + t_2 B_2 = 2 \cdot g_0 + g_1 + g_2. \tag{10.27}$$

(As previously noted, t_0 is redundant in a unitary state.) If we assume that the social welfare function in (10.26) is maximized by the unitary state government, its MCFs will have the following forms:

$$MCF_{t_1} = \frac{(1 - m_{n1})b_1 + m_c[Ib_2 + (1 - I)b_1]}{B_1 - t_1\alpha_{11} + t_2\alpha_{21}}, \tag{10.28}$$

$$MCF_{t_2} = \frac{(1 - m_{n2})b_2 - m_c[Ib_2 + (1 - I)b_1]}{B_2 - t_2\alpha_{22} + t_1\alpha_{12}}. \tag{10.29}$$

The numerators of these expressions indicate the welfare losses from an increase in t_1 or t_2 on the residents of the region where these taxes are imposed as well as the residents of the other region who engage in cross-border shopping. The denominators of these expressions include the effects of an increase in tax rate in region i on total tax revenues from tax base i (the first two terms) as well as the additional tax revenues collected from the other tax base. The optimal set of taxes for the unitary state government will satisfy the condition $MCF_{t_1} = MCF_{t_2}$. Appealing to the Ramsey rule of optimal taxation as discussed in section 3.3, the optimal set of taxes will cause the tax bases in the two regions, B_1 and B_2, to shrink in the same proportion. Depending on the relative tax sensitivities of the two bases, the unitary state may levy different tax rates in the two regions. We will discuss this further in the section that deals with the simulation results. The optimal expenditure levels on the three public services would be determined by the condition $MCF = MB_{g_i}$, $i = 0, 1, 2$, where the marginal benefit from each public service is

$$MB_{g_i} = \Gamma - \gamma g_i, \qquad i = 0, 1, 2. \tag{10.30}$$

10.3.2   Federation without Intergovernmental Transfers

In the absence of intergovernmental grants, each government in a federation would face the budget constraint $t_i B_i = g_i$ for $i = 0, 1$, and 2. It is assumed that the central government has to set a uniform tax rate across the country. The MCFs of the three governments would be

$$MCF_{t_0} = \frac{(1 - m_{n1})b_1 + (1 - m_{n2})b_2 + MB_{g_1} \cdot t_1 \cdot \alpha_{10} + MB_{g_2} \cdot t_2 \cdot \alpha_{20}}{B_0 - t_0 \alpha_{00}}, \tag{10.31}$$

$$MCF_{t_1} = \frac{(1 - m_{n1} + (1 - I)m_c)b_1 + MB_{g_0} \cdot t_0 \cdot \alpha_{01}}{B_1 - t_1 \alpha_{11}}, \tag{10.32}$$

$$MCF_{t_2} = \frac{(1 - m_{n2} - I \cdot m_c)b_1 + MB_{g_0} \cdot t_0 \cdot \alpha_{02}}{B_2 - t_2 \alpha_{22}}. \tag{10.33}$$

The federal government takes the tax rates of the state governments as given, but takes into account how an increase in t_0 will affect the provision of state public services through its effects on their tax bases. These effects are reflected in the third and fourth terms in the numerator of (10.31). The first term in the numerators of each state's MCF reflects the impact of a tax increase on its residents. The state governments are assumed to ignore the effect of their taxes on the residents of the other state who are engaged in cross-border shopping, namely tax exporting. The state governments are also assumed to take into account the impact of their taxes on the level of federal services provided in their state (the second terms in equations 10.32 and 10.33), but they ignore the impact of their taxes on the tax revenues and the level of services of other states. Each level of government is assumed to adjust its taxes, given its budget constraint, to satisfy the condition $MB_{g_i} = MCF_{t_i}$. As in the model in section 9.5 there are both vertical and horizontal tax externalities, and there can be either too much or too little state spending relative to federal spending. In addition this model allows for the possibility of a horizontal fiscal imbalance because in general the MCFs of the two state governments will not be equalized. The simulation results reported at the end of this section will focus on these imbalances.

10.3.3   Federation with a Net Equalization Grant System

As was noted in section 10.2, many federations provide equalization grants to states with below average tax bases. We investigate the implications of two alternative methods of financing the equalization grants. First, we present a model of what is known in the literature as a "net" equalization grant system in which states either contribute or receive equalization grants. With this system the federal government does not finance the pool of equalization grants. This is the type of financing assumed in Bucovetsky and Smart (2006). In section 10.3.4 we consider a "gross" equalization system in which the federal government finances the equalization payments to recipient states, and the "rich" state governments do not directly contribute to the equalization pool.

In the context of the current model where both states have the same population, the equalization grant formula can be written as

$$E_i = t_s[B_s - B_i] = t_s B_0 \left(0.5 - \frac{B_i}{B_0} \right), \qquad i = 1, 2, \tag{10.34}$$

where $B_s = 0.5 B_0$ is the standard tax base and t_s is the standard tax rate,

$$t_s = t_1 \frac{B_1}{B_0} + t_2 \frac{B_2}{B_0}. \tag{10.35}$$

Each state's budget constraint is

$$t_i B_i + E_i = g_i, \qquad i = 1, 2. \tag{10.36}$$

If state i has more than 50 percent of the total tax base, B_0, then E_i is negative, and the state is a net contributor to the equalization pool. If the state has less than 50 percent of the total tax base, E_i is positive and the state receives an equalization grant. Note that $E_1 + E_2 = 0$.

The equalization grants not only represent an additional source of revenues for recipient states, or additional expenditure for contributing states, they also affect the states' perceived MCF because the state's tax rates affect its equalization grant or contribution. Building on the framework developed in section 10.2, we have incorporated the equalization rate effect and the equalization base effect in the MCFs of the two state governments as shown in the equations below:

$$MCF_{t_1} = \frac{(1 - m_{n1} + (1 - I)m_c)b_1 + MB_{g_0} \cdot t_0 \cdot \alpha_{01}}{B_1 - t_1\alpha_{11} + B_1\left[\left(0.5 - \frac{B_1}{B_0}\right) + t_s\left(\frac{\alpha_{11}}{B_1} - \frac{\alpha_{01}}{B_0}\right)\right]},$$ (10.37)

$$MCF_{t_2} = \frac{(1 - m_{n2} - I \cdot m_c)b_1 + MB_{g_0} \cdot t_0 \cdot \alpha_{02}}{B_2 - t_2\alpha_{22} + B_2\left[\left(0.5 - \frac{B_2}{B_0}\right) + t_s\left(\frac{\alpha_{22}}{B_2} - \frac{\alpha_{02}}{B_0}\right)\right]},$$ (10.38)

where the first terms in the square brackets in the denominators are the equalization rate effects and the second term are the equalization base effects.

Although the federal government does not finance the equalization grants under the net RTS system, we assume that the federal government takes into account the effect of its tax rate increase on the equalization grants of the states and the consequent effect on the provision of state public services. Therefore the MCF for the federal government has the following form:

$$MCF_{t_0} = \frac{(1 - m_{n1})b_1 + (1 - m_{n2})b_2 + MB_{g_1}\left(t_1 \cdot \alpha_{10} + \frac{dE_1}{dt_0}\right) + MB_{g_2}\left(t_2 \cdot \alpha_{20} + \frac{dE_2}{dt_0}\right)}{B_0 - t_0\alpha_{00}},$$ (10.39)

where

$$\frac{dE_i}{dt_0} = [t_s\alpha_{00} - t_1\alpha_{10} - t_2\alpha_{20}]\left(0.5 - \frac{B_i}{B_0}\right) + t_s(\alpha_{i0} - 0.5\alpha_{00}).$$ (10.40)

10.3.4 Federation with a Gross Equalization Grant System

The net equalization system has a theoretical appeal because of its symmetric treatment of states. However, in practice, most central governments fund equalization grants, and states with above average tax bases do not directly contribute to the equalization pool. With a central government-funded or gross equalization system the grant formula and the budget constraints of the three governments become

$$E_i = \max\left[t_sB_0\left(0.5 - \frac{B_i}{B_0}\right), 0\right], \quad i = 1, 2,$$ (10.41)

$$g_0 + E_1 + E_2 = t_0B_0,$$ (10.42)

$$g_i = t_iB_i + E_i, \quad i = 1, 2.$$ (10.43)

The switch to a gross RTS system from a net RTS system means that the state with the above average tax base does not have to fund equalization grants out of its own tax revenue. It also affects the state's MCF because it is no longer affected by the equalization rate and equalization base effects. Therefore the MCFs of the two state governments are asymmetric and can be written in general form as

$$MCF_{t_1} = \frac{(1 - m_{n1} + (1 - I)m_c)b_1 + MB_{g_0} \cdot t_0 \cdot \alpha_{01}}{B_1 - t_1\alpha_{11} + B_1\left[\left(0.5 - \frac{B_1}{B_0}\right) + t_s\left(\frac{\alpha_{11}}{B_1} - \frac{\alpha_{01}}{B_0}\right)\right] \cdot t_1}, \tag{10.44}$$

$$MCF_{t_2} = \frac{(1 - m_{n2} - I \cdot m_c)b_1 + MB_{g_0} \cdot t_0 \cdot \alpha_{02}}{B_2 - t_2\alpha_{22} + B_2\left[\left(0.5 - \frac{B_2}{B_0}\right) + t_s\left(\frac{\alpha_{22}}{B_2} - \frac{\alpha_{02}}{B_0}\right)\right] \cdot t_2}, \tag{10.45}$$

where ι_i is an indicator variable with $\iota_i = 0$ if $E_i = 0$ and $\iota_i = 1$ if $E_i > 0$. The marginal cost of funds expression for the federal government also has to be modified by the switch to central government funding of equalization grants because the net amount of revenue that the federal government receives and that can be used to finance federal public services is affected by dE_i/dt_0. Therefore the federal MCF becomes

MCF_{t_0}

$$= \frac{(1 - m_{n1})b_1 + (1 - m_{n2})b_2 + MB_{g_1}\left(t_1 \cdot \alpha_{10} + \iota_1 \frac{dE_1}{dt_0}\right) + MB_{g_2}\left(t_2 \cdot \alpha_{20} + \iota_2 \frac{dE_2}{dt_0}\right)}{B_0 - t_0\alpha_{00} - \iota_1 \frac{dE_1}{dt_0} - \iota_2 \frac{dE_2}{dt_0}}.$$

$$\tag{10.46}$$

10.3.5 Simulation Model of the Effects of Equalization Grants

Tables 10.2 and 10.3 show the results from simulating the model with the parameter values $\delta = 1$, $Y = 1$, $p = 0$, $\Gamma = 3$, and $\gamma = 20$. The last two parameters were chosen so that the elasticity of demand for the public services is -0.50 if the MCF were one and that the first-best provision for each type of public service, g_i^*, would be 10 percent of income, that is $g_0^* = g_1^* = g_2^* = 0.10$.

Table 10.2 contains simulations where state 1 would have a 50 percent larger tax base than state 2 if all governments imposed lump-sum taxes, and both states' tax bases had the same tax sensitivity. The particular parameter values used in these simulations are $b_1 = 1.20$, $b_2 = 0.80$, and $\delta_{n1} = \delta_{n2} = 1.15$. In the unitary state case the MCFs for both taxes would be equal to 1.287 and the same tax rate, 0.210, would be imposed in both regions. This tax policy is optimal because it implements the Ramsey rule by causing both tax bases to shrink in the same proportion; that is, both tax bases are 81.8 percent of their value with a lump-sum tax. The use of the

Table 10.2
VFI and HFI when states have different per capita tax bases

	Unitary state	Federal state		
		No inter-governmental grants	Net RNAS equalization grant	Gross RNAS equalization grant
MCF_0	na	1.283	1.293	1.266
MCF_1	1.287	1.302	1.360	1.321
MCF_2	1.287	1.580	1.130	1.143
VFI_1 [b]	na	0.019	0.067	0.055
VFI_2 [b]	na	0.297	−0.190	−0.123
HFI [b]	na	0.278	−0.257	−0.178
g_0/g_0^*	0.857	0.858	0.854	0.867
g_1/g_1^*	0.857	0.849	0.820	0.840
g_2/g_2^*	0.857	0.710	0.948	0.929
t_0	na	0.104	0.105	0.119
t_1	0.210	0.082	0.102	0.082
t_2	0.210	0.114	0.119	0.121
B_1/b_1	0.818	0.857	0.831	0.850
B_2/b_2	0.818	0.779	0.789	0.753
E_1	na	na	−0.020	0
E_2	na	na	0.020	0.020
E_2/g_2	na	na	0.210	0.217
S/S_{LS}	0.98946	0.98846	0.98903	0.98866

a. Key parameter values are $\delta_I = 1.00$, $\delta_{n1} = 1.15$, $\delta_{n2} = 1.15$, $b_1 = 1.20$, and $b_2 = 0.80$.
b. $VFI_1 = MCF_1 - MCF_0$, $VFI_2 = MCF_2 - MCF_0$, and $HFI = MCF_2 - MCF_1$.

distortionary tax to finance the provision of the three public services reduces their provision to 85.7 percent of their first-best levels. As a consequence social welfare is 98.946 percent of what could be achieved with lump-sum taxes, S_{LS}.

In a federal state that did not provide intergovernmental transfers, the MCFs of the three governments would diverge. Even though its per capita tax base is higher than the federal government's, state 1 would have a slightly higher MCF than the federal government because its tax base is more tax sensitive than the federal tax base because of cross-border shopping with state 2. State 2 would have a much higher MCF than either federal government or state 1. There would be significant vertical fiscal imbalances (VFI) and horizontal fiscal imbalances (HFI) in the federation as measured by the differentials in the governments' MCFs. As result of these differentials in the MCFs, the relative underprovision of g_2 would be particularly significant—71 percent of the first-best level compared to 84.9 percent for state 1 and 85.8 percent for the federal public good. The "misallocation" of the tax burden

Table 10.3
VFI and HFI when states' tax bases have different tax sensitivity

	Unitary state	Federal state		
		No inter-governmental grants	Net RNAS equalization grant	Gross RNAS equalization grant
MCF_0	na	1.285	1.291	1.302
MCF_1	1.289	1.413	1.209	1.390
MCF_2	1.289	1.485	1.227	1.236
$VFI_1{}^b$	na	0.128	−0.082	0.088
$VFI_2{}^b$	na	0.200	−0.064	−0.066
HFI^b	na	0.073	0.018	−0.154
g_0/g_0^*	0.856	0.857	0.854	0.849
g_1/g_1^*	0.856	0.794	0.895	0.805
g_2/g_2^*	0.856	0.757	0.886	0.882
t_0	na	0.104	0.105	0.106
t_1	0.215	0.094	0.110	0.094
t_2	0.204	0.093	0.109	0.108
B_1/b_1	0.817	0.840	0.826	0.854
B_2/b_2	0.817	0.814	0.797	0.782
E_1	na	na	−0.0016	0
E_2	na	na	0.0016	0.0036
E_2/g_2	na	na	0.018	0.041
S/S_{LS}	0.98939	0.98901	0.98929	0.98915

a. Key parameter values are $\delta_I = 1.00$, $\delta_{n1} = 1.25$, $\delta_{n2} = 1.05$, $b_1 = 1.00$, and $b_2 = 1.00$. Other parameter values are described in the text.
b. $VFI_1 = MCF_0 - MCF_1$, $VFI_2 = MCF_0 - MCF_2$, and $HFI = MCF_2 - MCF_1$.

in the federation is reflected in the 22.1 percent reduction in state 2's tax base compared to the 14.3 percent reduction in state 1's tax base. As a result of these vertical and horizontal fiscal imbalances, social welfare would be lower in the federal state than in the unitary state.

With a net equalization grant system, state 1's MCF would increase slightly from 1.302 to 1.360 and state 2's MCF would drop from 1.580 to 1.13. The main reasons for these changes in the states' MCFs are the equalization rate effect and equalization base effect. For state 1 the two effects almost completely offset each other, with the equalization rate effect equal to −0.112 and the equalization base effect equal to 0.131. As a result of these offsetting effects, state 1's contribution to equalization would go down by 1.9 cents for each additional dollar in taxes that it raises. Thus the net incentive effect of the RTS formula would tend to lower state 1's MCF, but the overall increase in its MCF arises principally because it now has to impose a higher tax rate to finance the transfer to state 2. State 2's MCF declines dramatically with the net RTS grant because its equalization rate effect is 0.112 and its equalization base effect is 0.211 implying that state 2 would get 32.3 cents in additional equalization grants if it increased its taxes by an additional dollar. As a result of these large incentive effects, state 2's MCF would be lower than the MCFs for both the federal government and state 2. This would result in a negative vertical and horizontal fiscal imbalance with too much spending by state 2 relative to state 1 and the federal government. State 2 would receive an equalization grant equal to 21 percent of its spending on public services, and this would improve the regional allocation of the tax burden in the federation, as indicated by a narrowing of the differential "shrinkage" rate of the two states' tax bases. Overall, social welfare, as measured by the utilitarian social welfare function, would be higher with the net equalization grants than in a federal state without intergovernmental transfers.

With the gross equalization system the MCF for state 1 declines to 1.321 from 1.360 under the net equalization system because it no longer has to fund the equalization transfer. The MCF for the federal government also declines slightly to 1.266. Consequently the vertical and horizontal fiscal imbalances that arose with the net equalization grant still exit. The allocation of the tax burden in the federation deteriorates slightly compared to the net equalization grant and social welfare is slightly lower than with the net equalization grant, but there would still be an improvement compared to the federal state without equalization grants. Overall, there would be a gain of 12.7 cents per dollar transferred to state 2 from state 1 with the net equalization grant system and a gain of 4 cents per dollar transferred to state 2 from the federal government with the gross equalization grant.

To summarize, the simulations in this table show that an equalization grant system, while not capable of replicating the unitary state allocation of taxes and public services, would produce a net social gain, based on a utilitarian social welfare function, and that the funding of the equalization system by the central government would reduce the welfare gains by only a small amount.

Table 10.3 contains the simulations when the tax sensitivities of the states' tax bases differ. Specially, in these simulations $b_1 = b_2 = 1.00$, and $\delta_{n1} = 1.25$ and $\delta_{n2} = 1.05$, with state 2 having a more tax sensitive tax base because the costs of travel to its neighboring foreign country for cross-border shopping are lower than for state 1. Note that in this case, any differences in the states' tax bases will be induced by the taxes that are levied. In the absence of taxation, the two states would have the same potential tax base.

In a unitary state the MCFs for the two tax bases would be equalized at 1.289 by levying a tax rate of 0.215 in region 1 and 0.204 in region 2. The higher tax rate would be imposed in the region with the less sensitive tax base to implement the equivalent of the Ramsey rule for optimal taxation by shrinking the tax bases of the two regions in the same proportion. This shows why regional variations in tax rates may be an important characteristic of an efficient tax system in a country where regions have significantly different tax base elasticities.

In a federal state without equalization grants, these differences in the tax base elasticities would result in a somewhat higher MCF for state 2 than state 1, but in these simulations the main distortion is the vertical fiscal imbalance that emerges between the federal government and the two state governments. That is, the states' public services are under-provided relative to the federal public services. In addition the allocation of the tax burden across the regions worsens, compared to the unitary state, because state 2's tax base declines relative to state 1's tax base. As a result of these horizontal and vertical imbalances, social welfare declines relative to the unitary state.

The RTS equalization grants were not designed to deal with differences in tax base elasticities between states. (Indeed one of the underlying assumptions of the RTS is that tax bases are exogenous and not affected by tax rates.) Therefore one might think that the RTS equalization grants would not be capable of improving the allocation of resources in the federal system when the only differences between states is the tax sensitivity of their tax bases. However, equalization grants can have incentive effects that improve (or possibly worsen) the allocation of resources in a federation. With the net equalization grants, table 10.3 indicates that the MCFs of both state governments are significantly lowered because of these incentive effects. Note that this occurs even though the equalization transfers are very small—less than 2 percent of state 2's spending on public services. For both states the equalization rate effects are very small because the differences the states' tax bases are relatively small. However, the equalization base effects of 0.185 for state 1 and 0.214 for state 2 significantly reduce their MCFs, such that they are lower than the federal governments, thus creating a "negative vertical fiscal imbalance" in the federation. Tax rates levied by both states increase and the imbalances in spending by the two levels of government are ameliorated. The misallocation of the tax burden across the states remains more or less the same. Overall, the net equalization grant system produces an improvement in social welfare compared to the federal state without intergovernmental transfers.

With the gross equalization grant system, state 1's MCF is 1.39, much higher than the federal government's MCF or state 2's MCF, which is reduced because of the incentive effects. A significant horizontal fiscal imbalance emerges in which the state with the above average tax base provides a lower level of public services than the state with the low average tax base. Furthermore the allocation of the tax burden across the tax bases worsens, as indicated by a divergence in the shrinkage rates of the tax bases—the tax base in state 1 is 85.4 percent of its before-tax value whereas the state 2's tax base is 78.2 percent of its before-tax values. Despite exacerbating these tax base distortions, we see that the gross equalization grant system still generates a welfare improvement over the federal state without intergovernmental grants.

In summary, these simulations give us some insights into the role that equalization grant systems can play in addressing the problems of horizontal and fiscal imbalances in a federation when states tax bases differ in terms of the size and the tax sensitivity of their tax bases.

Notes

Chapter 2

1. On the measurement of the excess burden of taxation, see Boadway and Bruce (1984), Mayshar (1990), and Auerbach and Hines (2002).

2. The total effect of a price change can be decomposed into a substitution effect and an income effect. The substitution effect shows how the consumer's consumption changes in response to a change in relative prices, holding utility constant. The substitution effect of an increase in the price of x_i always reduces the quantity of x_i demanded, except when the consumer has Leontief indifference curves and in this special case there is no substitution effect. The income effect shows how a price change affects demand through its effect on the purchasing power of the consumer's budget. The income effect of a price increase reduces the demand for a normal good, but increases the demand for an inferior good.

3. A head tax is a form of lump-sum taxation, provided that emigration to avoid the tax is not possible. However, a head tax would not raise nearly as much revenue as is collected by modern governments, and it would be highly regressive.

4. Figure 2.4 shows why the EB_{CV} is defined using the compensated revenues. If the EB_{CV} were defined by subtracting the actual tax revenues from the CV, it would equal the area *dabf*, which is potentially much larger than *abc*.

5. For example, pacifists are worse off when there is an increase in military expenditures, holding tax rates and other public services constant.

6. Further discussion of the linkage between the MCF and the shape of the Laffer curve is contained in section 3.1.

7. Figure 2.8 shows the gain from replacing a tariff with a general sales tax, t_j. See section 2.5 and table 2.1 for more details. Because it is always more efficient to raise tax revenues with the sales tax than the tariff, the MCF curves for the two taxes do not intersect and the MCFs for both taxes decline as the consumption tax replaces the tariff.

8. This important result, linking the MCF and the MEB_{EV}, was derived by Triest (1990). See also Håkonsen (1998).

9. Calculations based on data in Agbeyegbe, Stotsky, and WoldeMariam (2004, tab. 1, p. 6).

10. On the welfare and revenue effects of tariff reform, see Keen and Ligthart (2002).

11. In this model, the consumption tax is distorts the labor–leisure decision by reducing the workers' real wage rate and ε equals $-\eta_L$, the labor supply elasticity. In section 3.2.1 and 4.2, we discuss the connection between commodity taxes and labor market distortions in more detail.

12. This is based on the notion that if individuals receive a dollar of lump-sum income, they "spend" it on goods and leisure. Some labor supply studies indicate that the marginal propensity to earn income is -0.20. This implies that the marginal propensity to spend on goods is 0.80.

13. See the Further Reading section at the end of this chapter for more discussion about tariff reform.

14. See also Sandmo (1998) on incorporating distributional concerns in the evaluation of taxation and public expenditure.

15. For further analysis of the equity component of the SMCF, see Sandmo (1998).

16. An alternative approach to determining distributional weights is to try to infer them from previous public policy decisions involving the redistribution of income. See, for example, Christiansen and Jansen (1978) on the calculation of implicit distributional weights in the Norwegian tax system.

17. Other early contributions dealing with definition and interpretation of the MCF include Usher (1982, 1984), Topham (1984), and Wildasin (1979, 1984).

18. Browning's "error" in formulating his expression for the MCF is reminiscent of the error that Stigler made in adopting the assumption of a fixed sample size in his Nobel prize-winning contribution on consumer search. As Stigler noted, one can make a major contribution by asking the right question, even if one does not supply the right answer.

19. What does a dollar of cost really mean when cigarettes are $2.00 per pack instead of $10.00, a beer is $0.75 a bottle, and the opportunity cost of my time is 67 percent higher than today? Not only is it difficult to think about what a dollar is worth at these unfamiliar prices, we economists should admit that we really don't know what these prices would be in the absence of taxes.

20. See also Snow and Warren (1996) who tried to reconcile the alternative approaches by developing a measure which they referred to as the marginal welfare cost and which incorporated expenditure effects.

21. See also Christiansen (1981) and Boadway and Keen (1993) on the validity of the Samuelson condition under an optimal income tax.

Chapter 3

1. An exception to this prohibition against operating on the downward-sloping section of the Laffer curve is the case where the taxed good produces strong negative externalities.

2. See Ramsey (1927).

3. For a discussion of the conditions in which uniform commodity taxation is optimal, see Besley and Jewitt (1995).

4. See Corlett and Hague (1953).

5. On the computation of optimal commodity tax rates, see Ray (1986), Murty and Ray (1987, 1989), and Majumder (1988).

6. See Parry and Small (2005) for the calculation of the optimal gasoline excise tax. They concluded that the optimal excise tax for the United States was twice its existing rate and that the optimal rate in the United Kingdom was half its existing rate.

7. For further discussion of environmental and nonenvironmental tax distortions, see Bovenberg and de Mooij (1994) and Ballard et al. (2005).

8. A formal derivation of the MCF under imperfect competition is contained in Dahlby (1992).

9. See Dahlby (1992).

10. For a derivation of this result, see Delipalla and Keen (1992).

11. See Stern (1987) on the use of conjectural variations models and Auerbach and Hines (2001, pp. 57–74) on imperfect competition and the efficiency effects of taxation.

12. See Delipalla and O'Donnell (2001).

13. Bernheim and Rangel (2005, p. 39).

14. See Joossens et al. (2000) for a survey of the issues concerning tobacco smuggling.

15. Norton (1988) has developed an economic model of smuggling and Usher (1986) and Ray (1997, pp. 380–84) have incorporated tax evasion into the calculation of the MCF.

Chapter 4

1. Calculations based on data in Tanzi and Zee (2000, tab. 2, p. 304). See also Burgess and Stern (1993, tab. 5, p. 773) on developing countries' reliance on goods and services taxation.

2. See Leung and Phelps (1993) and Badenes-Plá and Jones (2003, tab. 3, p. 140) for a summary of empirical estimates of the price elasticity of alcohol consumption in the United States and other countries.

3. A recent study by Decker and Schwartz (2000) using US household level data indicated that the demand for cigarettes declines when alcohol prices increase while the demand for alcohol increases when the price of cigarettes increase. An early study using aggregate US data by Goel and Morey (1995) had indicated that alcohol and tobacco were substitutes, while a study using UK data by Jones (1989) indicated that tobacco was a complement for alcohol. Gruber, Sen, and Stabile (2002) based on Canadian data found that higher cigarette prices reduced alcohol consumption.

4. See N. Badenes-Plá and Jones (2003, tab. 2, p. 139) for a summary of empirical estimates of the elasticity of cigarette consumption, which are in the −0.40 to −0.60 range.

5. See Parry and Small (2005, p. 1283).

6. Madden calculated the marginal revenue cost of increasing welfare, which is the inverse of the MCF.

7. See section 4.2.

8. Parry (2003) has provided an extensive review of the empirical literature on the externalities generated by the consumption of gasoline, alcohol, and cigarettes in the United States and the United Kingdom. While there is still a great deal of uncertainty concerning the magnitudes of these parameters, Parry's choices for his base case estimates seem reasonable, but their applicability to Thailand is unknown. Based on his review of the literature, Parry concluded that tobacco products impose the largest harmful externalities, representing 28.3 percent of the consumer price of the product, followed by petrol at 17.8 percent, and alcohol at 11 percent of the product price. It should be noted that Parry treated all externalities as direct consumption externalities even though his discussion and the literature indicate that these externalities, especially for smoking and alcohol consumption, take the form of higher public expenditures on health care, and in our framework would be included in the δ_G parameters.

9. See Pogue and Sgontz (1989), Grossman et al. (1993), Irvine and Sims (1993), Kenkel (1996), Cook and Moore (2002), and Chaloupka, Grossman, and Saffer (2002).

10. This benefit transfer technique (the value transfer method) is used to convert the study site values (United Kingdom in this case) to policy site values (Thailand in this case). The conversion using real per capita GDP is widely applied in environmental assessment in Thailand. See Rosenberger and Loomis (2003) for more details of the technique.

11. These figures are from the Health and Welfare Survey (HWS) in 2003. The survey is conducted by National Statistical Office of Thailand. It surveys health status, health care insurance coverage, health care expenditure, and health-related behavior.

12. From the Thailand Health and Welfare Survey in 2003.

13. See Delipalla and O'Donnell (2001) on the concentration of EU cigarette markets.

14. In the TDRI study the price elasticities for color liquor, white liquor, imported liquor, beer, and wine were −1.56, −2.73, −0.61, −2.68, and −0.60, respectively.

15. Delipalla and O'Donnell (2001) used a conjectural variations framework to estimate the responsiveness of cigarette prices to tax changes in European countries. Their estimates of the tax shifting parameters were consistent with the theoretical prediction that ad valorem taxes produce smaller price increases than per unit taxes in an imperfectly competitive market. The ratio of the tax-shifting effects for per unit and ad valorem taxes yields an estimate of the market power distortion of 0.219 if the price elasticity of demand for cigarettes is −0.40.

16. If one assumes that the mobile phone market is a Cournot duopoly, then the δ_M parameter could be calculated as 0.5 (1/0.183)0.35 = 0.956, where the 0.5 is one divided by the number of firms and 0.183 is my estimate of the elasticity of demand for telecom services and 35 percent is the mobile phone share of the total market for telecom services (International Telecommunication Union 2002, tab. 2.3). This estimate of the market power distortion is very high because the estimate of the demand elasticity for telecommunications is so low. The range of values that we have used in the calculation is more realistic.

17. See Smith (2005, p. 77) for the UK figure.

18. In July 2002 one Baht was worth approximately US$0.024.

19. The tax rate for alcohol is a weighted average of the ad valorem equivalent tax rates for beer (31.8 percent), wine (52.9 percent), and spirits (63.5 percent) where beer has a 50 percent weighting and wine and spirits have 25 percent weights.

20. The average tax rate on all other goods is below the VAT rate because many goods are zero-rated or exempt from VAT. Chennells, Dilnot, and Roback (1999, tab. 6, p. 8) indicate that the reduction in tax revenue due to zero-rating, exemption, and reduced VAT rates for domestic fuels was £26.9 billion in 1998–99.

21. Sensitivity analysis indicated that allocating the externalities between the environmental and public expenditures did not have a large effect on the computed MCFs.

22. A pdf file describing the calculations is available from the author upon request.

23. These results seem consistent with the conclusion, reached by Parry and Small (2005), that the UK tax rates on petrol are "too high."

24. Recall that Parry did not model or compute the MEBs for taxes on all other goods.

Chapter 5

1. A more detailed analysis of the incidence of a tax on labor in a one-sector model is contained in Feldstein (1974).

2. Auerbach and Hines (2002) provide an alternative explanation for the size of the MCF in terms of the "tax normalization," that is, whether commodities are taxed and labor is the numéraire or whether labor is taxed and consumption is the numéraire. See also Gahvari (2006).

3. Ballard (1990) and Ballard and Fullerton (1992) provide an alternative explanation of the relationship between the MEB and the MCF.

4. Reviews of the empirical literature on the labor supply elasticity are contained in Blundell and MaCurdy (1999) and Fortin and Lacroix (2002).

5. See Feldstein (1974).

6. See, for example, Wildasin (1984) and Browning (1987).

7. In some countries low-income individuals face the highest marginal tax rates because of reductions in their social benefits when their income increases. In the analysis in this section it will be assumed that marginal tax rates are not decreasing as individual income rises.

8. Also see Sandmo (1998) and Allgood and Snow (1998) on the marginal cost of funds under a progressive tax system.

9. See Dahlby (1998, tab. 1, p. 112).

10. For an overview of models of the political economy of taxation, see Hettich and Winer (1999, ch. 2).

11. On the MCF and the median voter model, see Fuest and Huber (2001) and Usher (2006).

12. Data in Fuest and Huber (2001, tab. A1, p. 113) for ten European countries indicate that the ratio of median to average income ranges from 0.80 in Ireland and 0.935 in Belgium.

13. See Harms and Zink (2003) for a survey of theoretical models explaining why redistribution has been more limited than predicted by the simple median voter model.

Chapter 6

1. See Freebairn (1995) who developed a model of the MCF that incorporates wage stickiness in the calculation of the MCF using parameter values for Australia. In the Freebairn model the degree of wage stickiness is treated as an exogenous parameter.

2. Our analysis is based on Poapongsakorn et al. (2000).

3. Fortin and Lacroix (1994) calculated the $SMCF_p$ to be 1.47. However, as they acknowledged, their calculation understates the $SMCF_p$ because they did not deduct MC from MR in calculating the net additional revenue from increased tax enforcement.

4. For an overview of the optimal income tax problem, see Salanié (2003).

5. See Saez (2002) on bunching of individuals at kink points in the US income tax schedule.

Chapter 7

1. A tax on leisure would imply that wage rates are subsidized. A general wage subsidy could lead to wide spread abuse, such as neighbors hiring each other to collect more subsidy. See Coleman (2000, p. 12) on the feasibility of wage subsidies.

2. It is useful to think of $(\varepsilon_{22}^c - \varepsilon_{12}^c) = -\sigma_{21} < 0$, where σ_{21} is the elasticity of substitution between good 1 and good 2.

3. This assumption does not affect the computed value of the optimal tax rate.

4. See, for example, Gordon (1986) and Bruce (1992).

5. A major debate concerning the degree of international capital mobility was spawned by Feldstein and Horioka (1980) who concluded that capital was immobile because national investment and savings rates are highly correlated. See Coakley et al. (2003) for a recent empirical study of the Feldstein-Horioka puzzle.

6. See, for example, Huizinga and Nielsen (1996) and Keen and Marchand (1997).

7. All of the own and cross price elasticities of demand are negative and $\varepsilon_{Lw} < \varepsilon_{Kw} < 0$ and $\varepsilon_{Kc} < \varepsilon_{Lc} < 0$. See Keen and Marchand (1997).

8. The restrictions on the demand elasticities mentioned in note 7 imply that the denominator is positive and the numerator is greater than or equal to zero. See Sorensen (2001) for a derivation of the optimal tax rate on capital in a model with imperfect capital flows between countries.

9. See Mintz and Leechor (1993) for a detailed analysis of the user cost of capital for a foreign subsidiary.

10. Calculations performed by the Technical Committee on Business Taxation (the Mintz Committee) indicated that pure profits represent roughly one-third of total corporate profits in Canada.

11. It should also be noted that the Damus-Hobson-Thirsk model also assumed that the demands for Canadian exports were not perfectly elastic, which provided another avenue for exporting the corporate income tax burden.

12. Excess foreign tax credits can be carried forward to offset taxes in future years, but future tax credits are obviously worth less than an immediate tax credit.

13. A large open economy, such as that of the United States, may be able to affect capital flows and the degree of tax competition through its choice of a deduction, exemption, or tax credit. See Feldstein and Hartman (1979) and Dahlby (2002b).

Chapter 8

1. Most of the papers in this debate appear in Ferguson (1964). The debate was largely confined to the question of whether a public debt could impose a burden on future generations in a closed economy where there is no trade or capital flow with other countries. Even the orthodox Keynesians acknowledged that foreign borrowing—an external public debt—could impose a burden on future generations.

2. It is interesting to note that with his assumption of "public debt illusion" Vickrey explicitly assumed Ricardian equivalence does not hold.

3. Eisner (1987, p. 294) still argued in the 1980s that in a closed economy "the public debt would be irrelevant, except for distributional effects" if it could be financed by lump-sum (i.e., nondistortionary) taxes.

4. Rankin and Roffia (2003, tab. 1, p. 228) used a somewhat different approach to calculate the maximum sustainable debt in the Diamond overlapping generations model. Their approach yields the same numerical values as results (8.3), but they did not derive a formula for the maximum sustainable debt.

5. In 1994, interest payments on the public debt in Canada were about 9 percent of GDP, or $69.597 billion, based on calculations by the author from Department of Finance, Fiscal Reference Tables (tab. 33, p. 40).

6. There is an error in the way that Elmendorf and Mankiw specified the government's budget constraint; see Mankiw (2005). A properly specified budget constraint is used in this version of the model.

7. If interest payments on the government's debt are taxed, the government's tax revenue would be $\tau(Y + rB)$ and its expenditures would be $rB + G$. Consequently whether or not interest payments on government bonds are taxed, the government's budget constraint is $\tau Y = \rho B + G$.

8. See, for example, McGrattan (1998) and Durlauf and Quah (1999).

9. See Hall (1988) and Patterson and Pesaran (1992).

10. See Ireland (1994), Bruce and Turnovsky (1999), and Agell and Persson (2000) on the slope of the dynamic Laffer curve in endogenous growth models.

11. It can be shown that the slope of OC is $d\tau/dg = -c[(1 - \sigma)Abg] - 1$.

12. All data were taken from the IMF's *International Financial Statistics*. The program expenditure ratio is the ratio of consumptive government spending to GDP.

13. All data were taken from the IMF's *International Financial Statistics*. The program expenditure ratio is the ratio of consumptive government spending to GDP.

Chapter 9

1. See Buettner (2003) for an empirical study of horizontal fiscal externalities in Germany.

2. This section is based on Dahlby (1996). In this section we focus on tax externalities rather than expenditure externalities.

3. See Arnott and Grieson (1981), Fujii, Khaled, and Mak (1985), and Wildasin (1987) on tax exporting.

4. See Bruekner (2003) for a general model of the strategic interactions of subnational governments caused by horizontal externalities and a survey of the econometric literature on estimating subnational governments' reaction functions.

5. See Besley and Rosen (1998), Goodspeed (2000), Hayashi and Boadway (2001), Esteller-Moré and Solé-Ollé (2001, 2002), Andersson et al. (2004), and Brülhart and Jametti (2006) for econometric studies of the vertical tax externalities and the interdependence of tax policies in federations.

6. This section is based on Dahlby (2005b).

7. In Australia, vertical fiscal imbalance has also been a prominent policy issue.

8. See, for example, Bird and Tarasov (2004) and Rodden and Wibbels (2002).

9. See Dahlby, Mintz, and Wilson (2000) on the vertical fiscal externalities from the deductibility of state taxes from federal income taxes.

10. For further discussion of the allocative effects of tax competition, see Wilson (1999) and Wilson and Wildasin (2004).

11. See section 2.2 on the optimal provision of public goods financed by distortionary taxation.

12. See Boadway (2004) for a survey article on efficiency and equity effects of intergovernmental equalization grants and Bucovetsky and Smart (2006) on the role that an equalization grant system can play in offsetting the distortions caused by horizontal tax competition.

13. See Flochel and Madies (2002) on Leviathan governments in a federation.

14. In Dahlby and Wilson (2003) the state governments also provide a public good that enhances firm's productivity creating a vertical expenditure externality. They show that this vertical expenditure externality can be either positive or negative and that it is independent of the sign or magnitude of the vertical tax externality.

15. The main difference between the model presented in this section and the Keen and Kotsogiannis (2002) model is that their model has state government taxes on profits generated by production in the state. This tax is omitted here because it raises the question of whether the federal tax on capital should be deductible in calculating taxable profits and whether the future profit tax revenue has to be discounted.

16. This was first noted by Keen and Kotsogiannis (2002) in proposition 1.

17. Note that $(1 - \tau_i)\varepsilon = \rho K' K^{-1}$ and therefore can be interpreted as the elasticity of demand for capital with respect to the after-tax rate of return.

18. In some models of vertical fiscal interactions between state and central governments, the federal government is modeled as a Stackelberg leader. See, for example, Boadway and Keen (1996) or Boadway and Tremblay (2006). Whether federal governments deliberately manipulate states' fiscal decisions is an interesting empirical question. In a democracy, where voters have limited knowledge about the interactions of the two levels of government, one might question whether Stackelberg leadership behavior would emerge.

19. The VFI index was 0.284 with fifty state governments. Therefore the model indicated that most of the increase in the VFI occurred when there are ten or fewer states.

20. See Boadway and Keen (1996) for a model of fiscal transfers from state governments to a central government.

Chapter 10

1. This section is based on Dahlby (2005a).

2. A detailed description of Canadian federal and provincial tax incentives for R&D is contained in McKenzie (2005).

3. A similar point was made in section 3.4.1.

4. Measuring the private and social rates of depreciation on R&D investment is particularly problematic. Various studies have assumed that depreciation rates vary between 10 and 30 percent.

5. See Mohnen (1999) for a survey of the literature on the incentive of effects of R&D.

6. Alberta currently does not offer tax credits for R&D but allows the deduction of current and capital expenditures on R&D. Consequently Alberta's tax regime may be considered close to neutral with respect to R&D spending. Computations by McKenzie (2005) indicate that the marginal effective subsidy rate on R&D in Alberta is −0.40. If it is assumed that this is entirely due to the federal tax treatment of R&D, then the $t_{RD_0} = -0.029$ given that the opportunity cost of private funds invested in R&D, ρ, is 0.10.

7. See Courchene and Beavis (1973), Swan and Garvey (1995), Smart (1998), and Dahlby (2002a).

8. In the rest of the section we will refer to the territories as states.

9. See Winer and Hettich (1998) on the interpretation of the ω as the marginal political cost of taxation.

10. Since the social welfare function is only unique up to a positive monotonic transformation, we can chose the values of the function so that $\omega_{i1} = 1$.

References

Agbeyegbe, T., J. Stotsky, and A. WoldeMariam. 2004. Trade liberalization, exchange rate changes, and tax revenue in sub-Saharan Africa. Working paper WP/04/178. IMF.

Agell, J., and M. Persson. 2000. On the analytics of the dynamic Laffer curve. Working paper 383. CESifo.

Ahmad, E., and N. Stern. 1984. The theory of reform and Indian indirect taxes. *Journal of Public Economics* 25: 259–98.

Ahmad, E., and N. Stern. 1987. Alternative sources of government revenue: Illustrations for India, 1979–80. In D. Newbery and N. Stern, eds., *The Theory of Taxation in Developing Countries*. Oxford: Oxford University Press, pp. 281–332.

Ahmad, E., and N. Stern. 1990. Tax reform and shadow prices for Pakistan. *Oxford Economic Papers* 42: 135–59.

Ahmed, S., and D. Croushore. 1996. The marginal cost of funds with nonseparable public spending. *Public Finance Quarterly* 24: 216–36.

Aiyagari, S. R., A. Marcet, T. Sargent, and J. Seppala. 2002. Optimal tax without state-contingent debt. *Journal of Political Economy* 110: 1222–54.

Allgood, S., and A. Snow. 1998. The marginal cost of raising tax revenue and redistributing income. *Journal of Political Economy* 106: 1246–73.

Altig, D., A. Auerbach, L. Kotlikoff, K. Smetters, and J. Walliser. 2001. Simulating fundamental tax reform in the United States. *American Economic Review* 91: 574–95.

Anderson, J. 2002. Trade reform diagnostics with many households, quotas, and tariffs. *Review of International Economics* 10: 215–36.

Andersson, L., T. Aronsson, and M. Wikström. 2004. Testing for vertical fiscal externalities. *International Tax and Public Finance* 11: 243–63.

Ardagna, S., F. Caselli, and T. Lane. 2004. Fiscal discipline and the cost of public debt service: Some estimates for OECD countries. Working paper 10788. NBER.

Arnott, R., and R. Grieson. 1981. Optimal fiscal policy for a state or local government. *Journal of Urban Economics* 9: 23–48.

Atkinson, A., and A. Sandmo. 1980. Welfare implications of the taxation of savings. *Economic Journal* 90: 529–49.

Atkinson, A., and N. Stern. 1974. Pigou, taxation and public goods. *Review of Economic Studies* 41: 119–28.

Auerbach, A., and J. Hines. 2002. Taxation and economic efficiency. In A. Auerbach and M. Feldstein, eds., *Handbook of Public Economic*. Amsterdam: North Holland, pp. 1347–1421.

Auerbach, A., and K. Hassett. 1993. Taxation and foreign direct investment in the United States: A reconsideration of the evidence. In A. Giovannini, G. Hubbard, and J. Slemrod, eds., *Studies in International Taxation*. Chicago: University of Chicago Press, pp. 119–44.

Auerbach, A., and L. Kotlikoff. 1987. *Dynamic Fiscal Policy.* Cambridge: Cambridge University Press.

Badenes-Plá, N., and A. Jones. 2003. Addictive goods and taxes: A survey from an economic perspective. *Hacienda Pública Española/Revista de Economía Pública* 167: 123–53.

Ballard, C. 1990. Marginal welfare cost calculations: Differential analysis vs. balanced-budget analysis. *Journal of Public Economics* 41: 263–76.

Ballard, C., and D. Fullerton. 1992. Distortionary taxes and the provision of public goods. *Journal of Economic Perspectives* 6: 117–31.

Ballard, C., and S. Medema. 1993. The marginal efficiency effects of taxes and subsidies in the presence of externalities: A computational general equilibrium approach. *Journal of Public Economics* 52: 199–216.

Ballard, C., J. Goddeeris, and S.-K. Kim. 2005. Non-homothetic preferences and the non-environmental effects of environmental taxes. *International Tax and Public Finance* 12: 115–30.

Ballard, C., J. Shoven, and J. Whalley. 1985. General equilibrium computations of the marginal welfare costs of taxes in the United States. *American Economic Review* 75 (1): 128–38.

Bank of Thailand. ⟨http://www.bot.or.th/bothomepage/databank/EconData/Econ&Finance/⟩.

Barro, R. 1974. Are government bonds net wealth? *Journal of Political Economy* 82: 1095–1117.

Baylor, M., and L. Beausejour. 2004. Taxation and economic efficiency: Results from a Canadian CGE model. Working paper 2004-10. Department of Finance, Ottawa.

Bernheim, B. 2002. Taxation and saving. In A. Auerbach and M. Feldstein, eds., *Handbook of Public Economics*, vol. 3. Amsterdam: North-Holland, pp. 1173–1249.

Bernheim, B., and A. Rangel. 2005. Behavioral public economics: Welfare and policy analysis with non-standard decision makers. Working paper 11518. NBER.

Besley, T., and H. Rosen. 1998. Vertical externalities in tax setting: Evidence from gasoline and cigarettes. *Journal of Public Economics* 70: 383–98

Besley, T., and I. Jewitt. 1995. Uniform taxation and consumer preferences. *Journal of Public Economics* 58: 73–85.

Bessho, S., and M. Hayahi. 2005. The social cost of public funds: the case of Japanese progressive income taxation. Policy Research Institute Discussion paper 05A-16. Ministry of Finance, Japan.

Binswanger, H., and D. Sillers. 1983. Risk aversion and credit constraints in farmers' decision-making: A reinterpretation. *Journal of Development Studies* 20: 5–21.

Bird, R., and A. Tarasov. 2004. Closing the gap: Fiscal imbalances and intergovernmental transfers in developed federations. *Environment and Policy C: Government and Policy* 22: 77–102.

Bloom, N., R. Griffith, and J. Van Reenen. 2002. Do R&D tax credits work? Evidence from a panel of countries 1979–1997. *Journal of Public Economics* 85: 1–31.

Blundell, R. 1996. Labour supply and taxation. In M. Devereux ed., *The Economics of Tax Policy*. Oxford: Oxford University Press, pp. 107–36.

Blundell, R., and I. Walker. 1983. Limited dependent variables in demand analysis: An application to modeling family labour supply and commodity demand behaviour. Discussion paper in Econometrics 126. University of Manchester.

Blundell, R., and T. MaCurdy. 1999. Labor supply: A review of alternative approaches. In O. Ashenfelter and D. Card, eds., *Handbook of Labor Economics*, vol. 3. Amsterdam: North-Holland, pp. 1559–1695.

Boadway, R. 2004. The theory and practice of equalization. *CESifo Economic Studies* 50: 211–54.

Boadway, R. and J.-F. Tremblay. 2006. A theory of fiscal imbalance. *FinanzArchiv* 62: 1–27.

Boadway, R., and M. Keen. 1993. Public goods, self-selection, and optimal income taxation. *International Economic Review* 34: 463–78.

Boadway, R., and M. Keen. 1996. Efficiency and the optimal direction of federal–state transfers. *International Tax and Public Finance* 3: 137–55.

Boadway, R., and N. Bruce. 1984. *Welfare Economics*. Oxford: Blackwell.

Boadway, R., M. Marchand, and M. Vigneault. 1998. The consequences of overlapping tax bases for redistribution and public spending in a federation. *Journal of Public Economics* 68: 453–78.

Borge, L.-E. and J. Rattsø. 2002. Spending growth with vertical fiscal imbalance: Decentralized government spending in Norway, 1880–1990. *Economics and Politics* 14: 351–73.

Bovenberg, A. 1999. Green tax reforms and the double dividend: An updated reader's guide. *International Tax and Public Finance* 6: 421–43.

Bovenberg, L., and R. de Mooij. 1994. Environmental levies and distortionary taxation. *American Economic Review* 84: 1085–89.

Bowen, W., R. Davis, and D. Kopf. 1960. The public debt: A burden on future generations? *American Economic Review* 50: 701–706.

Brennan, G., and J. Buchanan. 1980. *The Power to Tax: Analytical Foundations of a Fiscal Constitution.* Cambridge: Cambridge University Press.

Breton, A. 1996. *Competitive Governments.* Cambridge: Cambridge University Press.

Browning, E. 1976. The marginal cost of public funds. *Journal of Political Economy* 84: 283–98.

Browning, E. 1987. On the marginal welfare cost of taxation. *American Economic Review* 77: 11–23.

Browning, E., and L. Liu. 1998. The optimal supply of public goods and the distortionary cost of taxation: comment. *National Tax Journal* 51: 103–16.

Browning, E., T. Gronberg, and L. Liu. 2000. Alternative measures of the marginal cost of funds. *Economic Inquiry* 38: 591–99.

Bruce, N. 1992. A note on the taxation of international capital income flows. *Economic Record* 68: 217–21.

Bruce, N., and S. Turnovsky. 1999. Budget balance, welfare, and the growth rate: "Dynamic Scoring" of the long-run government budget. *Journal of Money, Credit, and Banking* 31: 162–86.

Brueckner, J. 2003. Strategic interaction among governments: An overview of empirical studies. *International Regional Science Review* 26: 175–88.

Brülhart, M., and M. Jametti. 2006. Vertical versus horizontal tax externalities: An empirical test. *Journal of Public Economics* 90: 2027–62.

Buchanan, J. 1958. *Public Principles of Public Debt.* New York: Irwin.

Bucovetsky, S., and M. Smart. 2006. The efficiency consequences of local revenue equalization: Tax competition and tax distortions. *Journal of Public Economic Theory* 8: 119–44.

Buettner, T. 2003. Tax base effects and fiscal externalities of local capital taxation: Evidence from a panel of German jurisdictions. *Journal of Urban Economics* 54: 110–28.

Buettner, T. 2006. The incentive effect of fiscal equalization transfers on tax policy. *Journal of Public Economics* 90: 477–97.

Burgess, R., and N. Stern. 1993. Taxation and development. *Journal of Economic Literature* 31: 762–830.

Calvo, G. 2003. Explaining sudden stop, growth collapse, and bop crisis: The case of distortionary output taxes. *IMF Staff Papers* 50: 1–20.

Campbell, H. 1975. Deadweight loss and commodity taxation in Canada. *Canadian Journal of Economics* 8: 441–47.

Campbell, H., and K. Bond. 1997. The cost of public funds in Australia. *Economic Record* 73: 22–34.

Cassing, J., and A. Hillman. 1982. State-federal resource tax rivalry: The Queensland railway and the federal export tax. *Economic Record* 58: 235–41.

Chaloupka, F., M. Grossman, and H. Saffer. 2002. The effects of price on alcohol consumption and alcohol-related problems. *Alcohol Research and Health* 26: 22–34.

Chandoevwit, W., and B. Dahlby. 2007. The marginal cost of public funds for excise taxes in Thailand. *eJournal of Tax Research* 5: 135–67. http://www.atax.unsw.edu.au/ejtr/

Chennells, L., and R. Griffith. 1997. *Taxing Profits in a Changing World.* London: Institute for Fiscal Studies.

Chennells, L., A. Dilnot, and N. Roback. 1999. A survey of the UK tax system. London: Institute for Fiscal Studies.

Christiansen, V. 1981. Evaluation of public projects under optimal taxation. *Review of Economic Studies* 48: 447–57.

Christiansen, V., and E. Jansen. 1978. Implicit social preferences in the Norwegian system of indirect taxation. *Journal of Public Economics* 10: 217–45.

Cnossen, S. 2005a. The role and rationale of excise taxes in the ASEAN countries. *International Bulletin of Fiscal Documentation:* 503–13.

Cnossen, S. 2005b. *Theory and Practice of Excise Taxation—Smoking, Drinking, Gambling, Polluting, and Driving.* Oxford: Oxford University Press.

Cnossen, S., and M. Smart. 2005. Taxation of tobacco. In S. Cnossen, ed., *Theory and Practice of Excise Taxation—Smoking, Drinking, Gambling, Polluting, and Driving.* Oxford: Oxford University Press, pp. 20–55.

Coakley, J., A. Fuertes, and F. Spagnolo. 2003. The Feldstein-Horioka puzzle is not as bad as you think. Working paper. Department of Accounting, Finance, and Management, University of Essex.

Coleman, W. J. II. 2000. Welfare and optimum dynamic taxation of consumption and income. *Journal of Public Economics* 76: 1–39.

Cook, P., and M. Moore. 2002. The economics of alcohol abuse and alcohol-control policies. *Health Affairs* 21: 120–33.

Cooley, T., and L. Ohanian. 1997. Postwar British economic growth and the legacy of Keynes. *Journal of Political Economy* 105: 439–72.

Corlett, W., and D. Hague. 1953. Complementarity and the excess burden of taxation. *Review of Economic Studies* 21: 21–30.

Courchene, T., and D. Beavis. 1973. Federal-provincial tax equalization: An evaluation. *Canadian Journal of Economics* 6: 483–502.

Coyne, A. 2005. Defining the "fiscal imbalance." *National Post.* April 13, p. A18.

Cragg, M. 1991. Do we care? A study of Canada's indirect tax system. *Canadian Journal of Economics* 24: 124–43.

Creedy, J. 2000. Measuring welfare changes and the excess burden of taxation. *Bulletin of Economic Research* 52: 1–47.

Dahlby, B. 1977. The measurement of consumer surplus and the path dependence problem. *Public Finance* 32: 293–311. (Reprinted in John Creedy, ed., *Economic Welfare: Concepts and Measurement*, vol. 1. Aldershot, UK: Edward Elgar, 1999.)

Dahlby, B. 1992. The efficiency effects of an excise tax in a generalized Cournot oligopoly model with an application to the U.S. cigarette industry. *Public Finance/Finances Publiques* 47: 378–89.

Dahlby, B. 1994. The distortionary effect of rising taxes. In R. Robson and W. Scarth, eds., *Deficit Reduction: What Pain; What Gain?* C.D. Howe Institute, Toronto, pp. 44–72.

Dahlby, B. 1996. Fiscal externalities and the design of intergovernmental grants. *International Tax and Public Finance* 3: 397–412.

Dahlby, B. 1998. Progressive taxation and the social marginal cost of public funds. *Journal of Public Economics* 67: 105–22.

Dahlby, B. 2002a. Globalization and the choice between the foreign tax credit and the exemption system. Working paper. University of Alberta.

Dahlby, B. 2002b. The incentive effects of fiscal equalization grants. In P. Boothe, ed., *Equalization: Welfare Trap or Helping Hand?* Atlantic Institute for Market Studies, Halifax.

Dahlby, B. 2005a. A framework for evaluating provincial R&D tax subsidies. *Canadian Public Policy* 31: 45–58.

Dahlby, B. 2005b. Dealing with the fiscal imbalances: Vertical, horizontal, and structural. Working paper. C.D. Howe Institute, Toronto.

Dahlby, B., and L. S. Wilson. 1994. Fiscal capacity, tax effort, and optimal equalization grants. *Canadian Journal of Economics* 27: 657–72.

Dahlby, B., and L. S. Wilson. 2003. Vertical fiscal externalities in a federation. *Journal of Public Economics* 87: 917–30.

Dahlby, B., and N. Warren. 2003. The fiscal incentive effects of the Australian equalisation system. *Economic Record* 79: 435–46.

Dahlby, B., J. Mintz, and L. S. Wilson. 2000. The deductibility of provincial business taxes in a federation with vertical fiscal externalities. *Canadian Journal of Economics* 33: 677–94.

Damus, S., P. Hobson, and W. Thirsk. 1991. Foreign tax credits, the supply of foreign capital, and tax exporting. *Journal of Public Economics* 45: 29–46.

Deaton, A., and J. Muellbauer. 1980. *Economics and Consumer Behavior*. Cambridge: Cambridge University Press.

Decker, S., and A. Schwartz. 2000. Cigarettes and alcohol: substitutes or complement? Working paper 7535. NBER.

Decoster, A., and E. Schokkaert. 1990. Tax reform results with different demand systems. *Journal of Public Economics* 41: 277–96.

Delipalla, S., and M. Keen. 1992. The comparison between ad valorem and specific taxes in noncompetitive environments. *Journal of Public Economics* 53: 53–71.

Delipalla, S., and O. O'Donnell. 2001. Estimating tax incidence, market power and market conduct: The European cigarette industry. *International Journal of Industrial Organization* 19: 885–908.

Desai, M., F. Foley, and J. Hines Jr. 2001. Repatriation taxes and dividend distortions. *National Tax Journal* 54: 829–51.

Devarajan, S., K. Thierfelder, and S. Suthiwart-Narueput. 2002. The marginal cost of public funds in developing countries. In A. Fossati and W. Wiegard., eds., *Policy Evaluations with Computable General Equilibrium Models*. London: Routledge, pp. 39–55.

Diamond, P. 1965. National debt in a neoclassical growth model. *American Economic Review* 55: 1126–50.

Diamond, P. 1976. A many-person Ramsey tax rule. *Journal of Public Economics* 4: 227–44.

Diamond, P. 1998. Optimal income taxation: An example with a U-shaped pattern of optimal marginal tax rates. *American Economic Review* 88: 83–95.

Diamond, P., and J. Mirrlees. 1971. Optimal taxation and public production. *American Economic Review* 61: 8–27 and 261–278.

Diewert, E., and D. Lawrence. 1996. The deadweight costs of taxation in New Zealand. *Canadian Journal of Economics* 29: S658–73.

Diewert, E., and D. Lawrence. 1998. The deadweight costs of capital taxation in Australia. Discussion paper 98-01. Department of Economics, University of British Columbia.

Diewert, E., and D. Lawrence. 2000. New measures of the excess burden of capital taxation in Canada. Paper presented at the CERF and IRPP Conference held in Ottawa, May 4–6, 2000.

Durlaf, S., and D. Quah. 1999. The new empirics of economic growth. In J. Taylor and M. Woodford, eds., *Handbook of Marcroeconomics*, vol. 1A. Amsterdam: Elsevier, pp. 235–308.

Ebel, R., and S. Yilmaz. 2002. Concept of fiscal decentralization and worldwide overview. *International Symposium on Fiscal Imbalance: A Report*. Commission on Fiscal Imbalance, Quebec City: pp. 145–74.

Ebrahimi, A., and C. Heady. 1988. Tax design and household composition. *Economic Journal* 98: 83–96.

Eisner, R. 1987. The burden of the public debt. In J. Eatwell, M. Milgate, and P. Newman, eds., *The New Palgrave: A Dictionary of Economics*, vol. 1. London: Macmillan, pp. 294–96.

Elmendorf, D., and G. Mankiw. 1999. Government debt. In J. Taylor and M. Woodford, eds., *Handbook of Macroeconomics*. Amsterdam: Elsevier, pp. 1615–69.

Engen, E., and R. Hubbard. 2004. Federal government debts and interest rates. Working paper 10681. NBER.

Erbil, C. 2004. Trade taxes are expensive. Working paper. Brandeis University.

Esteller-Mor, A., and A. Solé-Ollé. 2001. Vertical income tax externalities and fiscal interdependence: Evidence from the U.S. *Regional Science and Urban Economics* 31: 247–72.

Esteller-Moré, E., and A. Solé-Ollé. 2002. An empirical analysis of vertical tax externalities: The case of personal income taxation in Canada. *International Tax and Public Finance* 9: 235–57.

Feldstein, M. 1978. The welfare cost of capital income taxation. *Journal of Political Economy* 86 (suppl.): S29–51.

Feldstein, M. 1995. The effect of marginal tax rates on taxable income: A panel study of the 1986 Tax Reform Act. *Journal of Political Economy* 103: 551–72.

Feldstein, M. 1997. How big should government be? *National Tax Journal* 50: 197–213.

Feldstein, M. 1999. Tax avoidance and the deadweight loss of the income tax. *Review of Economics and Statistics* 81: 674–80.

Feldstein, M., and C. Horioka. 1980. Domestic saving and international capital flows. *Economic Journal* 90: 314–29.

Feldstein, M., and D. Hartman. 1979. The optimal taxation of foreign source investment income. *Quarterly Journal of Economics* 93: 613–29.

Feldstein, M. S. 1974. Tax incidence in a growing economy with variable factor supply. *Quarterly Journal of Economics* 88: 551–73.

Ferguson, J. 1964. *Public Debt and Future Generations*. Raleigh: University of North Carolina Press.

Findlay, C., and R. Jones. 1982. The marginal cost of Australian income taxation. *Economic Record* 58: 253–62.

Flochel, L., and T. Madies. 2002. Interjurisdictional tax competition in a federal system of overlapping revenue maximizing governments. *International Tax and Public Finance* 9: 121–41.

Flowers, M. 1988. Shared tax sources in a leviathan model of federalism. *Public Finance Quarterly* 16: 67–77.

Fortin, B., and G. Lacroix. 1994. Labour supply, tax evasion, and the marginal cost of public funds: an empirical investigation. *Journal of Public Economics* 55: 407–31.

Fortin, B., and G. Lacroix. 2002. Assessing the impact of tax and transfer policies on labour supply: A survey. Discussion paper 2002RP-10. CIRANO, Montreal, Quebec.

Freebairn, J. 1995. Reconsidering the marginal welfare cost of taxation. *Economic Record* 71: 121–31.

Fuest, C., and B. Huber. 2001. Tax competition and tax coordination in a median voter model. *Public Choice* 107: 97–113.

Fuest, C., B. Huber, and J. Mintz. 2003. Capital mobility and tax competition: A survey. Working paper 956. CESifo, Munich.

Fujii, E., M. Khaled, and J. Mak. 1985. The exportability of hotel occupancy and other tourist taxes. *National Tax Journal* 38: 169–77.

Fullerton, D. 1991. Reconciling recent estimates of the marginal welfare cost of taxation. *American Economic Review* 81: 302–308.

Fullerton, D., and Y. Henderson. 1989. The marginal excess burden of differential capital tax instruments. *Review of Economics and Statistics* 71: 435–42.

Gahvari, F. 2006. On the marginal cost of public funds and the optimal provision of public goods. *Journal of Public Economics* 90: 1251–62.

Galbraith, J., and M. Kaiserman. 1997. Taxation, smuggling and demand for cigarettes in Canada: Evidence from time-series data. *Journal of Health Economics* 16: 287–301.

Goel, R. and M. Morey. 1995. The interdependence of cigarette and liquor demand. *Southern Economic Journal* 62: 451–59.

Goodspeed, T. 2000. Tax structure in a federation. *Journal of Public Economics* 75: 493–506.

Goolsbee, A. 1999. Evidence on the high-income Laffer curve from six decades of tax reform. *Brookings Papers on Economic Activity* 2: 1–47.

Goolsbee, A. 2000. What happens when you tax the rich? Evidence from executive compensation. *Journal of Political Economy* 108: 352–78.

Gordon, R. 1983. An optimal taxation approach to fiscal federalism. *Quarterly Journal of Economics* 97: 567–86.

Gordon, R. 1986. Taxation of investment and saving in a world economy. *American Economic Review* 76: 1086–1102.

Gordon, R. 2000. Taxation of capital income vs. labor income: An overview. In S. Cnossen, ed., *Taxing Capital Income in the European Union*. Oxford: Oxford University Press, pp. 15–45.

Gordon, R., and J. Hines. 2002. International taxation. In A. Auerbach and M. Feldstein eds., *Handbook of Public Economics*, vol. 4. Amsterdam: North-Holland, pp. 1935–95.

Gordon, R., and J. MacKie-Mason. 1994. Why is there corporate taxation in a small open economy? The role of transfer pricing and income shifting. In M. Feldstein, J. Hines Jr. and G. Hubbard, eds., *The Effects of Taxation on Multinational Corporations*. Chicago: University of Chicago Press and NBER.

Griliches, Z. 1958. Research cost and social returns: Hybrid corn and related innovations. *Journal of Political Economy* 66: 419–31.

Grisley, W. 1980. Effect of risk and risk aversion on farm decision-making: farmers in northern Thailand. PhD dissertation. University of Illinois.

Grossman, M. 2004. Individual behaviors and substance use: the role of price. Working paper 10948. NBER.

Grossman, M., J. Sindelar, J. Mullahy, and R. Anderson. 1993. Policy watch: Alcohol and cigarette taxes. *Journal of Economic Perspectives* 7: 211–22.

Gruber, J., A. Sen, and M. Stabile. 2002. Estimating price elasticities when there is smuggling: The sensitivity of smoking to price in Canada. Working paper 8962. NBER.

Gruber, J., and B. Kőszegi. 2004. Tax incidence when individuals are time-inconsistent: The case of cigarette excise taxes. *Journal of Public Economics* 88: 1959–87.

Gruber, J., and E. Saez. 2000. The elasticity of taxable income: Evidence and implications. NBER working paper 7512.

Gruber, J., and E. Saez. 2002. The elasticity of taxable income: Evidence and implications. *Journal of Public Economics* 84: 1–32.

Gruber, J., and S. Mullainathan. 2005. Do cigarette taxes make smokers happier? *Advances in Economic Analysis and Policy*. 5: article 4.

Guindon, G., S. Tobin, and D. Yach. 2002. Trends and affordability of cigarette prices: Ample room for tax increases and related health gains. *Tobacco Control* 11: 35–43.

Håkonsen, L. 1998. An investigation into alternative representations on the marginal cost of public funds. *International Tax and Public Finance* 5: 329–43.

Hall, B. 1996. The private and social return to research and development: What have we learned? In B. Smith and C. Barfield, eds., *Technology, R&D, and the Economy*. Washington: Brookings Institute and the American Enterprise Institute, pp. 140–83.

Hall, B., and J. van Reenen. 2000. How effective are fiscal incentives for R&D? A new review of the evidence. *Research Policy* 29: 449–69.

Hall, G., and S. Krieger. 2000. The tax smoothing implications of the federal debt paydown. *Brookings Papers on Economic Activity*: 253–84.

Hall, R. 1988. Intertemporal substitution in consumption. *Journal of Political Economy* 96: 339–57.

Hall, R., and A. Rabushka. 1995. *The Flat Tax*, 2nd ed. Stanford: Hoover Institution.

Hallwood, P., and R. MacDonald. 2005. The economic case for fiscal federalism. In: B. Ashcroft, D. Coyle, and W. Alexander, eds., *New Wealth for Old Nations*. Princeton: Princeton University Press, pp. 96–116.

Hansson, I., and C. Stuart. 1985. Tax revenue and the marginal cost of public funds in Sweden. *Journal of Public Economics* 27: 331–53.

Hansson, I., and C. Stuart. 1987. The suboptimality of local taxation under two-tier fiscal federalism. *European Journal of Political Economy* 3: 407–11.

Harberger, A. 1964. Taxation, resource allocation, and welfare. In *The Role of Direct and Indirect Taxes in the Federal Revenue System: A Conference Report of the National Bureau of Economic Research and the Brookings Institution*, Princeton: Princeton University Press, pp. 25–75.

Harberger, A. 1971. Three basic postulates for applied welfare economics: An interpretive essay. *Journal of Economic Literature* 9: 785–97.

Harberger, A. 1978. On the use of distributional weights in social cost-benefit analysis. *Journal of Political Economy* 86: S87–120.

Harms, P., and S. Zink. 2003. Limits to redistribution in a democracy: A survey. *European Journal of Political Economy* 19: 651–68.

Hartman, D. 1985. Tax policy and foreign direct investment. *Journal of Public Economics* 26: 107–21.

Hayakawa, T., and P. Zak. 2002. Debt, death and taxes. *International Tax and Public Finance* 9: 157–73.

Hayashi, M., and R. Boadway. 2001. An empirical analysis of intergovernmental tax interaction: The case of business income taxes. *Canadian Journal of Economics* 34: 481–503.

Heckman, J. 1993. What has been earned about labor supply in the past twenty years? *American Economic Review* 83: 116–21.

Hettich, W., and S. Winer. 1986. Vertical imbalance in the fiscal systems of federal states. *Canadian Journal of Economics* 19: 745–65.

Hettich, W., and S. Winer. 1999. *Democratic Choice and Taxation*. Cambridge: Cambridge University Press.

Hines, J. 1996. Altered states: Taxes and the location of foreign direct investment in America. *American Economic Review* 86: 1076–94.

Hines, J. 1999. Lessons from behavioral responses to international taxation. *National Tax Journal* 52: 305–22.

Huizinga, H., and S. Nielsen. 1996. Capital income and profit taxation with foreign ownership of firms. Working paper. Economic Policy Research Institute, Copenhagen Business School.

Hunter, J. 1977. *Federalism and Fiscal Balance*. Australian National University Center for research on Federal Financial Relations, Canberra.

Immervoll, H., H. Kleven, C. Kreiner, and E. Saez. 2007. Welfare reform in European countries: A microsimulation analysis. *Economic Journal* 117: 1–44.

International Telecommunication Union. 2002. Bits and Bahts: Thailand internet case study. Geneva, Switzerland, March. ⟨www.itu.int/asean2001/reports/material/THA%20CS.pdf⟩.

Ireland, P. 1994. Supply-side economics and endogenous growth. *Journal of Monetary Economics* 33: 559–71.

Irvine, I., and W. Sims. 1993. The welfare effects of alcohol taxation. *Journal of Public Economics* 52: 83–100.

Ivanov, A., M. Keen, and A. Klemm. 2005. Russia's "Flat Tax." *Economic Policy* July: 399–444.

Johnson, W. 1988. Income redistribution in a federal system. *American Economic Review* 78: 570–73.

Johnson, W. 1991. Decentralized income redistribution reconsidered. *Economic Inquiry* 29: 69–78.

Jones, A. 1989. A systems approach to the demand for alcohol and tobacco. *Bulletin of Economic Research* 41: 85–105.

Jones, C. 2005. *Applied Welfare Economics*. Oxford University Press.

Jones, S. 1993. Cyclical and seasonal properties of Canadian gross flows of labour. *Canadian Public Policy* 19: 1–17.

Joossens, L., F. Chaloupka, D. Merriman, and A. Yureki. 2000. Issues in the smuggling of tobacco products. In P. Jha and F. Chaloupka, eds., *Tobacco Control in Developing Countries*. Oxford: Oxford University Press, pp. 393–406.

Jorgenson, D., and K. Yun. 1991. The excess burden of U.S. taxation. *Journal of Accounting, Auditing, and Finance* 6: 487–508.

Jorgenson, D., and K. Yun. 2001. *Investment: Lifting the Burden*, vol. 3. Cambridge: MIT Press.

Judd, K. 1987. The welfare cost of factor taxation in a perfect-foresight model. *Journal of Political Economy* 95: 675–709.

Judd, K. 1999. Optimal taxation and spending in growing economy. *Journal of Public Economics* 71: 1–25.

Kanbur, R., and M. Keen. 1993. Jeux sans frontieres: Tax competition and tax coordination when countries differ in size. *American Economic Review* 83: 877–92.

Kaplow, L. 1996. The optimal supply of public goods and the distortionary cost of taxation. *National Tax Journal* 49: 513–33.

Kaplow, L. 2004. On the (ir)relevance of distribution and labor supply distortion to government policy. *Journal of Economic Perspectives* 18: 159–75.

Keen, M. 1998. Vertical tax externalities in the theory of fiscal federalism. *IMF Staff Papers* 45: 454–85.

Keen, M., and C. Kotsogiannis. 2002. Does federalism lead to excessively high taxes? *American Economic Review* 92: 363–70.

Keen, M., and J. Ligthart. 2002. Coordinating tariff reduction and domestic tax reform. *Journal of International Economics* 56: 489–507.

Kenkel, D. 1996. New estimates of the optimal tax on alcohol. *Economic Inquiry* 34: 296–319.

Keuschnigg, C. 2007. Exports, foreign direct investment and the costs of corporate taxation. Discussion paper, University of St. Gallen.

Kleven, H., and C. Kreiner. 2006. The marginal cost of public funds: hours of work versus labor force participation. *Journal of Public Economics* 90: 1955–73.

Kopczuk, W. 2003. Tax bases, tax rates and the elasticity of reported income. Working paper 10044. NBER.

Kydland, F., and E. Prescott. 1977. Rules rather than discretion: The inconsistency of optimal plans. *Journal of Political Economy* 85: 473–92.

Leechor, C., and J. Mintz. 1993. On the taxation of multinational corporate investment when the deferral method is used by the capital exporting country. *Journal of Public Economics* 51: 75–96.

Lerner, A. 1948. The burden of the national debt. In L. Metzler, ed., *Income, Employment, and Public Policy: Essays in Honor of Alvin H. Hansen*, New York: Norton, pp. 255–75.

Leung, S., and C. Phelps. 1993. My kingdom for a drink . . . ? A review of estimates of the price sensitivity of demand for alcoholic beverage. National Institute of Health Publication 93-3513, pp. 1–31.

Lin, S. 2000. Government debt and economic growth in an overlapping generations model. *Southern Economic Journal* 66: 754–63.

Lin, S., and K. Sosin. 2001. Foreign debt and economic growth. *Economics of Transition* 9: 635–55.

Liu, L. 2002. The marginal cost of funds: Incorporating public sector inputs. Working paper 0203. Private Enterprise Research Center, Texas A&M University.

Liu, L. 2003. A marginal cost of funds approach to multi-period public project evaluation: Implications for the social discount rate. *Journal of Public Economics* 87: 1707–18.

Liu, L. 2004. The marginal cost of funds and the shadow prices of public sector inputs and outputs. *International Tax and Public Finance* 11: 17–29.

Lucas, R., and N. Stokey. 1983. Optimal fiscal and monetary policy in an economy without capital. *Journal of Monetary Economics* 12: 55–93.

Ma, J. 1997. Intergovernmental fiscal transfers in nine countries: Lessons for developing countries. Policy research working paper 1822. Macroeconomic Management and Policy Division, Economic Development Institute, The World Bank.

Madden, D. 1995. Labour supply, commodity demand and marginal tax reform. *Economic Journal* 105: 485–97.

Majumder, A. 1988. A note on optimal commodity taxation in India. *Economic Letters* 27: 167–71.

Mankiw, G. 2000. The savers-spenders theory of fiscal policy. *American Economic Review* 90: 120–25.

Mankiw, G. 2005. The savers-spenders theory of fiscal policy: Corrigendum. *American Economic Review* 95: 1752.

Mankiw, N. G., and M. Weinzierl. 2006. Dynamic scoring: A back-of-the-envelope guide. *Journal of Public Economics* 90: 1415–33.

Manning, W., E. Keeler, J. Newhouse, E. Sloss, and J. Wasserman. 1989. The taxes of sin: Do smokers and drinkers pay their way? *Journal of American Medical Association* 261: 1604–09.

Mansfield, E., J. Rapoport, A. Romeo, S. Wagner, and G. Beardsley. 1977. Social and private rates of return from industrial innovations. *Quarterly Journal of Economics* 91: 221–40.

Martinez-Vazquez, J. and B. Searle, eds. 2007. *Fiscal Equalization: Challenges in the Design of Intergovernmental Transfer.* New York: Springer.

Mayshar, J. 1990. On measures of excess burden and their application. *Journal of Public Economics* 43: 263–89.

Mayshar, J. 1991. On measuring the marginal cost of funds analytically. *American Economic Review* 81: 1329–35.

Mayshar, J., and S. Yitzhaki. 1995. Dalton-improving indirect tax reform. *American Economic Review* 85: 793–807.

McGrattan, E. 1998. A defense of AK growth models. *Federal Reserve Bank of Minneapolis Quarterly Review* 22: 13–27.

McGrattan, E., and J. Schmitz Jr. 1999. Explaining cross-country income differences. In J. Taylor and M. Woodford, eds., *Handbook of Macroeconomics,* vol. 1A. Amsterdam: Elsevier, pp. 669–737.

McKenzie, K. 2005. Tax subsidies for R&D in Canadian provinces. *Canadian Public Policy* 31: 29–44.

McKenzie, K., M. Mansour, and A. Brule. 1997. The calculation of marginal effective tax rates. Working paper 97-15. Technical Committee on Business Taxation, Department of Finance.

Meltzer, A., and S. Richard. 1981. A rational theory of the size of government. *Journal of Political Economy* 89: 914–27.

Mendoza, E., A. Razin, and L. Tesar. 1994. Effective tax rates in macroeconomics: Cross-country estimates of tax rates on factor incomes and consumption. *Journal of Monetary Economics* 34: 297–323.

Ministry of Public Health. 2004. *Public Health in Thailand 1999–2004.* Bangkok, Thailand.

Mintz, J. 1992. Is there a future for capital income taxation? Working paper 108. Economics Department, OECD, Paris.

Mintz, J., and M. Smart. 2004. Income shifting, investment, and tax competition: Theory and evidence from provincial taxation in Canada. *Journal of Public Economics* 88: 1149–68.

Mirrlees, J. 1971. An exploration in the theory of optimal income taxation. *Review of Economic Studies* 38: 175–208.

Modigliani, F. 1961. Long-run implications of alternative fiscal policies and the burden of the national debt. *Economic Journal* 71: 730–55.

Mohnen, P. 1999. Tax incentives: Issue and evidence. Working paper 99-32. CIRANO.

Murty, M., and R. Ray. 1987. Sensitivity of optimal commodity taxes to relaxing leisure/goods separability and to the wage rate. *Economic Letters* 24: 273–77.

Murty, M., and R. Ray. 1988. A computational procedure for calculating optimal commodity taxes with illustrative evidence from Indian budget data. *Scandinavian Journal of Economics* 91: 655–70.

Myles, G. 1987. Tax design in the presence of imperfect competition: An example. *Journal of Public Economics* 34: 367–78.

Myles, G. 1989. Ramsey tax rules for economies with imperfect competition. *Journal of Public Economics* 38: 95–115.

Nadiri, M. 1993. Innovations and technological spillovers. Working paper 4423. NBER.

National Statistical Office. 2002. Socio-economic survey data tape 2002. Bangkok, Thailand.

National Statistical Office. 2003. Health and welfare survey data tape 2003. Bangkok, Thailand.

Newbery, M. 2005. Road user and congestion charges. In S. Cnossen, ed., *Theory and Practice of Excise Taxation—Smoking, Drinking, Gambling, Polluting, and Driving.* Oxford: Oxford University Press, pp. 193–229.

Ng, Y.-K. 2000. The optimal size of public spending and the distortionary cost of taxation. *National Tax Journal* 53: 253–72.

O'Donoghue, T., and M. Rabin. 2006. Optimal sin taxes. *Journal of Public Economics* 90: 1825–49.

Parry, I. 2003. On the costs of excise taxes and income taxes in the UK. *International Tax and Public Finance* 10: 281–304.

Parry, I., and K. Small. 2005. Does Britain or the United States have the right gasoline tax? *American Economic Review* 95: 1276–89.

Pattamasiriwat, D. 1989. A study of consumption pattern using national income account. *Chulalongkorn Journal of Economics* 1: 244–64. (in Thai).

Pigou, A. C. 1920 [1960]. *The Economics of Welfare*. London: Macmillan.

Pigou, A. C. 1947. *A Study in Public Finance*, 3rd ed. London: Macmillan.

Poapongsakorn, N. 1979. Labor supply, demand for children and wage rates of paid employees in Thailand. PhD dissertation. Department of Economics, University of Hawaii.

Poapongsakorn, N., K. Charnvitayapong, D. Laovakul, S. Suksiriserekul, and B. Dahlby. 2000. A cost–benefit analysis of the Thailand taxpayer survey. *International Tax and Public Finance* 7: 63–82.

Pogue, T., and L. Sgontz. 1989. Taxing to control social costs: The case of alcohol. *American Economic Review* 79: 235–43.

Ramsey, F. 1927. A contribution to the theory of taxation. *Economic Journal* 37: 47–61.

Rankin, N., and B. Roffia. 2003. Maximum sustainable government debt in the overlapping generations model. *Manchester School* 71: 217–41.

Ray, R. 1986. Sensitivity of "optimal" commodity tax rates to alternative demand functional forms: An econometric case study of India. *Journal of Public Economics* 31: 253–68.

Ray, R. 1997. Issues in the design and reform of commodity taxes: Analytical results and empirical evidence. *Journal of Economic Surveys* 11: 353–88.

Rodden, J., and E. Wibbels. 2002. Beyond the fiction of federalism: Macroeconomic management in multi-tiered systems. *World Politics* 54: 494–531.

Rosenberger, R., and J. Loomis. 2003. Benefit transfer. In P. Shamp, K. Boyle, and T. Brown, eds., *A Primer on Nonmarket Valuation*. Boston: Kluwer Academic Publishers, pp. 445–82.

Ruggeri, G. 1999. The marginal cost of public funds in closed and small open economies. *Fiscal Studies* 20: 41–60.

Saez, E. 2001. Using elasticities to derive optimal income tax rates. *Review of Economic Studies* 68: 205–29.

Saez, E. 2004. Reported incomes and marginal tax rates, 1960–2000: Evidence and policy implications. Working paper 10273. NBER.

Saint-Paul, G. 1992. Fiscal policy in an endogenous growth model. *Quarterly Journal of Economics* 107: 1243–59.

Salanié, B. 2003. *The Economics of Taxation*. Cambridge: MIT Press.

Sandmo, A. 1998. Redistribution and the marginal cost of public funds. *Journal of Public Economics* 70: 365–82.

Sarntisart, I. 2003. *Economic Analysis for Tobacco Control in Thailand*. A Report for Discussion: Health, Nutrition and Population, Tobacco Free Initiative. World Health Organization. (in Thai)

Scarth, W. 2004. What should we do about the debt? In C. Ragan and W. Watson, eds., *Is the Debt War Over? Dispatches from Canada's Fiscal Frontline*. Institute for Research on Public Policy, Montreal, pp. 243–68.

Shah, A., and J. Slemrod. 1991. Do taxes matter for foreign direct investment? *The World Bank Economic Review* 5: 473–91.

Shapiro, C., and J. Stiglitz. 1984. Equilibrium unemployment as a worker discipline device. *American Economic Review* 74: 433–44.

Skeath, S., and G. Trandel. 1994. A Pareto comparison of ad valorem and unit taxation under imperfect competition. *Journal of Public Economics* 49: 351–67.

Slemrod, J. 1990. Optimal taxation and optimal tax systems. *Journal of Economic Perspectives* 4: 157–78.

Slemrod, J. 1990. Tax effects on foreign direct investment in the United States: Evidence from cross-country comparison. In A. Razin and J. Slemrod, eds., *Taxation in the Global Economy*. Chicago: University of Chicago Press, pp. 79–117.

Slemrod, J., and S. Yitzhaki. 1987. The optimal size of a tax collection agency. *Scandinavian Journal of Economics* 89: 183–92.

Slemrod, J., and S. Yitzhaki. 2001. Integrating expenditure and tax decisions: The marginal cost of funds and the marginal benefit of projects. *National Tax Journal* 54: 189–201.

Slemrod, J., S. Yitzhaki, J. Mayshar, and M. Lundholm. 1994. The optimal two-bracket linear income tax. *Journal of Public Economics* 53: 269–90.

Smart, M. 1998. Taxation and deadweight loss in a system of intergovernmental transfers. *Canadian Journal of Economics* 31: 189–206.

Smart, M. 2006. Raising taxes through equalization. Working paper. Department of Economics, University of Toronto.

Smith, S. 2005. Economic issues in alcohol taxation. In S. Cnossen, ed., *Theory and Practice of Excise Taxation—Smoking, Drinking, Gambling, Polluting, and Driving*. Oxford: Oxford University Press, pp. 56–83.

Snoddon, T. 2003. On equalization and incentives: An empirical assessment. Working paper 2003-06 EC. School of Business and Economics, Wilfred Laurier University.

Snow, A., and R. Warren Jr. 1996. The marginal welfare cost of public funds: Theory and estimates. *Journal of Public Economics* 61: 289–305.

Sorensen, P. 2001. International tax coordination: Regionalism versus globalism. Working paper. Economic Policy Research Unit (EPRU), University of Copenhagen.

Sriyookrat, P. 2001. A study of market structure and factor affecting demand for alcoholic beverages in Thailand. Master of Science thesis (Agricultural Economics), Department of Agricultural and Resource Economics, Kasetsart University.

Stern, N. 1976. On the specification of models of optimum taxation. *Journal of Public Economics* 6: 123–62.

Stern, N. 1987. The effects of taxation, price control, and government contracts in oligopoly and monopolistic competition. *Journal of Public Economics* 32: 133–58.

Stiglitz, J., and P. Dasgupta. 1971. Differential taxation, public goods, and economic efficiency. *Review of Economic Studies* 38: 151–74.

Stuart, C. 1984. Welfare costs per dollar of additional tax revenue in the United States. *American Economic Review* 74: 352–62.

Summers, L. 1981. Taxation and capital accumulation in a life cycle growth model. *American Economic Review* 71: 533–54.

Sunley, E., A. Yurekli, and F. Chaloupka. 2000. The design, administration, and potential of tobacco excises. In P. Jha and F. Chaloupka, eds., *Tobacco Control in Developing Countries*. Oxford: Oxford University Press, pp. 409–26.

Swan, P., and G. Garvey. 1995. The equity and efficiency implications of fiscal equalization. Swan Consultants Pty Ltd., Tamarama, NSW.

Tanzi, V., and H. Zee. 2000. Tax policy for emerging markets: Developing countries. *National Tax Journal* 53: 299–322.

Tanzi, V., and P. Shome. 1993. A primer on tax evasion. *IMF Staff Papers* 40: 807–28.

Thai Beverage PCL. 2005. *Prospectus: ThaiBev PCL*. ⟨www.bangkokbiznew.com/2005/special/beerchang/⟩. Accessed on Februaury 21, 2006 (in Thai).

Thailand Development Research Institute. 2005. *Alcoholic Beverage Consumption in Thailand.* Bangkok, Thailand (in Thai).

Thailand Development Research Institute. 2006. *An Impact Assessment of Alcoholic Beverage Tax on Its Price and Consumption.* Bangkok, Thailand (in Thai).

Thirsk, W. 1986. The marginal welfare cost of corporate taxation in Canada. *Public Finance* 41: 78–95.

Thirsk, W., and J. Moore. 1991. The social cost of Canadian labour taxes. *Canadian Tax Journal* 39: 554–66.

Topham, N. 1984. A reappraisal and recalculation of the marginal cost of public funds. *Public Finance/ Finances Publiques* 39: 394–405.

Tridimas, G., and S. Winer. 2005. The political economy of government size. *European Journal of Political Economy* 21: 643–66.

Triest, R. 1990. The relationship between the marginal cost of public funds and marginal excess burden. *American Economic Review* 80: 557–66.

Tuomala, M. 1990. *Optimal Income Tax and Redistribution.* Oxford: Clarendon Press.

Turnovsky, S. 1997. Equilibrium growth in a small economy facing an imperfect world capital market. *Review of Development Economics* 1: 1–22.

Usher, D. 1982. The private cost of public funds: Variations on themes by Browning, Atkinson, and Stern. Discussion paper 481. Institute for Economic Research. Queen's University.

Usher, D. 1984. An instructive derivation of the expression for the marginal cost of public funds. *Public Finance/Finances Publiques* 39: 406–11.

Usher, D. 1986. Tax evasion and the marginal cost of public funds. *Economic Inquiry* 24: 563–86.

Usher, D. 2006. The marginal cost of public funds is the ratio of mean income to median income. *Public Finance Review* 34: 687–711.

van der Ploeg, F. 1996. Budgetary policies, foreign indebtedness, the stock market, and economic growth. *Oxford Economic Papers* 48: 382–96.

Wade, S. 2003. Price responsiveness in the AEO2003 NEMS residential and commercial buildings sector models. *Energy Information Administration Publication.* ⟨www.eia.doe.gov/oiaf/analysispaper/elasticity/ pdf buildings.pdf downloaded on Aug. 30, 2006⟩.

Warlters, M., and E. Auriol. 2005. The marginal cost of public funds in Africa. Working paper 3679. World Bank Policy Research.

Warren, N. 2002. Removing the effects of interstate tax policy differences from land values. A report commissioned by the New South Wales Treasury.

Webb, R. 2002. Public finance and vertical fiscal imbalance. Research Note 13. Canberra: Department of the Parliamentary Library.

West, S., and R. Williams III. 2007. Optimal taxation and cross-price effects on labor supply: Estimates of the optimal gas tax. *Journal of Public Economics* 91: 593–617.

Wildasin, D. 1979. Public good provision with optimal and non-optimal commodity taxation: The single-consumer case. *Economic Letters* 4: 59–64.

Wildasin, D. 1984. On public good provision with distortionary taxation. *Economic Inquiry* 22: 227–43.

Wildasin, D. 1984. The welfare effects of intergovernmental grants in an economy with distortionary local taxes. *Journal of Public Economics* 25: 103–25.

Wildasin, D. 1987. The demand for public goods in the presence of tax exporting. *National Tax Journal* 40: 591–601.

Wildasin, D. 1989. Interjurisdictional capital mobility: Fiscal externality and a corrective subsidy. *Journal of Urban Economics* 25: 193–212.

Wilson, J. 1986. A theory of interregional tax competition. *Journal of Urban Economics* 19: 296–315.

Wilson, J. 1991. Optimal public good provision with limited lump-sum taxation. *American Economic Review* 81: 153–66.

Wilson, J. 1999. Theories of tax competition. *National Tax Journal* 52: 269–304.

Wilson, J., and D. Wildasin. 2004. Capital tax competition: Bane or boon? *Journal of Public Economics* 88: 1065–91.

Young, D., and A. Bielińska-Kwapisz. 2002. Alcohol and beverage prices. *National Tax Journal* 55: 57–73.

Zeckhauser, R. 1971. Optimal mechanisms for income transfer. *American Economic Review* 61: 324–34.

Zodrow, G., and P. Mieszkowski 1986. Pigou, Tiebout, property taxation, and the underprovision of local public goods. *Journal of Urban Economics* 19: 356–70.

Index